OECD Tax Policy Studies

Taxation of Household Savings

No.25

OECD
BETTER POLICIES FOR BETTER LIVES

Please cite this publication as:
OECD (2018), *Taxation of Household Savings*, OECD Tax Policy Studies, No. 25, OECD Publishing, Paris.
http://dx.doi.org/10.1787/9789264289536-en

ISBN 978-92-64-28952-9 (print)
ISBN 978-92-64-28953-6 (PDF)

Series: OECD Tax Policy Studies
ISSN 1990-0546 (print)
ISSN 1990-0538 (online)

Photo credits: Cover © selensergen/Thinkstock.

Corrigenda to OECD publications may be found on line at: *www.oecd.org/about/publishing/corrigenda.htm*.

Foreword

In 1994, following widespread reforms to the taxation of capital income and wealth in member countries, the OECD released a landmark report on Taxation and Household Savings. *A range of recent developments make a re-examination of the topic timely. In particular, income and wealth inequality has increased in many countries. This has been brought into particular focus as a result of the 2008 global financial and economic crisis, leading to strong calls for greater taxation of capital income and wealth in many countries. Furthermore, ground-breaking changes are being made in the international tax environment to prevent capital income and wealth being hidden offshore. Meanwhile, concern about low levels of retirement savings persist, particularly in light of continued population ageing.*

This report provides a detailed review of the taxation of household savings in 40 OECD and key partner countries in light of these and other developments. It examines the different approaches that countries take to taxing savings and calculates marginal effective tax rates to quantify the incentives created by these approaches; examines the distribution of asset holdings in a range of OECD countries; examines the recent changes in the international tax environment; and discusses the implications of the analysis for savings tax policy.

While countries do not necessarily need to tax savings more, the analysis shows that there is significant scope to improve the way countries tax savings to foster inclusive growth. Most significantly, there are opportunities for countries to increase neutrality in taxation across assets and thereby improve both the efficiency and fairness of their tax systems. At the same time, there remains a case for preferential tax treatment of private pensions in order to encourage retirement savings. There are also opportunities for improvement in tax design regarding private pensions and in a number of other areas such as residential property.

This report provides policymakers with the empirical evidence and the practical policy recommendations needed to ensure a more coherent and effective approach to the taxation of household savings.

Acknowledgements

This study was produced by the Tax Policy and Statistics Division of the OECD Centre for Tax Policy and Administration (CTPA) with the financial support of the Korea Institute of Public Finance (KIPF).

The study was led by Alastair Thomas of the CTPA, under the supervision of Bert Brys. Chapters 1, 2 and 3 were prepared by Alastair Thomas. Chapters 4 and 6 were prepared by Pierce O'Reilly and Alastair Thomas. Chapter 5 was prepared by Sarita Gomez and Pierce O'Reilly. The underlying METR methodology was developed by Bert Brys.

The study has drawn on information and comments received from delegates to Working Party No. 2 on Tax Policy Analysis and Tax Statistics of the OECD Committee on Fiscal Affairs. The project was carried out under the guidance of David Bradbury. It has also benefitted from comments and suggestions provided by Monica Bhatia, Anzhela Cédelle, Dónal Godfrey, Eric Hantala, Michelle Harding, Radhanath Housden, Philip Kerfs, Jeremy Maddison, Giorgia Maffini, Dario Oriolo, Stéphanie Payet, Sarah Perret and Achim Pross. Background research and assistance provided by Melanie Marten and Bethany Millar-Powell is also gratefully acknowledged. Michael Sharratt provided support on graphical issues. Carrie Tyler assisted with the publication process. Violet Sochay provided administrative assistance.

Table of contents

Tables

Figures

Boxes

Executive summary

Following the 2008 financial and economic crisis, there has been renewed interest in the taxation of household savings as a means of strengthening the efficiency and fairness of countries' tax systems. Strong calls have come from civil society to increase capital taxation to address income and wealth inequality. Meanwhile, the recent move towards the automatic exchange of financial account information between tax administrations is likely to make it harder for taxpayers to evade tax by hiding income and wealth offshore.

This report provides a detailed and timely review of the taxation of household savings in OECD and five key partner countries in light of these and other developments. The report finds that, while countries do not necessarily need to tax savings more, there is significant scope to improve the way they tax savings. Most significantly, there are opportunities for countries to increase the neutrality of taxation across assets and thereby improve both the efficiency and fairness of their tax systems.

The lack of neutrality in the taxation of savings is illustrated by marginal effective tax rate (METR) modelling undertaken for 40 OECD and key partner countries across a range of potential savings options. METR modelling enables the impact of a wide range of taxes and tax design features to be incorporated into a single indicator. The results highlight significant variation in METRs across assets, with tax systems creating significant incentives to alter savings portfolio allocation away from that which would be optimal in the absence of taxation.

Private pension funds tend to be the most tax-favoured form of saving, with owner-occupied residential property also significantly tax-favoured. In contrast to owner-occupied residential property, rental property is often subject to relatively high METRs due to the application of progressive marginal personal income tax rates, capital gains taxes and property taxes. Bank accounts and corporate bonds also tend to be relatively heavily taxed in many countries.

Analysis of asset holding microdata shows that a move towards greater neutrality in the taxation of savings can often also improve the fairness of tax systems. Drawing on microdata for 18 European countries from the Eurosystem Household Finance and Consumption Survey (HFCS), the report finds that patterns of asset holdings vary significantly across both income and wealth distributions. Matching these asset holding patterns with METRs shows that current tax systems often favour the savings of households that are financially better-off. For example, poorer households tend to hold a significantly greater proportion of their wealth than richer households in bank accounts, which are typically highly-taxed, whereas richer households tend to hold a greater proportion of their wealth in investment funds, pension funds and shares, which are all often taxed relatively lightly.

While acknowledging the difficulty in achieving perfect neutrality across assets, the report discusses a number of ways in which countries can look to increase neutrality, such as through inflation indexation and consistent application of taxes across assets. A number of more fundamental reforms are also discussed, including exemption of the normal return on savings, imposition of an interest charge on deferred capital gains, and adoption of expenditure-based taxation.

The report also finds that opportunities may exist for some countries to increase progressivity in their taxation of capital income as a result of major changes to the international tax environment. The report argues that the recent move towards the automatic exchange of financial account information between tax administrations is likely to make it harder in years to come for taxpayers to evade tax by hiding income and wealth offshore – making it less distortive for countries to levy taxes on capital income. This may present a particular opportunity for countries that previously moved away from progressive taxation of capital income (due to concerns regarding such tax evasion) to reintroduce a degree of progressivity. The ability to implement such reforms and the degree to which progressivity should be increased will depend on a range of country-specific factors including existing levels of inequality and preferences for redistribution.

While the main conclusion of the report is the need for greater neutrality in the tax treatment of savings, there are exceptions. Encouraging retirement savings is the clearest example. Most countries encourage retirement savings by providing highly concessionary expenditure tax regimes for private pensions that often result in negative METRs. As societies in most OECD countries continue to age, and public pension systems come under increasing strain, there remains a case to maintain these concessionary tax regimes to encourage private savings. However, the tax treatment of voluntary private pension savings should be considered in a coordinated way with the financial advantages and generosity of public pension systems. For example, where public pension provision is substantial, there may be less need to incentivise the use of private pensions.

Finally, the report also highlights opportunities for equity-enhancing improvements in the design of taxes on household savings. For example, tax deductions provided for private pension contributions and mortgage interest payments could be turned into tax credits so that richer taxpayers do not benefit disproportionately from these concessions as compared to poorer taxpayers. Ideally tax credits would be refundable to ensure that taxpayers without sufficient tax liability in a particular year would still receive the full benefit of the tax credit.

Chapter 1

Introduction

This chapter sets the scene for a detailed analysis of the taxation of savings in OECD and partner economies. The chapter examines recent trends in inequality and population ageing. It then summarises the economic literature on the impact of taxation on household savings. Finally, it provides an outline of the structure of the rest of the report.

The taxation of household savings has long been an important issue for tax policymakers. This is unsurprising because how a country taxes household savings can have significant effects on both the efficiency and fairness of the tax system. This report examines in detail the taxation of household savings in OECD and five key partner countries and discusses the resulting implications for savings tax policy.

Such a review is very timely in light of a range of trends and recent developments that have significant implications for tax policy. In particular, inequality continues to increase in many countries leading to strong calls for greater taxation of savings and wealth; while recent changes in the international tax environment regarding the exchange of financial account information between tax administrations can be expected to significantly alter the ability of countries to tax capital income. Meanwhile, continued population ageing is placing significant pressure on public pension systems, with many countries therefore looking to further encourage private pension savings.

This introductory chapter provides a range of background information to aid the analysis to follow. First, it examines recent trends in inequality and population ageing. Second, it summarises the economic literature on the impact of taxation on savings. Finally, the chapter also provides an outline of the structure of the report to follow.

1.1. Background

Inequality is increasing

Within-country income inequality has increased over recent years in many countries due to a wide range of factors including technological change and globalisation, as well as tax, benefit and other policy settings.[1] These increases have been brought into particular focus as a result of the 2008 global financial and economic crisis, and have led to strong calls for greater taxation of savings and wealth in many countries (see, e.g., Piketty, 2014).

The Gini coefficient of disposable income inequality stood at 0.29 on average across OECD countries in the mid-1980s. By 2013, it had increased by about 10% or three points to 0.32 (OECD, 2015a). The latest available data shows that inequality has risen since the mid-1980s in 19 of the 22 OECD countries for which long-time series data are available (Figure 1.1).

Wealth is much more unequally distributed than income. In the 18 OECD countries for which comparable data is available, the bottom 40% of the wealth distribution own only 3% of total household wealth (Figure 1.2). In comparison, the bottom 40% of the income distribution receives 20% of total household income. The top 10% of the wealth distribution hold half of total household wealth and the wealthiest 1% own almost a fifth. The wealth share of the top 1% of the wealth distribution is almost as large as the income share of the top decile in the income distribution (OECD, 2015a).[2]

Figure 1.1. **Disposable income Gini coefficients, mid-1980s and 2015 (or latest available year) in 22 OECD countries**

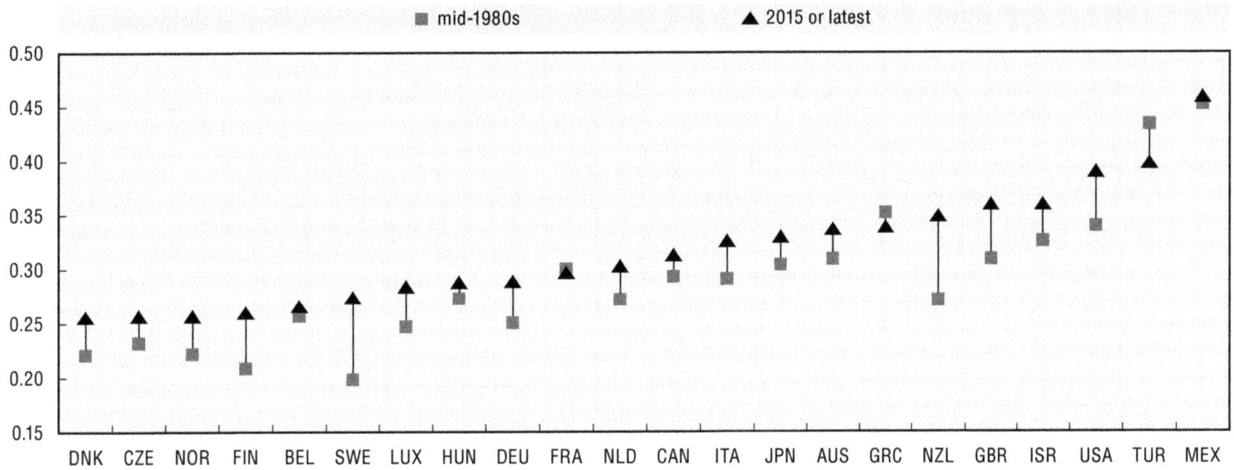

Source: OECD Income Distribution Database

StatLink http://dx.doi.org/10.1787/888933660279

Figure 1.2. **Distributions of household disposable income and net wealth across deciles**

Average of 18 OECD countries, 2010 or latest available year

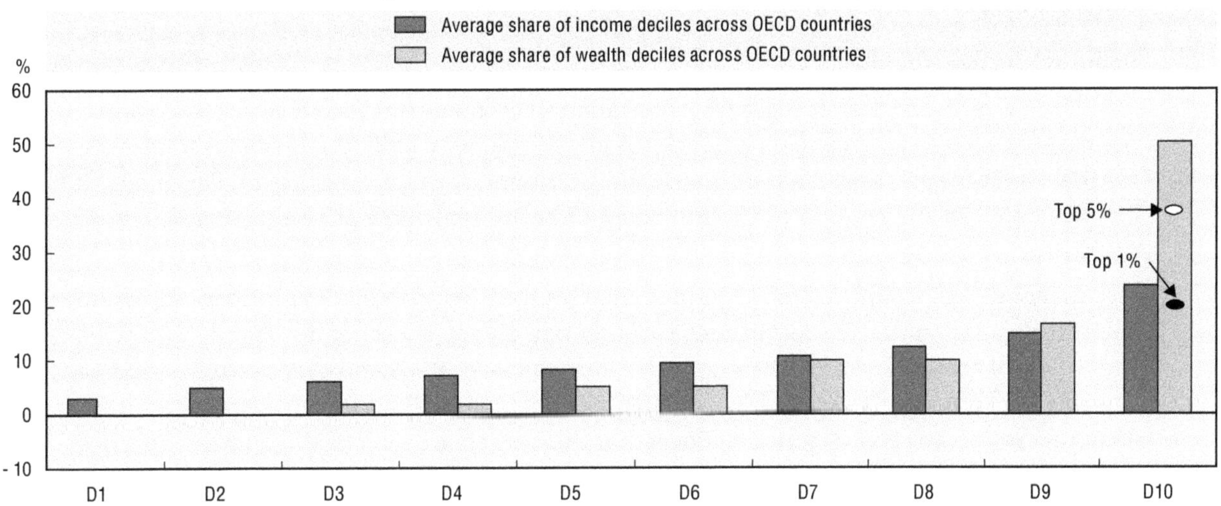

Note: OECD18 includes Australia, Austria, Belgium, Canada, Finland, France, Germany, Greece, Italy, Korea, Luxembourg, the Netherlands, Norway, Portugal, the Slovak Republic, Spain, the United Kingdom and the United States.

Source: OECD (2015) based on OECD Wealth Distribution Database and Income Distribution Database

StatLink http://dx.doi.org/10.1787/888933660298

There is also some evidence that wealth inequality has been worsening over time. Using data from eight OECD countries since the 1970s, Piketty (2014) concluded that private wealth has tended to become more unequally distributed in recent decades, reversing a long-term decline throughout much of the 20th century.

Some caution is necessary when considering measures of income and wealth inequality – with potential for both under- and over-estimation of levels and trends in income inequality. For example, some studies have suggested that commonly used data sources – including those cited above – underestimate the levels of income inequality by not accounting for tax evasion and avoidance, and by not valuing wealth held inside businesses (Piketty and

Saez, 2006). Some studies suggest that tax evasion is higher for high income and high net wealth households than for lower income and net wealth households, meaning that a larger percentage of total income and wealth go unreported at the top of the income and net wealth distribution than at the bottom (Zucman, 2014). This suggests that when concealed wealth and income is taken into account, income and wealth inequality is even greater than the many existing estimates suggest. In contrast, several studies of income inequality in the United States find lower levels and smaller increases in inequality using broader measures of income and correcting for factors such as declining marriage rates and increasing transfer payments (Auten and Splinter, 2017; Bricker et al., 2016; Burkhauser, et al., 2012).[3]

Additionally, trends across time – such as those illustrated in Figure 1.1 – may be affected by tax avoidance and evasion behaviour. For example, part of the increases in measured Gini inequality in the late 1980s may be due to the base broadening reforms that occurred in many countries in that period, resulting in previously undeclared income of higher-income taxpayers being brought into the tax base (and reflected to some degree in survey responses).[4] The choice of start and end points in such a comparison across time may also influence trends.[5] Furthermore, the causes of changes in inequality over time are likely to be important in assessing policy concern (Ball and Creedy, 2016). For example, changes in population structure, such as the increasing size of older cohorts, may increase Gini inequality. However, if the (now larger) older cohort is no worse off than previous (smaller) older cohorts, policymakers may be less concerned by the measured increase in Gini inequality.

Populations are ageing

The current discussion regarding the taxation of household savings occurs against the backdrop of the ageing of our societies. A key reason why individuals save is to provide for their retirement. Thus, the tax treatment of retirement pensions in particular needs to be considered in the context of the financing of both public and private pensions across countries.

In many OECD countries, demographic changes have led to a smaller number of workers supporting a larger number of retirees through pay-as-you-go schemes. Figure 1.3 shows the old-age dependency ratio (the number of individuals aged 65 and over per 100 people of working age) across OECD countries. In 2015, the average old-age dependency ratio across OECD countries was 27.6. Figure 1.4 shows that this ratio has been steadily increasing since 1950. Projections beyond 2015 suggest even greater increases, with more than 50 retirees per 100 people of working age on average by 2050.

OECD research shows that securing adequate pension arrangements requires a diversity of pension retirement financing. This includes public pension arrangements as well as private financing. This is particularly true in the context of high public deficits across the OECD. Diversification of public and private retirement provision allows for greater security of retirement provision, because different kinds of schemes are more or less exposed to different kinds of risks. For example, population ageing may create fiscal sustainability pressures for pay-as-you-go defined benefit arrangements, solvency problems for funded defined benefit arrangements, and adequacy problems for funded defined contribution pension arrangements (OECD, 2016).

These demographic trends have led to an increasing focus on private pension provision, and on defined contribution schemes. These factors should be considered when examining the merits of tax incentives for private pensions.

Figure 1.3. **Old-age dependency ratios, 2015**

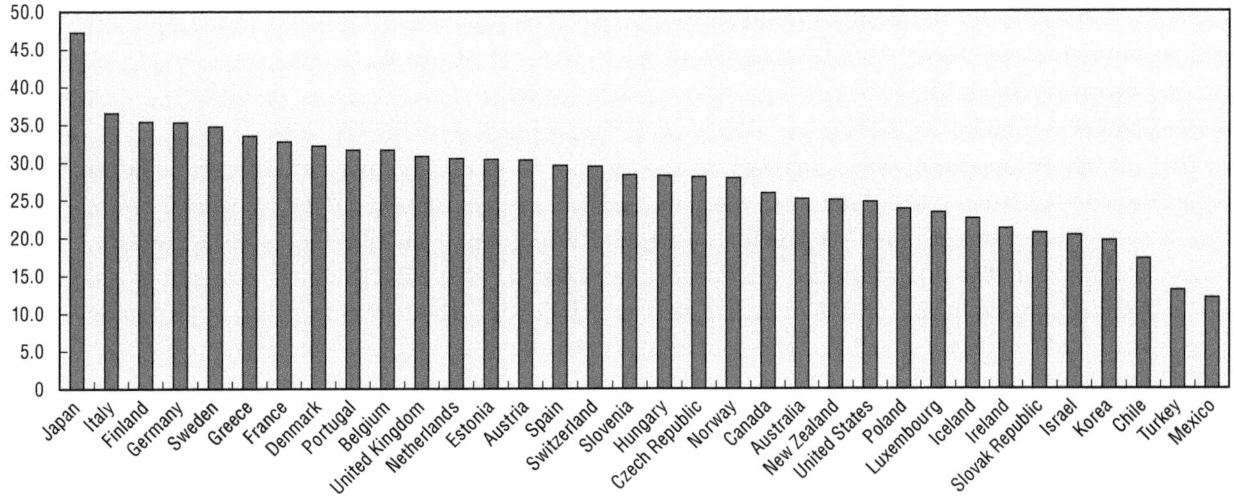

Note: The old-age dependency ratio is defined as the number of individuals aged 65 and over per 100 people of working age defined as those aged between 20 and 64.

Source: OECD Pensions at a Glance, 2015

StatLink http://dx.doi.org/10.1787/888933660317

Figure 1.4. **Old-age dependency ratio over time, OECD average**

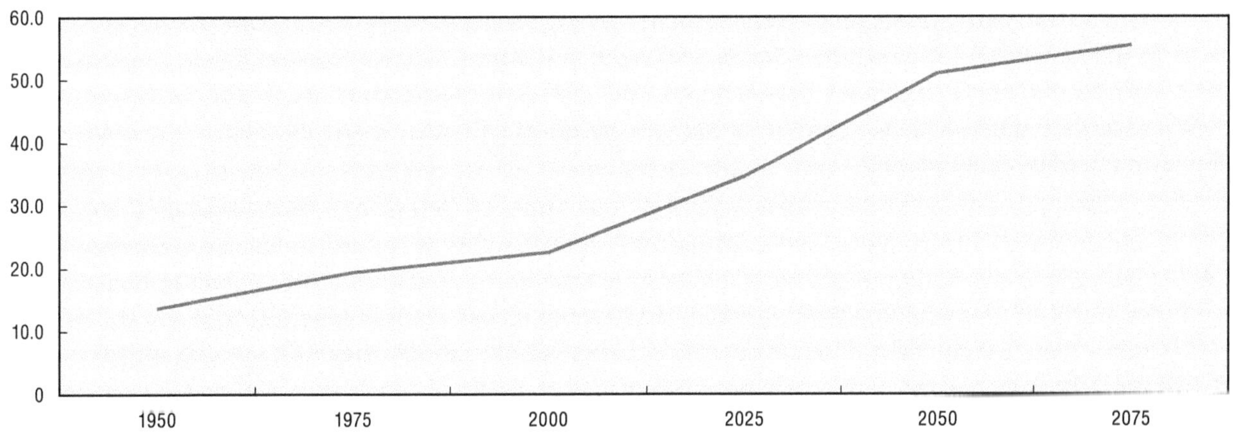

Note: The old-age dependency ratio is defined as the number of individuals aged 65 and over per 100 people of working age defined as those aged between 20 and 64. Actual figures for 1950-2000. Projections for 2025-2075. Projections are based on the most recent "medium-variant" population projections drawn from the United Nations, World Population Prospects – 2012 Revision. Latest data available is for 2015, where the average old-age dependency ratio across OECD countries was 27.6.

Source: OECD Pensions at a Glance, 2015

StatLink http://dx.doi.org/10.1787/888933660336

1.2. The effects of taxation on savings

A key concern for tax policymakers is the potentially distortionary impact of taxation on savings. Taxation can potentially affect savings in two ways. It may affect the allocation of savings across different assets (i.e. "portfolio composition"); and the allocation of savings over the lifecycle (and hence on the total level of savings of an individual and in an economy). This section provides a brief summary of the empirical evidence examining the effect of taxation on savings behaviour.

The effect of taxation on portfolio composition

There is a long history of empirical analysis investigating the impact of taxation on household savings portfolio composition. While these studies vary in the strength of their findings, a clear conclusion can be reached that taxpayers do respond to incentives in the tax system and alter portfolio composition towards more tax-favoured assets.

The first econometric analysis of the impact of taxation on portfolio composition was by Feldstein (1976). He found the personal income tax to have a "very powerful effect on individuals' demands for portfolio assets, after adjusting for the effects of net wealth, age, sex, and the ratio of human to non-human capital." However, Feldstein disregards the methodological implications of incomplete portfolios (i.e. the fact that many households will hold only a subset of the group of assets considered in a study) – a shortcoming that may lead to sample selection bias. Cross-sectional studies from the early eighties through the nineties utilise the Heckman (1979) two-step approach to overcome the methodological limitations in Feldstein's analysis.

The Heckman two-step approach suggests that households make two decisions when making savings decisions that affect the composition of their portfolios. First, households decide whether to hold a particular asset or not (the discrete asset allocation choice). Conditional on deciding to hold an asset, the household then decides how much of that asset to hold (the continuous asset allocation choice).

Cross-sectional studies following the Heckman two-step approach include Dicks-Mireaux and King (1983) for Canada; Hubbard (1985), King and Leape (1998) and Poterba and Samwick (2002) for the United States; and Agell and Edin (1990) for Sweden. These papers consistently find that taxes have a significant effect on the decision to hold a particular asset, although evidence is more mixed on the effect of taxes on the decision as to how much of an asset to hold.

More recent studies (e.g. Samwick, 2000; Alan and Leth-Petersen, 2006; Alan et al., 2010; and Zoutman, 2014) have tended to be 'natural experiment' type studies, utilising time series data and the variation in tax rates following a tax reform to estimate the impact of taxes on portfolio composition. Findings from these more recent studies generally indicate that taxes have a significant effect on portfolio composition, though they find smaller effects than those suggested in cross-sectional studies.

Most studies have focused primarily on the impact of taxation on the portfolio composition of high-income and wealthy households. An exception is the field experiment of Duflo et al. (2006) where low- and middle-income households are considered. While this study did find evidence that taxes impact the asset allocation decisions of lower income households, the study concluded that factors such as information costs and framing also play an important role.

The effect of taxation on the level of savings[6]

Empirical evidence is vastly more mixed regarding whether taxation affects the level of savings in an economy. In this regard, most empirical analysis has focused on tax incentives for retirement savings.

OECD (2018) undertakes a detailed review of the literature since the mid-1990s, and finds two disparate groupings of papers.[7] A first set of papers generally finds that tax incentives for retirement savings produce at least moderate increases in national savings. For example,

Poterba et al. (1996) find that the tax incentives associated with IRA and 401(k) plans in the United States have led to increased national savings. Other papers with similar findings include: Hubbard and Skinner (1996); Benjamin (2003), Ayuso et al. (2007), Guariglia and Markose (2000), Rossi (2009), Gelber (2011) and Beshears et al. (2014).

In contrast, a similarly large group of studies finds that tax incentives for retirement savings mostly result in reallocation rather than new savings. Engen et al. (1996), for example, who also consider IRAs in the United States, find instead that most of the reported increase in financial assets in IRAs can be attributed to stock market booms, higher real interest rates, and shifts in non-financial assets, debt, pensions and social security wealth. Papers with similar findings include: Attanasio and DeLeire (2002), Pence (2002), Attanasio et al. (2004), Antón et al. (2014), Chetty et al. (2014) and Paiella and Tiseno (2014).

Interestingly, there is more consistent evidence that tax incentives tend to increase the level of savings of low-income individuals, while high-income individuals tend to reallocate their savings (Engelhardt, 2000; Engen and Gale, 2000; Chernozhukov and Hansen, 2004; Engelhardt and Kumar, 2011).

1.3. Outline of the report

The rest of this report is structured as follows. Chapter 2 investigates how countries actually tax savings, finding wide variation in approaches both across and within countries, and across different asset types. Broad trends in design approaches are examined and a summary of the key design features adopted by countries is provided.

Chapter 3 quantifies the incentives created by these tax systems by presenting marginal effective tax rates (METRs) on a wide range of assets / savings vehicles. METR modelling enables the impact of a wide range of taxes and tax design features to be incorporated into the one indicator. The results for the 40 countries examined highlight significant variation in METRs across savings vehicles, with tax systems creating significant incentives to alter portfolio allocation away from that which would be optimal in the absence of taxation, with some assets tending to be particularly tax-favoured as compared to others.

Chapter 4 analyses patterns of asset holdings in selected OECD countries across both income and wealth distributions. The analysis draws on income and asset-holdings microdata for 18 countries from the Eurosystem Household Finance and Consumption Survey (HFCS). Patterns of asset holdings are found to vary substantially across both income and wealth distributions, with significant implications regarding the distributional effects of the taxation of household savings.

Chapter 5 discusses the taxation of household savings from an international perspective, and considers the impact of exchange of information on the taxation of capital income internationally. The recent move towards the automatic exchange of financial account information between tax administrations suggests that it will be harder in years to come for taxpayers to engage in tax evasion, and thus will make it easier to levy taxes on capital income without income and assets necessarily shifting offshore in response.

Finally, Chapter 6 brings together the key insights from the preceding chapters and discusses their implications for savings tax policy. It concludes that, while countries do not necessarily need to tax savings more, there is significant scope to improve the way countries tax savings. Most significantly, there are opportunities for countries to increase coherency and consistency in taxation across assets and thereby improve both the efficiency and fairness of their tax systems. There may also be opportunities for many countries to increase progressivity in their taxation of savings. At the same time, there remains a case for well-designed preferential tax treatment of private pensions in order to encourage retirement savings.

Notes

1. An analysis of the various causes of changes in income inequality over time is beyond the scope of this report.
2. Commonly used measures of wealth generally include only private wealth. Most developed countries have public pension systems that provide wealth in the form of the capitalised value of future pensions. For example, in the United States the formula is based on the highest 35 years of qualified earnings so that each year of work adds to this form of wealth. Social Security wealth represents a major form of wealth for much of the population and reduces the perceived need to accumulate private wealth for retirement. While researchers note the importance of such wealth (e.g., Bricker et al., 2016), conventional wealth measures generally do not include it.
3. Saez and Zucman (2016) estimate that the share of total household wealth owned by the top 0.1% in the United States increased from 7% in the late 1970s to 22% in 2012. In contrast, Bricker et al. (2016) conclude that top wealth shares are lower and growing more slowly in the United States. For example, their preferred estimate is that the top 0.1 percent's wealth share increased from about 11 percent in 1992 to 15 percent in 2013. Bricker et al. conclude that all of the difference in estimated growth of the top 0.1% share is due to the gross capitalisation rate used for fixed income assets in Saez and Zucman (2016). This capitalisation rate generated the result that fixed income assets (bank accounts and bonds) accounted for nearly half of the total assets of the top 0.1% in 2013 and virtually all of the increase in the top 0.1% share between 2001 and 2013.
4. Auten and Splinter (2017), for example, find base broadening in the 1980s to have had a significant impact on income reported in tax returns leading to overestimation of increases in the share of income held by the top 1% in the United States by studies that fail to correct for changes in the tax base.
5. For example, while survey data for New Zealand shows a higher disposable income Gini coefficient in 2013 than in 1984, much of the increase occurred in the late 1980s – such that the Gini is lower in 2013 than in 1993 (Ball and Creedy, 2016).
6. This section draws heavily on OECD (2018)
7. OECD (1994) finds similar mixed evidence from earlier studies.

References

Agell, J. and P. Edin (1990), "Marginal taxes and the asset portfolios of Swedish households", *Scandinavian Journal of Economics*, Vol. 92/1, Wiley, pp. 47-64.

Alan, S., K. Atalay, T. Crossley and S-H. Jeon (2010), "New evidence on taxes and portfolio choice", *Journal of Public Economics*, Vol. 94/11-12,, Elsevier, pp. 813-823.

Alan, S. and S. Leth-Petersen (2006), "Tax Incentives and Household Portfolios: A Panel Data Analysis", SEDAP *Research Paper*, No. 163, McMaster University.

Antón, J., R. Muñoz de Bustillo and E. Fernández-Macías (2014), "Supplementary private pensions and saving: evidence from Spain", *Journal of Pension Economics and Finance*, Vol. 13/4, Cambridge University Press, pp. 367-388.

Attanasio, O., J. Banks and M. Wakefield (2004), "Effectiveness of tax incentives to boost (retirement) saving: Theoretical motivation and empirical evidence", *IFS Working Paper*, W04/33.

Attanasio, O. and T. DeLeire (2002), "The effect of individual retirement accounts on household consumption and national saving", *The Economic Journal*, Vol. 112/481, Wiley, pp. 504-538.

Auten, G. and D. Splinter (2017), "Income inequality in the United States: Using tax data to measure long-term trends", US Treasury Department and Joint Committee on Taxation (unpublished paper)

Ayuso, J., J. Jimeno and E. Villanueva (2007), "The effects of the introduction of tax incentives on retirement savings", *Bank of Spain Working Papers*, No. 0724, Banco de España, Madrid,.

Ball, C. and J. Creedy (2016), "Inequality in New Zealand 1983/84 to 2012/13", *New Zealand Economic Papers*, Vol. 50/3, pp. 323-342.

Benjamin, D. (2003), "Does 401(k) eligibility increase saving? Evidence from propensity score subclassification", *Journal of Public Economics*, Vol. 87/5-6, Elsevier, pp. 1259-1290.

Beshears, J., J. Choi, D. Laibson and B. Madrian (2014), "Does front-loading taxation increase savings? Evidence from Roth 401(k) introductions", *NBER Working Paper Series*, No. 20738, The National Bureau of Economic Research.

Bricker, J., A. Henriques, J. Krimmel and J. Sabelhaus (2016), "Measuring Income and Wealth at the Top Using Administrative and Survey Data", *Brookings Papers on Economic Activity*, Brookings, pp. 261-312.

Burkhauser, R., S. Feng, S. Jenkins and J. Larrimore (2012), "Recent Trends in Top Income Shares in the United States: Reconciling Estimates from March CPS and IRS Tax Return Data", *The Review of Economics and Statistics*, Vol. 44/2, pp. 371-388.

Chernozhukov, V. and C. Hansen (2004), "The effect of 401(k) participation on the wealth distribution: An instrumental quantile regression analysis", *The Review of Economics and Statistics*, 86/3, pp. 735-751.

Chetty, R., J. Friedman, S. Leth-Petersen, T. Nielsen and T. Olsen (2014), "Active vs. passive decisions and crowdout in retirement savings accounts: Evidence from Denmark", *The Quarterly Journal of Economics*, Vol. 129/3, pp. 1141-1219.

Congressional Budget Office (2016), *The Distribution of Household Income and Federal Taxes, 2013*, (supplemental tables) Congressional Budget Office, *www.cbo.gov/publication/* 51361.

Dicks-Mireaux, L. and M. King (1983), "Portfolio Composition and Pension Wealth: An Econometric Study", in Z. Bodie and J. Shoven (eds.), *Financial Aspects of the United States Pension System*, University of Chicago Press.

Duflo, E., W. Gale, J. Liebman, P. Orszag and E. Saez (2006), "Saving Incentives for Low- and Middle-Income Families: Evidence from a Field Experiment with H&R Block", *The Quarterly Journal of Economics*, Vol. 121/4, pp. 1311-1346.

Engelhardt, G. (2000), "Have 401(k)s raised household saving? Evidence from the Health and Retirement Study", *Syracuse Centre for Policy Research Working Paper*.

Engelhardt, G. and A. Kumar (2011), "Pensions and household wealth accumulation", *The Journal of Human Resources*, Vol. 46/ 1.

Engen, E. and W. Gale (2000), "The effects of 401(k) plans on household wealth: Differences across earnings groups", *NBER Working Paper Series*, No. 8032.

Feldstein, M. (1976), "Personal taxation and portfolio composition: an econometric analysis", *Econometrica*, Vol. 44/4, JSTOR, pp. 631–650.

Gelber, A.M. (2011), "How do 401(k)s affect saving? Evidence from changes in 401(k) eligibility", *American Economic Journal: Economic Policy*, American Economic Association, Vol. 3/4, pp. 103-122.

Guariglia, A. and S. Markose (2000), "Voluntary contributions to personal pension plans: Evidence from the British Household Panel Survey", *Fiscal Studies*, Vol. 21/4, pp. 469-488.

Heckman, J. (1979), "Sample Selection Bias as a Specification Error", *Econometrica*, Vol. 47/1, JSTOR, pp. 153-161.

Hubbard, R. (1985), "Personal taxation, pension wealth, and portfolio composition", *Review of Economics and Statistics*, Vol. 67/1, JSTOR, pp. 53-60.

Hubbard, R. and J. Skinner (1996), "Assessing the effectiveness of saving incentives", *Journal of Economic Perspectives*, American Economic Association, Vol. 10/4, pp. 73-90.

King, M. and J. Leape (1998), "Wealth and portfolio composition: theory and evidence", *Journal of Public Economics*, Vol. 69/2, pp. 155-193.

OECD (2018), *OECD Pensions Outlook 2018*, OECD Publishing, Paris (forthcoming).

OECD (2016), *OECD Pensions Outlook, 2016*. OECD Publishing, Paris, *http://dx.doi.org/10.1787/pens_outlook-2016-en*.

OECD (2015a), *In It Together: Why Less Inequality Benefits All*, OECD Publishing, Paris, *http://dx.doi.org/10.1787/9789264235120-en*.

OECD (2015b), *Pensions at a Glance 2015: OECD and G20 indicators*, OECD Publishing, Paris, *http://dx.doi.org/10.1787/pension_glance-2015-en*.

OECD (1994), "Taxation and Household Saving", OECD Publishing, Paris.

Paiella, M. and A. Tiseno (2014), "Evaluating the impact on saving of tax-favored retirement plans", *Journal of Pension Economics and Finance*, Vol. 13/1, pp. 62-87.

Pence, K. (2002), "401(k)s and household saving: New evidence from the Survey of Consumer Finances", *Finance and Economics Discussion Series*, Vol. 2002/6, Board of Governors of the Federal Reserve System, Washington, D.C.

Piketty, T. (2014), *Capital in the 21st century*, Harvard University Press.

Piketty, T. and E. Saez (2006), "The Evolution of Top Incomes: A Historical and International Perspective", *American Economic Review, Papers and Proceedings*, Vol. 96/2, pp. 200-205.

Poterba, J. and A. Samwick (2002), "Taxation and household portfolio composition: US evidence from the 1980s and 1990s", *Journal of Public Economics*, Vol. 87/1, pp. 5-38.

Poterba, J., S. Venti and D. Wise (1996), "How retirement saving programs increases saving", *The Journal of Economic Perspectives*, Vol. 10 /4, pp. 91-112.

Rossi, M. (2009), "Examining the interaction between saving and contributions to personal pension plans: Evidence from the BHPS", *Oxford Bulletin of Economics and Statistics*, Vol. 71/2, pp. 253-271.

Saez, E. and G. Zucman (2016), "Wealth inequality in the United States since 1913: Evidence from capitalized income tax data", *Quarterly Journal of Economics*, Vol. 131/2, pp. 519-578.

Samwick, A. (2000), "Portfolio responses to taxation: Evidence from the end of the rainbow", in: J. Slemrod (ed.), *Does Atlas Shrug*, Harvard University Press, Cambridge, MA.

Scholz, J. (1994), "Portfolio choice and tax progressivity: Evidence from the Surveys of Consumer Finances", in: J. Slemrod (ed.), *Tax Progressivity and Income Inequality*, Cambridge University Press, New York.

Zoutman, F. (2014), "The Effect of Capital Taxation on Households' Portfolio Composition and Intertemporal Choice: Evidence from the Dutch 2001 Capital Income Tax Reform", *NHH Dept. of Business and Management Science Discussion Paper*, No. 2014/23, Norwegian School of Economics.

Zucman, G. (2014), "Taxing across Borders: Tracking Personal Wealth and Corporate Profits", *Journal of Economic Perspectives*, Vol. 28/4, pp. 121-148.

Chapter 2

How countries tax savings

This chapter investigates how countries tax household savings. Broad trends in design approaches are identified and a summary of the key design features adopted by countries is provided. The chapter finds wide variation in approaches to taxing household savings both across and within countries, and across different asset types.

2.1. Introduction

Countries adopt a range of approaches to taxing household savings. This chapter provides a summary of the general design features adopted by the 40 countries covered in this study. The magnitude of taxes that are imposed is not discussed in this chapter; this is the focus of Chapter 3, which combines the impact of the various features of savings taxation to calculate marginal effective tax rates.

This chapter focuses on the following assets / savings vehicles, which can be expected to cover the majority of household savings in most countries:

- Bank deposits
- Corporate and government bonds
- Equities (purchase of corporate shares)
- Investment fund assets (marketable collective investment vehicles)
- Private pensions
- Deposits in individual tax-favoured savings accounts
- Residential property

The chapter proceeds as follows: section 2.2 first frames the discussion by presenting, in a stylised manner, the types of approaches that countries take to taxing household savings; section 2.3 then summarises the broad trends in the approaches that countries take, before section 2.4 examines the taxation of each asset / savings vehicle individually.

2.2. Approaches taken to taxing household savings

Based on current capital income tax systems in OECD countries, it is possible to distinguish several "stylised approaches" to taxing savings that are useful in comparing and contrasting the ways different countries tax household savings, both in a broad sense and with regard to specific assets / savings vehicles. The list below focuses is on taxation at the individual level and does not, for example, consider the integration of personal and corporate level taxation (which is however briefly discussed in Chapter 3).

We distinguish seven broad approaches: a comprehensive income tax, a flat rate capital income tax; an expenditure tax, a tax exempt savings approach; a tax deferral approach; a rate of return allowance approach; and a deemed return approach. Most countries implement a combination of these approaches.

- Under a **comprehensive income tax (CT)** approach, labour and capital income are taxed together at progressive rates. No tax relief is provided when the saving is made. A pure CT system is based on the Schanz-Haig-Simons comprehensive definition of income, and would require all income and gains to be taxed on an accrual basis. However, in practice this is extremely rare with capital gains being taxed instead on realisation. As such we refer to such systems, where they are in place, as "broadly comprehensive".

- Under a **flat rate capital income tax** approach, labour and capital income are taxed separately, with capital taxed at a flat rate. Like a CT system, no tax relief is provided when the saving is made. Two subsets of this system are a dual income tax system and a final withholding tax system.
  - A **dual income tax** system taxes labour under a progressive rate schedule and capital income at a proportional rate. In its original form, labour and capital income are taxed together at a flat rate, and then a separate progressive tax is applied on labour income only.
  - A **final withholding tax** system applies (typically) progressive rates on labour income, and a flat rate on capital income which is withheld at source to minimise compliance costs.
- Under an **expenditure tax** approach, taxation only occurs when income is spent.[1] An expenditure tax approach is often taken in relation to private pensions within a system that taxes labour income. In such a case, upfront tax relief tax is given for amounts saved, returns from savings are untaxed as they accrue, but both savings and returns are taxed when a pension is paid.
- Under a **tax exempt savings** approach, no relief is provided when savings are made. However, returns are untaxed as they accrue, and both savings and accrued returns are untaxed on distribution.
- Under a **tax deferral** approach, no tax relief is provided when the saving is made, returns from savings are untaxed as they accrue, but the accrued returns are taxed on distribution (either at flat rates, or together with labour income at progressive rates). This approach is typically applied when intermediaries manage the household savings on behalf of the individual.
- Under a **rate of return allowance** (RRA) approach, taxation occurs as with a CT or a flat rate capital income tax system except that an allowance is provided for the normal return on savings. As such, only economic rents from savings are taxed at the individual level. Any unutilised allowance amount would be carried forward to future years.
- Under a **deemed return** approach, the actual return on savings is not taxed but a presumptive return is taxed instead. No tax relief is provided when the saving is made, and there is also no taxation on distribution or when capital gains are realised. A single or multiple deemed return can be applied and can be taxed at a flat or progressive rates.

In practice, no country implements any one of these approaches consistently across all potential assets / savings vehicles. Furthermore, the exact implementation of each stylised approach tends to vary across countries. For example, two countries can apply a broadly similar approach but with significantly different magnitudes of taxation.

Tax systems also get more complicated in practice due to the cumulative impact of additional taxes on different bases. For example, in addition to taxes on income and capital gains, transaction taxes, net wealth taxes, and recurrent property taxes may apply to certain assets. These additional taxes may also be contingent on income/wealth levels. The next section summarises the approaches to taxing savings that have been taken in the 40 countries considered in this study, drawing on the above classifications.

2.3. Overall trends in countries' approaches to taxing savings

Most countries tax the majority of savings vehicles broadly following either a comprehensive income tax or flat rate capital income tax approach. However, even within these two broad approaches there can be significant differences in taxation, particularly in relation to the size of statutory tax rates on income and the tax treatment of capital gains (which are often taxed at concessionary rates, potentially subject to a holding period requirement).

The greatest degree of consistency in approach is across savings in bank accounts, bonds and shares. Residential rental property is typically also taxed consistently with other assets on a comprehensive basis or flat rate capital tax basis, but is generally also subject to recurrent property taxes, and often transaction taxes.

Irrespective of the broad approach applied to most assets / savings vehicles, private pensions and owner-occupied residential property are typically taxed very differently. Private pensions are almost always taxed following an expenditure tax approach, with the degree of concessionary treatment relative to other assets varying depending on the country. Meanwhile, capital income from owner-occupied residential property is typically exempt but, as with rental property, recurrent property taxes and in many cases transaction taxes are applied. Unlike other savings vehicles, tax relief is often also provided for interest expenses incurred in relation to residential property.

There is less consistency across countries with respect to tax-favoured savings accounts and investment funds. 17 of the 40 countries considered in this study provide some type of tax-favoured savings account. Tax treatment varies from a tax exempt approach (but with a limit on contributions), to a comprehensive income tax approach with concessionary rates, to an expenditure tax approach in a small number of countries. There is no clear link between the general approach to savings taxation that a county applies and the approach applied to tax-favoured savings accounts.

Regarding investment funds, in some countries there is consistency with the broader approach taken – e.g. some countries that apply broadly comprehensive approaches for other assets do so also for investment funds. However, in many cases there is less consistency across assets. For example, a tax deferral approach is often adopted for investment funds when a comprehensive or flat rate capital tax approach is taken for other assets. A tax exempt approach is also sometimes followed for investment funds.

Broad trends in approaches across the majority of assets / savings vehicles are highlighted in Table 2.1. Broadly comprehensive approaches with progressive rates applying to capital income, though not necessarily to capital gains, are applied in 11 countries. In another 21 countries, flat rates are applied to capital income either as part of a dual income tax or a final withholding tax system. In these countries, tax rates are almost always at a significantly lower level than the top marginal rate applying to labour income.

In three countries, a mixed approach is broadly adopted – with low income taxpayers subject to flat final withholding taxes on most capital income, but higher income taxpayers subject to progressive rates.

Finally, there are a range of less common approaches. The Netherlands applies a deemed return approach to most assets / savings vehicles (excluding private pensions and owner-occupied residential property). In Argentina, only a net wealth tax (which implicitly taxes a deemed return on savings) is applied to most savings. Norway applies a dual income tax system, but for equity investment a rate of return allowance is applied. In Estonia and Hungary, personal income tax rates are broadly applied, but as they have flat rate personal income tax systems, the impact on capital income is the same as if a flat rate capital income tax approach was applied.

Table 2.1. **Broad approaches to taxation of savings**
(as at 1 July 2016)

Broadly comprehensive / progressive rate approach	Flat-rate approach	Mixed flat-rate/ progressive	Deemed-return approach	Rate of return allowance
Australia	Austria	Finland	Argentina	Norway (shares)
Canada	Belgium	Korea	Netherlands	
Chile	Bulgaria	Mexico		
France	Colombia			
Ireland	Czech Republic			
New Zealand	Denmark			
South Africa	Estonia*			
Spain	Germany			
Switzerland	Greece			
United Kingdom	Hungary*			
United States	Iceland			
	Israel			
	Italy			
	Japan			
	Latvia			
	Lithuania*			
	Luxembourg			
	Poland			
	Portugal			
	Slovak Republic			
	Slovenia			
	Sweden			
	Turkey			

*A flat-rate personal income tax applies to both labour and capital income.
Source: Country responses to Taxation of Household Savings questionnaire

Again, for each of these groupings in Table 2.1, private pensions tend to follow an expenditure tax approach; owner –occupied property tends to be only subject to recurrent property and transaction taxes; while the tax treatment of investment funds and tax-favoured savings accounts varies considerably.

Regarding the application of specific taxes a number of common themes are also apparent. As already noted, income taxes are applied on either a progressive or flat rate basis depending on the broad approach adopted to taxing savings. That said, a degree of progressivity is also applied in several countries through the application of basic allowances or exempt amounts for a specified level of savings income (typically interest or dividend income).

Capital gains are more commonly taxed at flat rates, even in broadly comprehensive systems. Furthermore, countries often provide concessionary treatment for capital gains that have been held longer than a specified minimum holding period. Capital gains are almost universally taxed on a realisation rather than an accrual basis.[2]

Transaction taxes are applied almost exclusively to residential property, though a small number of countries apply them to bank accounts, bonds and shares. They are generally applied at flat rates, but occasionally can depend on the value of the asset.

Recurrent taxes on immovable property, by definition apply only to immovable property. They are typically implemented at a sub-central level and can consequently vary substantially within a country. In the majority of countries they are levied on a tax base closely linked to the value of the property, though in many cases these valuations lag behind the real value of the property and often remain significantly out of date. Meanwhile the tax base in a small number of countries is based on characteristics of the property, such as size of property or location, rather than value.

Net wealth taxes are rare, being applied in only six countries. In general they exclude private pensions, and have a considerable minimum wealth threshold before a positive rate or rates apply.

2.4. Results across asset types

This section examines the taxation of each asset type in more detail. Tables 2.2-2.9 present key features of the tax treatment of each asset across the three broad stages at which savings may be taxed: acquisition; holding; and disposal. Categories are signified as Y for yes; N for no; or NA if not applicable. Additional details are provided in footnotes where relevant. The tables reflect the rules in place in each country as of 1 July 2016.

Bank accounts

As noted above, most countries tax bank accounts following either a broadly comprehensive or flat rate capital income tax approach. Table 2.2 provides further detail on the design features across the 40 countries covered in this report.

Tax treatment on acquisition (i.e. on deposit of savings in a bank account) is very simple: in no country is the amount of any deposit deductible, and no country imposes a transaction tax.

At the holding stage, marginal personal income tax rates are applied to interest income as it is earned in 13 countries. In three of these countries (Chile, South Africa and the United Kingdom) an allowance or exemption is first applied to a specified amount of interest income. In 25 countries, a flat withholding tax rate applies to interest income. In three of these countries (Germany, Iceland, Lithuania) an allowance or exemption is similarly applied to a specified amount on interest income. Uniquely amongst the 40 countries, Colombia provides relief for the inflationary component of bank interest. Interest earned on bank account deposits is untaxed in Argentina and Estonia.

In Korea, a final withholding tax is applied if combined interest and dividend income is less than KRW 20 million. Otherwise marginal personal income tax rates apply. Similarly, in Mexico, the withholding tax is final if the taxpayer has other income less than MXN 400 000 and interest income less than MXN 100 000. Furthermore, if the average account balance does not exceed five times the minimum average wage (MXN 133 298 in 2016) then no tax will be applied. Otherwise, the withholding tax is provisional and personal income tax rates will be applied at the end of the year.

The Netherlands exempts the first EUR 24 437 (in 2016) of savings from tax. Beyond this amount, a 30% tax rate is applied on a deemed return of 4% of the bank balance (under the deemed return approach).[3]

Colombia, France, Norway, Spain and Switzerland apply net wealth taxes on bank account holdings, but with large exempt amounts or allowances so that only high wealth taxpayers are subject to them.[4] Argentina has a wealth tax but does not apply it to bank account balances.

Bonds

Most countries also tax corporate and government bonds following either a broadly comprehensive or flat rate capital income tax approach. Table 2.3 provides further detail on the design features across the 40 countries covered in this report.

Tax treatment on acquisition (i.e. purchase of a bond) is again very simple: in no country is the amount of any deposit deductible, while only in Belgium and Italy are transaction taxes payable. Meanwhile, if saving is debt-financed, the interest is deductible in Australia, New Zealand, Norway and the United States.

At the holding stage, marginal personal income tax rates are applied to interest income on bonds as it is earned in 15 countries. In two of these countries (South Africa and the United Kingdom) an allowance or exemption is first applied to a specified amount of interest income. In 22 countries, a flat withholding tax rate applies to interest income. In three countries (Germany, Iceland, Lithuania) an allowance or exemption is similarly applied to a specified amount of interest income.

As with bank interest, in Mexico the withholding tax is only final if the taxpayer has other income less than MXN 400 000 and interest income less than MXN 100 000. As with bank interest, the Netherlands exempts the first EUR 24 437 (in 2016) of savings from tax, and beyond this amount the deemed return approach applies.

Argentina, Colombia, France, Norway, Spain and Switzerland apply net wealth taxes on bonds, but typically with large exempt amounts or allowances so that only high wealth taxpayers are subject to them.

On disposal, capital gains (derived when bonds have been issued below par) are taxed in 36 of 40 countries. However, in Chile, the Czech Republic, Hungary and Luxembourg, concessionary rates (or even exemptions) apply for bonds held longer than a minimum period or for capital gains of less than a specified amount. In Iceland, Lithuania, South Africa and the United Kingdom, an allowance or exempt amount applies to both interest and capital gains.

In a number of countries (e.g. Belgium, Korea, Mexico, Slovenia), capital gains on bonds are taxed on realisation as interest income, rather than being subject to a separate capital gains tax. In Belgium, while accrued interest is subject to taxation, there is no other taxation of capital gains. In Korea, as with bank interest, a final withholding tax is applied if combined interest and dividend income is less than KRW 20 million. Otherwise marginal personal income tax rates apply.

In New Zealand, capital gains on bonds are also taxed as interest income on a realisation basis as long as the difference in the person's annual income on a cash basis and on an accrual basis does not exceed NZD 40 000, and either the taxpayer has less than NZD 100 000 of income from financial arrangements or less than NZD 1 million held in financial arrangements. Otherwise they are taxed on an accrual basis.

Differential treatment is applied for government bonds in five countries. In Greece both interest and capital gains from government bonds are exempt. Capital gains on government bonds are exempt in Chile and Ireland, and subject to a reduced rate in Italy. Government bonds are not subject to the wealth tax in Argentina.

Equities (purchase of corporate shares)

Shares are also taxed following either a broadly comprehensive or flat rate capital income tax approach in most countries. Table 2.4 provides further detail on the design features across the 40 countries covered in this report.

Tax treatment on acquisition (i.e. purchase of a share) is very simple: in no country is the amount of any share purchase deductible, while only in Belgium, Ireland and Italy are transaction taxes payable. Meanwhile, if saving is debt-financed, the interest is deductible in Australia, New Zealand and the United States.

At the holding stage, marginal personal income tax rates are applied to dividend income in 15 countries. In two of these countries (Finland and Switzerland) only part of the dividend is exempt; while in the United Kingdom an allowance is first applied. In Norway a rate of return allowance is applied before income is subject to tax.

In 18 countries a flat withholding tax rate applies to dividend income. In Germany a tax-free allowance is first applied; while in Turkey 50% of dividends are exempt. In Japan the taxpayer has the choice whether to apply a flat rate or marginal personal income tax rates. In Korea, as with bank accounts and bonds, a final withholding tax is applied if combined interest and dividend income is less than KRW 20 million. Otherwise marginal personal income tax rates apply. Once again, the Netherlands exempts the first EUR 24 437 (in 2016) of savings from tax, and beyond this amount the deemed return approach applies.

In some cases publicly listed and non-publicly listed shares are treated differently. For example, in Argentina, dividends from publicly listed shares are exempt, but dividends from non-public offer shares are taxed.

Argentina, Colombia, France, Norway, Spain and Switzerland apply net wealth taxes on shareholdings, but typically with large exempt amounts or allowances so that only high wealth taxpayers are subject to them.

On disposal, capital gains on shares are taxed in 33 of 40 countries. However, in many countries concessionary rates (or even exemptions) apply for shares held longer than a minimum period or for capital gains of less than a specified amount. Greece applies a transaction tax on sale. In Estonia, while dividends are exempt from tax, capital gains are taxable.

Investment funds

A range of approaches are taken to the taxation of investment funds across countries. Some countries apply a broadly comprehensive approach; many apply a tax deferral approach; while a tax exempt approach is also applied in some countries. Table 2.5 provides further detail on the design features across the 40 countries covered in this report.

On acquisition (i.e. purchase of a share in an investment fund), France is the only country to provide tax relief – and then only in relation to savings placed in specified funds and subject to a ceiling. No country imposes transaction taxes on investment funds. If saving is debt-financed, the interest is deductible in Australia, New Zealand and the United States.

At the holding stage, 10 countries tax income as it accrues in the investment fund. This is either achieved by treating the fund as a pass-through entity (as in Australia, Canada, the United Kingdom and the United States); by deeming a distribution to have occurred each year if income has not been actually distributed (as in Germany); or by requiring distribution each year (as in Korea). Eight of these countries impose progressive personal income tax rates and the other three impose flat rates. The Netherlands applies its exempt savings amount and deemed return method. In Argentina, no tax is imposed in the fund if returns are dividends from publicly listed companies. In contrast, tax is only imposed on the fund in Bulgaria if it receives dividend income.

Argentina, Colombia, France, Norway, Spain and Switzerland apply net wealth taxes on investment fund holdings, but with typically large exempt amounts or allowances so that only high wealth taxpayers are subject to them.

Six countries impose tax at both the fund level and on distribution. Meanwhile, 19 countries only tax income accrued in the fund upon distribution – either as interest, dividends or capital gains, depending on the fund and the form of the return. In many cases, distributions are tax preferred, especially capital gains.

Private pension funds

Private pensions are taxed following an expenditure tax approach in most countries, though the exact degree of concessionary treatment (as compared to a comprehensive or flat rate capital income tax approach) varies significantly. Exceptions include Argentina which follows a tax exempt approach; Sweden and the Slovak Republic that follow tax deferral approaches; and New Zealand and Turkey that follow broadly comprehensive approaches. Table 2.6 provides further detail on the design features across the 40 countries covered in this report.

At the acquisition stage, 35 of 40 countries provide tax relief for contributions made to private pension funds. In most countries relief is provided as a deduction, although in several countries a tax credit is provided instead. Limits are placed on the size of the tax relief in all but two countries (Chile and Greece). Transaction taxes are not imposed in any country.

At the holding stage, income accruing in the pension fund is only taxed in six countries, and generally at flat rates. Colombia applies its net wealth tax to assets in pension funds, but the remaining countries with net wealth taxes do not.

On distribution, both contributions and accumulated returns are taxed in most countries, though often at concessionary rates. Distributions are exempt in countries following a comprehensive approach (New Zealand, Turkey). Additionally, several countries that provide tax relief up front also exempt distributions resulting in highly concessionary tax treatment. For example, Austria exempt distributions if an annuity is paid out; Lithuania exempt distributions if retirement age has been reached; and Argentina exempt distributions unconditionally.

Tax-favoured savings accounts

Tax-favoured savings accounts are present in 17 out of 40 countries covered in this study, with the type of concessionary treatment (as compared to a comprehensive approach) varying across countries. Some countries apply a tax exempt approach; some a broadly comprehensive approach but with concessionary rates at the holding stage, while a small number of countries apply an expenditure tax approach. Table 2.7 provides further detail on the design features across the 17 countries with such accounts.

On acquisition (i.e. deposit in a tax-favoured savings account), five countries provide tax relief. Deposits are deductible up to a specified limit in Colombia, Finland and Luxembourg, while tax credits are applied in Austria and Norway, again up to a specified limit. Transaction taxes are not imposed in any country.

At the holding stage, no tax is imposed in 12 out of the 17 countries, while the remaining five impose taxes at concessionary rates. Net wealth taxes are applied in Colombia, France and Spain. On distribution, no tax is imposed in 14 out of the 17 countries.

To receive tax relief, various requirements are often imposed (as specified in footnotes to the tables). Austria, Colombia, Finland, Hungary and Spain impose minimum holding period requirements, while distributed funds can only be used for specified purposes in Israel, Luxembourg, Norway and the United States. Meanwhile, contribution limits are applied in Canada, Japan, Korea, the United States[5], South Africa and the United Kingdom.

Owner-occupied residential property

The tax treatment of owner-occupied residential property is complicated. While capital income is typically untaxed, recurrent property taxes and in many cases transaction taxes are applied. Table 2.8 provides further detail on the design features across the 40 countries covered in this report.

On acquisition, while purchase costs are never deductible, 21 out of 40 countries provide tax relief (either a deduction or tax credit) for the interest expense incurred in purchasing a property with debt, though in many cases the available tax relief is capped. Meanwhile, transaction taxes are applied in 30 out of 40 countries.

At the holding stage, only four countries (Denmark, Greece, the Netherlands and Switzerland) tax imputed rental income (generally at low rates, and only when at least partially debt-financed in the case of the Netherlands). A net wealth tax is imposed on owner-occupied property in all six countries with net wealth taxes (Argentina, Colombia, France, Norway, Spain and Switzerland), but a 30% rate reduction applies in France and only 25% of the property value is subject to the tax in Norway. Spain applies a specific exemption threshold to the main residence of up to EUR 300 000, which is additional to the EUR 700 000 general exemption threshold. Meanwhile, recurrent property taxes are imposed in all 40 countries, though not all sub-central areas apply a tax in some countries (e.g. Hungary, Switzerland).

At disposal, only 14 countries tax capital gains. Furthermore, these taxes are often imposed at concessionary (or zero) rates, often subject to a minimum holding period test.

Rented residential property

A broadly comprehensive approach is typically applied to rented residential property. In addition, recurrent property taxes and in many cases transaction taxes are also applied. Table 2.9 provides further detail on the design features across the 40 countries covered in this report.

On acquisition, while purchase costs are never deductible, 27 out of 40 countries provide tax relief (either a deduction or tax credit) for the interest expense incurred in purchasing a property with debt. In many cases, though less frequently than with owner-occupied property, the available tax relief is capped. In addition, Belgium provides tax relief for mortgage principal repayments (but not for interest payments). Transaction taxes are again applied in 30 out of 40 countries.

At the holding stage, 34 out of 40 countries tax rental income, while two (Belgium and the Netherlands) apply a tax on imputed rather than actual rental income. Rental income is typically taxed at progressive rates, but at flat rates in four countries (Denmark, Iceland, Italy and Slovenia). That said, in some cases rates are applied at concessionary levels, or on a reduced base (e.g. Latvia, Spain, Iceland, Italy). There are also income-based exemptions applied to rental income in Korea and the Slovak Republic.

A net wealth tax is imposed on rented property in all six countries with net wealth taxes (Argentina, Colombia, France, Norway, Spain and Switzerland), but only 80% of the property value is subject to the tax in Norway. Recurrent property taxes are imposed in all countries, though as with owner-occupied property, not all sub-central areas apply a tax in some countries (e.g. Hungary, Switzerland).

At disposal, at least some capital gains are taxed in 34 out of 40 countries. However, concessionary (or zero) rates are often applicable, often subject to a minimum holding period test.

Table 2.2. **Tax treatment of different forms of saving: bank accounts**

(as at 1 July 2016)

Country	Acquisition of asset			Holding of asset			Disposal of asset		
	PIT treatment		Transaction tax	PIT	Other taxes		PIT or CGT		
	Interest expense deductible	Amount of acquisition deductible		Income from asset	Income from asset	Value of asset	Realised income from asset	Original value of asset	Capital gains
Australia	N	N	N	Y	N	N	N	N	NA
Austria	N	N	N	N	Y[1]	N	N	N	NA
Belgium	N	N	N	N	Y[1]	N	N	N	NA
Canada	N	N	N	Y	N	N	N	N	NA
Chile	N	N	N	Y[2]	N	N	N	N	NA
Czech Republic	N	N	N	N	Y[1]	N	N	N	NA
Denmark	N	N	N	N	Y[3]	N	N	N	NA
Estonia	N	N	N	N	N	N	N	N	NA
Finland	N	N	N	N	Y[1]	N	N	N	NA
France	N	N	N	Y	N	Y[4]	N	N	NA
Germany	N	N	N	N	Y[1,5]	N	N	N	NA
Greece	N	N	N	N	Y[1]	N	N	N	NA
Hungary	N	N	N	Y	N	N	N	N	NA
Iceland	N	N	N	N	Y[6]	N	N	N	NA
Ireland	N	N	N	N	Y[1]	N	N	N	NA
Israel	N	N	N	N	Y[1]	N	N	N	NA
Italy	N	N	N	N	Y[1]	Y[7]	N	N	NA
Japan	N	N	N	N	Y[1]	N	N	N	NA
Korea	N	N	N	Y[8]	Y[8]	N	N	N	NA
Latvia	N	N	N	N	Y[1]	N	N	N	NA
Luxembourg	N	N	N	N	Y[1]	N	N	N	NA
Mexico	N	N	N	N	Y[9]	N	N	N	NA
Netherlands	N	N	N	N	Y[10]	N	N	N	NA
New Zealand	N	N	N	Y	N	N	N	N	NA
Norway	N	N	N	Y	N	Y[11]	N	N	NA
Poland	N	N	N	N	Y[1]	N	N	N	NA
Portugal	N	N	N	N	Y[1]	N	N	N	NA
Slovak Republic	N	N	N	N	Y[1]	N	N	N	NA
Slovenia	N	N	N	N	Y[1]	N	N	N	NA
Spain	N	N	N	Y	N	Y[12]	N	N	NA
Sweden	N	N	N	N	Y	N	N	N	NA
Switzerland	N	N	N	Y	N	Y[13]	N	N	NA
Turkey	N	N	N	N	Y[1]	N	N	N	NA
United Kingdom	N	N	N	Y[14]	N	N	N	N	NA
United States	N	N	N	Y	N	N	N	N	NA
Argentina	N	N	N	N	N	N	N	N	NA
Bulgaria	N	N	N	N	Y[1]	N	N	N	NA
Colombia	N	N	N	N	Y[1]	Y[15]	N	N	NA
Lithuania	N	N	N	Y[16]	N	N	N	N	NA
South Africa	N	N	N	Y[17]	N	N	N	N	NA

Table 2.2. **Tax treatment of different forms of saving: bank accounts** *(cont.)*

(as at 1 July 2016)

Notes

1. Final withholding tax.
2. Interest income is exempt for "small taxpayers" or taxpayers whose only other income is from employment and pensions, and where interest income is less than CLP 923 660 (in 2016).
3. Taxed at flat rate as "net capital income" under semi-dual system.
4. Net wealth tax. The taxable threshold is set at EUR 1.3 million, but once this threshold has been achieved, the assets are taxed as of EUR 800 000.
5. EUR 801 tax-free allowance for interest and dividend income.
6. Flat capital income tax rate. The first ISK 125 000 of interest income is exempt from taxation.
7. Retail bank deposits and deposit passbooks in excess of EUR 5 000 are subject to a fixed stamp duty tax of EUR 34.20 per year. Custody or holding accounts are charged a proportional stamp duty tax: 0.2% tax rate on deposits in excess of EUR 5 000.
8. Final withholding tax if interest and dividend income less than 20 million won. Otherwise marginal PIT rates apply.
9. Provisional withholding tax of 0.50%. Final for individuals who have no other income (or other income less than MXN 400 000 per year) and interest income does not exceed MXN 100 000. Interest paid on bank accounts where individuals received their salary, savings, and pensions are not taxed whenever the average balance does not exceed five times the annual minimum wage (MXN 133 298 in 2016). Interest from other types of bank accounts (certificates of deposit, money market accounts, etc.) and government bonds are not eligible for this exemption.
10. Deemed return on asset value is taxed. The first EUR 24 437 (in 2016) of total assets excluding pensions and owner-occupied housing is exempt.
11. Net wealth tax. The tax-free allowance is NOK 1 400 000.
12. Net wealth tax. Each resident taxpayer is entitled to a general exemption of EUR 700 000.
13. Net wealth tax applied at the cantonal level.
14. GBP 1 000 savings allowance; otherwise progressive PIT rates.
15. Net wealth tax.
16. First EUR 500 of interest per year is exempt.
17. Exempt if interest income of less than SAR 28 300.

Table 2.3. **Tax treatment of different forms of saving: bonds**

(as at 1 July 2016)

Country	Acquisition of asset			Holding of asset			Disposal of asset		
	PIT treatment		Transaction tax	PIT	Other taxes		PIT or CGT		
	Interest expense deductible	Amount of acquisition deductible		Income from asset	Income from asset	Value of asset	Realised income from asset	Original value of asset	Capital gains
Australia	Y	N	N	Y	N	N	N	N	Y
Austria	N	N	N	N	Y[1]	N	N	N	Y[1]
Belgium	N	N	Y	N	Y[1]	N	N	N	Y[1]
Canada	N	N	N	Y	N	N	N	N	Y
Chile	N	N	N	Y[2]	N	N	N	N	Y[3]
Czech Republic	N	N	N	N	Y[1]	N	N	N	Y[4]
Denmark	N	N	N	N	Y[4]	N	N	N	Y[5]
Estonia	N	N	N	Y	N	N	N	N	Y
Finland	N	N	N	N	Y[1]	N	N	N	Y
France	N	N	N	Y	N	Y[6]	N	N	Y
Germany	N	N	N	N	Y[1,7]	N	N	N	Y[1]
Greece	N	N	N	N	Y[1,8]	N	N	N	Y[8]
Hungary	N	N	N	Y	N	N	N	N	Y[9]
Iceland	N	N	N	N	Y[10]	N	N	N	Y[10]
Ireland	N	N	N	Y	N	N	N	N	Y[8]
Israel	N	N	N	N	Y[1]	N	N	N	Y
Italy	N	N	Y	N	Y[1]	N	N	N	Y[11]
Japan	N	N	N	N	Y[1]	N	N	N	Y[1]
Korea	N	N	N	Y[12]	Y[12]	N	N	N	Y[12]
Latvia	N	N	N	N	Y[1]	N	N	N	Y
Luxembourg	N	N	N	N	Y[1]	N	N	N	Y[13]
Mexico	N	N	N	N	Y[14]	N	N	N	Y
Netherlands	N	N	N	N	Y[15]	N	N	N	N
New Zealand	Y	N	N	Y	N	N	N	N	Y[16]
Norway	Y	N	N	Y	N	Y[17]	N	N	Y
Poland	N	N	N	N	Y[1]	N	N	N	Y
Portugal	N	N	N	N	Y[1]	N	N	N	Y
Slovak Republic	N	N	N	N	Y[1]	N	N	N	Y
Slovenia	N	N	N	N	Y[1]	N	N	N	Y[1]
Spain	N	N	N	Y	N	Y[18]	N	N	Y
Sweden	N	N	N	N	Y	N	N	N	Y
Switzerland	N	N	N	Y	N	Y[19]	N	N	Y
Turkey	N	N	N	N	Y[1]	N	N	N	Y
United Kingdom	N	N	N	Y[20]	N	N	N	N	Y[21]
United States	Y[22]	N	N	Y	N	N	N	N	Y
Argentina	N	N	N	N	N	Y[23]	N	N	N
Bulgaria	N	N	N	N	N	N	N	N	N
Colombia	N	N	N	N	Y[1]	Y[24]	N	N	Y[25]
Lithuania	N	N	N	Y[26]	N	N	N	N	Y[27]
South Africa	N	N	N	Y[28]	N	N	N	N	Y[29]

Table 2.3. **Tax treatment of different forms of saving: bonds** *(cont.)*

(as at 1 July 2016)

Notes

1. Final withholding tax
2. Interest income is exempt for "small taxpayers" or taxpayers whose only other income is from employment and pensions, and where interest income is less than CLP 923 660 (in 2016).
3. Capital gains are exempt if not "habitual in the trade of bonds" and if capital gain is less than CLP 5 541 960 (in 2016). Otherwise "business profits" tax rate is applied. Capital gains on "public offer debt instruments" from Central Bank of Chile or General Treasury of Republic of Chile are exempt.
4. Subject to flat rate cap gains tax if gain greater than CZK 100 000 and held for three years or less.
5. Taxed at flat rate as "net capital income" under semi-dual system
6. Net wealth tax. The taxable threshold is set at EUR 1.3 million, but once this threshold has been achieved, the assets are taxed as of EUR 800 000.
7. EUR 801 tax-free allowance for interest and dividend income.
8. Government bonds are exempt from all taxation in Greece, and from capital gains tax in Ireland.
9. Treated as interest. Preferential capital income tax rate of 10% and healthcare rate of 6% if held 3+ years; Exempt from capital income tax if held 5+ years. Healthcare tax only applies if income above HUF 450 000.
10. Flat capital income tax rate. The first ISK 125 000 of interest income is exempt from taxation
11. Government bonds subject to 12.5% rate instead of 26% on capital gains
12. Final withholding tax if interest and dividend income less than 20 million won. Otherwise marginal PIT rates apply. Capital gains treated as interest income.
13. If the asset is sold more than 6 months after purchase there is no capital gains taxation applicable
14. Provisional withholding tax of 0.50%. Final for individuals who have no other income (or other income less than MXN 400 000 per year) and interest income does not exceed MXN 100 000. Interest paid on bank accounts where individuals received their salary, savings, and pensions are not taxed whenever the average balance does not exceed five times the annual minimum wage (MXN 133 298 in 2016). Interests from other types of bank accounts (certificates of deposit, money market accounts, etc.) and government bonds are not eligible for this exemption.
15. Deemed return on asset value is taxed. The first EUR 24 437 (in 2016) of total assets excluding pensions and owner-occupied housing is exempt.
16. Taxed under the financial arrangements rules at marginal PIT rates on a realisation basis if less than NZD 100 000 of income from financial arrangements or NZD 1 million in value held in financial arrangements, otherwise on an accrual basis.
17. Net wealth tax. The tax-free allowance is NOK 1 400 000.
18. Net wealth tax. Each resident taxpayer is entitled to a general exemption of EUR 700 000.
19. Net wealth tax applied at the cantonal level.
20. GBP 1 000 savings allowance; otherwise progressive PIT rates
21. GBP 11 100 capital gain "annual exempt amount"
22. Interest expense is generally deductible up to the amount of investment income.
23. Corporate bonds subject to wealth tax (not Government bonds).
24. Net wealth tax
25. Capital gain taxed as interest income (final withholding tax) on realisation
26. First EUR 500 of interest per year is exempt.
27. Exempt if less than EUR 500 of capital gain.
28. Exempt if interest income of less than SAR 28 300
29. Exempt if capital gain of less than SAR 40 000. Otherwise subject to marginal rates after 40% exclusion.

Table 2.4. **Tax treatment of different forms of saving: shares**

(as at 1 July 2016)

Country	Acquisition of asset			Holding of asset			Disposal of asset		
	PIT treatment		Transaction tax	PIT	Other taxes		PIT or CGT		
	Interest expense deductible	Amount of acquisition deductible		Income from asset	Income from asset	Value of asset	Realised income from asset	Original value of asset	Capital gains
Australia	Y	N	N	Y	N	N	N	N	Y
Austria	N	N	N	N	Y[1]	N	N	N	Y[1]
Belgium	N	N	Y	N	Y[1]	N	N	N	N[2]
Canada	N	N	N	Y	N	N	N	N	Y
Chile	N	N	N	Y[3]	N	N	N	N	Y[4]
Czech Republic	N	N	N	N	Y[1]	N	N	N	Y[5]
Denmark	N	N	N	N	Y[6]	N	N	N	Y[6]
Estonia	N	N	N	N	N	N	N	N	Y
Finland	N	N	N	Y[7]	N	N	N	N	Y
France	N	N	N	Y	N	Y[8]	N	N	Y
Germany	N	N	N	N	Y[1,9]	N	N	N	Y[1]
Greece	N	N	Y	N	Y[1]	N	Y[10]	Y[10]	Y
Hungary	N	N	N	Y	N	N	N	N	Y[11]
Iceland	N	N	N	N	Y[12]	N	N	N	Y[12]
Ireland	N	N	Y	Y	N	N	N	N	Y
Israel	N	N	N	N	Y[1]	N	N	N	Y[13]
Italy	N	N	Y	N	Y[1]	N	N	N	Y
Japan	N	N	N	Y[14]	Y[14]	N	N	N	Y[1]
Korea	N	N	Y	Y[15]	Y[15]	N	N	N	Y[16]
Latvia	N	N	N	N	Y[1]	N	N	N	Y
Luxembourg	N	N	N	Y[17]	N	N	N	N	Y[18]
Mexico	N	N	N	Y	N	N	N	N	Y[1]
Netherlands	N	N	N	N	Y[19]	N	N	N	N
New Zealand	Y	N	N	Y	N	N	N	N	N
Norway	N	N	N	Y[20]	N	Y[21]	N	N	Y
Poland	N	N	N	N	Y[1]	N	N	N	Y
Portugal	N	N	N	N	Y[1]	N	N	N	Y
Slovak Republic	N	N	N	N	N	N	N	N	Y[22]
Slovenia	N	N	N	N	Y[1]	N	N	N	Y[23]
Spain	N	N	N	Y	N	Y[24]	N	N	Y
Sweden	N	N	N	N	Y	N	N	N	Y
Switzerland	N	N	N	Y[25]	N	Y[26]	N	N	Y
Turkey	N	N	N	N	Y[27]	N	N	N	N[28]
United Kingdom	N	N	N	Y[29]	N	N	N	N	Y[30]
United States	Y[31]	N	N	Y	N	N	N	N	Y[31]
Argentina	N	N	N	N	N	Y[32]	N	N	N
Bulgaria	N	N	N	N	Y	N	N	N	N
Colombia	N	N	N	N	N	Y[32]	N	N	N
Lithuania	N	N	N	Y	N	N	N	N	Y[33]
South Africa	N	N	N	N	Y[1]	N	N	N	Y[34]

Table 2.4. **Tax treatment of different forms of saving: shares** *(cont.)*

(as at 1 July 2016)

Notes

1. Final withholding tax.
2. Unless shares held for less than six months.
3. Dividend income is exempt for "small taxpayers" or taxpayers whose only other income is from employment and pensions, and where interest income is less than CLP 923 660 (in 2016).
4. Capital gains are exempt if not "habitual in the trade of shares", shares are held for at least one year and if capital gain is less than CLP 5 541 960. Otherwise "business profits" tax rate is applied.
5. Subject to flat rate cap gains tax if shares held for three years or less.
6. Taxed at flat rate as "net capital income" under semi-dual system
7. 85% of dividend income is taxed as investment income. 15% of income is exempt.
8. Net wealth tax. The taxable threshold is set at EUR 1.3 million, but once this threshold has been achieved, the assets are taxed as of EUR 800 000.
9. EUR 801 tax-free allowance for interest and dividend income.
10. 2% tax on sale
11. Preferential capital income tax rate of 10% and healthcare rate of 6% if held 3+ years; Exempt from capital income tax if held 5+ years. Healthcare tax only applies if income above HUF 450 000.
12. Flat capital income tax rate.
13. Capital gains are indexed for inflation
14. Taxpayer can choose "taxation on aggregate" where taxed at marginal PIT rates, or "separate taxation", where taxed at flat 20% rate.
15. Final withholding tax if interest and dividend income less than 20 million won. Otherwise marginal PIT rates apply.
16. Exempt from capital gains tax if listed shares held by minority (<1%) shareholder and less than KRW 250 million market capitalisation.
17. A 15% withholding tax is applied on dividend income. However, this withholding tax is imputed with other taxes in the tax return. The dividend income is included with other revenues and subject to the global personal income tax rate. 50% of distributed dividend income is included in the personal income tax base.
18. If the asset is sold more than 6 months after purchase there is no capital gains taxation applicable
19. Deemed return on asset value is taxed. The first EUR 24 437 (in 2016) of total assets excluding pensions and owner-occupied housing is exempt.
20. Only the portion of the return above the risk-free rate is taxed
21. Net wealth tax. The tax-free allowance is NOK 1 400 000.
22. Capital gains less than EUR 500 are exempt
23. The tax rate for capital gains depends on the holding period: 25% for a holding period of up to 5 years, 15% for a holding period from 5 to 10 years, 10% for a holding period from 10 to 15 years, 5% for a holding period from 15 to 20 years, resulting in non-taxation of capital gains derived after a holding period greater than 20 years.
24. Net wealth tax. Each resident taxpayer is entitled to a general exemption of EUR 700 000.
25. Only 50% of dividends are taxed
26. Net wealth tax applied at the cantonal level.
27. Dividends are subject to a 15% withholding tax and half of the dividends is exempt from tax. The remaining half is declared if it exceeds the declaration limit for that year and is subject to progressive tax rate.
28. Capital gains earned from sale of equities quoted in the ISE and held for longer than 1 year (2 years for unquoted shares) are not subject to withholding tax and are not declared
29. GBP 5 000 dividend allowance.
30. GBP 11 100 capital gain "annual exempt amount"
31. Interest expense is generally deductible up to the amount of investment income. A lower rate schedule applies for long term capital gains of more than one year. However, the taxpayer must choose between deducting the interest expense and claiming the preferential capital gains tax rate.
32. Net wealth tax
33. Exempt if less than EUR 500 of capital gain.
34. Exempt if capital gain of less than SAR 40 000. Otherwise subject to marginal rates after 40% exclusion.

Table 2.5. Tax treatment of different forms of saving: investment funds

(as at 1 July 2016)

Country	Acquisition of asset			Holding of asset			Disposal of asset		
	PIT treatment		Transaction tax	PIT	Other taxes		PIT or CGT		
	Interest expense deductible	Amount of acquisition deductible		Income from asset	Income from asset	Value of asset	Realised income from asset	Original value of asset	Capital gains
Australia	Y	N	N	Y	N	N	N	N	N
Austria	N	N	N	N	Y[1]	Y[2]	Y[1]	N	Y[2]
Belgium	N	N	N	N	N	N	N	N	N[3]
Canada	N	N	N	Y[4]	N	N	N	N	Y[4]
Chile	N	N	N	N	N	N	Y	N	Y[5]
Czech Republic	N	N	N	N	Y[1]	N	Y[1]	N	Y[6]
Denmark	N	N	N	N	Y[7]	N	Y[8]	N	N
Estonia	N	N	N	N	N	N	Y	N	Y
Finland	N	N	N	N	N	N	Y	N	Y
France	N	Y[9]	N	N	N	Y[10]	Y	N	N[11]
Germany	N	N	N	N	Y[1,12]	N	N	N	Y[1,12]
Greece	N	N	N	N	N	N	Y	N	Y
Hungary	N	N	N	N	N	N	Y	N	Y[13]
Iceland	N	N	N	N	N	N	Y[14]	N	Y[14]
Ireland	N	N	N	N	N	N	Y[15]	N	Y[15]
Israel	N	N	N	N	N	N	Y	N	Y[16]
Italy	N	N	N	N	N	N	Y	N	Y
Japan	N	N	N	N	N	N	Y	N	Y
Korea	N	N	N	Y[17]	N	N	Y[18]	N	Y[18]
Latvia	N	N	N	N	Y[1]	N	N	N	Y
Luxembourg	N	N	N	N	N	N	Y[19]	N	Y[20]
Mexico	N	N	N	N	N	N	Y	N	Y
Netherlands	N	N	N	N	Y[21]	N	N	N	N
New Zealand	Y	N	N	N	Y[22]	N	N	N	N
Norway	N	N	N	N	N	Y[23]	Y	N	Y
Poland	N	N	N	N	N	N	Y	N	Y
Portugal	N	N	N	N	Y[1]	N	N	N	N
Slovak Republic	N	N	N	N	N	N	Y	N	Y
Slovenia	N	N	N	N	N	N	Y[1]	N	Y[24]
Spain	N	N	N	N[25]	N	Y[26]	Y	N	Y
Sweden	N	N	N	N	Y[27]	N	Y	N	Y
Switzerland	N	N	N	Y[4]	N	N	N	N	Y[4]
Turkey	N	N	N	N	Y[28]	N	Y[28]	N	Y[28]
United Kingdom	N	N	N	Y[29]	N	N	N	N	Y[29]
United States	Y[30]	N	N	Y	N	N	N	N	Y[30]
Argentina	N	N	N	N	N	Y	N	N	N
Bulgaria	N	N	N	N	N	N	N	N	N
Colombia	N	N	N	N	N	Y	N	N	N
Lithuania	N	N	N	N	N	N	Y	N	Y
South Africa	N	N	N	Y	N	N	N	N	Y

Table 2.5. **Tax treatment of different forms of saving: investment funds** *(cont.)*

(as at 1 July 2016)

Notes

1. Final withholding tax
2. 60% of capital gains retained in a fund are taxed at 27.5%; and this is credited against capital gains tax to be paid on distribution to the investor
3. For a SICAVs/BEVEKS fund having invested at least 25% of the portfolio in interest-bearing debt securities, capital gains obtained through the repurchase of own shares or through a partial or total distribution of the social assets of the SICAV/BEVEK, are liable to the 27% withholding tax in respect of the part corresponding to, on the one hand, the interest received by the SICAV/BEVEK and, on the other hand, capital gains generated by the debt securities portfolio, after deduction of losses.
4. Flow through treatment, so taxed each year in hands of the investor
5. All distributions are treated as dividends and taxed at progressive PIT rates. Dividend income is exempt for "small taxpayers" or taxpayers whose only other income is from employment and pensions, and where interest income is less than CLP 923 660 (in 2016).
6. Subject to flat rate cap gains tax if gain greater than CZK 100 000 and held for three years or less.
7. Taxed at flat rate as "net capital income" under semi-dual system
8. Flat final withholding tax
9. For investment in innovation-focused mutual funds (FCPI) or proximity investments funds (FIP), taxpayers benefit from a reduction of their income tax equal to 18% of the cash subscriptions, up a ceiling of EUR 12 000 for single person (i.e. a EUR 2 160 reduction) and EUR 24 000 for a married couple (i.e. a EUR 4 320 reduction). The rate is increased to 38% if the investment is in Corse, and 42% if it is in overseas territories. Investment in Sofica also provides a reduction of 30% of the cash subscription on the income tax. The cash subscription eligible for the reduction is subject to a double ceiling: EUR 12 000 for single person or EUR 24 000 for a married couple and less than 25% of the global income. The rate is increased to 36% if the Sofica realizes at least 10% of the investments in production societies before December 31 of the year following the subscription.
10. Net wealth tax. The taxable threshold is set at EUR 1.3 million, but once this threshold has been achieved, the assets are taxed as of EUR 800 000.
11. No CGT if investment in innovation-focused mutual funds (FCPI) or proximity investments funds (FIP).
12. Deemed distribution annually
13. Preferential capital income tax rate of 10% and healthcare rate of 6% if held 3+ years; Exempt from capital income tax if held 5+ years. Healthcare tax only applies if income above HUF 450 000.
14. Flat capital income tax rate.
15. Flat rate exit tax on distribution
16. Capital gains are indexed for inflation
17. Non-qualified funds are treated as pass-through entities.
18. Qualified funds taxed on distribution
19. A 15% withholding tax is applied on dividend income. However, this withholding tax is imputed with other taxes in the tax return. The dividend income is included with other revenues and subject to the global personal income tax rate. 50% of distributed dividend income is included in the personal income tax base.
20. If the asset is sold more than 6 months after purchase there is no capital gains taxation applicable
21. Deemed return on asset value is taxed. The first EUR 24 437 (in 2016) of total assets excluding pensions and owner-occupied housing is exempt.
22. Portfolio investment entity (PIE) regime: income earned by the PIE is attributed to the investor each year and taxed annually at progressive "prescribed investor rates". Final distribution to the investor is not taxed.
23. Net wealth tax. The tax-free allowance is NOK 1 400 000.
24. The tax rate for capital gains depends on the holding period: 25% for up to 5 years; 15% from 5 to 10 years; 10% from 10 to 15 years; 5% from 15 to 20 years; and non-taxation for greater than 20 years.
25. Untaxed if dividend income.
26. Net wealth tax. Each resident taxpayer is entitled to a general exemption of EUR 700 000.
27. Imputed income of the investment fund is taxed at the flat 30% tax rate for capital income
28. 10% tax applied at fund level if held <1 year. 10% withholding tax is not applied on distribution from the investment fund if held for >1 year if the equity portion of investment fund's portfolio is at least 51% at all times. If applicable, the withholding tax is final.
29. GBP 1 000 savings allowance for interest income; GBP 5 000 dividend allowance; GBP 11 100 capital gain "annual exempt amount".
30. Interest expense is generally deductible up to the amount of investment income. A lower rate schedule applies for long term capital gains of more than one year. However, the taxpayer must choose between deducting the interest expense and claiming the preferential capital gains tax rate.

Table 2.6. **Tax treatment of different forms of saving: private pensions**

(as at 1 July 2016)

Country	Acquisition of asset			Holding of asset			Disposal of asset		
	PIT treatment		Transaction tax	PIT	Other taxes		PIT or CGT		
	Interest expense deductible	Amount of acquisition deductible		Income from asset	Income from asset	Value of asset	Realised income from asset	Original value of asset	Capital gains
Australia	N	Y[1]	N	N	Y	N	N[2]	N	NA
Austria	N	Y[3]	N	N	N	N	N[4]	N[4]	NA
Belgium	N	Y[1]	N	N	N	N	Y[5]	Y[5]	NA
Canada	N	Y[3]	N	N	N	N	Y	Y	NA
Chile	N	Y	N	N	N	N	Y	Y	NA
Czech Republic	N	Y[3]	N	N	N	N	Y	Y	NA
Denmark	N	Y[3]	N	N	Y	N	Y	Y	NA
Estonia	N	Y[3]	N	N	N	N	Y	Y	NA
Finland	N	Y[3]	N	N	N	N	Y	Y	NA
France	N	Y[3]	N	N	N	N	Y	Y	NA
Germany	N	Y[3]	N	N	N	N	Y	Y	NA
Greece	N	Y	N	N	N	N	Y	Y	NA
Hungary	N	Y[3]	N	N	N	N	N	N	NA
Iceland	N	Y[3]	N	N	N	N	Y	Y	NA
Ireland	N	Y[3]	N	N	N	N	Y	Y	NA
Israel	N	Y[1]	N	N	N	N	N	N	NA
Italy	N	Y[3]	N	N	Y[6]	N	Y[5]	Y[5]	NA
Japan	N	Y[3]	N	N	N	N	Y[7]	Y[7]	NA
Korea	N	Y[1]	N	N	N	N	Y[5]	Y[5]	NA
Latvia	N	Y[3]	N	N	Y[8]	N	N	N	NA
Luxembourg	N	Y[3]	N	N	N	N	Y	Y	NA
Mexico	N	Y[3]	N	N	N	N	Y[9]	Y[9]	NA
Netherlands	N	Y[3]	N	N	N	N	Y[10]	Y[10]	NA
New Zealand	N	N	N	Y	N	N	N	N	NA
Norway	N	Y[3]	N	N	N	N	Y	Y	NA
Poland	N	Y[3]	N	N	N	N	Y[5]	Y[5]	NA
Portugal	N	Y[1]	N	N	N	N	Y[5]	Y[5]	NA
Slovak Republic	N	N	N	N	N	N	Y	N	NA
Slovenia	N	Y[3]	N	N	N	N	Y[11]	Y[11]	NA
Spain	N	Y[3]	N	N	N	N	Y	Y	NA
Sweden	N	N	N	N	Y[12]	N	Y	N	NA
Switzerland	N	Y[3]	N	N	N	N	Y[13]	Y[13]	NA
Turkey	N	N	N	N	N	N	N[14]	N	NA
United Kingdom	N	Y[3]	N	N	N	N	Y[15]	Y[15]	NA
United States	N	Y[3]	N	N	N	N	Y	Y	NA
Argentina	N	N	N	N	N	N	N	N	NA
Bulgaria	N	Y[3]	N	N	N	N	N[16]	N[16]	NA
Colombia	N	Y	N	N	N	Y	N	N	NA
Lithuania	N	Y[3]	N	N	N	N	N	N	NA
South Africa	N	Y[3]	N	N	N	N	Y[17]	Y[17]	NA

Table 2.6. **Tax treatment of different forms of saving: private pensions** *(cont.)*

(as at 1 July 2016)

Notes

1. Tax credit, subject to limit.
2. Taxed if above threshold.
3. Deduction, subject to limit.
4. Untaxed as long as transformed into a life-long annuity.
5. Flat rate on distribution.
6. Rate is 20%; but returns from government bonds are only taxed at 12.5% (technically is a 62.5% inclusion).
7. Taxable at marginal PIT rates, but taxpayer receives a deduction (that is lower for higher income taxpayers).
8. Withholding tax on dividend and interest income earned by pension fund.
9. Exempt up to a daily amount not exceeding fifteen times the minimum wage. For the excess amount the tax is paid accordingly to the standard personal income tax rates. If paid in one lump sum, exempt for a total amount of ninety annual minimum wages for every year worked and the amount in excess is taxed according to the personal income tax table.
10. The EET-system (pension is taxed when the pension is payed) only applies if the pension savings do not exceed the allowed limit of 1.875 percent of the annual wage, above a fixed threshold. The EET-system applies as far as the maximum annual wage does not exceed the amount of EUR 103 317 per year.
11. Only 50% of pension distribution is included in the tax base.
12. Imputed income of the pension fund is taxed at a flat 15% tax rate.
13. 1/5 of rates applied to pension distributions if annuities.
14. Untaxed unless withdraw from plan early (less than 10 years), or before eligible for pension benefits.
15. 25% of distributions (up to lifetime limit of GBP1m) can be withdrawn at age 55 tax free (which the majority of people do); remainder is taxed at the taxpayer's marginal tax rate.
16. Distributions are untaxed if reached retirement age, otherwise are taxed at 10% rate.
17. One third of pension wealth is immediately distributable as a lump sum and taxed at reduced PIT rates; two thirds is taxed at normal marginal PIT rates.

Table 2.7. **Tax treatment of different forms of saving: tax-favoured savings accounts**

(as at 1 July 2016)

Country	Acquisition of asset			Holding of asset			Disposal of asset		
	PIT treatment		Transaction tax	PIT	Other taxes		PIT or CGT		
	Interest expense deductible	Amount of acquisition deductible		Income from asset	Income from asset	Value of asset	Realised income from asset	Original value of asset	Capital gains
Australia	NA	NA	NA	NA	NA	NA	NA	NA	NA
Austria	N	Y[1]	N	N	Y[2]	N	N	N	NA
Belgium	N	N	N	N	Y[2,3]	N	N	N	NA
Canada	N	N	N	N[4]	N	N	N	N	NA
Chile	NA	NA	NA	NA	NA	NA	NA	NA	NA
Czech Republic	NA	NA	NA	NA	NA	NA	NA	NA	NA
Denmark	NA	NA	NA	NA	NA	NA	NA	NA	NA
Estonia	NA	NA	NA	NA	NA	NA	NA	NA	NA
Finland	N	Y[5]	N	N	N	N	Y[5]	Y[5]	NA
France	N	N	N	N[6]	N	Y[7]	N	N	NA
Germany	NA	NA	NA	NA	NA	NA	NA	NA	NA
Greece	NA	NA	NA	NA	NA	NA	NA	NA	NA
Hungary	N	N	N	Y[8]	N	N	N	N	NA
Iceland	NA	NA	NA	NA	NA	NA	NA	NA	NA
Ireland	NA	NA	NA	NA	NA	NA	NA	NA	NA
Israel	N	N	N	N	N	N	Y[9]	N	NA
Italy	NA	NA	NA	NA	NA	NA	NA	NA	NA
Japan	N	N	N	N[10]	N	N	N	N	NA
Korea	N	N	N	Y[11]	N	N	N	N	NA
Latvia	NA	NA	NA	NA	NA	NA	NA	NA	NA
Luxembourg	N	Y[12]	N	Y[13]	N	N	N	N	NA
Mexico	NA	NA	NA	NA	NA	NA	NA	NA	NA
Netherlands	NA	NA	NA	NA	NA	NA	NA	NA	NA
New Zealand	NA	NA	NA	NA	NA	NA	NA	NA	NA
Norway	N	Y[14]	N	N	N	N	Y	Y	NA
Poland	NA	NA	NA	NA	NA	NA	NA	NA	NA
Portugal	NA	NA	NA	NA	NA	NA	NA	NA	NA
Slovak Republic	NA	NA	NA	NA	NA	NA	NA	NA	NA
Slovenia	NA	NA	NA	NA	NA	NA	NA	NA	NA
Spain	N	N	N	N[15]	N	Y[16]	N	N	NA
Sweden	N	N	N	N	Y[17]	N	N	N	NA
Switzerland	NA	NA	NA	NA	NA	NA	NA	NA	NA
Turkey	NA	NA	NA	NA	NA	NA	NA	NA	NA
United Kingdom	N	N	N	N[18]	N	N	N	N	NA
United States	N	N[19]	N	N[20]	N	N	N	N	NA
Argentina	NA	NA	NA	NA	NA	NA	NA	NA	NA
Bulgaria	NA	NA	NA	NA	NA	NA	NA	NA	NA
Colombia	N	Y	N	N	N	Y	N[21]	N[21]	NA
Lithuania	NA	NA	NA	NA	NA	NA	NA	NA	NA
South Africa	N	N	N	N[22]	N	Y	N	N	NA

Table 2.7. **Tax treatment of different forms of saving: tax-favoured savings accounts** *(cont.)*

(as at 1 July 2016)

Notes

1. A refundable tax credit is given for contributions to special housing savings bank accounts where held for a minimum of six years. Contributions up to EUR 1 200 per year receive the tax credit. The tax credit rate varies with the average interest rate of Austrian government bonds.
2. Final withholding tax
3. First EUR 1 880 of interest is tax free.
4. Max contribution of CAD 5 500 per year (as of 2016), but unutilised contribution room is carried forward to future years.
5. Treated like pension income (EET, max deduction of EUR 5 000) if retained until paid out in instalments over at least 10 years following retirement age
6. Certain regulated savings income is expressly exempt from income tax: "A passbook", people's savings passbooks (LEP), youth passbooks, savings accounts for sustainable development (LDD), housing savings accounts (CEL). Interest on home-ownership savings plans (plans d'épargne-logement, PEL) is subject to the progressive income tax scale (or, optionally, a flat rate of 24%) for the portion of accrued interest as from the plan's twelfth anniversary. Interest from PEL and CEL are subject to social taxes.
7. Net wealth tax. The taxable threshold is set at EUR 1.3 million, but once this threshold has been achieved, the assets are taxed as of EUR 800 000.
8. Interest income is exempt if held for 5+ years. Healthcare tax due if income above HUF 450 000.
9. Advanced-study funds ("Keren Hishtalmut"). These funds are enjoyed by around 40% of the wage earners where the employer pays 7.5% of the worker's salary and the employee contributes 2.5% - up to a ceiling of ILS 15 712 per month. The employer contribution is tax exempt although there is no tax benefit on the employee contribution. The fund gains are tax exempt. Distributions are tax exempt after six years for any purpose. The self-employed enjoy an equivalent benefit.
10. Exempt up to JPY 5 500 000
11. Reduced rate for savings of up to KRW 20 million per year if account maintained for 5 years. Up to KRW 50 million if aged 15-29, and for business income earners whose global income is KRW 35 million or less and who maintain account for 3 years. Those aged 65 or older, disabled persons, and persons of distinguished service to the State, may invest up to KRW 50 million.
12. The contributions to building societies are deductible up to an amount of EUR 672 per year, only if the assets of this account are used to finance the construction, the purchasing or the transformation of an apartment or a dwelling for own needs.
13. Interest attributed to a building society account are exempted from taxation, however only if the assets of this account are used to finance the construction, the purchasing or the transformation of an apartment or a dwelling for own needs.
14. 20% tax credit for persons under the age of 34 for deposits in special home savings bank accounts. Maximum annual deposit is NOK 20 000 and maximum total deposit is NOK 150 000. In order to keep the tax credit the deposit must be used to acquire a dwelling or to pay instalments on loans on a dwelling that has been acquired after the home savings account was established.
15. Earnings are tax exempt as long as held for five years and then withdrawn in the form of a lump sum. Contributions cannot exceed EUR 5 000 per year.
16. Net wealth tax. Each resident taxpayer is entitled to a general exemption of EUR 700 000.
17. Imputed income of the investment savings account is taxed at a flat 30% tax rate.
18. Maximum total savings of GBP 20 000
19. However, some states have a limited deduction for contributions to tax preferred 529 plans for saving for future college expenses.
20. Some limitations depending on scheme
21. Requires a 5 year investment and then money to be used to purchase house otherwise distributions are taxable.
22. Annual contributions limited to SAR 30 000

Table 2.8. **Tax treatment of different forms of saving: owner-occupied residential property**

(as at 1 July 2016)

Country	Acquisition of asset			Holding of asset			Disposal of asset		
	PIT treatment		Transaction tax	PIT	Other taxes		PIT or CGT		
	Interest expense deductible	Amount of acquisition deductible		Income from asset	Income from asset	Value of asset	Realised income from asset	Original value of asset	Capital gains
Australia	N	N	Y	N	N	Y	N	N	N
Austria	N	N	Y	N	N	Y	N	N	N
Belgium	Y[1]	N	Y	N	N	Y	N	N	N
Canada	N	N	Y	N	N	Y	N	N	N
Chile	Y[2]	N	N	N	N	Y[3]	N	N	N
Czech Republic	Y	N	Y	N	N	Y	N	N	Y[4]
Denmark	Y	N	Y	N	Y[5]	Y	N	N	N
Estonia	Y[6]	N	N	N	N	Y	N	N	N
Finland	Y[7]	N	Y	N	N	Y	N	N	N
France	N	N	Y	N	N	Y[8]	N	N	N
Germany	N	N	Y	N	N	Y	N	N	Y[9]
Greece	Y	N	Y[10]	N	Y[5]	Y	N	N	N
Hungary	N	N	Y[10]	N	N	Y[11]	N	N	Y[12]
Iceland	N	N	Y	N	N	Y	N	N	N
Ireland	N	N	Y	N	N	Y	N	N	N
Israel	N	N	Y	N	N	Y	N	N	Y[13]
Italy	Y[14]	N	Y	N	N	Y[15]	N	N	Y[16]
Japan	Y[17]	N	N	N	N	Y	N	N	Y
Korea	Y[18]	N	Y	N	N	Y	N	N	Y[19]
Latvia	N	N	Y	N	N	Y	N	N	N
Luxembourg	Y[20]	N	N	N	N	Y	N	N	N
Mexico	Y	N	Y	N	N	Y	N	N	N[21]
Netherlands	Y	N	Y	Y[5]	N	Y[22]	N	N	N
New Zealand	N	N	N	N	N	Y	N	N	N
Norway	Y	N	Y	N	N	Y[23]	N	N	N
Poland	N	N	Y	N	N	Y	N	N	N
Portugal	N	N	Y	N	N	Y	N	N	N
Slovak Republic	N	N	N	N	N	Y	N	N	N
Slovenia	N	N	Y	N	N	Y	N	N	Y[24]
Spain	N[25]	N	Y	N	N	Y[26]	N	N	Y[27]
Sweden	Y	N	Y	N	N	Y[28]	N	N	Y[29]
Switzerland	Y	N	Y[30]	Y[5]	N	Y[30,31]	N	N	N
Turkey	N	N	Y	N	N	Y	N	N	N
United Kingdom	N	N	Y	N	N	Y	N	N	N
United States	Y	N	Y	N	N	Y	N	N	Y[32]
Argentina	Y	N	N	N	N	Y[31]	N	N	N
Bulgaria	Y[33]	N	Y	N	N	Y	N	N	N
Colombia	Y	N	N	N	N	Y[31]	N	N	Y
Lithuania	N	N	N	N	N	Y	N	N	Y[34]
South Africa	N	N	Y	N	N	Y	N	N	Y[35]

Table 2.8. **Tax treatment of different forms of saving: owner-occupied residential property** *(cont.)*

(as at 1 July 2016)

Notes

1. Tax credit received equals EUR 0.45 for every euro of interest paid. Cap of EUR 2 300 tax credit amount.
2. Interest not deductible if taxpayer earns above CLP 83 129 400 (in 2016).
3. Recurrent property tax applies if house value of CLP 21 934 249 or greater.
4. Gains are taxable if held for five years or less; or two years or less if the taxpayer's main residence (unless the gains are used to finance a new residence in which case not taxable even if held for two years or less).
5. Tax on imputed rental income.
6. Mortgage interest is deductible up to EUR 1 200 per year.
7. 55% of mortgage interest is deductible against capital income. Remaining interest is deductible against earned income up to EUR 1 400 per year.
8. Recurrent property tax plus net wealth tax. The taxable threshold for the net wealth tax is set at EUR 1.3 million, but once this threshold has been achieved, the assets are taxed as of EUR 800 000.
9. No CGT if held more than 10 years.
10. First-time house buyers are exempt from the transaction tax.
11. Recurrent property tax (building tax on dwellings) due in only some municipalities. In 2017 only 548 municipalities out of 3 178 levied building tax on dwellings.
12. The taxable capital gain is reduced by an increasing percentage each year and is exempt after five years.
13. CGT only applies on gains above a sale price of ILS 4.5 million.
14. A tax credit of 19% of mortgage interest is provided up to a max of EUR 4 000 of interest payment
15. Only luxury homes subject to recurrent property tax
16. Exempt from CGT if held at least five years
17. Tax credit equal to 1% of mortgage value
18. Deductible at taxpayer's marginal rate unless house cost more than KRW 400 million, and up to a limit depending on years being paid off.
19. 40% tax rate for short term holdings of less than 1 year. No CGT if held for 2 years or more. CGT is however still applicable if house is worth more than KRW 900 million.
20. Mortgage interest is deductible below a threshold (EUR 1 500 years 1-5; EUR 1 125 years 5-10; then EUR 750).
21. Unless gain exceeds 700 thousand investment units, or have sold a house within the previous five years.
22. Recurrent property tax
23. Recurrent property tax and net wealth tax. The tax-free allowance for the net wealth tax is NOK 1 400 000.
24. The tax rate for capital gains depends on the holding period: 25% for up to 5 years; 15% from 5 to 10 years; 10% from 10 to 15 years; 5%; and non-taxation for greater than 20 years.
25. A tax credit (which covered interest and amount of acquisition) was repealed in 2013. However, it can still be applied as a temporary regime by taxpayers who were applying the credit prior to 2013. According to their legal competences the mayority of regional governments (Comunidades Autónomas) apply the tax credit.
26. Recurrent property tax and net wealth tax. For net wealth tax, an exemption threshold of EUR 300 000 applies for the main residence.
27. However, full roll-over relief applies in respect of capital gains from disposals by any taxpayer of his primary residence. The exemption requires that the entire proceeds be reinvested within a 2-year period in the acquisition of another primary residence. Full exemption applies for taxpayers over 65 years old (see above).
28. Recurrent property tax has a maximum amount of SEK 7 412 for a house and SEK 1 268 for an apartment.
29. Only a proportion (22/30) of the capital gain is taxable.
30. Transaction taxes and recurrent property taxes are applied in many, but not all cantons. Neither are applied in Zurich which is used as the representative canton in the METR modelling in Chapter 3.
31. Recurrent property tax plus net wealth tax.
32. Untaxed if capital gain of less than USD 250 000 (or USD 500 000 for married filing jointly) and held for at least 2 of the last 5 years. Otherwise taxed at marginal PIT rates for short-term gains, and at preferential long-term rates for long-term gains.
33. Mortgage interest is deductible (for a married investor only) if either the investor or the spouse was under 35 years of age (and they were already married) at the start of the mortgage.
34. Taxable unless place of residence for at least 2 years; or if less than 2 years and income is used within one year to purchase a new place of residence.
35. Exempt if capital gain of less than SAR 2 million. Otherwise subject to marginal rates after 40% exclusion.

Table 2.9. **Tax treatment of different forms of saving: rented residential property**

(as at 1 July 2016)

Country	Acquisition of asset			Holding of asset			Disposal of asset		
	PIT treatment		Transaction tax	PIT	Other taxes		PIT or CGT		
	Interest expense deductible	Amount of acquisition deductible		Income from asset	Income from asset	Value of asset	Realised income from asset	Original value of asset	Capital gains
Australia	Y	N[1]	Y	Y	N	Y	N	N	Y
Austria	Y	N	Y	Y	N	Y	N	N	Y
Belgium	Y[2]	N	Y	Y[3]	N	Y	N	N	Y[4]
Canada	Y	N	Y	Y	N	Y	N	N	Y
Chile	Y[5]	N	N	N	N	Y6	N	N	N
Czech Republic	Y	N	Y	Y	N	Y	N	N	Y[7]
Denmark	Y	N	Y	N	Y[8]	Y	N	N	Y[9]
Estonia	Y[10]	N	N	Y[11]	N	Y	N	N	Y
Finland	Y[12]	N	Y	Y[13]	N	Y	N	N	Y
France	N	N	Y	Y	N	Y[14]	N	N	Y[15]
Germany	Y	N	Y	Y	N	Y	N	N	Y[16]
Greece	Y	N	Y[17]	Y	N	Y	N	N	Y
Hungary	N	N	Y	Y	N	Y[18]	N	N	Y[19]
Iceland	N	N	Y	N	Y[20]	Y	N	N	Y
Ireland	Y	N	Y	Y	N	Y	N	N	Y
Israel	N	N	Y	Y[21]	N	Y	N	N	Y
Italy	N	N	Y[22]	Y[23]	Y[23]	Y	N	N	Y[24]
Japan	Y	N	N	Y	N	Y	N	N	Y
Korea	Y[25]	N	Y	Y[26]	N	Y	N	N	Y[27]
Latvia	N	N	Y	Y[28]	N	Y	N	N	Y
Luxembourg	Y	N	N	Y	N	Y	N	N	Y
Mexico	Y	N	Y	Y	N	Y	N	N	Y
Netherlands	N	N	Y	N	Y[29]	Y	N	N	N
New Zealand	Y	N	N	Y	N	Y	N	N	N
Norway	Y	N	Y	Y	N	Y[30]	N	N	Y
Poland	Y	N	Y	Y	N	Y	N	N	Y
Portugal	N	N	Y	Y	N	Y	N	N	Y[31]
Slovak Republic	N	N	N	Y[32]	N	Y	N	N	N
Slovenia	N	N	Y	N	Y[1]	Y	N	N	Y[33]
Spain	Y	N	Y	Y[34]	N	Y[35]	N	N	Y
Sweden	Y	N	Y	Y	N	Y[36]	N	N	Y[37]
Switzerland	Y	N	Y[38]	Y	N	Y[38,39]	N	N	Y
Turkey	Y	N	Y	Y	N	Y	N	N	N
United Kingdom	Y	N	Y	Y	N	Y	N	N	Y
United States	Y	N	Y	Y	N	Y	N	N	Y[40]
Argentina	N	N	N	Y	N	Y	N	N	N
Bulgaria	N	N	Y	Y	N	Y	N	N	Y[41]
Colombia	Y	N	N	Y	N	Y	N	N	Y
Lithuania	N	N	N	Y	N	Y	N	N	Y[42]
South Africa	Y	N	Y	Y	N	Y	N	N	Y[43]

Table 2.9. **Tax treatment of different forms of saving: rented residential property** *(cont.)*

(as at 1 July 2016)

Notes

1. No general depreciation deduction. But cost of depreciable assets in a rental property are deductible
2. While mortgage interest is not deductible, a tax credit is provided equal to EUR 0.45 for every euro of mortgage principle paid, limited to the first EUR 76 780 of the loan.
3. Imputed income is taxed at progressive PIT rates
4. If held less than five years.
5. Interest not deductible if taxpayer earns above CLP 83 129 400 (90 UTA).
6. Recurrent property tax applies if house value of CLP 21 934 249 or greater.
7. Taxable if held <5 years; or <2 years if taxpayer's main residence (unless used to finance new residence).
8. A splitting system applies. See Chapter 3 for further detail.
9. Taxed at flat rate as "net capital income" under semi-dual system
10. Mortgage interest is deductible up to EUR 1 200 per year.
11. Income tax only applies to 80% of rental income
12. Deductible against capital income
13. Rental income is taxed as investment income, but at a flat 30% rate.
14. Recurrent property tax plus net wealth tax. The taxable threshold for the net wealth tax is set at EUR 1.3 million, but once this threshold has been achieved, the assets are taxed as of EUR 800 000.
15. Subject to flat withholding tax plus social taxes. A reduction is provided if held more than six years. Untaxed if held for more than 22 years (withholding tax) and 30 years (social taxes).
16. No CGT if held more than 10 years
17. First-time house buyers are exempt from the transaction tax.
18. Recurrent property tax (building tax on dwellings) due in only some municipalities. In 2017 only 548 municipalities of 3178 levied building tax on dwellings.
19. The taxable capital gain is reduced by an increasing percentage each year and is exempt after five years.
20. 50% of rental income is exempt and 50% is subject to a flat 20% capital income tax rate
21. Taxpayer has three options: exemption of rental income up to a ceiling of ILS 5,030; 10% tax on gross rental income, with no deductions; or marginal tax rate (30% to 48%) on rental income net of expenses
22. Higher transaction tax rate for second homes than owner-occupied home
23. Actual rental income from residential property is taxed under ordinary PIT, with 95% of the annual rent included in the tax base. Alternatively, the taxpayer can choose to pay a 21% "coupon tax" on rental income (10% in the case of pre-agreed controlled rents).
24. Exempt from CGT if held at least five years
25. 40% of interest and principle is deductible against salary and wage income.
26. Exempt if rental income does not exceed KRW 20 million income until 2016.
27. 40% tax rate if held <1 year. For 5 years, taxable but get 15% reduction; if 10 years get 38% reduction
28. Special PIT rate applied at flat concessionary rate.
29. Deemed return on net asset value (value less debt) is taxed. First EUR 24 437 of total assets excluding pensions and owner-occupied housing is exempt.
30. Recurrent property tax and net wealth tax. The tax-free allowance for the net wealth tax is NOK 1 400 000.
31. Half of capital gains are indexed.
32. Rental income less than EUR 500 is untaxed.
33. The tax rate for capital gains depends on the holding period: 25% for up to 5 years; 15% from 5 to 10 years; 10% from 10 to 15 years; 5%; and non-taxation for greater than 20 years.
34. 60% reduction in tax on rental income
35. Recurrent property tax and net wealth tax. For net wealth tax, an exemption threshold of EUR 700 000 is applied in general for all assets, including rented residential property.
36. Recurrent property tax has a maximum amount of SEK 7 412 for a house and SEK 1 268 for an apartment.
37. Only 90% of the capital gain is taxable when used mainly for business
38. Transaction taxes and recurrent property taxes are applied in many, but not all cantons. Neither are applied in Zurich which is used as the representative canton in the METR modelling in chapter 3.
39. Recurrent property tax plus net wealth tax.
40. Lower rate schedule applies for long term gains of more than one year. Gain attributable to any accelerated depreciation is taxable at ordinary rates. Gain attributable to straight-line depreciation is taxed at ordinary rates up to 25%.
41. No CGT if held more than three years, but only for one house sold per year.
42. If held less than 10 years.
43. Subject to marginal PIT rates after 40% exclusion.

Notes

1. An expenditure tax can be implemented either by taxing consumption directly (e.g. with a VAT) or indirectly by taxing income but exempting savings from the tax base.
2. In the United States, capital gains in the lowest brackets (currently 10% and 15%) are taxed at a zero rate. Capital gains in the middle brackets are taxed at 15%. Capital gains of the highest income taxpayers are taxed at 20%. As of 2017, capital gains of high income taxpayers are also subject to a 3.8% tax on net investment income.
3. Note that, as of 2017, the deemed return applied on net assets increases with the net value of the assets. The tax rate applied continues to be 30%.
4. Note that exemption thresholds can vary across asset types. For instance, Spain provides a general threshold (which covers all assets, including bank account balances), and a specific threshold for the main residence. Both thresholds are compatible.
5. The United States has a number of limited purpose savings accounts for education and health expenses which have limits on contributions.

Chapter 3

Marginal effective tax rates on household savings

This chapter presents estimates of marginal effective tax rates (METRs) across a range of savings vehicles for 40 OECD and key partner countries to assess the effect of tax systems on the incentives individuals face to save in different forms. The results highlight significant variation in METRs across savings vehicles, with tax systems creating significant incentives to alter portfolio allocation away from that which would be optimal in the absence of taxation. Private pension funds tend to be the most tax-favoured, with owner-occupied residential property also significantly tax-favoured. In contrast to owner-occupied residential property, rental property is often subject to relatively high METRs due to the application of progressive marginal personal income tax rates, capital gains taxes and significant property taxes. Bank accounts and corporate bonds also tend to be relatively heavily taxed in many countries.

3.1. Introduction

An individual can choose to save in a wide range of different forms. Typical options include putting money in a bank account, pension scheme or investment fund, and purchasing bonds, equities or residential property. However, these different savings vehicles may be taxed in very different ways, potentially distorting the savings portfolio choices that individuals and households make. Given the strong empirical evidence, highlighted in Chapter 1, that taxes do affect household portfolio allocation decisions, the differential taxation of savings vehicles is likely to lead to significant welfare costs. There may be a specific policy rationale for the provision of tax concessions to certain savings vehicles, while tax differentials may also have arisen over time through piecemeal reform processes. In either case, it is important to be able to quantify the tax differentials in place so that the incentive effects of the tax system are clear, and the merits of the underlying tax provisions can be properly assessed.

Any assessment of the impact of tax systems on the incentives individuals face to save in different forms is complicated by the range of different taxes and tax designs that are applied to different savings vehicles. A focus on statutory tax rates, for example, will not capture the impact of multiple taxes on a particular savings vehicle, of deductions and variations in the tax base, of different holding periods and the potential build-up of untaxed or tax-deferred returns, and of variation in the type of return generated (e.g. interest, dividends, or capital gains). In addition, statutory tax rates do not take account of inflation which can impose a substantial additional tax on the return to savings. In contrast, marginal effective tax rate (METR) modelling enables the impact of a wide range of taxes and tax design features to be summarised in the one indicator.

This chapter presents estimates of METRs across a range of savings vehicles for 40 OECD and key partner countries to assess the effect of tax systems on the incentives individuals face to save in different forms. METR calculations are based on rules in place as of 1 July 2016 as described in country responses to a questionnaire sent to country delegates to Working Party No. 2 on Tax Policy Analysis and Tax Statistics of the OECD's Committee on Fiscal Affairs.

The results for the 40 countries highlight significant variation in METRs across savings vehicles, with tax systems creating significant incentives to alter portfolio allocation away from that which would be optimal in a no-tax world. Some assets tend to be particularly tax-favoured as compared to others. Pension funds tend to be the most tax-favoured, with owner-occupied residential property also significantly tax-favoured. In contrast to owner-occupied residential property, rental property is often subject to relatively high METRs due to the application of progressive marginal personal income tax (PIT) rates, capital gains taxes and significant property taxes. Bank accounts and corporate bonds also tend to be relatively heavily taxed in many countries. As noted above, while there may be a clear policy rationale for the provision of some concessions, the merits of these concessions need to be weighed against the resulting welfare costs. In this regard, country-specific circumstances are likely to be particularly important.

The chapter proceeds as follows: Section 3.2 outlines the METR methodology and key assumptions made, before section 3.3 presents the METR results.

3.2. Methodology

The METR methodology in this report follows broadly the approach of the OECD's 1994 *Taxation and Household Savings* study (OECD, 1994), which itself drew on the methods used by King and Fullerton (1984).[1] This section describes this methodology, including the key assumptions that have been made as well as the limitations of the approach. The underlying METR equations derived under this methodology and used to calculate the METRs for each savings vehicle are presented in Annex A.

Marginal Investment

As emphasised in the OECD (1994) study, the appropriate way to analyse the effect of tax on savings decisions is to examine the incentives faced by the taxpayer at the margin. The analysis therefore focuses on a saver who is contemplating investing an additional currency unit in one of a range of potential savings vehicles. The investment is a marginal investment, both in terms of being an incremental purchase of the asset, and in terms of generating a net return just sufficient to make the investment worthwhile (as compared to the next best savings opportunity).

The approach assumes a fixed pre-tax real rate of return and calculates the minimum post-tax real rate of return that will for that asset, at the margin, make the investment worthwhile. The METR can then be calculated as the difference between the pre- and post-tax rates of return (the savings income tax wedge) divided by the pre-tax rate of return.

The post-tax rate of return is determined by explicitly modelling the stream of returns and taxes associated with a marginal investment over time. The modelling incorporates the impact of a wide range of taxes, including income taxes (at the personal level as well as at the level of the savings intermediary such as an investment or pension fund), taxes on realised capital gains (with or without indexation), taxes on gross asset purchases and/or sales, transaction taxes and taxes on the stock of an asset (i.e. wealth taxes). The tax gain as a result of the deductibility of savings from taxable income as well as of interest payments that have to be paid if the investment is partly or fully financed with borrowed funds are modelled as well.

Types of savings vehicles modelled

While it is not practicable to cover all possible types of savings vehicles present in all countries, this report does extend considerably beyond the five-asset scope of the original OECD (1994) study. METRs are calculated for the following different savings vehicles, which can be expected to cover the majority of household savings in most countries:

- Bank deposits
- Corporate bonds
- Government bonds
- Equities (purchase of corporate shares)

- Investment fund assets (marketable collective investment vehicles)
- Private pensions
- Deposits in individual tax-favoured savings accounts
- Equity-financed owner-occupied residential property
- Equity-financed rented residential property
- Debt-financed owner-occupied residential property
- Debt-financed rented residential property

Fixed pre-tax rate of return approach

The adoption of a fixed pre-tax rate of return follows the approach taken in the OECD (1994) study. This approach is conventionally denoted the *fixed-p* (or *fixed-r*) approach and focuses on investments that would yield the same pre-tax return at the margin and thus be equally attractive in the absence of tax. As emphasised in the OECD (1994) study, the fixed-p approach effectively assumes that arbitrage between different assets in international capital markets results in all assets generating the same rates of return before taxes. Individual savers then arrange their portfolios in light of the individual-level tax rules.

This approach is consistent with the highly integrated nature of modern international capital markets and the predominantly residence-based taxation of international portfolio savings. The main alternative approach would have been to fix the post-tax rate of return (and then calculate the required pre-tax rate of return to generate this; i.e. a *fixed-s* approach). However, such an approach would be more appropriate in the case where international portfolio savings were predominantly taxed on a source basis – as arbitrage would then equate post-tax returns across assets. Meanwhile, in closed economies, any tax would change the interest rate in that economy, and so unless the elasticities of saving and investment with respect to the interest rate were known, any assumption about fixing either the pre- or post-tax rates of return would necessarily be only approximate.

The pre-tax real rate of return adopted in calculating the preliminary METRs presented in the next section is three percent. Results were also calculated for a pre-tax real rate of return of two and four percent to examine the sensitivity of the results to the pre-tax real rate of return. For completeness, these additional results are presented in Annex B.

Inflation rate

Results are presented for the different savings vehicles first allowing inflation to vary across countries (reflecting the actual inflation rates in each country). To aid cross-country comparison, results are also shown for a common inflation rate (the OECD average). In both cases, inflation rates are based on the five-year average from Q3 2011 to Q2 2016.[2] Results were also calculated for a zero rate of inflation to examine the sensitivity of the results to inflation. For completeness, these additional results are also presented in Annex B.

Tax rates

METR results are presented for three different taxpayer types to account for potential variation in statutory marginal tax rates depending on an individual's situation. In the majority of cases, simply specifying an income level is sufficient to determine the appropriate marginal tax rate to apply for each taxpayer type. However, in some cases the appropriate statutory marginal tax rate, or even the applicability of a tax, may also depend on the amount and type of capital income or wealth held by the taxpayer.[3] As such, each taxpayer type is defined by both an income level and a wealth level held at the time their investment decision is being made (with wealth further split between housing and non-housing wealth). Capital income levels, when necessary, are then determined by applying a 3% real return on wealth (under the assumption that all non-property income is from wealth held in the particular asset being modelled).[4] The three taxpayer types are defined as follows:

- **Low-rate taxpayer**: a single individual earning annual combined (labour plus capital) income equal to 67% of the average wage, with no or minimal net wealth such that their marginal currency unit of savings always benefits from a tax free allowance or tax credit, if one is provided.
- **Average-rate taxpayer**: a single individual earning annual combined (labour plus capital) income equal to 100% of the average wage, with net wealth equal to six times the average wage, of which three-quarters is held in residential property.
- **High-rate taxpayer**: a single individual earning annual combined (labour plus capital) income equal to 500% of the average wage, with net wealth equal to twenty times the average wage, of which half is held in residential property.

Holding period

The length of time that an asset is held can be crucial in determining the taxes paid on the investment. The approach taken here again follows broadly the approach of OECD (1994) in applying a fixed probability of sale to each period. The expected return is then calculated for each asset, on a risk-neutral basis. The expected holding period of the asset is equal to the reciprocal of the fixed probability of sale in each period.

This "endogenous asset holding period" approach has a number of advantages. First, it allows the modelling of different holding periods while avoiding the presence of time-related variables in the analytical solution of the derived effective tax rates. Second, it allows for the impact of deferral of taxes that only have to be paid when the asset is sold. Third, where tax rates vary with the holding period, the method could be potentially extended to implicitly weight the different tax rates according to the different holding periods. The latter extension is not pursued in this report to allow for the possibility of showing METRs for different holding periods.

The expected holding period adopted in calculating the METRs presented in the next section is five years for all savings vehicles with the exception of pension funds and housing where the expected holding period is 20 years. The probability of sale applied to each period is therefore 0.05 for pension funds and housing, and 0.2 for all other assets. Results for additional expected holding periods are presented in Annex B.

For capital gains taxes that vary with the holding period, a simplifying assumption has been made in the modelling. Rather than modelling for each year the particular capital gains tax rate that would apply if the asset was sold in that particular year, the calculations use for each year the tax rate that matches the expected holding period. As pointed out, this modelling simplification allows results to be presented for assets held for different expected holding periods.

Type of returns generated

The return to investment in equities may be in the form of dividends, capital gains or a combination of the two. The OECD (1994) study assumed a fixed proportion of returns were derived as dividends and as capital gains. A different approach is taken here, with METRs presented separately for three different scenarios: 100% of the return as dividends; 100% of the return as capital gains; and 50% of the return as each.

Similarly, the return on bonds can be in the form of interest or, when sold below par, as capital gains. A similar approach to that applied to equities has been adopted, with results presented for bonds issued at par (where 100% of the return is in the form of interest) and for bonds issued below par (where 75% of the return is in the form of interest and 25% is capital gains).

Investment funds and pension funds

A simplified approach has been taken regarding the taxation of investment funds. These are modelled under the assumption that all income earned in the fund is retained and reinvested each year until final disposition. Many countries do not impose any tax at the level of the investment fund. However, for countries that impose a fixed rate annual tax at the level of the investment fund, this is modelled with the remaining funds then assumed to be immediately reinvested. If different tax rates are applied at the investment fund level depending on the type of income earned, all income is assumed to be from dividends. In countries where distribution is legally required each year, all income is again assumed to be from dividends, with the remaining funds then being immediately reinvested as a new investment within in the same type of fund.

Income received within a pension fund is also currently assumed to be taxed at a single rate (if it is taxed at all), with the remaining funds then immediately reinvested. On final distribution, the most concessionary tax treatment available is modelled. For example, lower rates (or exemptions) may be provided if a private pension is paid out as an annuity rather than a lump sum, or if payments are not made until a specific retirement age is reached. In such cases, an annuity is assumed to have been chosen and the required retirement age is assumed to have been reached.

For countries that tax distributions from private pension funds at progressive marginal rates, we model two scenarios: first, income in retirement is assumed to be the same as when contributions are made (so marginal tax rates will remain the same); and second, income in retirement is assumed to be lower than when making contributions (potentially resulting in a lower marginal tax rate at retirement). The assumed income reductions are as follows:

- A high-rate taxpayer's income is assumed to fall in retirement from 500% of the average wage to 250% of the average wage.
- An average-rate taxpayer's income is assumed to fall in retirement from 100% of the average wage to 67% of the average wage.
- A low-rate taxpayer's income is assumed to fall in retirement from 67% of the average wage to 50% of the average wage.

Social security contributions

In addition to income taxes, social security contributions (SSCs) may in some cases be payable on income from capital. Following the approach of the OECD (1994) study, the current study focuses on personal taxes on household savings, and hence SSCs are beyond its scope.

As such, SSCs are not taken account of in the modelling, either in terms of their imposition on income from capital, or on whether certain payments (e.g. pension contributions, mortgage interest deductions) reduce the base on which contributions are due. There are two exceptions to this general approach: France and the Netherlands[5] considered SSCs applicable on capital income to be sufficiently close in nature to pure taxes as to warrant their inclusion in the modelling.

Recurrent property taxes

In most countries, recurrent property taxes are implemented at the sub-central level and rates and bases can vary across the country. Consequently one of two simplified modelling approaches has been adopted on a country-by-country basis. Countries have either applied an estimated average tax rate for the entire country, or a representative municipality/region has been chosen to be adopted in the modelling.

In most countries, the tax base is related closely to the property value. However, the base is often lower than current market value (which is effectively the tax base in the METR calculations – see the methodological annex). Where available, an estimate has consequently been made of the degree to which the actual tax base is undervalued as compared to current market value. In countries where an estimate of undervaluation was not available (Bulgaria, Germany, Iceland, Spain, Turkey) recurrent property tax figures are likely to be overstated. In some countries the tax base depends predominantly on house or property size rather than value, in which case an assumption has been made regarding a "representative" property size, again on a country-by-country basis.

Given the variation in approaches taken, the recurrent property tax modelling should be considered indicative and approximate only.

Limitations of the methodology

While there is great analytical utility in being able to summarise complex tax systems into a single comparable parameter, the METR methodology is not without limitations. In particular, the METRs are scenario and assumption driven, with results sensitive to those scenarios (e.g. the income level chosen) and assumptions (e.g. on inflation, the real rate of return, expected holding period, split between income and capital gains).

For simplicity, the modelling also effectively assumes certainty as to the pre-tax rate of return, the tax system and other parameters that in reality may be subject to change over time. While there is uncertainty over the holding period of an asset, savers are assumed to be risk neutral to this uncertainty – which may not be the case in reality. More fundamentally, the fixed-p approach ignores differences in risk among alternative investments (i.e. higher risk assets are likely to require higher pre-tax rates of return) and that rates of return may vary with household wealth (e.g. because of better quality information of investment opportunities).

The study is also limited to examining the impact of taxes directly imposed at the personal level on savings. It therefore does not account for the possible impact of other taxes, such as taxes directly on labour and consumption, or estate and gift taxes, on savings behaviour at the margin. That said, such effects (if any) are likely to be small.

The omission of the corporate income tax (CIT) from the modelling means that the METRs may not present a full picture of all the taxes imposed on equity investment. The degree to which the METRs capture the total tax burden on equity investment will vary across countries, depending on the mix of taxes imposed at the corporate and personal level and the country's approach to integration of corporate and personal level taxation. Using the METRs to compare the total tax imposed on equity with tax imposed on other assets, or to compare across countries, should therefore be undertaken with great caution.

Table 3.1 highlights the degree of variation in approaches to the integration of corporate and personal level taxation. A number of countries apply pure classical systems, while many apply a modified classical system where dividends are taxed at a lower rate than other forms of capital income (thereby providing partial relief from double taxation). Many countries apply fixed withholding rates that may be lower than the tax that would have been due if they were subject to marginal PIT rates. Partial tax relief is also applied in various other ways at either corporate level (Allowance for Corporate Equity) or individual level (partial inclusion, dividend exemption, or via the provision of a rate of return allowance). Partial imputation systems may give full relief from corporate level tax to some taxpayers but not to all, while full imputation gives full relief from corporate level tax at the personal level.

Table 3.1. **Approaches to integration of corporate and personal level taxation**

Classical system	Modified classical	Final withholding	Allowance for Corporate Equity	Partial inclusion	Rate of Return allowance	Dividend exemption	Partial imputation	Full imputation
Bulgaria	Denmark	Argentina	Belgium	Finland	Norway	Colombia	Korea	Australia
Germany	Japan	Austria	Italy	France		Estonia	United Kingdom	Canada
Iceland	Lithuania	Czech Republic	Turkey	Luxembourg		Slovak Republic		Chile
Ireland	Norway	Greece						Mexico
Latvia	Switzerland	Hungary						New Zealand
Netherlands	United States	Israel						
Spain		Poland						
Sweden		Portugal						
		Slovenia						
		South Africa						

Note: For more detail on different approaches to the integration of corporate and personal level taxes, see Harding and Marten (2018).
Source: Harding and Marten (2018), OECD Tax Database, IBFD Tax Research Platform.

3.3. Results

This section presents detailed METR results for all countries and all asset types. Tables 3.2-3.4 present results using the actual country inflation rate for the three different taxpayer types (low-rate, average-rate and high-rate taxpayers). These results are used for within-country comparison of METRs across asset types, but not for cross-country comparison. Tables 3.5-3.7 instead present results using a common (OECD average) inflation rate to aid cross-country comparison of METRs for a particular asset type (by removing variations in inflation as a cause of METR differences). Overall results from Tables 3.2-3.4 are first summarised below in box-and-whisker plot form, while results are also presented separately for each country in graphical form at the end of the section.

Overall, the results show significant variation in METRs across asset types, with tax systems creating significant incentives to alter portfolio allocation away from that which would be optimal in a no-tax world. This variation can be seen in Figure 3.1, which summarises the distribution of METR results across countries in box-and-whisker plots for each asset type. The bold horizontal line within each "box" represents the median METR for that asset type, while the box itself reflects the inter-quartile range (the distance between the first and third quartile). The extreme points of each "whisker" show the minimum and maximum METR values for each asset type (excluding outliers[6]).

Figure 3.1 highlights that some asset types tend to be particularly tax-favoured as compared to others. Pension funds tend to be the most tax-favoured, with owner-occupied residential property, and tax-favoured savings accounts (when present) also tending to be significantly tax-favoured. The tax advantage towards pension funds tends to increase with income, though there is considerable variation across countries. In contrast to owner-occupied residential property, rental property is often subject to relatively high METRs due to the application of progressive marginal personal income tax (PIT) rates, capital gains taxes and significant property taxes. Bank accounts and corporate bonds tend to be relatively heavily taxed in many countries.

METRs are often significantly higher than statutory tax rates because they combine the impact of multiple taxes – as well as the impact of inflation – in a single indicator. (Box 3.1 discusses further the differences between METRs and statutory tax rates.)

The rest of this section examines in detail the results for each asset type, in turn, before discussing the sensitivity of the results to the underlying modelling assumptions.

Box 3.1. **Comparing effective and statutory marginal tax rates**

The marginal **effective** tax rates (METRs) presented in Tables 3.2-3.7 are often significantly higher than marginal **statutory** tax rates applicable to income from saving in a particular asset. As presented in detail in the methodology section and Annex A, this is because METRs combine various factors – including the impact of multiple taxes, deductions and variations in tax bases, and the impact of inflation – in a single tax burden indicator. As such, METRs provide a far more complete picture of the tax-induced incentives individuals face to save in different assets.

Factors that increase METRs include:

- The presence of multiple taxes on saving in a particular asset, such as income taxes, capital gains taxes, transaction taxes, and wealth or property taxes (if applicable in a particular country).
- Where savings occurs through an intermediary, the imposition of taxes on the same income at both the intermediate and personal level.
- Inflation, where taxes are imposed on nominal rather than real returns.

Factors that reduce METRs include:

- Tax deferral effects – where statutory tax rates are imposed only once income is realised as opposed to when it accrues (e.g. capital gains); or where lower statutory tax rates apply beyond a specified holding period.
- Reductions in the tax base – such as basic allowances or exemptions for an amount of savings income, tax deductions or tax credits (e.g. for contributions to private pension schemes or for mortgage interest payments).

The impact of these different factors may also vary with the underlying assumptions of the specific METR being calculated – e.g. the taxpayer type (and corresponding income and wealth levels), how long the asset is owned, and the type of return generated (e.g. interest, dividends or capital gains).

The METR calculations presented in this chapter show that, in general, factors increasing METRs above statutory tax rates tend to outweigh factors decreasing them below statutory rates, particularly for higher income taxpayers. The most significant exception to this is tax relief for private pension contributions which often more than outweighs the tax paid when the pension is received in retirement, resulting in negative METRs.

Figure 3.1. **Distribution of marginal effective tax rates across countries for each asset type, 2016**

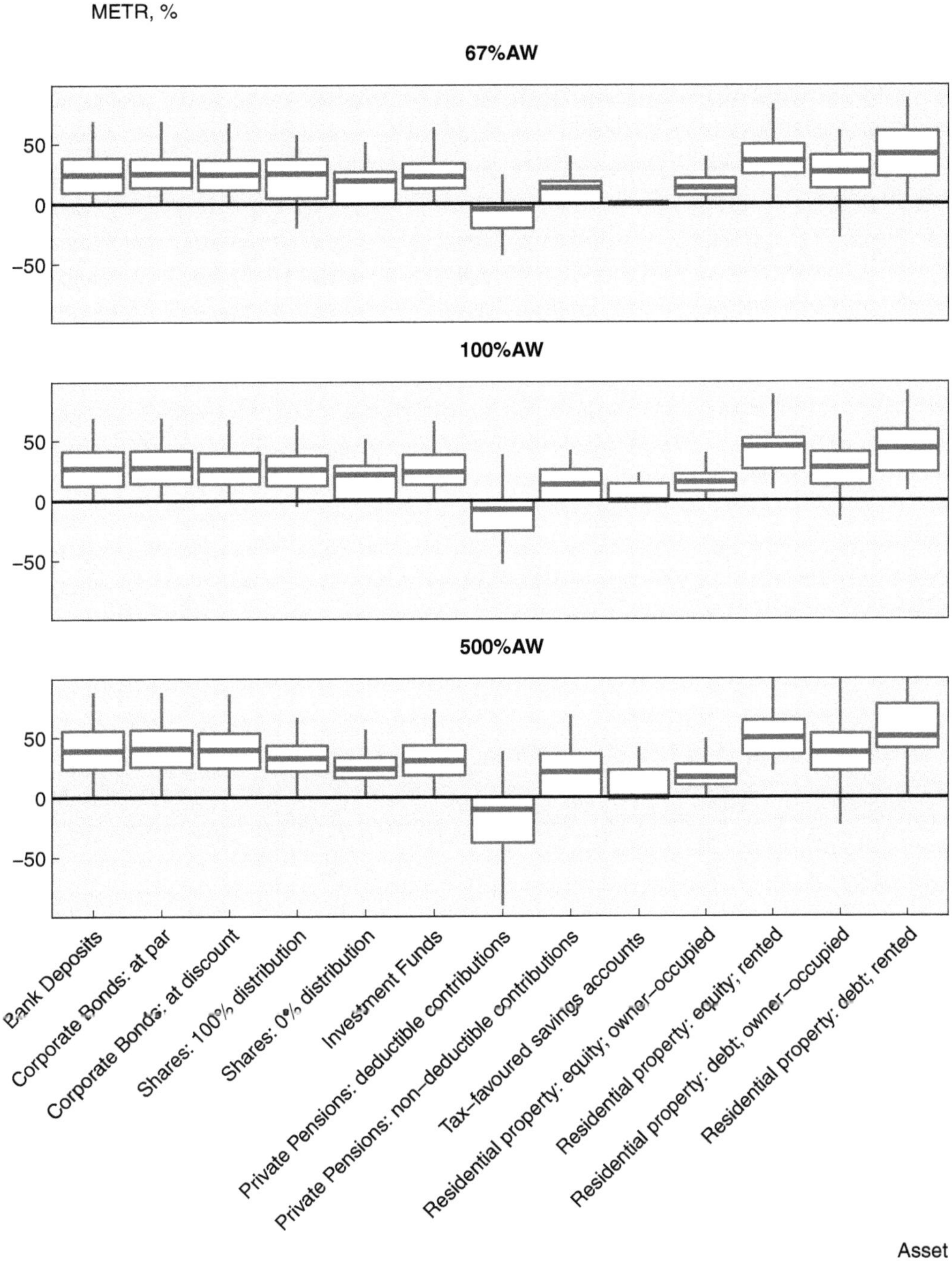

Explanatory note: The bold horizontal line within each "box" represents the median METR for that asset type, while the box itself reflects the inter-quartile range. The extreme points of each "whisker" show the minimum and maximum METR values for each asset type, excluding outliers. An outlier is defined as a result more than 1.5 times the inter-quartile range below the first quartile or above the third quartile.

StatLink http://dx.doi.org/10.1787/888933660355

Table 3.2. **Marginal effective tax rates by asset, 2016 – Personal tax rate: 67% of average wage case; Inflation: country actual**

Country	Bank deposits	Corporate bonds		Government bonds		Shares		
		Issued at par	Issued at discount	Issued at par	Issued at discount	100% distribution	50% distribution	0% distribution
Australia	58.4%	58.4%	56.3%	58.4%	56.3%	7.6%	15.7%	24.0%
Austria	40.3%	44.3%	42.6%	44.3%	42.6%	44.3%	40.9%	37.3%
Belgium	40.8%	41.5%	40.0%	41.5%	40.0%	42.9%	22.3%	1.8%
Canada	30.3%	30.1%	25.7%	30.1%	25.7%	0.0%	6.2%	12.6%
Chile	0.0%	0.0%	0.0%	0.0%	0.0%	-52.6%	-26.3%	0.0%
Czech Republic	21.6%	21.6%	16.2%	21.6%	16.2%	21.6%	10.8%	0.0%
Denmark	50.9%	50.9%	49.4%	50.9%	49.4%	57.8%	54.6%	51.2%
Estonia	0.0%	30.9%	29.7%	30.9%	29.7%	0.0%	12.8%	25.9%
Finland	43.9%	43.9%	42.4%	43.9%	42.4%	37.3%	37.5%	37.8%
France	37.4%	37.4%	36.3%	37.4%	36.3%	30.1%	27.3%	24.5%
Germany	0.0%	0.0%	0.0%	0.0%	0.0%	0.0%	0.0%	0.0%
Greece	13.4%	13.4%	13.0%	0.0%	0.0%	22.2%	23.0%	23.9%
Hungary	24.1%	24.1%	18.0%	24.1%	18.0%	16.0%	14.6%	13.1%
Iceland	0.0%	0.0%	8.0%	0.0%	8.0%	41.7%	37.4%	33.0%
Ireland	50.3%	31.3%	32.4%	31.3%	23.5%	38.8%	40.5%	42.4%
Israel	19.3%	19.3%	18.6%	19.3%	18.6%	25.7%	24.1%	22.4%
Italy	37.9%	37.9%	36.6%	19.1%	18.3%	37.3%	34.8%	32.1%
Japan	24.7%	24.7%	23.9%	24.7%	23.9%	13.1%	17.2%	21.4%
Korea	21.4%	21.4%	20.5%	21.4%	20.5%	29.3%	18.0%	6.6%
Latvia	13.3%	13.3%	14.2%	13.3%	14.2%	13.3%	15.1%	17.0%
Luxembourg	14.8%	14.8%	11.1%	14.8%	11.1%	25.2%	12.6%	0.0%
Mexico	1.1%	1.1%	1.0%	1.1%	1.0%	-20.0%	-1.8%	16.7%
Netherlands	40.0%	40.0%	40.0%	40.0%	40.0%	40.0%	40.0%	40.0%
New Zealand	23.9%	23.9%	23.0%	23.9%	23.0%	-14.4%	-7.2%	0.0%
Norway	68.8%	68.8%	67.5%	68.8%	67.5%	28.3%	28.3%	28.3%
Poland	25.8%	25.8%	24.9%	25.8%	24.9%	25.8%	23.9%	22.0%
Portugal	37.9%	37.9%	36.7%	37.9%	36.7%	37.9%	35.4%	32.8%
Slovak Republic	27.1%	27.1%	26.1%	27.1%	26.1%	0.0%	11.3%	23.0%
Slovenia	32.9%	32.9%	31.8%	32.9%	31.8%	32.9%	25.0%	16.8%
Spain	27.0%	27.0%	25.5%	27.0%	25.5%	27.0%	24.0%	21.0%
Sweden	35.0%	35.0%	34.0%	35.0%	34.0%	35.0%	33.0%	31.0%
Switzerland	13.9%	15.0%	11.5%	15.0%	11.5%	15.0%	8.0%	1.0%
Turkey	55.7%	55.7%	51.2%	55.7%	51.2%	38.5%	19.3%	0.0%
United Kingdom	0.0%	0.0%	0.0%	0.0%	0.0%	0.0%	0.0%	0.0%
United States	22.6%	22.6%	21.6%	22.6%	21.6%	0.0%	0.0%	0.0%
Argentina	0.0%	25.0%	25.0%	0.0%	0.0%	25.0%	25.0%	25.0%
Bulgaria	10.2%	0.0%	0.0%	0.0%	0.0%	6.4%	3.2%	0.0%
Colombia	7.0%	9.0%	8.5%	9.0%	8.5%	0.0%	0.0%	0.0%
Lithuania	0.0%	0.0%	0.0%	0.0%	0.0%	22.9%	11.4%	0.0%
South Africa	0.0%	0.0%	0.0%	0.0%	0.0%	45.6%	23.6%	16.4%

Table 3.2. **Marginal effective tax rates by asset, 2016 – Personal tax rate: 67% of average wage case; Inflation: country actual** *(cont.)*

Country	Investment funds	Pension funds		Tax-favoured savings accounts	Residential property			
					Equity-financed		Debt-financed	
		Deductible contributions	Non-deductible contributions		Owner-occupied	Rented	Owner-occupied	Rented
Australia	58.4%	-15.0%	25.4%	n.a.	14.7%	82.5%	58.5%	82.5%
Austria	39.1%	-7.4%	0.0%	40.3%	15.5%	53.2%	46.3%	40.0%
Belgium	0.0%	-52.4%	13.3%	0.0%	49.3%	50.6%	25.7%	79.2%
Canada	30.1%	0.0%	16.7%	0.0%	38.9%	62.9%	60.6%	62.9%
Chile	0.0%	0.0%	0.0%	n.a.	0.0%	0.0%	0.0%	0.0%
Czech Republic	7.2%	0.0%	12.1%	n.a.	11.1%	22.1%	11.1%	22.1%
Denmark	57.8%	21.1%	21.1%	n.a.	21.3%	47.5%	16.3%	53.2%
Estonia	25.9%	-20.8%	16.7%	n.a.	0.0%	22.4%	-28.4%	22.4%
Finland	37.8%	0.0%	25.4%	0.0%	12.1%	48.9%	29.5%	48.9%
France	32.7%	-2.3%	15.7%	0.0%	22.8%	39.6%	53.6%	69.3%
Germany	0.0%	0.0%	28.1%	n.a.	19.4%	57.4%	19.4%	16.5%
Greece	12.0%	0.0%	0.0%	n.a.	27.2%	26.2%	30.7%	29.8%
Hungary	13.1%	-41.7%	0.0%	0.0%	14.9%	30.2%	33.7%	48.4%
Iceland	33.0%	0.0%	39.7%	n.a.	15.5%	36.1%	43.4%	63.2%
Ireland	45.0%	11.5%	19.3%	n.a.	6.6%	37.0%	51.8%	60.3%
Israel	22.4%	-89.7%	0.0%	0.0%	10.0%	28.4%	26.7%	44.3%
Italy	27.1%	-2.0%	36.0%	n.a.	1.8%	47.2%	13.2%	76.4%
Japan	21.4%	-4.9%	5.7%	0.0%	20.8%	31.4%	12.8%	41.7%
Korea	21.4%	-19.6%	4.0%	0.0%	5.6%	9.3%	4.3%	27.2%
Latvia	13.3%	-36.5%	13.3%	n.a.	17.8%	29.5%	28.8%	40.4%
Luxembourg	0.0%	-42.9%	13.9%	0.0%	0.3%	40.8%	12.8%	9.1%
Mexico	16.7%	-20.3%	0.0%	n.a.	11.0%	34.5%	-4.9%	19.0%
Netherlands	40.0%	-61.6%	0.0%	n.a.	10.5%	49.8%	-7.3%	49.8%
New Zealand	23.9%	23.9%	23.9%	n.a.	20.0%	35.2%	39.4%	35.2%
Norway	63.6%	-3.9%	68.8%	41.7%	16.7%	66.6%	41.3%	87.6%
Poland	22.0%	-16.3%	16.7%	n.a.	5.9%	15.0%	28.2%	26.1%
Portugal	37.9%	-25.0%	0.0%	n.a.	10.0%	39.8%	42.2%	69.4%
Slovak Republic	23.0%	15.4%	15.4%	n.a.	0.4%	20.6%	23.7%	42.8%
Slovenia	16.8%	-15.9%	13.3%	n.a.	7.9%	34.2%	36.4%	60.5%
Spain	21.0%	0.0%	17.9%	0.0%	36.7%	45.6%	43.2%	57.8%
Sweden	34.1%	18.7%	18.7%	14.0%	6.1%	24.1%	6.1%	24.1%
Switzerland	13.9%	-22.6%	13.9%	n.a.	11.6%	15.0%	11.6%	15.0%
Turkey	24.4%	0.0%	0.0%	n.a.	7.2%	29.1%	34.1%	17.8%
United Kingdom	32.7%	-10.4%	12.9%	0.0%	28.4%	55.5%	28.4%	31.0%
United States	0.0%	0.0%	25.0%	0.0%	45.0%	60.0%	45.0%	60.0%
Argentina	25.0%	0.0%	0.0%	n.a.	28.3%	52.9%	-18.4%	52.9%
Bulgaria	0.0%	-18.5%	0.0%	n.a.	9.6%	23.2%	18.4%	31.8%
Colombia	0.0%	0.0%	0.0%	0.0%	17.4%	17.2%	21.9%	21.8%
Lithuania	0.0%	-29.4%	0.0%	n.a.	2.7%	18.7%	2.7%	18.7%
South Africa	43.4%	-12.2%	13.1%	0.0%	22.9%	47.5%	22.9%	18.0%

StatLink http://dx.doi.org/10.1787/888933661704

Table 3.3. Marginal effective tax rates by asset, 2016 – Personal tax rate: 100% of average wage case; Inflation: country actual

Country	Bank deposits	Corporate bonds		Government bonds		Shares		
		Issued at par	Issued at discount	Issued at par	Issued at discount	100% distribution	50% distribution	0% distribution
Australia	66.0%	66.0%	63.8%	66.0%	63.8%	15.2%	21.1%	27.2%
Austria	40.3%	44.3%	42.6%	44.3%	42.6%	44.3%	40.9%	37.3%
Belgium	40.8%	41.5%	40.0%	41.5%	40.0%	42.9%	22.3%	1.8%
Canada	44.9%	44.5%	38.1%	44.5%	38.1%	9.7%	14.1%	18.7%
Chile	0.0%	0.0%	0.0%	0.0%	0.0%	-43.8%	-21.9%	0.0%
Czech Republic	21.6%	21.6%	16.2%	21.6%	16.2%	21.6%	10.8%	0.0%
Denmark	50.9%	50.9%	49.4%	50.9%	49.4%	57.8%	54.6%	51.2%
Estonia	0.0%	30.9%	29.7%	30.9%	29.7%	0.0%	12.8%	25.9%
Finland	43.9%	43.9%	42.4%	43.9%	42.4%	37.3%	37.5%	37.8%
France	57.2%	57.2%	55.7%	57.2%	55.7%	41.6%	37.3%	32.9%
Germany	0.0%	0.0%	0.0%	0.0%	0.0%	0.0%	0.0%	0.0%
Greece	13.4%	13.4%	13.0%	0.0%	0.0%	22.2%	23.0%	23.9%
Hungary	24.1%	24.1%	18.0%	24.1%	18.0%	16.0%	14.6%	13.1%
Iceland	41.7%	41.7%	39.6%	41.7%	39.6%	41.7%	37.4%	33.0%
Ireland	50.3%	55.8%	51.0%	55.8%	41.9%	63.1%	53.0%	42.4%
Israel	19.3%	19.3%	18.6%	19.3%	18.6%	25.7%	24.1%	22.4%
Italy	37.9%	37.9%	36.6%	19.1%	18.3%	37.3%	34.8%	32.1%
Japan	24.7%	24.7%	23.9%	24.7%	23.9%	20.0%	20.7%	21.4%
Korea	21.4%	21.4%	20.5%	21.4%	20.5%	29.3%	18.0%	6.6%
Latvia	13.3%	13.3%	14.2%	13.3%	14.2%	13.3%	15.1%	17.0%
Luxembourg	14.8%	14.8%	11.1%	14.8%	11.1%	28.9%	14.4%	0.0%
Mexico	1.1%	1.1%	1.0%	1.1%	1.0%	-4.7%	5.9%	16.7%
Netherlands	40.0%	40.0%	40.0%	40.0%	40.0%	40.0%	40.0%	40.0%
New Zealand	41.0%	41.0%	39.7%	41.0%	39.7%	2.7%	1.4%	0.0%
Norway	68.8%	68.8%	67.5%	68.8%	67.5%	28.3%	28.3%	28.3%
Poland	25.8%	25.8%	24.9%	25.8%	24.9%	25.8%	23.9%	22.0%
Portugal	37.9%	37.9%	36.7%	37.9%	36.7%	37.9%	35.4%	32.8%
Slovak Republic	27.1%	27.1%	26.1%	27.1%	26.1%	0.0%	11.3%	23.0%
Slovenia	32.9%	32.9%	31.8%	32.9%	31.8%	32.9%	25.0%	16.8%
Spain	27.0%	27.0%	25.5%	27.0%	26.1%	27.0%	25.1%	23.3%
Sweden	35.0%	35.0%	34.0%	35.0%	34.0%	35.0%	33.0%	31.0%
Switzerland	26.5%	27.5%	22.7%	27.5%	22.7%	27.5%	17.9%	8.3%
Turkey	55.7%	55.7%	51.2%	55.7%	51.2%	51.5%	25.8%	0.0%
United Kingdom	0.0%	0.0%	0.0%	0.0%	0.0%	0.0%	0.0%	0.0%
United States	37.6%	37.6%	36.2%	37.6%	36.2%	22.6%	20.7%	18.8%
Argentina	0.0%	25.0%	25.0%	0.0%	0.0%	25.0%	25.0%	25.0%
Bulgaria	10.2%	0.0%	0.0%	0.0%	0.0%	6.4%	3.2%	0.0%
Colombia	7.0%	9.0%	8.5%	9.0%	8.5%	0.0%	0.0%	0.0%
Lithuania	0.0%	0.0%	0.0%	0.0%	0.0%	22.9%	11.4%	0.0%
South Africa	0.0%	0.0%	0.0%	0.0%	0.0%	45.6%	34.5%	23.1%

Table 3.3. **Marginal effective tax rates by asset, 2016 – Personal tax rate: 100% of average wage case; Inflation: country actual** *(cont.)*

Country	Investment funds	Pension funds		Tax-favoured savings accounts	Residential property			
					Equity-financed		Debt-financed	
		Deductible contributions	Non-deductible contributions		Owner-occupied	Rented	Owner-occupied	Rented
Australia	66.0%	-27.2%	25.4%	n.a.	14.7%	88.2%	64.2%	88.2%
Austria	39.1%	-7.4%	0.0%	40.3%	15.5%	59.0%	46.3%	36.5%
Belgium	0.0%	-52.4%	13.3%	22.7%	49.3%	50.6%	25.7%	79.2%
Canada	44.5%	0.0%	25.5%	0.0%	38.9%	74.6%	71.0%	74.6%
Chile	6.6%	0.0%	3.8%	n.a.	21.2%	21.2%	18.7%	18.6%
Czech Republic	7.2%	0.0%	12.1%	n.a.	11.1%	22.1%	11.1%	22.1%
Denmark	57.8%	21.1%	21.1%	n.a.	21.3%	48.9%	16.3%	53.5%
Estonia	25.9%	-20.8%	16.7%	n.a.	0.0%	22.4%	-28.4%	22.4%
Finland	37.8%	0.0%	25.4%	0.0%	12.1%	49.9%	29.5%	49.9%
France	51.1%	-9.0%	27.5%	0.0%	22.8%	47.4%	69.8%	91.2%
Germany	0.0%	0.0%	35.3%	n.a.	19.4%	65.8%	19.4%	15.7%
Greece	12.0%	0.0%	0.0%	n.a.	27.2%	26.2%	30.7%	29.8%
Hungary	13.1%	-41.7%	0.0%	0.0%	14.9%	30.2%	33.7%	48.4%
Iceland	33.0%	0.0%	39.7%	n.a.	15.5%	36.1%	43.4%	63.2%
Ireland	45.0%	15.3%	36.8%	n.a.	6.6%	58.5%	51.8%	59.6%
Israel	22.4%	-89.7%	0.0%	0.0%	10.0%	28.4%	26.7%	44.3%
Italy	27.1%	-2.0%	36.0%	n.a.	1.8%	47.2%	13.2%	76.4%
Japan	21.4%	-8.1%	8.9%	0.0%	20.8%	37.4%	12.8%	41.6%
Korea	21.4%	-13.3%	4.0%	13.8%	5.6%	9.3%	4.3%	27.2%
Latvia	13.3%	-36.5%	13.3%	n.a.	21.8%	33.2%	32.7%	43.9%
Luxembourg	0.0%	-53.3%	16.1%	0.0%	0.3%	46.9%	12.8%	8.3%
Mexico	16.7%	-36.2%	0.0%	n.a.	11.1%	45.6%	-16.9%	19.4%
Netherlands	40.0%	-7.2%	0.0%	n.a.	10.5%	49.8%	-7.3%	49.8%
New Zealand	38.3%	38.3%	38.3%	n.a.	20.0%	46.0%	53.3%	46.0%
Norway	63.6%	-3.9%	68.8%	41.7%	16.7%	66.6%	41.3%	87.6%
Poland	22.0%	-16.3%	16.7%	n.a.	5.9%	15.0%	28.2%	26.1%
Portugal	37.9%	-25.0%	0.0%	n.a.	15.0%	44.4%	46.6%	73.4%
Slovak Republic	23.0%	15.4%	15.4%	n.a.	0.4%	20.6%	23.7%	42.8%
Slovenia	16.8%	-30.8%	22.5%	n.a.	7.9%	34.2%	36.4%	60.5%
Spain	23.3%	0.0%	22.2%	0.0%	36.7%	47.6%	43.2%	57.7%
Sweden	34.1%	21.5%	21.5%	14.0%	6.1%	24.1%	6.1%	24.1%
Switzerland	26.5%	-38.1%	19.2%	n.a.	23.3%	27.8%	31.0%	35.4%
Turkey	24.4%	0.0%	0.0%	n.a.	7.2%	36.5%	34.1%	10.7%
United Kingdom	32.7%	-10.4%	12.9%	0.0%	28.4%	55.5%	28.4%	31.0%
United States	22.6%	0.0%	41.7%	0.0%	39.8%	58.0%	39.8%	58.0%
Argentina	25.0%	0.0%	0.0%	n.a.	28.3%	57.1%	-28.5%	57.1%
Bulgaria	0.0%	-18.5%	0.0%	n.a.	9.6%	23.2%	18.4%	31.8%
Colombia	0.0%	0.0%	0.0%	0.0%	17.4%	17.2%	21.9%	21.8%
Lithuania	0.0%	-29.4%	0.0%	n.a.	2.7%	18.7%	2.7%	18.7%
South Africa	43.4%	-19.5%	19.1%	0.0%	22.9%	58.6%	22.9%	15.3%

StatLink http://dx.doi.org/10.1787/888933661723

Table 3.4. **Marginal effective tax rates by asset, 2016 – Personal tax rate: 500% of average wage case; Inflation: country actual**

Country	Bank deposits	Corporate bonds		Government bonds		Shares		
		Issued at par	Issued at discount	Issued at par	Issued at discount	100% distribution	50% distribution	0% distribution
Australia	83.0%	83.0%	80.5%	83.0%	80.5%	32.2%	33.3%	34.5%
Austria	40.3%	44.3%	42.6%	44.3%	42.6%	44.3%	40.9%	37.3%
Belgium	40.8%	41.5%	40.0%	41.5%	40.0%	42.9%	22.3%	1.8%
Canada	81.0%	80.3%	69.1%	80.3%	69.1%	59.5%	47.2%	34.4%
Chile	50.4%	50.4%	48.2%	50.4%	37.8%	-26.2%	-3.1%	21.5%
Czech Republic	21.6%	21.6%	16.2%	21.6%	16.2%	21.6%	10.8%	0.0%
Denmark	57.8%	57.8%	56.2%	57.8%	56.2%	57.8%	54.6%	51.2%
Estonia	0.0%	30.9%	29.7%	30.9%	29.7%	0.0%	12.8%	25.9%
Finland	43.9%	43.9%	43.7%	43.9%	43.7%	37.3%	40.1%	43.1%
France	87.4%	87.4%	86.3%	87.4%	86.3%	66.1%	61.4%	56.4%
Germany	36.7%	36.7%	35.4%	36.7%	35.4%	36.7%	34.2%	31.6%
Greece	13.4%	13.4%	13.0%	0.0%	0.0%	22.2%	23.0%	23.9%
Hungary	24.1%	24.1%	18.0%	24.1%	18.0%	16.0%	14.6%	13.1%
Iceland	41.7%	41.7%	39.6%	41.7%	39.6%	41.7%	37.4%	33.0%
Ireland	50.3%	58.9%	53.3%	58.9%	44.2%	66.1%	54.5%	42.4%
Israel	19.3%	19.3%	18.6%	19.3%	18.6%	25.7%	24.1%	22.4%
Italy	37.9%	37.9%	36.6%	19.1%	18.3%	37.3%	34.8%	32.1%
Japan	24.7%	24.7%	23.9%	24.7%	23.9%	24.7%	23.1%	21.4%
Korea	58.1%	58.1%	56.3%	58.1%	56.3%	65.7%	36.1%	6.6%
Latvia	13.3%	13.3%	14.2%	13.3%	14.2%	13.3%	15.1%	17.0%
Luxembourg	14.8%	14.8%	11.1%	14.8%	11.1%	29.6%	14.8%	0.0%
Mexico	65.4%	65.4%	63.2%	65.4%	63.2%	21.8%	19.3%	16.7%
Netherlands	40.0%	40.0%	40.0%	40.0%	40.0%	40.0%	40.0%	40.0%
New Zealand	45.1%	45.1%	43.7%	45.1%	43.7%	6.8%	3.4%	0.0%
Norway	68.8%	68.8%	67.5%	68.8%	67.5%	28.3%	28.3%	28.3%
Poland	25.8%	25.8%	24.9%	25.8%	24.9%	25.8%	23.9%	22.0%
Portugal	37.9%	37.9%	36.7%	37.9%	36.7%	37.9%	35.4%	32.8%
Slovak Republic	27.1%	27.1%	26.1%	27.1%	26.1%	0.0%	11.3%	23.0%
Slovenia	32.9%	32.9%	31.8%	32.9%	31.8%	32.9%	25.0%	16.8%
Spain	29.5%	29.5%	28.0%	29.5%	28.0%	29.5%	26.4%	25.6%
Sweden	35.0%	35.0%	34.0%	35.0%	34.0%	35.0%	33.0%	31.0%
Switzerland	46.7%	47.8%	39.7%	47.8%	39.7%	47.8%	31.7%	15.6%
Turkey	55.7%	55.7%	51.2%	55.7%	51.2%	66.4%	33.2%	0.0%
United Kingdom	73.5%	73.5%	62.2%	73.5%	62.2%	77.3%	54.3%	30.4%
United States	55.3%	55.3%	53.6%	55.3%	53.6%	28.3%	26.0%	23.8%
Argentina	0.0%	41.7%	41.7%	0.0%	0.0%	41.7%	41.7%	41.7%
Bulgaria	10.2%	0.0%	0.0%	0.0%	0.0%	6.4%	3.2%	0.0%
Colombia	7.0%	9.0%	8.5%	9.0%	8.5%	0.0%	0.0%	0.0%
Lithuania	22.9%	22.9%	21.9%	22.9%	21.9%	22.9%	21.0%	19.0%
South Africa	118.5%	118.5%	98.1%	118.5%	98.1%	45.6%	40.9%	35.9%

Table 3.4. **Marginal effective tax rates by asset, 2016 – Personal tax rate: 500% of average wage case; Inflation: country actual** *(cont.)*

Country	Investment funds	Pension funds		Tax-favoured savings accounts	Residential property			
					Equity-financed		Debt-financed	
		Deductible contributions	Non-deductible contributions		Owner-occupied	Rented	Owner-occupied	Rented
Australia	83.0%	-13.7%	25.4%	n.a.	14.7%	100.9%	76.9%	100.9%
Austria	39.1%	-7.4%	0.0%	40.3%	15.5%	65.7%	46.3%	32.1%
Belgium	0.0%	-52.4%	13.3%	22.7%	49.3%	50.6%	77.2%	79.2%
Canada	80.3%	0.0%	50.2%	0.0%	40.0%	105.2%	97.7%	105.2%
Chile	39.7%	0.0%	23.2%	n.a.	24.8%	24.8%	43.0%	43.5%
Czech Republic	7.2%	0.0%	12.1%	n.a.	11.1%	22.1%	11.1%	22.1%
Denmark	57.8%	21.1%	21.1%	n.a.	21.3%	58.1%	23.1%	62.1%
Estonia	25.9%	-20.8%	16.7%	n.a.	3.8%	26.3%	3.8%	26.3%
Finland	43.1%	0.0%	25.4%	0.0%	17.0%	54.3%	31.4%	54.3%
France	82.7%	-15.9%	36.3%	87.4%	33.9%	68.6%	102.4%	129.4%
Germany	36.7%	0.0%	38.4%	n.a.	19.4%	69.3%	51.1%	47.5%
Greece	12.0%	0.0%	0.0%	n.a.	38.5%	37.5%	41.8%	40.8%
Hungary	13.1%	-41.7%	0.0%	0.0%	14.9%	30.2%	33.7%	48.4%
Iceland	33.0%	0.0%	49.3%	n.a.	15.5%	36.1%	43.4%	63.2%
Ireland	45.0%	22.2%	39.2%	n.a.	6.6%	61.2%	51.8%	62.3%
Israel	22.4%	-89.7%	0.0%	0.0%	22.2%	28.4%	38.2%	44.3%
Italy	27.1%	-56.5%	36.0%	n.a.	1.8%	47.2%	13.2%	76.4%
Japan	21.4%	-43.0%	30.1%	0.0%	20.8%	74.7%	12.8%	40.8%
Korea	58.1%	-13.3%	4.0%	13.8%	10.6%	55.1%	57.1%	81.2%
Latvia	13.3%	-36.5%	13.3%	n.a.	25.8%	36.8%	36.5%	47.4%
Luxembourg	0.0%	-55.6%	16.5%	0.0%	0.3%	48.1%	12.8%	8.2%
Mexico	16.7%	-20.6%	21.4%	n.a.	13.6%	63.4%	13.6%	63.4%
Netherlands	40.0%	0.0%	0.0%	n.a.	10.5%	49.8%	-14.5%	49.8%
New Zealand	38.3%	38.3%	38.3%	n.a.	20.0%	48.6%	56.7%	48.6%
Norway	63.6%	0.0%	68.8%	41.7%	16.7%	66.6%	41.3%	87.6%
Poland	22.0%	-53.9%	16.7%	n.a.	5.9%	15.0%	28.2%	23.6%
Portugal	37.9%	-25.0%	0.0%	n.a.	26.8%	57.5%	56.9%	85.2%
Slovak Republic	23.0%	15.4%	15.4%	n.a.	0.4%	27.0%	23.7%	48.6%
Slovenia	16.8%	-83.3%	41.7%	n.a.	7.9%	34.2%	36.4%	60.5%
Spain	25.6%	0.0%	35.9%	0.0%	37.0%	53.8%	45.7%	59.7%
Sweden	34.1%	50.6%	50.6%	14.0%	6.1%	24.1%	6.1%	24.1%
Switzerland	46.7%	-90.0%	32.1%	n.a.	41.5%	48.3%	56.5%	62.8%
Turkey	24.4%	0.0%	0.0%	n.a.	7.2%	44.9%	34.1%	1.4%
United Kingdom	73.5%	-34.1%	30.7%	73.5%	28.4%	86.2%	81.4%	86.2%
United States	28.3%	0.0%	55.0%	0.0%	33.7%	51.3%	33.7%	51.3%
Argentina	41.7%	0.0%	0.0%	n.a.	45.0%	82.3%	45.0%	82.3%
Bulgaria	0.0%	-18.5%	0.0%	n.a.	9.6%	23.2%	18.4%	31.8%
Colombia	0.0%	-64.8%	0.0%	-259.3%	19.6%	49.4%	-23.3%	10.4%
Lithuania	19.0%	-29.4%	0.0%	n.a.	16.0%	32.0%	34.0%	49.3%
South Africa	43.4%	-4.7%	46.3%	0.0%	41.0%	85.7%	99.7%	85.7%

StatLink http://dx.doi.org/10.1787/888933661742

Table 3.5. Marginal effective tax rates by asset, 2016 – Personal tax rate: 67% of average wage case; Inflation: OECD average

Country	Bank deposits	Corporate bonds		Government bonds		Shares		
		Issued at par	Issued at discount	Issued at par	Issued at discount	100% distribution	50% distribution	0% distribution
Australia	52.8%	52.8%	51.0%	52.8%	51.0%	6.9%	14.4%	22.1%
Austria	38.3%	42.1%	40.6%	42.1%	40.6%	42.1%	39.0%	35.8%
Belgium	41.3%	42.0%	40.5%	42.0%	40.5%	43.4%	22.6%	1.8%
Canada	30.7%	30.7%	26.3%	30.7%	26.3%	0.0%	6.3%	12.7%
Chile	0.0%	0.0%	0.0%	0.0%	0.0%	-36.7%	-18.4%	0.0%
Czech Republic	23.0%	23.0%	17.2%	23.0%	17.2%	23.0%	11.5%	0.0%
Denmark	56.6%	56.6%	54.8%	56.6%	54.8%	64.3%	60.3%	56.1%
Estonia	0.0%	30.6%	29.4%	30.6%	29.4%	0.0%	12.6%	25.7%
Finland	45.9%	45.9%	44.3%	45.9%	44.3%	39.0%	39.1%	39.2%
France	44.0%	44.0%	42.5%	44.0%	42.5%	35.5%	31.8%	28.1%
Germany	0.0%	0.0%	0.0%	0.0%	0.0%	0.0%	0.0%	0.0%
Greece	23.0%	23.0%	22.0%	0.0%	0.0%	28.6%	29.4%	30.1%
Hungary	23.0%	23.0%	17.2%	23.0%	17.2%	15.3%	14.0%	12.6%
Iceland	0.0%	0.0%	6.3%	0.0%	6.3%	30.6%	28.2%	25.7%
Ireland	62.7%	39.0%	40.1%	39.0%	29.3%	46.7%	48.3%	49.9%
Israel	23.0%	23.0%	22.0%	23.0%	22.0%	26.3%	24.4%	22.4%
Italy	41.4%	41.4%	39.9%	20.8%	19.9%	40.8%	37.8%	34.6%
Japan	30.7%	30.7%	29.5%	30.7%	29.5%	16.3%	20.9%	25.7%
Korea	21.4%	21.4%	20.5%	21.4%	20.5%	29.3%	18.0%	6.6%
Latvia	15.3%	15.3%	16.2%	15.3%	16.2%	15.3%	17.2%	19.1%
Luxembourg	15.3%	15.3%	11.5%	15.3%	11.5%	26.0%	13.0%	0.0%
Mexico	0.8%	0.8%	0.7%	0.8%	0.7%	-14.0%	-0.8%	12.6%
Netherlands	40.0%	40.0%	40.0%	40.0%	40.0%	40.0%	40.0%	40.0%
New Zealand	26.8%	26.8%	25.8%	26.8%	25.8%	-16.1%	-8.1%	0.0%
Norway	66.6%	66.6%	65.5%	66.6%	65.5%	28.3%	28.3%	28.3%
Poland	29.1%	29.1%	27.9%	29.1%	27.9%	29.1%	26.8%	24.4%
Portugal	42.8%	42.8%	41.3%	42.8%	41.3%	42.8%	39.7%	36.5%
Slovak Republic	29.1%	29.1%	27.9%	29.1%	27.9%	0.0%	12.0%	24.4%
Slovenia	38.3%	38.3%	36.8%	38.3%	36.8%	38.3%	28.8%	19.1%
Spain	32.1%	32.1%	30.2%	32.1%	30.2%	32.1%	28.3%	24.4%
Sweden	45.9%	45.9%	44.3%	45.9%	44.3%	45.9%	42.6%	39.2%
Switzerland	25.4%	26.6%	20.2%	26.6%	20.2%	26.6%	13.8%	1.0%
Turkey	23.0%	23.0%	22.0%	23.0%	22.0%	15.9%	7.9%	0.0%
United Kingdom	0.0%	0.0%	0.0%	0.0%	0.0%	0.0%	0.0%	0.0%
United States	23.0%	23.0%	22.0%	23.0%	22.0%	0.0%	0.0%	0.0%
Argentina	0.0%	25.0%	25.0%	0.0%	0.0%	25.0%	25.0%	25.0%
Bulgaria	12.2%	0.0%	0.0%	0.0%	0.0%	7.7%	3.8%	0.0%
Colombia	7.0%	6.1%	5.8%	6.1%	5.8%	0.0%	0.0%	0.0%
Lithuania	0.0%	0.0%	0.0%	0.0%	0.0%	23.0%	11.5%	0.0%
South Africa	0.0%	0.0%	0.0%	0.0%	0.0%	24.9%	13.3%	10.7%

Table 3.5. **Marginal effective tax rates by asset, 2016 – Personal tax rate: 67% of average wage case; Inflation: OECD average** *(cont.)*

Country	Investment funds	Pension funds		Tax-favoured savings accounts	Residential property			
		Deductible contributions	Non-deductible contributions		Equity-financed		Debt-financed	
					Owner-occupied	Rented	Owner-occupied	Rented
Australia	52.8%	-17.4%	23.0%	n.a.	14.7%	81.0%	56.3%	81.0%
Austria	37.2%	-7.4%	0.0%	38.3%	15.5%	51.7%	45.5%	39.0%
Belgium	0.0%	-52.4%	13.3%	0.0%	49.3%	50.6%	25.5%	79.4%
Canada	30.7%	0.0%	16.9%	0.0%	38.9%	63.0%	60.7%	63.0%
Chile	0.0%	0.0%	0.0%	n.a.	0.0%	0.0%	0.0%	0.0%
Czech Republic	7.7%	0.0%	12.5%	n.a.	11.1%	22.1%	11.1%	22.1%
Denmark	64.3%	23.4%	23.4%	n.a.	21.3%	50.4%	15.8%	56.4%
Estonia	25.7%	-20.8%	16.7%	n.a.	0.0%	22.3%	-28.2%	22.3%
Finland	39.2%	0.0%	26.1%	0.0%	12.1%	49.9%	29.9%	49.9%
France	37.5%	-2.3%	17.2%	0.0%	22.8%	41.3%	56.4%	73.6%
Germany	0.0%	0.0%	29.6%	n.a.	19.4%	57.4%	19.4%	13.9%
Greece	19.1%	0.0%	0.0%	n.a.	27.2%	32.0%	32.0%	36.9%
Hungary	12.6%	-41.7%	0.0%	0.0%	14.4%	29.7%	32.8%	47.5%
Iceland	25.7%	0.0%	34.3%	n.a.	15.5%	31.5%	39.5%	55.1%
Ireland	54.7%	11.5%	21.8%	n.a.	6.6%	42.7%	57.6%	69.2%
Israel	22.4%	-89.7%	0.0%	0.0%	10.0%	28.4%	28.4%	45.9%
Italy	29.2%	0.4%	39.0%	n.a.	1.8%	47.2%	13.7%	77.8%
Japan	25.7%	-4.9%	6.5%	0.0%	23.7%	34.5%	21.3%	46.0%
Korea	21.4%	-19.6%	4.0%	0.0%	5.6%	9.3%	4.3%	27.2%
Latvia	15.3%	-34.5%	15.3%	n.a.	17.8%	31.0%	29.7%	42.8%
Luxembourg	0.0%	-42.9%	14.2%	0.0%	0.3%	41.3%	13.0%	8.9%
Mexico	12.6%	-20.3%	0.0%	n.a.	11.0%	28.5%	-2.3%	15.4%
Netherlands	40.0%	-61.6%	0.0%	n.a.	10.5%	49.8%	-7.0%	49.8%
New Zealand	26.8%	26.8%	26.8%	n.a.	20.0%	35.2%	40.7%	35.2%
Norway	62.0%	-3.9%	66.6%	41.7%	16.7%	65.5%	41.8%	87.0%
Poland	24.4%	-16.3%	16.7%	n.a.	5.9%	15.0%	29.6%	26.2%
Portugal	42.8%	-25.0%	0.0%	n.a.	10.0%	41.2%	44.4%	72.7%
Slovak Republic	24.4%	16.0%	16.0%	n.a.	0.3%	20.6%	24.6%	43.6%
Slovenia	19.1%	-15.9%	13.3%	n.a.	7.9%	34.2%	38.8%	62.8%
Spain	24.4%	0.0%	19.7%	0.0%	39.2%	48.3%	46.4%	61.7%
Sweden	42.3%	21.3%	21.3%	14.0%	10.1%	30.5%	10.1%	30.5%
Switzerland	25.4%	-22.6%	25.4%	n.a.	11.6%	22.0%	11.6%	22.0%
Turkey	12.6%	0.0%	0.0%	n.a.	7.2%	29.1%	25.9%	21.7%
United Kingdom	30.7%	-10.4%	12.5%	0.0%	28.4%	54.6%	28.4%	30.9%
United States	0.0%	0.0%	25.0%	0.0%	45.0%	60.2%	45.0%	60.2%
Argentina	25.0%	0.0%	0.0%	n.a.	28.3%	52.9%	-1.1%	52.9%
Bulgaria	0.0%	-18.5%	0.0%	n.a.	9.6%	23.2%	19.3%	32.7%
Colombia	0.0%	0.0%	0.0%	0.0%	14.7%	14.4%	20.3%	20.2%
Lithuania	0.0%	-29.4%	0.0%	n.a.	2.7%	18.7%	2.7%	18.7%
South Africa	23.0%	-12.2%	9.9%	0.0%	22.9%	44.1%	22.9%	22.4%

StatLink http://dx.doi.org/10.1787/888933661761

Table 3.6. **Marginal effective tax rates by asset, 2016 – Personal tax rate: 100% of average wage case; Inflation: OECD average**

Country	Bank deposits	Corporate bonds		Government bonds		Shares		
		Issued at par	Issued at discount	Issued at par	Issued at discount	100% distribution	50% distribution	0% distribution
Australia	59.7%	59.7%	57.8%	59.7%	57.8%	13.8%	19.3%	25.0%
Austria	38.3%	42.1%	40.6%	42.1%	40.6%	42.1%	39.0%	35.8%
Belgium	41.3%	42.0%	40.5%	42.0%	40.5%	43.4%	22.6%	1.8%
Canada	45.4%	45.5%	38.9%	45.5%	38.9%	9.8%	14.3%	18.9%
Chile	0.0%	0.0%	0.0%	0.0%	0.0%	-30.6%	-15.3%	0.0%
Czech Republic	23.0%	23.0%	17.2%	23.0%	17.2%	23.0%	11.5%	0.0%
Denmark	56.6%	56.6%	54.8%	56.6%	54.8%	64.3%	60.3%	56.1%
Estonia	0.0%	30.6%	29.4%	30.6%	29.4%	0.0%	12.6%	25.7%
Finland	45.9%	45.9%	44.3%	45.9%	44.3%	39.0%	39.1%	39.2%
France	67.3%	67.3%	65.3%	67.3%	65.3%	48.9%	43.5%	37.8%
Germany	0.0%	0.0%	0.0%	0.0%	0.0%	0.0%	0.0%	0.0%
Greece	23.0%	23.0%	22.0%	0.0%	0.0%	28.6%	29.4%	30.1%
Hungary	23.0%	23.0%	17.2%	23.0%	17.2%	15.3%	14.0%	12.6%
Iceland	30.6%	30.6%	29.4%	30.6%	29.4%	30.6%	28.2%	25.7%
Ireland	62.7%	69.6%	63.3%	69.6%	52.2%	77.0%	63.9%	49.9%
Israel	23.0%	23.0%	22.0%	23.0%	22.0%	26.3%	24.4%	22.4%
Italy	41.4%	41.4%	39.9%	20.8%	19.9%	40.8%	37.8%	34.6%
Japan	30.7%	30.7%	29.5%	30.7%	29.5%	24.8%	25.3%	25.7%
Korea	21.4%	21.4%	20.5%	21.4%	20.5%	29.3%	18.0%	6.6%
Latvia	15.3%	15.3%	16.2%	15.3%	16.2%	15.3%	17.2%	19.1%
Luxembourg	15.3%	15.3%	11.5%	15.3%	11.5%	29.8%	14.9%	0.0%
Mexico	0.8%	0.8%	0.7%	0.8%	0.7%	-3.3%	4.6%	12.6%
Netherlands	40.0%	40.0%	40.0%	40.0%	40.0%	40.0%	40.0%	40.0%
New Zealand	46.0%	46.0%	44.4%	46.0%	44.4%	3.1%	1.5%	0.0%
Norway	66.6%	66.6%	65.5%	66.6%	65.5%	28.3%	28.3%	28.3%
Poland	29.1%	29.1%	27.9%	29.1%	27.9%	29.1%	26.8%	24.4%
Portugal	42.8%	42.8%	41.3%	42.8%	41.3%	42.8%	39.7%	36.5%
Slovak Republic	29.1%	29.1%	27.9%	29.1%	27.9%	0.0%	12.0%	24.4%
Slovenia	38.3%	38.3%	36.8%	38.3%	36.8%	38.3%	28.8%	19.1%
Spain	32.1%	32.1%	30.2%	32.1%	30.9%	32.1%	29.6%	27.0%
Sweden	45.9%	45.9%	44.3%	45.9%	44.3%	45.9%	42.6%	39.2%
Switzerland	42.3%	43.5%	34.7%	43.5%	34.7%	43.5%	25.9%	8.3%
Turkey	23.0%	23.0%	22.0%	23.0%	22.0%	21.2%	10.6%	0.0%
United Kingdom	0.0%	0.0%	0.0%	0.0%	0.0%	0.0%	0.0%	0.0%
United States	38.3%	38.3%	36.8%	38.3%	36.8%	23.0%	21.1%	19.1%
Argentina	0.0%	25.0%	25.0%	0.0%	0.0%	25.0%	25.0%	25.0%
Bulgaria	12.2%	0.0%	0.0%	0.0%	0.0%	7.7%	3.8%	0.0%
Colombia	7.0%	6.1%	5.8%	6.1%	5.8%	0.0%	0.0%	0.0%
Lithuania	0.0%	0.0%	0.0%	0.0%	0.0%	23.0%	11.5%	0.0%
South Africa	0.0%	0.0%	0.0%	0.0%	0.0%	24.9%	19.9%	14.8%

Table 3.6. **Marginal effective tax rates by asset, 2016 – Personal tax rate: 100% of average wage case; Inflation: OECD average** *(cont.)*

Country	Investment funds	Pension funds		Tax-favoured savings accounts	Residential property			
					Equity-financed		Debt-financed	
		Deductible contributions	Non-deductible contributions		Owner-occupied	Rented	Owner-occupied	Rented
Australia	59.7%	-29.7%	23.0%	n.a.	14.7%	86.5%	61.7%	86.5%
Austria	37.2%	-7.4%	0.0%	38.3%	15.5%	57.5%	45.5%	35.6%
Belgium	0.0%	-52.4%	13.3%	23.0%	49.3%	50.6%	25.5%	79.4%
Canada	45.5%	0.0%	25.8%	0.0%	38.9%	74.7%	71.2%	74.7%
Chile	5.0%	0.0%	3.2%	n.a.	21.2%	21.2%	18.1%	18.0%
Czech Republic	7.7%	0.0%	12.5%	n.a.	11.1%	22.1%	11.1%	22.1%
Denmark	64.3%	23.4%	23.4%	n.a.	21.3%	52.1%	15.8%	56.9%
Estonia	25.7%	-20.8%	16.7%	n.a.	0.0%	22.3%	-28.2%	22.3%
Finland	39.2%	0.0%	26.1%	0.0%	12.1%	51.1%	29.9%	51.1%
France	59.0%	-9.0%	30.1%	0.0%	22.8%	49.0%	74.1%	96.8%
Germany	0.0%	0.0%	37.2%	n.a.	19.4%	65.8%	19.4%	12.4%
Greece	19.1%	0.0%	0.0%	n.a.	27.2%	32.0%	32.0%	36.9%
Hungary	12.6%	-41.7%	0.0%	0.0%	14.4%	29.7%	32.8%	47.5%
Iceland	25.7%	0.0%	34.3%	n.a.	15.5%	31.5%	39.5%	55.1%
Ireland	54.7%	15.3%	41.7%	n.a.	6.6%	64.6%	57.6%	65.9%
Israel	22.4%	-89.7%	0.0%	0.0%	10.0%	28.4%	28.4%	45.9%
Italy	29.2%	0.4%	39.0%	n.a.	1.8%	47.2%	13.7%	77.8%
Japan	25.7%	-8.1%	10.0%	0.0%	23.7%	40.5%	21.3%	45.2%
Korea	21.4%	-13.3%	4.0%	13.8%	5.6%	9.3%	4.3%	27.2%
Latvia	15.3%	-34.5%	15.3%	n.a.	21.8%	34.7%	33.5%	46.3%
Luxembourg	0.0%	-53.3%	16.4%	0.0%	0.3%	47.4%	13.0%	8.0%
Mexico	12.6%	-36.2%	0.0%	n.a.	11.1%	37.7%	-12.1%	15.7%
Netherlands	40.0%	-7.2%	0.0%	n.a.	10.5%	49.8%	-7.0%	49.8%
New Zealand	42.9%	42.9%	42.9%	n.a.	20.0%	46.0%	55.5%	46.0%
Norway	62.0%	-3.9%	66.6%	41.7%	16.7%	65.5%	41.8%	87.0%
Poland	24.4%	-16.3%	16.7%	n.a.	5.9%	15.0%	29.6%	26.2%
Portugal	42.8%	-25.0%	0.0%	n.a.	15.0%	45.8%	48.8%	76.7%
Slovak Republic	24.4%	16.0%	16.0%	n.a.	0.3%	20.6%	24.6%	43.6%
Slovenia	19.1%	-30.8%	22.5%	n.a.	7.9%	34.2%	38.8%	62.8%
Spain	27.0%	0.0%	24.4%	0.0%	39.2%	50.3%	46.4%	61.4%
Sweden	42.3%	24.6%	24.6%	14.0%	10.1%	30.5%	10.1%	30.5%
Switzerland	42.3%	-38.1%	35.0%	n.a.	23.3%	38.0%	29.6%	44.2%
Turkey	12.6%	0.0%	0.0%	n.a.	7.2%	36.5%	25.9%	19.8%
United Kingdom	30.7%	-10.4%	12.5%	0.0%	28.4%	54.6%	28.4%	30.9%
United States	23.0%	0.0%	41.7%	0.0%	39.8%	58.4%	39.8%	58.4%
Argentina	25.0%	0.0%	0.0%	n.a.	28.3%	57.1%	-7.0%	57.1%
Bulgaria	0.0%	-18.5%	0.0%	n.a.	9.6%	23.2%	19.3%	32.7%
Colombia	0.0%	0.0%	0.0%	0.0%	14.7%	14.4%	20.3%	20.2%
Lithuania	0.0%	-29.4%	0.0%	n.a.	2.7%	18.7%	2.7%	18.7%
South Africa	23.0%	-19.5%	14.5%	0.0%	22.9%	53.7%	22.9%	22.1%

StatLink http://dx.doi.org/10.1787/888933661780

Table 3.7. **Marginal effective tax rates by asset, 2016 – Personal tax rate: 500% of average wage case; Inflation: OECD average**

Country	Bank deposits	Corporate bonds		Government bonds		Shares		
		Issued at par	Issued at discount	Issued at par	Issued at discount	100% distribution	50% distribution	0% distribution
Australia	75.0%	75.0%	73.0%	75.0%	73.0%	29.1%	30.4%	31.7%
Austria	38.3%	42.1%	40.6%	42.1%	40.6%	42.1%	39.0%	35.8%
Belgium	41.3%	42.0%	40.5%	42.0%	40.5%	43.4%	22.6%	1.8%
Canada	81.9%	82.0%	70.6%	82.0%	70.6%	60.1%	47.7%	34.8%
Chile	35.2%	35.2%	34.2%	35.2%	26.4%	-12.4%	4.2%	21.5%
Czech Republic	23.0%	23.0%	17.2%	23.0%	17.2%	23.0%	11.5%	0.0%
Denmark	64.3%	64.3%	62.3%	64.3%	62.3%	64.3%	60.3%	56.1%
Estonia	0.0%	30.6%	29.4%	30.6%	29.4%	0.0%	12.6%	25.7%
Finland	45.9%	45.9%	45.6%	45.9%	45.6%	39.0%	41.8%	44.8%
France	99.9%	99.9%	98.3%	99.9%	98.3%	74.8%	68.8%	62.3%
Germany	40.4%	40.4%	38.9%	40.4%	38.9%	40.4%	37.4%	34.3%
Greece	23.0%	23.0%	22.0%	0.0%	0.0%	28.6%	29.4%	30.1%
Hungary	23.0%	23.0%	17.2%	23.0%	17.2%	15.3%	14.0%	12.6%
Iceland	30.6%	30.6%	29.4%	30.6%	29.4%	30.6%	28.2%	25.7%
Ireland	62.7%	73.4%	66.2%	73.4%	55.1%	80.8%	65.8%	49.9%
Israel	23.0%	23.0%	22.0%	23.0%	22.0%	26.3%	24.4%	22.4%
Italy	41.4%	41.4%	39.9%	20.8%	19.9%	40.8%	37.8%	34.6%
Japan	30.7%	30.7%	29.5%	30.7%	29.5%	30.7%	28.2%	25.7%
Korea	58.1%	58.1%	56.3%	58.1%	56.3%	65.7%	36.1%	6.6%
Latvia	15.3%	15.3%	16.2%	15.3%	16.2%	15.3%	17.2%	19.1%
Luxembourg	15.3%	15.3%	11.5%	15.3%	11.5%	30.6%	15.3%	0.0%
Mexico	45.9%	45.9%	45.0%	45.9%	45.0%	15.3%	14.0%	12.6%
Netherlands	40.0%	40.0%	40.0%	40.0%	40.0%	40.0%	40.0%	40.0%
New Zealand	50.6%	50.6%	48.9%	50.6%	48.9%	7.7%	3.8%	0.0%
Norway	66.6%	66.6%	65.5%	66.6%	65.5%	28.3%	28.3%	28.3%
Poland	29.1%	29.1%	27.9%	29.1%	27.9%	29.1%	26.8%	24.4%
Portugal	42.8%	42.8%	41.3%	42.8%	41.3%	42.8%	39.7%	36.5%
Slovak Republic	29.1%	29.1%	27.9%	29.1%	27.9%	0.0%	12.0%	24.4%
Slovenia	38.3%	38.3%	36.8%	38.3%	36.8%	38.3%	28.8%	19.1%
Spain	35.2%	35.2%	33.2%	35.2%	33.2%	35.2%	31.2%	29.7%
Sweden	45.9%	45.9%	44.3%	45.9%	44.3%	45.9%	42.6%	39.2%
Switzerland	73.4%	74.5%	59.7%	74.5%	59.7%	74.5%	45.0%	15.6%
Turkey	23.0%	23.0%	22.0%	23.0%	22.0%	27.4%	13.7%	0.0%
United Kingdom	69.0%	69.0%	58.5%	69.0%	58.5%	72.7%	51.3%	29.0%
United States	56.3%	56.3%	54.5%	56.3%	54.5%	28.8%	26.5%	24.1%
Argentina	0.0%	41.7%	41.7%	0.0%	0.0%	41.7%	41.7%	41.7%
Bulgaria	12.2%	0.0%	0.0%	0.0%	0.0%	7.7%	3.8%	0.0%
Colombia	7.0%	6.1%	5.8%	6.1%	5.8%	0.0%	0.0%	0.0%
Lithuania	23.0%	23.0%	22.0%	23.0%	22.0%	23.0%	21.1%	19.1%
South Africa	62.7%	62.7%	52.5%	62.7%	52.5%	24.9%	23.8%	22.6%

Table 3.7. **Marginal effective tax rates by asset, 2016 – Personal tax rate: 500% of average wage case; Inflation: OECD average** *(cont.)*

Country	Investment funds	Pension funds		Tax-favoured savings accounts	Residential property			
		Deductible contributions	Non-deductible contributions		Equity-financed		Debt-financed	
					Owner-occupied	Rented	Owner-occupied	Rented
Australia	75.0%	-16.1%	23.0%	n.a.	14.7%	98.7%	73.8%	98.7%
Austria	37.2%	-7.4%	0.0%	38.3%	15.5%	64.1%	45.5%	31.6%
Belgium	0.0%	-52.4%	13.3%	23.0%	49.3%	50.6%	77.4%	79.4%
Canada	82.0%	0.0%	50.8%	0.0%	40.0%	105.5%	98.0%	105.5%
Chile	29.7%	0.0%	19.5%	n.a.	24.8%	24.8%	34.7%	35.0%
Czech Republic	7.7%	0.0%	12.5%	n.a.	11.1%	22.1%	11.1%	22.1%
Denmark	64.3%	23.4%	23.4%	n.a.	21.3%	62.8%	23.1%	67.0%
Estonia	25.7%	-20.8%	16.7%	n.a.	3.8%	26.1%	3.8%	26.1%
Finland	44.8%	0.0%	26.1%	0.0%	17.0%	55.5%	31.8%	55.5%
France	93.0%	-15.9%	39.7%	99.9%	33.9%	70.3%	106.6%	134.7%
Germany	40.4%	0.0%	40.5%	n.a.	19.4%	69.3%	52.7%	46.0%
Greece	19.1%	0.0%	0.0%	n.a.	38.5%	43.5%	43.1%	48.2%
Hungary	12.6%	-41.7%	0.0%	0.0%	14.4%	29.7%	32.8%	47.5%
Iceland	25.7%	0.0%	42.6%	n.a.	15.5%	31.5%	39.5%	55.1%
Ireland	54.7%	22.2%	44.5%	n.a.	6.6%	67.3%	57.6%	68.6%
Israel	22.4%	-89.7%	0.0%	0.0%	22.2%	28.4%	39.8%	45.9%
Italy	29.2%	-54.1%	39.0%	n.a.	1.8%	47.2%	13.7%	77.8%
Japan	25.7%	-43.0%	34.1%	0.0%	23.7%	78.3%	21.3%	39.3%
Korea	58.1%	-13.3%	4.0%	13.8%	10.6%	55.1%	57.1%	81.2%
Latvia	15.3%	-34.5%	15.3%	n.a.	25.8%	38.4%	37.4%	49.8%
Luxembourg	0.0%	-55.6%	16.8%	0.0%	0.3%	48.6%	13.0%	7.9%
Mexico	12.6%	-20.6%	18.1%	n.a.	13.6%	54.0%	13.6%	54.0%
Netherlands	40.0%	0.0%	0.0%	n.a.	11.9%	50.9%	43.4%	50.9%
New Zealand	42.9%	42.9%	42.9%	n.a.	20.0%	48.6%	59.0%	48.6%
Norway	62.0%	0.0%	66.6%	41.7%	16.7%	65.5%	41.8%	87.0%
Poland	24.4%	-53.9%	16.7%	n.a.	5.9%	15.0%	29.6%	22.3%
Portugal	42.8%	-25.0%	0.0%	n.a.	26.8%	60.2%	58.9%	89.6%
Slovak Republic	24.4%	16.0%	16.0%	n.a.	0.3%	27.0%	24.6%	49.4%
Slovenia	19.1%	-83.3%	41.7%	n.a.	7.9%	34.2%	38.8%	62.8%
Spain	29.7%	0.0%	39.6%	0.0%	39.8%	56.8%	49.4%	63.3%
Sweden	42.3%	58.7%	58.7%	14.0%	10.1%	30.5%	10.1%	30.5%
Switzerland	73.4%	-90.0%	58.8%	n.a.	41.5%	67.3%	54.1%	79.4%
Turkey	12.6%	0.0%	0.0%	n.a.	7.2%	44.9%	25.9%	17.5%
United Kingdom	69.0%	-34.1%	29.7%	69.0%	28.7%	87.4%	83.6%	87.4%
United States	28.8%	0.0%	55.0%	0.0%	33.7%	52.0%	33.7%	52.0%
Argentina	41.7%	0.0%	0.0%	n.a.	45.0%	82.3%	45.0%	82.3%
Bulgaria	0.0%	-18.5%	0.0%	n.a.	9.6%	23.2%	19.3%	32.7%
Colombia	0.0%	-64.8%	0.0%	-259.3%	16.9%	46.4%	-15.8%	16.7%
Lithuania	19.1%	-29.4%	0.0%	n.a.	16.0%	32.0%	34.0%	49.3%
South Africa	23.0%	-4.7%	35.3%	0.0%	41.0%	78.1%	85.3%	78.1%

StatLink http://dx.doi.org/10.1787/888933661799

Results for different savings vehicles

Bank accounts

Income earned from savings in bank accounts often faces relatively high METRs as compared to other asset types. Nominal interest is taxed, either at marginal PIT rates (e.g. Australia, the United Kingdom and the United States), or at flat withholding rates (e.g. Germany, Italy and Korea). Countries with progressive PIT rate systems unsurprisingly tend to impose higher METRs on higher tax rate taxpayers than withholding rate countries or countries with flat-rate PIT systems (e.g. the Czech Republic and Hungary).[7]

The lowest METRs for bank account savings across all taxpayer types are observed in Argentina and Estonia, where interest income is exempt from any taxation, and in Colombia which imposes a flat 4% tax rate on all interest income.[8] Uniquely amongst the 40 countries modelled, Colombia taxes real rather than nominal interest income.

A number of other countries impose zero METRs on low-rate and (in some cases) average-rate taxpayers, but positive METRs on high-rate taxpayers (Chile, Germany, Iceland, Lithuania, the Netherlands, South Africa and the United Kingdom). This is generally due to the exemption of a fixed amount of interest income from taxation.[9] For example, in Iceland, the first ISK 125 000 (EUR 1 000) of interest income is tax exempt. In Lithuania, the exemption relates to interest accruing from a fixed annual deposit amount (EUR 500 in 2016). In South Africa, while a zero METR applies to low-rate and average-rate taxpayers (as they are assumed to earn less interest income than the ZAR 28 300 threshold), the combination of a high withholding tax rate and significant inflation results in a very high METR for high-rate taxpayers. In the Netherlands, a deemed return on asset value is taxed, rather than the actual income. The first EUR 24 437 (in 2016) of total assets excluding pensions and owner-occupied housing is exempt. For assets above this amount, a flat 30% tax is imposed on a deemed 4% return.[10]

Corporate bonds

The return on corporate (or government) bonds can be in the form of interest or, when issued below par, as capital gains. As such, METR results are presented for two scenarios: bonds issued at par (where 100% of the return is in the form of interest); and bonds issued below par (where 75% of the return is in the form of interest and 25% is capital gains).

Thirty-two of the forty countries tax interest from bank accounts identically to interest from corporate bonds, so that METRs are equivalent when bonds are issued at par. This is illustrated in Figure 3.2 which presents METRs for the average rate taxpayer case for bank accounts and corporate bonds (as detailed in Table 3.3).

Argentina, Austria, Belgium, Colombia, Estonia, and Switzerland impose higher METRs on interest income from corporate bonds than from bank accounts. Austria, for example, applies a higher withholding tax rate to interest from corporate bonds than to bank interest. In contrast, Bulgaria taxes interest on bank accounts, but exempts interest on corporate bonds as long as they are sold on a regulated exchange. Ireland, meanwhile, imposes a fixed withholding tax on bank interest, but imposes progressive marginal PIT rates on interest from corporate bonds. This results in a higher statutory tax rate (and METR) on bank interest than on corporate bonds for low-rate taxpayers, but the reverse is the case for average and high-rate taxpayers.

In almost all countries, corporate bonds issued below par face a lower tax rate than those issued at par. This, again, can be clearly seen in Figure 3.2 for the average rate taxpayer. At a minimum this is due to the deferral of tax payments until realisation of the capital gain. In addition, some countries tax capital gains at either a lower statutory tax rate than interest income (e.g. Hungary), or tax only part of the gain (e.g. Canada), which further reduces METRs. Meanwhile, some countries (e.g. the Czech Republic – if the bonds are held for three years or more) exempt capital gains entirely. In contrast, Latvia imposes a higher tax rate on capital gains than on interest from bonds, leading to a higher METR on bonds issued below par.

Figure 3.2. **Marginal effective tax rates for bank accounts and corporate bonds, 2016**

Personal tax rate: 100% of average wage case. Inflation: country actual

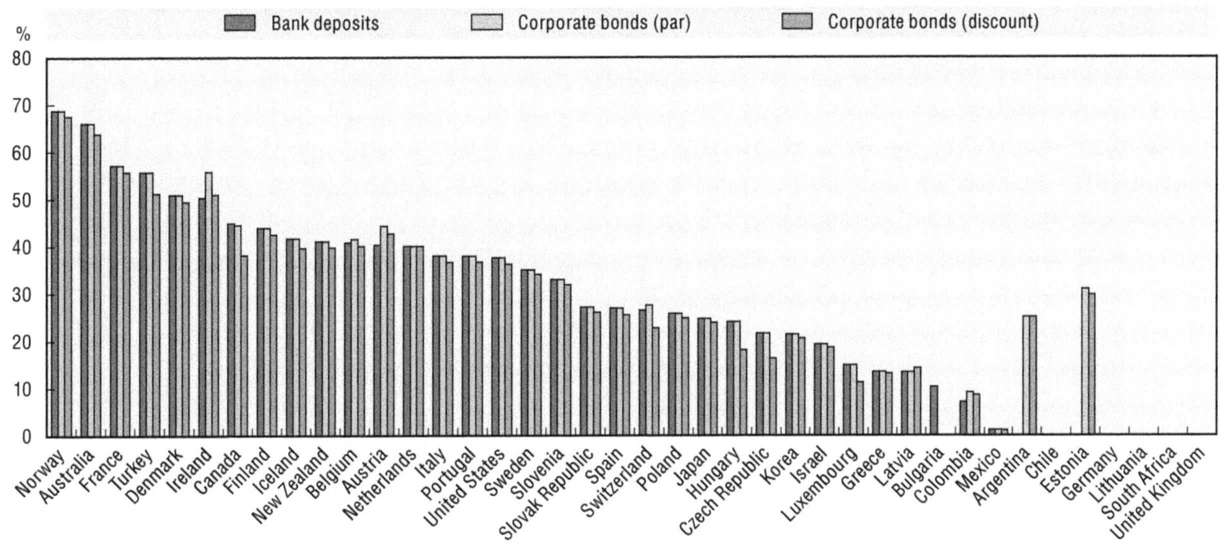

StatLink http://dx.doi.org/10.1787/888933660374

In Ireland, while interest income from corporate bonds is taxed at progressive marginal PIT rates, capital gains are taxed at a flat rate. As a result, bonds issued at a discount have a higher METR for low-rate taxpayers, but a lower METR for average and high-rate taxpayers. In Finland, while capital gains for high-rate taxpayers are taxed at a slightly higher statutory rate than interest is, this effect is outweighed by the tax deferral effect so that METRs remain slightly lower for bonds issued at a discount.

While not captured in the modelling results presented in this report, New Zealand's "financial arrangement" rules treat capital gains as interest income and tax this on an accrual basis. This leads to identical METRs for bonds issued at par and at a discount – as there is no deferral of tax liability. However, these rules only apply to high-income taxpayers meeting certain requirements.[11] Nevertheless, the financial arrangement rules do ensure that capital gains are treated as taxable income for all taxpayers, whereas they would otherwise be untaxed (as New Zealand does not tax capital gains on a comprehensive basis).

Government bonds

Only four countries (Chile, Greece, Ireland and Italy) tax government bonds differently to corporate bonds. In each case government bonds receive concessionary treatment. Chile and Ireland tax interest from corporate and government bonds identically, but exempt capital gains from government bonds. As Chile exempts a minimum amount of interest and capital gains income, this difference is only seen in the results for the high-rate taxpayer. Greece exempts government bonds from taxation on both interest and capital gains, while Italy imposes a lower withholding tax on interest and capital gains from government bonds.

Equities (purchase of corporate shares)

The return on an equity investment may take the form of either dividend income or capital gains. To take account of this, METR results for equity investments are presented for three different scenarios: 100%, 50% and 0% distribution of income as dividends, with the non-distributed income being taxed as a capital gain on realisation.

As noted earlier, the results do not take account of taxation at the corporate level, and therefore will not fully reflect the total tax imposed on an equity investment. Using the METRs to compare the total tax imposed on equity with tax imposed on other assets, or to compare across countries, should be undertaken with great caution. In particular, a country's approach to integrating corporate and personal level taxation needs to be considered when interpreting the results. For example, Colombia imposes zero METRs irrespective of the distribution policy for all three taxpayer types, while Germany and the United Kingdom impose zero METRs for low-rate and average-rate taxpayers. Nevertheless, tax is still paid at the corporate level in these countries.[12]

Overall, METRs for equity investments are generally lower than those on bank accounts and bonds. Furthermore, rates typically fall as capital gains make up a greater part of the overall return. This is illustrated in Figure 3.3, which presents METRs for the average rate taxpayer case for the three distribution scenarios (as detailed in Table 3.3).

Figure 3.3. **Marginal effective tax rates for shares, 2016**

Personal tax rate: 100% of average wage case. Inflation: country actual

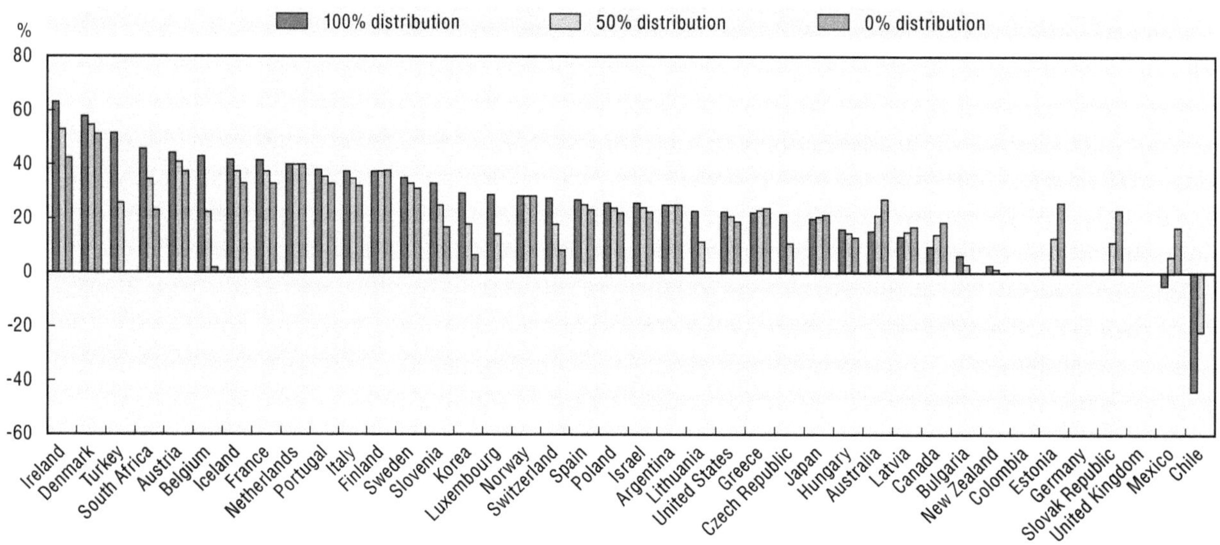

StatLink http://dx.doi.org/10.1787/888933660393

The fall in METRs highlights the fact that capital gains are typically taxed more favourably than dividend income. At the very least, as with bonds issued below par, this is due to the deferral of taxation of capital gains until realisation. More often, though, capital gains on equity investments are also taxed at lower rates than dividend income. These reduced rates typically apply only for "long term" capital gains held for longer than a specified minimum period. This period is typically between one and five years meaning that the reduced rates apply for all countries presented (as the results presented are based on a five-year expected holding period). In several countries (Bulgaria, the Czech Republic, Luxembourg, New Zealand and Turkey), capital gains are exempt, resulting in METRs of zero when capital gains make up the entire return. This is also the case for low and average rate taxpayers in Chile and Lithuania.

In several other countries (Estonia, Finland, Greece, Japan, Latvia, the Slovak Republic) METRs actually increase when capital gains make up a greater part of the overall return – as capital gains are taxed at higher rates than dividends (generally due to reductions in dividend taxation to reduce the extent of double taxation on corporate income). At the extreme, the METRs for Estonia and the Slovak Republic are zero when dividends make up the entire return, due to the non-taxation of dividend income at the personal level.

In Australia, only 50% of capital gains are taxable. However, this effect is outweighed by the impact of imputation ("franking") tax credits on dividend income, so that METRs increase slightly when capital gains make up a greater part of the overall return (as shown in Figure 3.3). Canada also applies a 50% capital gains tax reduction and an imputation system.[13] For low- and average-rate taxpayers, imputation credits also outweigh the impact of the capital gains tax reduction. However, the opposite occurs for high-rate taxpayers, so that METRs fall when capital gains make up a greater part of the overall return.

In Chile, Mexico and New Zealand, the impact of imputation credits outweighs the personal income tax due on dividend income for some taxpayer types. This results in negative METRs when income is fully distributed as dividends in all three countries for low-rate taxpayers, in Chile and Mexico for average-rate taxpayers, and also in Chile for high-rate taxpayers. METRs then increase as capital gains make up a greater part of the overall return. However, for average- and high-rate taxpayers in New Zealand, METRs fall when capital gains make up a greater part of the overall return because capital gains are untaxed. It should again be borne in mind that these results do not take account of taxation at the corporate level, and the combined corporate plus personal level tax burden would be positive in each country.

In Japan, the combination of taxation of dividend income at progressive PIT rates and flat-rate taxation of capital gains results in METRs decreasing as capital gains make up a greater part of the overall return for high-rate taxpayers, but increasing for low-rate and average-rate taxpayers (as shown in Figure 3.3). Similarly mixed results occur in Ireland.

METRs are constant irrespective of distribution policy in Argentina, the Netherlands and Norway. In Argentina, this is because only the wealth tax is imposed on shares. In Norway, no tax is applied directly on dividends or capital gains in the modelling due to Norway's risk-free return allowance and the assumption that, on the marginal euro of savings, the return generated is simply the risk-free return. (A non-marginal unit of savings with a return above the risk-free rate would be taxed). As such, only Norway's wealth tax is applied. In the Netherlands, shares are subject to the deemed return system, and hence the nature of the income is irrelevant.

Investment funds

Rather than investing directly in assets such as bonds and equities, a taxpayer may put their money into an investment fund that pools all the individual investors' money together and invests it "collectively" in a portfolio of assets, including bonds and equities. Countries may tax the income from such investment funds at two levels – each year as it is earned within the fund, and on distribution from the fund. In a small number of countries (Argentina, Colombia, France, Norway, Spain and Switzerland), a wealth tax is also applied to wealth held in investment funds above a threshold amount.[14]

Tax treatment of investment funds varies widely across the 40 countries considered in this report, with METRs consequently also varying significantly. Some countries tax investment funds annually in the hands of the individual investor. This is either achieved by treating the fund as a pass-through entity (as in Australia, Canada, the United Kingdom and the United States); by deeming a distribution to have occurred each year if income has not been actually distributed (as in Germany); or by requiring distribution each year (as in Korea). In most of these cases investors are taxed at marginal PIT rates, with METRs consequently varying depending on the applicable marginal PIT rate.

A larger number of countries only tax investment fund income on final distribution to the individual investor. These distributions (assumed in the modelling to be capital gains on the sale of shares/units in the investment fund) are then taxed at flat rates in the majority of cases so that METRs tend to be constant across the three taxpayer types. In a small number of cases, the distributed capital gains are untaxed which, together with the lack of taxation at the fund level, leads to zero METRs. This is the case in Belgium, Bulgaria and Colombia, and in Luxembourg as long as the shares in the investment fund are held for more than three years. In Lithuania, a tax-free threshold means that capital gains are only taxed in the high-rate taxpayer case. In the Slovak Republic, capital gains on investment funds are exempt if they are held for 15 years or more. However, this is not captured in Tables 3.2-3.7 which assume a five-year holding period.

France and Norway do not tax returns at the fund level either. However, in addition to taxing distributions to the investor, they impose a wealth tax on the investment fund wealth held by top-rate taxpayers. Colombia also imposes a wealth tax – but with a minimum wealth threshold that is so high as to not affect the three taxpayer types presented in Tables 3.2-3.7.

Meanwhile, some countries tax investment funds at both the fund level and separately on distribution. While in some cases this can result in particularly high METRs, in other cases taxation on distribution may be limited. For example, base investment funds in the Czech Republic are taxed at 5% at the fund level, and are taxed again on distribution, but if the return generated is a capital gain – as is modelled – then this will be tax free.

Argentina is the only country not to impose tax at either the fund level or on any type of distribution (i.e. not just capital gains). Argentina's wealth tax does apply to investment funds, although its minimum wealth threshold means that only the high-rate taxpayer type is subject to it.

Private pensions

Private pension schemes are highly tax-favoured in the majority of countries considered in this report. Most countries allow a deduction or tax credit for contributions made to an approved private pension scheme, though all countries have some limitation on the amount of eligible contributions. The majority of countries also do not tax the income accrued within a pension fund, and many countries provide concessionary treatment on distribution. The combined effect of these provisions is to produce zero or negative METRs for all three taxpayer types in 33 out of 40 countries, as shown in the "deductible contributions" pension fund columns in Tables 3.2-3.7.

A zero METR will occur when a country simply does not tax any income from a private pension. This is the case in Argentina and Turkey, where no tax relief is provided for pension contributions, but no tax is imposed on accumulation or on distribution (a "TEE" system). Zero rates will also occur when the tax rate at which deductions on contributions are provided matches the tax rate paid on distribution and there is no taxation on accumulation within the fund. The upfront tax saving in this "EET" system effectively funds the tax due on final distribution. However, where final taxation is at a rate lower than the initial deductions, the upfront tax saving more than compensates the taxpayer for their future tax liability – and hence a subsidy arises.[15]

The modelling results presented in Tables 3.2-3.7 assume that the taxpayer earns the same level of income when they make their contributions as when their pension is distributed, and hence face the same marginal PIT rate when making contributions and receiving distributions (when distributions are taxed at marginal PIT rates). Under this assumption, the results show that ten countries impose zero METRs for all three taxpayer types (Argentina, Canada, Chile, the Czech Republic, Finland, Germany[16], Greece, Iceland, Spain and the United States).[17]

In 22 countries, concessionary tax rates are applied on distributions (an "EEt" system, or "EEE" in the case of Austria, Bulgaria, Hungary and Lithuania), and hence METRs are negative for all three taxpayer types.[18] Even if accumulations within the fund are taxed, a lower tax rate on distribution can still result in a negative METR. For example, Italy taxes accumulations within a pension fund, but the concessionary rate on distribution is sufficient to outweigh this effect and still produce a negative METR (this can be categorised as an "Ett" system). In contrast, Denmark also taxes accumulations but provides no concessionary treatment on distribution, so overall METRs are positive despite the deductibility of contributions.

Examining the "deductible contributions" results across the three different taxpayer types, shows that in some countries the tax subsidy provided by pension schemes increases with income. This is the case in nine countries (Colombia, France, Italy, Japan, Luxembourg, Poland, Slovenia, Switzerland and the United Kingdom). The reason is that contributions are deducted at the taxpayer's marginal tax rate – so higher tax rate taxpayers get a larger upfront tax reduction, but face the same tax rate on distribution as lower-rate taxpayers. In Mexico, the METR is lowest for the average-rate taxpayer rather than the high-rate taxpayer as the high-rate taxpayer is subject to taxation on distribution whereas lower rate taxpayers are not.

To prevent such regressive effects, a number of countries (e.g. Austria, Belgium, Hungary, Korea and Israel) provide a tax credit rather than deduction for pension contributions. The Korean system goes even further, providing a larger tax credit (15%) for lower income taxpayers than higher income taxpayers (12%); METRs are consequently lower for the low-rate taxpayer case than the average-rate and high-rate taxpayer cases. A similar effect is achieved in Norway by allowing all taxpayers to claim a deduction for a surcharge, however, the surcharge is only applied to distributions to high-rate taxpayers. Meanwhile, Bulgaria, Estonia, Hungary, Latvia and Lithuania allow deductions at marginal PIT rates, but their flat rate PIT systems mean that all taxpayers benefit proportionately.

Several countries do not allow deductions for contributions, and consequently apply positive, and often progressive, METRs. For example, New Zealand applies a TTE system – where contributions are not deductible, income accumulating in the pension fund is taxed (at progressive rates), but distributions are not taxed. Meanwhile, the Slovak Republic and Sweden exempt accumulations, but tax distributions at flat and progressive rates, respectively (a "TET" system).

To take account of the varying limits in place on deductibility in almost all countries, results are also presented in Tables 3.2-3.7 for a marginal investment in a pension fund where the contribution is not deductible (in the "non-deductible contributions" column). Such an approach obviously limits the tax cost of EEt systems or EET systems where taxpayers can be subject to significantly lower marginal tax rates on distribution. The results highlight the importance of deductibility in providing concessional treatment. All METRs are now either zero or positive, with many rates increasing considerably. The main exceptions are the countries that apply TTE and TET systems, and therefore remain unchanged (New

Zealand, the Slovak Republic, Sweden, Turkey), and the Netherlands – which simply swaps an EET system for a TEE system on contributions in excess of a contribution threshold (EUR 100 000), so the METR remains at zero. Greece is the only country that has no limitation on deductibility.

The results presented so far highlight the significantly concessionary nature of EET systems. However, they may still understate the extent of the concession in countries that apply marginal PIT rates as it is very likely that distributions would be taxed at lower rates than deductions were granted at. This is because a taxpayer receiving pension payments is likely to be earning less income than when they were making contributions, if for no other reason than that they are likely to now be retired from the labour force.

Tables 3.8-3.10 present results where the taxpayer is assumed to earn less in retirement than when making contributions, and therefore potentially faces lower marginal PIT rates on distributions (although this depends on the interaction with the particular rate schedule). METRs fall in 4, 14 and 11 countries for low-rate, average-rate and high-rate taxpayers, respectively.

The reductions in METRs are also highlighted for the average-rate taxpayer case (for deductible contributions) in Figure 3.4. Six of the ten countries with EET systems previously producing zero METRs now have negative METRs. For example, the marginal tax rate on pension distributions for an average-rate taxpayer in the United States falls from 25% to 15%, resulting in a drop in the METR from zero to -22.2%.

Figure 3.4. **Marginal effective tax rates for private pensions (deductible contributions), 2016**

Personal tax rate: 100% of average wage case. Inflation: country actual

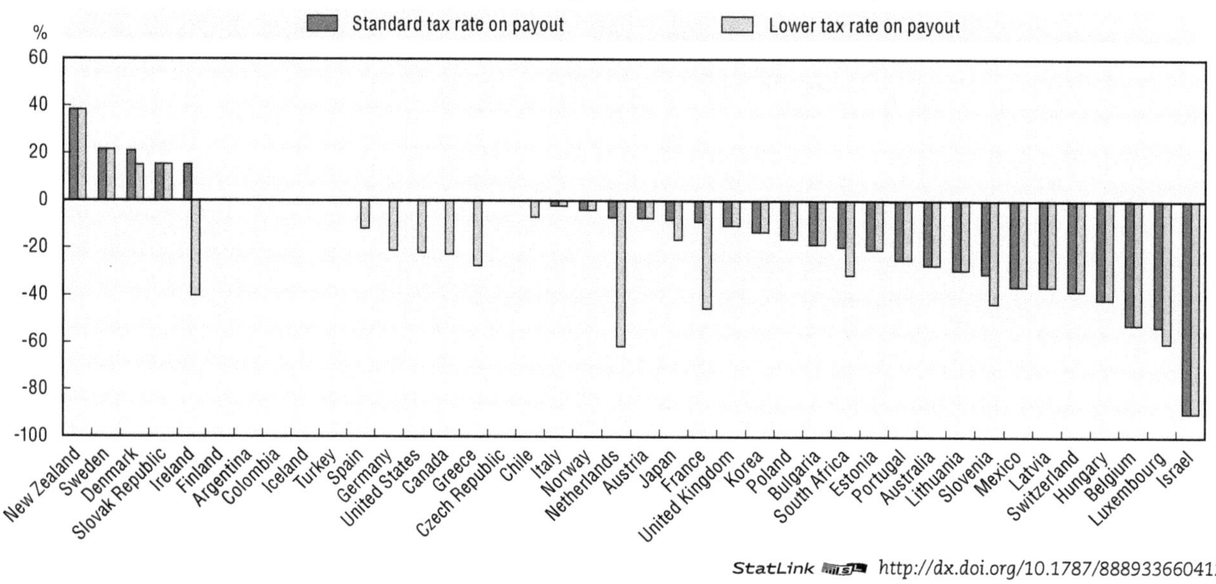

StatLink http://dx.doi.org/10.1787/888933660412

While countries with fixed withholding rates are unaffected, rates for some countries that were already providing concessionary treatment of distributions also fall. For example, the already negative METRs in Japan, France, Luxembourg, the Netherlands, Slovenia and South Africa fall further (for at least the average-rate taxpayer type) as the concessionary taxation of distributions in these countries is linked to the marginal tax rate (e.g. Luxembourg taxes distributions at a rate equal to 50% of the marginal PIT rate).

Table 3.8. **Marginal effective tax rates on private pensions, 2016 – Personal tax rate: 67% of average wage case; Inflation: country actual**

Country	Standard tax rate on payout		Lower tax rate on payout	
	Deductible contributions	Non-deductible contributions	Deductible contributions	Non-deductible contributions
Australia	-15.0%	25.4%	-15.0%	25.4%
Austria	-7.4%	0.0%	-7.4%	0.0%
Belgium	-52.4%	13.3%	-52.4%	13.3%
Canada	0.0%	16.7%	0.0%	16.7%
Chile	0.0%	0.0%	0.0%	0.0%
Czech Republic	0.0%	12.1%	0.0%	12.1%
Denmark	21.1%	21.1%	21.1%	21.1%
Estonia	-20.8%	16.7%	-20.8%	16.7%
Finland	0.0%	25.4%	0.0%	25.4%
France	-2.3%	15.7%	-2.3%	15.7%
Germany	0.0%	28.1%	-9.8%	24.6%
Greece	0.0%	0.0%	-4.8%	-4.8%
Hungary	-41.7%	0.0%	-41.7%	0.0%
Iceland	0.0%	39.7%	0.0%	39.7%
Ireland	11.5%	19.3%	6.3%	17.3%
Israel	-89.7%	0.0%	-89.7%	0.0%
Italy	-2.0%	36.0%	-2.0%	36.0%
Japan	-4.9%	5.7%	-4.9%	5.7%
Korea	-19.6%	4.0%	-19.6%	4.0%
Latvia	-36.5%	13.3%	-36.5%	13.3%
Luxembourg	-42.9%	13.9%	-55.6%	9.7%
Mexico	-20.3%	0.0%	-20.3%	0.0%
Netherlands	-61.6%	0.0%	-61.6%	0.0%
New Zealand	23.9%	23.9%	23.9%	23.9%
Norway	-3.9%	68.8%	-3.9%	68.8%
Poland	-16.3%	16.7%	-16.3%	16.7%
Portugal	-25.0%	0.0%	-25.0%	0.0%
Slovak Republic	15.4%	15.4%	15.4%	15.4%
Slovenia	-15.9%	13.3%	-15.9%	13.3%
Spain	0.0%	17.9%	0.0%	17.9%
Sweden	18.7%	18.7%	18.7%	18.7%
Switzerland	-22.6%	13.9%	-22.6%	13.9%
Turkey	0.0%	0.0%	0.0%	0.0%
United Kingdom	-10.4%	12.9%	-10.4%	12.9%
United States	0.0%	25.0%	0.0%	25.0%
Argentina	0.0%	0.0%	0.0%	0.0%
Bulgaria	-18.5%	0.0%	-18.5%	0.0%
Colombia	0.0%	0.0%	0.0%	0.0%
Lithuania	-29.4%	0.0%	-29.4%	0.0%
South Africa	-12.2%	13.1%	-12.2%	13.1%

StatLink http://dx.doi.org/10.1787/888933661818

Table 3.9. Marginal effective tax rates on private pensions, 2016 – Personal tax rate: 100% of average wage case; Inflation: country actual

Country	Standard tax rate on payout		Lower tax rate on payout	
	Deductible contributions	Non-deductible contributions	Deductible contributions	Non-deductible contributions
Australia	-27.2%	25.4%	-27.2%	25.4%
Austria	-7.4%	0.0%	-7.4%	0.0%
Belgium	-52.4%	13.3%	-52.4%	13.3%
Canada	0.0%	25.5%	-22.7%	16.7%
Chile	0.0%	3.8%	-6.9%	0.0%
Czech Republic	0.0%	12.1%	0.0%	12.1%
Denmark	21.1%	21.1%	15.0%	15.0%
Estonia	-20.8%	16.7%	-20.8%	16.7%
Finland	0.0%	25.4%	0.0%	25.4%
France	-9.0%	27.5%	-45.6%	15.7%
Germany	0.0%	35.3%	-21.3%	28.1%
Greece	0.0%	0.0%	-27.7%	-27.7%
Hungary	-41.7%	0.0%	-41.7%	0.0%
Iceland	0.0%	39.7%	0.0%	39.7%
Ireland	15.3%	36.8%	-40.3%	19.3%
Israel	-89.7%	0.0%	-89.7%	0.0%
Italy	-2.0%	36.0%	-2.0%	36.0%
Japan	-8.1%	8.9%	-16.4%	5.7%
Korea	-13.3%	4.0%	-13.3%	4.0%
Latvia	-36.5%	13.3%	-36.5%	13.3%
Luxembourg	-53.3%	16.1%	-60.1%	13.9%
Mexico	-36.2%	0.0%	-36.2%	0.0%
Netherlands	-7.2%	0.0%	-61.6%	0.0%
New Zealand	38.3%	38.3%	38.3%	38.3%
Norway	-3.9%	68.8%	-3.9%	68.8%
Poland	-16.3%	16.7%	-16.3%	16.7%
Portugal	-25.0%	0.0%	-25.0%	0.0%
Slovak Republic	15.4%	15.4%	15.4%	15.4%
Slovenia	-30.8%	22.5%	-43.4%	13.3%
Spain	0.0%	22.2%	-11.9%	17.9%
Sweden	21.5%	21.5%	21.5%	21.5%
Switzerland	-38.1%	19.2%	-38.1%	19.2%
Turkey	0.0%	0.0%	0.0%	0.0%
United Kingdom	-10.4%	12.9%	-10.4%	12.9%
United States	0.0%	41.7%	-22.2%	25.0%
Argentina	0.0%	0.0%	0.0%	0.0%
Bulgaria	-18.5%	0.0%	-18.5%	0.0%
Colombia	0.0%	0.0%	0.0%	0.0%
Lithuania	-29.4%	0.0%	-29.4%	0.0%
South Africa	-19.5%	19.1%	-31.5%	13.1%

StatLink http://dx.doi.org/10.1787/888933661837

Table 3.10. **Marginal effective tax rates on private pensions, 2016 – Personal tax rate: 500% of average wage case; Inflation: country actual**

Country	Standard tax rate on payout		Lower tax rate on payout	
	Deductible contributions	Non-deductible contributions	Deductible contributions	Non-deductible contributions
Australia	-13.7%	25.4%	-13.7%	25.4%
Austria	-7.4%	0.0%	-7.4%	0.0%
Belgium	-52.4%	13.3%	-52.4%	13.3%
Canada	0.0%	50.2%	-36.2%	39.1%
Chile	0.0%	23.2%	-32.5%	7.7%
Czech Republic	0.0%	12.1%	0.0%	12.1%
Denmark	21.1%	21.1%	20.7%	20.7%
Estonia	-20.8%	16.7%	-20.8%	16.7%
Finland	0.0%	25.4%	0.0%	25.4%
France	-15.9%	36.3%	-46.5%	27.5%
Germany	0.0%	38.4%	0.0%	38.4%
Greece	0.0%	0.0%	-5.6%	-5.6%
Hungary	-41.7%	0.0%	-41.7%	0.0%
Iceland	0.0%	49.3%	0.0%	49.3%
Ireland	22.2%	39.2%	22.2%	39.2%
Israel	-89.7%	0.0%	-89.7%	0.0%
Italy	-56.5%	36.0%	-56.5%	36.0%
Japan	-43.0%	30.1%	-61.1%	25.5%
Korea	-13.3%	4.0%	-13.3%	4.0%
Latvia	-36.5%	13.3%	-36.5%	13.3%
Luxembourg	-55.6%	16.5%	-55.6%	16.5%
Mexico	-20.6%	21.4%	-71.4%	0.0%
Netherlands	0.0%	0.0%	0.0%	0.0%
New Zealand	38.3%	38.3%	38.3%	38.3%
Norway	0.0%	68.8%	0.0%	68.8%
Poland	-53.9%	16.7%	-53.9%	16.7%
Portugal	-25.0%	0.0%	-25.0%	0.0%
Slovak Republic	15.4%	15.4%	15.4%	15.4%
Slovenia	-83.3%	41.7%	-98.3%	34.2%
Spain	0.0%	35.9%	0.0%	35.9%
Sweden	50.6%	50.6%	50.6%	50.6%
Switzerland	-90.0%	32.1%	-90.0%	32.1%
Turkey	0.0%	0.0%	0.0%	0.0%
United Kingdom	-34.1%	30.7%	-45.5%	26.9%
United States	0.0%	55.0%	-12.4%	46.7%
Argentina	0.0%	0.0%	0.0%	0.0%
Bulgaria	-18.5%	0.0%	-18.5%	0.0%
Colombia	-64.8%	0.0%	-64.8%	0.0%
Lithuania	-29.4%	0.0%	-29.4%	0.0%
South Africa	-4.7%	46.3%	-14.1%	41.9%

StatLink http://dx.doi.org/10.1787/888933661856

Tax-favoured savings accounts

Tax-favoured savings accounts are present in several countries and are subject to varying degrees of restriction. For example, in the United Kingdom, an individual can save up to GBP 20 000 (EUR 22 500) in an Individual Savings Account (ISA) tax free. Similarly Korea provides an "Individual Savings Account" which allows up to KOR 20 million (EUR 15 800) to be saved tax-free. Similarly, South Africa's "tax free savings accounts" provide an income exemption, with contributions limited to ZAR 30 000 (EUR 1 900) per year. In Belgium the first EUR 1 880 of interest income in qualified savings accounts is exempt, and any additional income is taxed at a concessionary (15%) withholding rate. In the United States, the tax-free "529 plan" and "Coverdell education savings account" are available, but are restricted to saving for particular education expenses.

In Spain, income from specified sources earned in "long-term savings plans" is exempt as long as the taxpayer does not withdraw any of the capital for at least five years. Contributions cannot exceed EUR 5 000 per year. In Hungary, interest, dividend and capital gain income earned in a "long-term investment account" is taxed at concessionary rates if the underlying assets are held for at least three years, and is exempt if held for at least five years. In Luxembourg, interest attributed to a building society account is exempt from taxation if the assets of the account are used to finance the construction, the purchasing, or the transformation of an apartment or a dwelling for the taxpayer's own needs. The contributions are deductible up to an amount of EUR 672 per year (the modelling assumes the taxpayer is contributing more than this amount per year).

In Colombia, income in "AFC" accounts is exempt if used to either cover mortgage payments or the acquisition of real estate. Contributions made are also deductible as long as they remain in the account for at least five years (10 years as of 2017). For the medium (5 year) investment presented in the main results, this concessionary tax treatment leads to zero METRs for the low and average rate taxpayer types (because they pay zero income tax, so get no benefit from the deductibility of contributions). However, a high rate taxpayer faces a METR of -259% because they benefit from the immediate deduction, but never pay any tax on the income during accumulation or distribution.[19]

Several countries also have schemes that are not covered by the modelling results. For example, Austria provides a tax credit (maximum EUR 1 200) for contributions to housing savings accounts, but these most be held for at least 6 years (and the results presented assume a five-year expected holding period). In Denmark, children's savings accounts are tax favoured, but they must be established before the child turns 14 years of age.

Equity-financed residential property

Using equity to save in owner-occupied residential property is highly tax-favoured in a majority of the 40 countries covered in this report. This is predominantly due to the non-taxation of imputed rental income and exemption of owner-occupied properties from capital gains taxation in most countries.

The significant impact of the non-taxation of imputed rental income can be seen when comparing owner-occupied with rented residential property. When a property is rented out, this rental income is taxed, typically at progressive marginal PIT rates. Additionally, most countries tax the capital gains from rented residential property, albeit some at reduced rates. These differences result in significantly higher METRs for rental properties than for primary residences, and are often higher than those that apply to other assets.

A key assumption necessary in modelling residential property is the split of the real return between rental income and capital gains. The base assumption made in the analysis is that 50% of the real return to residential property comes in the form of (imputed or actual) rental income and the remaining 50% as a capital gain. Where capital gains make up a significantly greater proportion of the overall return, METRs can be significantly lower than those presented in this section – due to the often concessionary taxation of capital gains. This is investigated further in the sensitivity analysis section.

Given the typically progressive taxation of rental income, METRs are generally higher for higher rate taxpayers than lower rate taxpayers for rental property, whereas METRs tend to be constant for owner-occupied properties. That said, rates are constant for rental property, for example, in the Czech Republic and Hungary due to their flat rate PIT systems. In some cases, progressivity in property taxes – whether based on income or value of the property – can lead to higher METRs on owner-occupied property for higher rate or higher wealth taxpayers, such as in Korea.[20] Meanwhile, in the United States, METRs on owner-occupied and rented property are actually lower for higher tax rate groups. This is due to the deductibility of sub-central property taxes against federal taxes which provides a greater benefit to taxpayers on higher marginal tax rates.

Transaction taxes (e.g. stamp duties) and recurrent property taxes typically apply to both owner-occupied and rented residential properties, and in some cases can be very substantial. For example, Belgium imposes a transaction tax of 12.5% on the purchase of all residential property, which even when spread over the entire expected holding period, leads – together with a significant recurrent property tax – to a substantial METR on owner-occupied residential property.[21] Canada (Ontario), the United Kingdom and United States also impose large recurrent property taxes relative to most other countries, resulting in comparatively high METRs on owner-occupied residential property. In contrast, for example, Italy exempts primary residences from recurrent property taxes and applies a reduced transaction tax rate to owner-occupied properties as compared to rental properties.

The inclusion in the METR calculations of recurrent property taxes effectively assumes that these taxes are a tax on the asset stock. However, it is arguable that in many cases these taxes may act like a "benefits tax" (i.e. as a payment for services) – and thus should not be included in the METRs. It is also arguable that recurrent property taxes may in some cases be capitalised into prices and hence are not borne by the prospective investor. We make no definitive conclusion on these issues in the report. Instead we present, for comparison, results both with and without recurrent property taxes in Tables 3.11-3.13. Results for the average-rate taxpayer case are also summarised in Figures 3.5 and 3.6 for (equity-financed) owner-occupied and rented residential property, respectively.

Figure 3.5. **Marginal effective tax rates for equity-financed owner-occupied residential property, 2016**

Personal tax rate: 100% of average wage case. Inflation: country actual

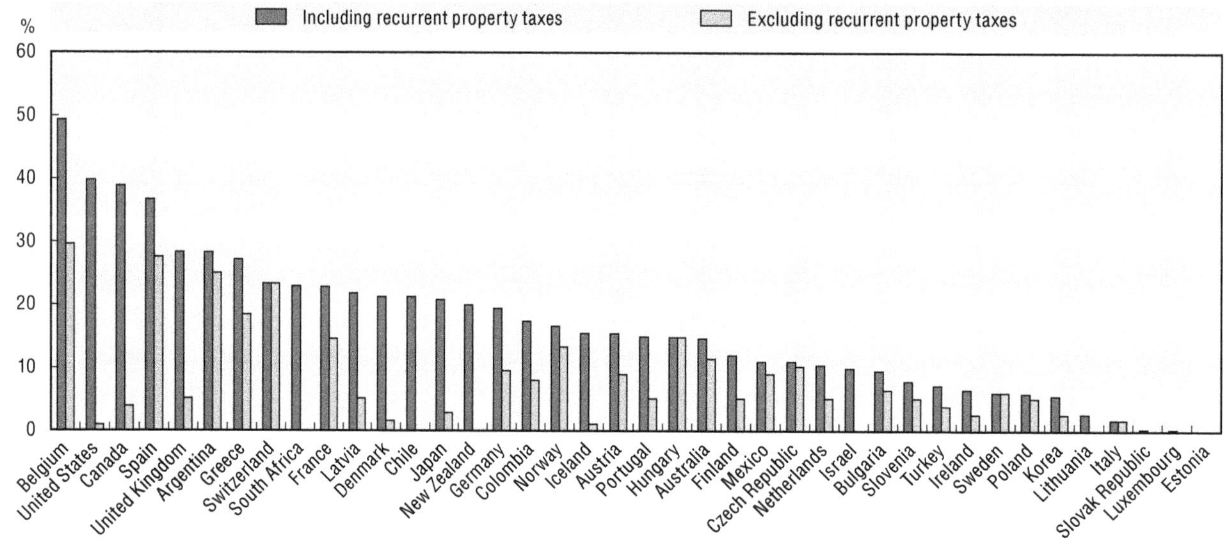

StatLink http://dx.doi.org/10.1787/888933660431

Figure 3.6. **Marginal effective tax rates for equity-financed rented residential property, 2016**

Personal tax rate: 100% of average wage case. Inflation: country actual

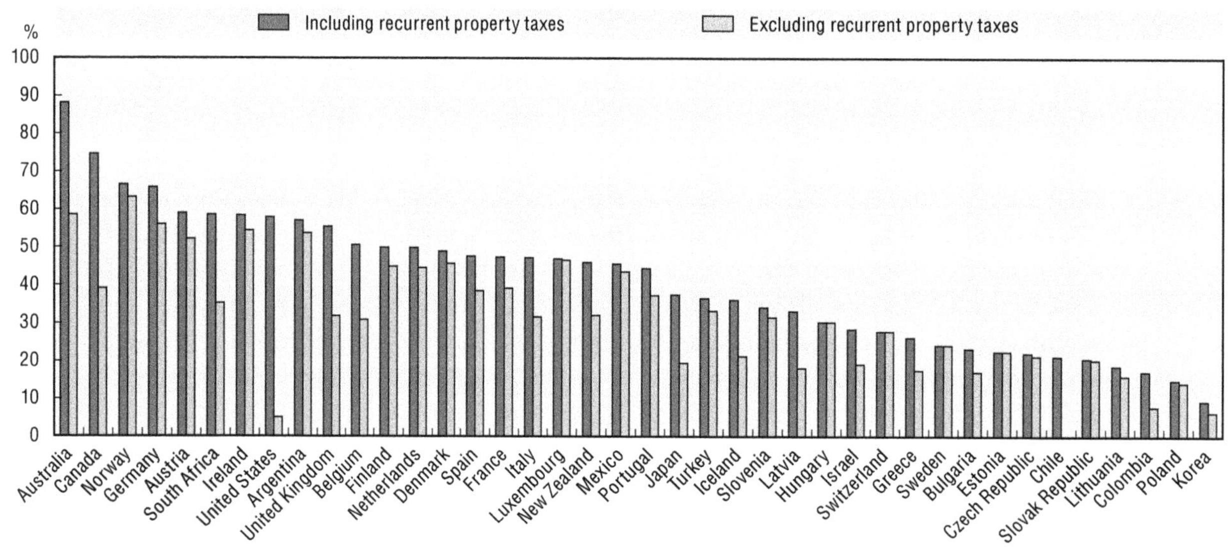

StatLink http://dx.doi.org/10.1787/888933660450

Results, in general, show a significant reduction in METRs in the absence of recurrent property taxes for both owner-occupied and rented residential property. Reductions are particularly large in Canada, Chile, South Africa, the United Kingdom and the United States. The reduction in Belgium is significant, but not as large as in these other countries as Belgium's comparatively large transaction tax remains.

Results without recurrent property taxes are unchanged in Hungary, Sweden and Switzerland. In Hungary, a representative tax rate of zero is modelled as only 548 out of 3 178 municipalities levy a recurrent property tax (in 2016). Sweden applies a relatively low maximum recurrent property tax amount and hence all three taxpayer types are assumed to pay no additional property tax at the margin. In Switzerland, no recurrent property tax is applied in Zurich, the representative canton applied in the modelling (although a number of other cantons do apply a recurrent property tax). In Italy, no recurrent property tax is applied to owner-occupied residential property (except for luxury homes). Meanwhile, a recurrent property tax is only modelled in Estonia for high-rate taxpayers due to an exemption for small properties (of less than 1 500 square metres).

Debt-financed residential property

It is common to at least partially supplement equity-financing of residential property with debt, and this may have significant tax implications. As such, METRs are also calculated for a marginal debt-financed investment in either owner-occupied or rented residential property. The modelling approach taken is to consider a saver choosing whether to finance a marginal investment with either debt or equity. If they choose to finance with debt, they must pay the market interest rate on the debt (the final cost of which may be reduced due to tax deductibility of the interest payments). They can then also invest the equity that they had available in an alternative investment and derive a return.[22] This alternative investment is assumed to be bank account interest earning the same pre-tax return as must be paid in mortgage interest (and as is assumed to be earned on all savings vehicles), and subject to the METRs as calculated in this report.

Table 3.11. **Marginal effective tax rates on residential property, 2016 – Personal tax rate: 67% of average wage case; Inflation: country actual**

Country	Including recurrent property taxes				Excluding recurrent property taxes			
	Equity-financed		Debt-financed		Equity-financed		Debt-financed	
	Owner-occupied	Rented	Owner-occupied	Rented	Owner-occupied	Rented	Owner-occupied	Rented
Australia	14.7%	82.5%	58.5%	82.5%	11.5%	53.1%	55.9%	53.1%
Austria	15.5%	53.2%	46.3%	40.0%	9.0%	46.5%	40.7%	32.9%
Belgium	49.3%	50.6%	25.7%	79.2%	29.6%	30.9%	3.8%	62.0%
Canada	38.9%	62.9%	60.6%	62.9%	3.9%	27.6%	29.0%	27.6%
Chile	0.0%	0.0%	0.0%	0.0%	0.0%	0.0%	0.0%	0.0%
Czech Republic	11.1%	22.1%	11.1%	22.1%	10.3%	21.3%	10.3%	21.3%
Denmark	21.3%	47.5%	16.3%	53.2%	1.6%	44.3%	-3.8%	50.1%
Estonia	0.0%	22.4%	-28.4%	22.4%	0.0%	22.4%	-28.4%	22.4%
Finland	12.1%	48.9%	29.5%	48.9%	5.2%	44.0%	23.1%	44.0%
France	22.8%	39.6%	53.6%	69.3%	14.6%	31.4%	46.4%	62.1%
Germany	19.4%	57.4%	19.4%	16.5%	9.6%	47.6%	9.6%	4.9%
Greece	27.2%	26.2%	30.7%	29.8%	18.4%	17.6%	22.0%	21.2%
Hungary	14.9%	30.2%	33.7%	48.4%	14.9%	30.2%	33.7%	48.4%
Iceland	15.5%	36.1%	43.4%	63.2%	1.1%	21.3%	30.6%	50.0%
Ireland	6.6%	37.0%	51.8%	60.3%	2.6%	33.0%	48.5%	56.7%
Israel	10.0%	28.4%	26.7%	44.3%	0.0%	19.2%	17.4%	35.7%
Italy	1.8%	47.2%	13.2%	76.4%	1.8%	31.6%	13.2%	62.7%
Japan	20.8%	31.4%	12.8%	41.7%	2.9%	13.5%	-5.7%	24.6%
Korea	5.6%	9.3%	4.3%	27.2%	2.6%	6.3%	1.3%	24.4%
Latvia	17.8%	29.5%	28.8%	40.4%	5.2%	18.1%	16.8%	29.5%
Luxembourg	0.3%	40.8%	12.8%	9.1%	0.0%	40.5%	12.5%	8.8%
Mexico	11.0%	34.5%	-4.9%	19.0%	9.1%	32.5%	-7.0%	16.9%
Netherlands	10.5%	49.8%	-7.3%	49.8%	5.2%	44.6%	-13.1%	44.6%
New Zealand	20.0%	35.2%	39.4%	35.2%	0.0%	18.7%	21.0%	18.7%
Norway	16.7%	66.6%	41.3%	87.6%	13.4%	63.2%	38.3%	84.6%
Poland	5.9%	15.0%	28.2%	26.1%	5.2%	14.2%	27.5%	25.4%
Portugal	10.0%	39.8%	42.2%	69.4%	0.0%	32.5%	33.5%	63.0%
Slovak Republic	0.4%	20.6%	23.7%	42.8%	0.0%	20.3%	23.4%	42.4%
Slovenia	7.9%	34.2%	36.4%	60.5%	5.2%	31.5%	34.1%	58.2%
Spain	36.7%	45.6%	43.2%	57.8%	27.6%	36.5%	34.4%	49.2%
Sweden	6.1%	24.1%	6.1%	24.1%	6.1%	24.1%	6.1%	24.1%
Switzerland	11.6%	15.0%	11.6%	15.0%	11.6%	15.0%	11.6%	15.0%
Turkey	7.2%	29.1%	34.1%	17.8%	3.9%	25.9%	31.1%	14.4%
United Kingdom	28.4%	55.5%	28.4%	31.0%	5.2%	31.9%	5.2%	4.8%
United States	45.0%	60.0%	45.0%	60.0%	0.9%	1.3%	0.9%	1.3%
Argentina	28.3%	52.9%	-18.4%	52.9%	25.0%	49.5%	-22.4%	49.5%
Bulgaria	9.6%	23.2%	18.4%	31.8%	6.5%	17.1%	15.4%	26.0%
Colombia	17.4%	17.2%	21.9%	21.8%	8.0%	7.8%	12.7%	12.6%
Lithuania	2.7%	18.7%	2.7%	18.7%	0.0%	16.0%	0.0%	16.0%
South Africa	22.9%	47.5%	22.9%	18.0%	0.0%	24.3%	0.0%	-8.2%

StatLink http://dx.doi.org/10.1787/888933661875

Table 3.12. **Marginal effective tax rates on residential property, 2016 – Personal tax rate: 100% of average wage case; Inflation: country actual**

Country	Including recurrent property taxes				Excluding recurrent property taxes			
	Equity-financed		Debt-financed		Equity-financed		Debt-financed	
	Owner-occupied	Rented	Owner-occupied	Rented	Owner-occupied	Rented	Owner-occupied	Rented
Australia	14.7%	88.2%	64.2%	88.2%	11.5%	58.6%	61.6%	58.6%
Austria	15.5%	59.0%	46.3%	36.5%	9.0%	52.3%	40.7%	29.0%
Belgium	49.3%	50.6%	25.7%	79.2%	29.6%	30.9%	3.8%	62.0%
Canada	38.9%	74.6%	71.0%	74.6%	3.9%	39.1%	41.0%	39.1%
Chile	21.2%	21.2%	18.7%	18.6%	0.0%	0.0%	-2.8%	-2.9%
Czech Republic	11.1%	22.1%	11.1%	22.1%	10.3%	21.3%	10.3%	21.3%
Denmark	21.3%	48.9%	16.3%	53.5%	1.6%	45.7%	-3.8%	50.4%
Estonia	0.0%	22.4%	-28.4%	22.4%	0.0%	22.4%	-28.4%	22.4%
Finland	12.1%	49.9%	29.5%	49.9%	5.2%	45.0%	23.1%	45.0%
France	22.8%	47.4%	69.8%	91.2%	14.6%	39.1%	63.2%	84.6%
Germany	19.4%	65.8%	19.4%	15.7%	9.6%	56.0%	9.6%	3.6%
Greece	27.2%	26.2%	30.7%	29.8%	18.4%	17.6%	22.0%	21.2%
Hungary	14.9%	30.2%	33.7%	48.4%	14.9%	30.2%	33.7%	48.4%
Iceland	15.5%	36.1%	43.4%	63.2%	1.1%	21.3%	30.6%	50.0%
Ireland	6.6%	58.5%	51.8%	59.6%	2.6%	54.5%	48.5%	55.6%
Israel	10.0%	28.4%	26.7%	44.3%	0.0%	19.2%	17.4%	35.7%
Italy	1.8%	47.2%	13.2%	76.4%	1.8%	31.6%	13.2%	62.7%
Japan	20.8%	37.4%	12.8%	41.6%	2.9%	19.5%	-5.7%	24.0%
Korea	5.6%	9.3%	4.3%	27.2%	2.6%	6.3%	1.3%	24.4%
Latvia	21.8%	33.2%	32.7%	43.9%	5.2%	18.1%	16.8%	29.5%
Luxembourg	0.3%	46.9%	12.8%	8.3%	0.0%	46.6%	12.5%	8.0%
Mexico	11.1%	45.6%	-16.9%	19.4%	9.1%	43.5%	-19.1%	17.2%
Netherlands	10.5%	49.8%	-7.3%	49.8%	5.2%	44.6%	-13.1%	44.6%
New Zealand	20.0%	46.0%	53.3%	46.0%	0.0%	32.0%	36.0%	32.0%
Norway	16.7%	66.6%	41.3%	87.6%	13.4%	63.2%	38.3%	84.6%
Poland	5.9%	15.0%	28.2%	26.1%	5.2%	14.2%	27.5%	25.4%
Portugal	15.0%	44.4%	46.6%	73.4%	5.2%	37.3%	38.0%	67.2%
Slovak Republic	0.4%	20.6%	23.7%	42.8%	0.0%	20.3%	23.4%	42.4%
Slovenia	7.9%	34.2%	36.4%	60.5%	5.2%	31.5%	34.1%	58.2%
Spain	36.7%	47.6%	43.2%	57.7%	27.6%	38.5%	34.4%	49.0%
Sweden	6.1%	24.1%	6.1%	24.1%	6.1%	24.1%	6.1%	24.1%
Switzerland	23.3%	27.8%	31.0%	35.4%	23.3%	27.8%	31.0%	35.4%
Turkey	7.2%	36.5%	34.1%	10.7%	3.9%	33.2%	31.1%	7.1%
United Kingdom	28.4%	55.5%	28.4%	31.0%	5.2%	31.9%	5.2%	4.8%
United States	39.8%	58.0%	39.8%	58.0%	0.9%	5.1%	0.9%	5.1%
Argentina	28.3%	57.1%	-28.5%	57.1%	25.0%	53.8%	-32.6%	53.8%
Bulgaria	9.6%	23.2%	18.4%	31.8%	6.5%	17.1%	15.4%	26.0%
Colombia	17.4%	17.2%	21.9%	21.8%	8.0%	7.8%	12.7%	12.6%
Lithuania	2.7%	18.7%	2.7%	18.7%	0.0%	16.0%	0.0%	16.0%
South Africa	22.9%	58.6%	22.9%	15.3%	0.0%	35.3%	0.0%	-12.7%

StatLink http://dx.doi.org/10.1787/888933661894

Table 3.13. Marginal effective tax rates on residential property, 2016 – Personal tax rate: 500% of average wage case; Inflation: country actual

Country	Including recurrent property taxes				Excluding recurrent property taxes			
	Equity-financed		Debt-financed		Equity-financed		Debt-financed	
	Owner-occupied	Rented	Owner-occupied	Rented	Owner-occupied	Rented	Owner-occupied	Rented
Australia	14.7%	100.9%	76.9%	100.9%	11.5%	71.0%	74.5%	71.0%
Austria	15.5%	65.7%	46.3%	32.1%	9.0%	59.0%	40.7%	24.3%
Belgium	49.3%	50.6%	77.2%	79.2%	29.6%	30.9%	60.1%	62.1%
Canada	40.0%	105.2%	97.7%	105.2%	5.2%	69.2%	71.8%	69.2%
Chile	24.8%	24.8%	43.0%	43.5%	0.0%	0.0%	20.1%	20.6%
Czech Republic	11.1%	22.1%	11.1%	22.1%	10.3%	21.3%	10.3%	21.3%
Denmark	21.3%	58.1%	23.1%	62.1%	1.6%	54.9%	3.6%	58.9%
Estonia	3.8%	26.3%	3.8%	26.3%	0.0%	22.4%	0.0%	22.4%
Finland	17.0%	54.3%	31.4%	54.3%	10.3%	49.5%	25.1%	49.5%
France	33.9%	68.6%	102.4%	129.4%	25.7%	60.3%	96.7%	123.6%
Germany	19.4%	69.3%	51.1%	47.5%	9.6%	59.5%	42.4%	36.7%
Greece	38.5%	37.5%	41.8%	40.8%	18.4%	17.6%	22.0%	21.2%
Hungary	14.9%	30.2%	33.7%	48.4%	14.9%	30.2%	33.7%	48.4%
Iceland	15.5%	36.1%	43.4%	63.2%	1.1%	21.3%	30.6%	50.0%
Ireland	6.6%	61.2%	51.8%	62.3%	2.6%	57.2%	48.5%	58.3%
Israel	22.2%	28.4%	38.2%	44.3%	12.7%	19.2%	29.3%	35.7%
Italy	1.8%	47.2%	13.2%	76.4%	1.8%	31.6%	13.2%	62.7%
Japan	20.8%	74.7%	12.8%	40.8%	2.9%	56.8%	-5.7%	19.8%
Korea	10.6%	55.1%	57.1%	81.2%	2.6%	47.0%	50.7%	74.1%
Latvia	25.8%	36.8%	36.5%	47.4%	5.2%	18.1%	16.8%	29.5%
Luxembourg	0.3%	48.1%	12.8%	8.2%	0.0%	47.8%	12.5%	7.8%
Mexico	13.6%	63.4%	13.6%	63.4%	11.1%	60.7%	11.1%	60.7%
Netherlands	10.5%	49.8%	-14.5%	49.8%	5.2%	44.6%	-20.6%	44.6%
New Zealand	20.0%	48.6%	56.7%	48.6%	0.0%	35.2%	39.6%	35.2%
Norway	16.7%	66.6%	41.3%	87.6%	13.4%	63.2%	38.3%	84.6%
Poland	5.9%	15.0%	28.2%	23.6%	5.2%	14.2%	27.5%	22.8%
Portugal	26.8%	57.5%	56.9%	85.2%	17.4%	50.7%	48.7%	79.2%
Slovak Republic	0.4%	27.0%	23.7%	48.6%	0.0%	26.7%	23.4%	48.3%
Slovenia	7.9%	34.2%	36.4%	60.5%	5.2%	31.5%	34.1%	58.2%
Spain	37.0%	53.8%	45.7%	59.7%	27.9%	44.7%	37.0%	50.8%
Sweden	6.1%	24.1%	6.1%	24.1%	6.1%	24.1%	6.1%	24.1%
Switzerland	41.5%	48.3%	56.5%	62.8%	41.5%	48.3%	56.5%	62.8%
Turkey	7.2%	44.9%	34.1%	1.4%	3.9%	41.6%	31.1%	-2.5%
United Kingdom	28.4%	86.2%	81.4%	86.2%	5.2%	62.1%	63.5%	62.1%
United States	33.7%	51.3%	33.7%	51.3%	0.9%	6.3%	0.9%	6.3%
Argentina	45.0%	82.3%	45.0%	82.3%	41.7%	79.0%	41.7%	79.0%
Bulgaria	9.6%	23.2%	18.4%	31.8%	6.5%	17.1%	15.4%	26.0%
Colombia	19.6%	49.4%	-23.3%	10.4%	8.0%	37.8%	-36.8%	-3.1%
Lithuania	16.0%	32.0%	34.0%	49.3%	0.0%	16.0%	19.1%	34.4%
South Africa	41.0%	85.7%	99.7%	85.7%	19.8%	72.8%	84.0%	72.8%

StatLink http://dx.doi.org/10.1787/888933661913

Under this scenario, if mortgage interest is deductible for tax purposes at the same rate as tax is paid on the taxpayer's alternative investment, then the financing cost will be zero – as the after-tax income earned on the alternative investment will exactly offset the after tax interest cost of the loan. This is the case, for example, in the Czech Republic, Sweden and the United States, and hence METRs are identical for debt-financed and equity-financed residential property. It is also the case for rental property in the Netherlands for taxpayers saving above the EUR 24 437 exemption amount, as residential rental property and bank accounts are taxed identically under the deemed return system.

If, however, mortgage interest is deductible at a lower rate than the tax rate on the alternative investment, the financing cost will be positive, and METRs will be higher for debt-financed housing. This will happen if the tax rate on rental income and hence the rate of deductibility of mortgage interest is lower than that on bank accounts.

In many countries (e.g. Austria, Germany and the United Kingdom) mortgage interest deductions are only allowed for rental property where the corresponding income is taxed, not owner-occupied property where imputed rental is not taxed. The financing cost will consequently be positive and METRs will increase for owner-occupied property. This will reduce the difference in METRs between owner-occupied and rental properties for debt-financed as compared to equity-financed investment. Mortgage interest deductions may also be disallowed for high income taxpayers or on more expensive houses, as is the case in Italy and Korea, thereby increasing METRs on debt-financed as compared to equity-financed housing.

Meanwhile, if mortgage interest is deductible at a higher rate than the tax rate on the alternative investment, the financing cost will be negative, and METRs will be lower for debt-financed housing. Effectively, the after-tax cost of borrowing is lower than the after-tax return made on the alternative investment. This will happen if the alternative investment is tax-favoured such as is modelled for low- and average-rate taxpayers in the United Kingdom (for rental property). This is also often the case in countries that apply a withholding tax on bank interest but marginal rates on rental income, such as in Germany and Italy, where marginal PIT rates on rental income are always higher than the withholding rate on bank interest.

These results, of course, are based on the assumption that the pre-tax rate of return on the bank account and the interest rate paid on the mortgage are the same. In reality, a bank will charge a higher rate of interest on a mortgage than they will pay on a bank deposit. However, for simplicity, and to illustrate the impact of the tax system rather than broader factors, we assume that both rates are the same. Even with a lower pre-tax rate of return being paid on a bank account, the tax saving on an alternative investment may still be sufficiently large as to outweigh the effect of the lower return, and so still reduce the financing cost.

In some countries (Argentina, Estonia, Mexico and the Netherlands) negative METRs can occur for debt-financed owner-occupied property. This is because there is no taxation of imputed rental income, but a mortgage interest deduction is still provided. The deduction is then assumed to be utilised against labour income in that year.

The ability to debt-finance a property may also open up leverage-based tax planning opportunities that may increase demand for residential rental property, without necessarily encouraging increased savings in residential rental property. Box 3.2 discusses the type of tax planning opportunities that may in some circumstances arise.

Box 3.2. **Debt financing and tax planning opportunities**

To examine the impact of tax on the composition of savings, the basic structure of the analysis throughout this chapter has been to focus on a taxpayer with one marginal currency unit of savings. This remains the case when considering the debt-financed purchase of residential property – with the opportunity return on that one currency unit of savings then partially, fully, or more than fully compensating for the interest costs of the debt, depending on tax rules in place. However, the ability to debt-finance residential property may also create leverage-based tax planning opportunities.

However, tax systems may provide tax-induced incentives to invest in immovable property even in the absence of own funds (i.e. savings) that can be invested. Consider, for example, a scenario where a rental property is expected to generate a significant return to pay for all ownership and financing costs, including taxes. The return may come predominantly in the form of a tax-preferred capital gain and through (possibly) tax-privileged rental income. Mortgage interest deductions are allowable against rental income, and operating losses can be offset against other sources of income. The taxpayer fully debt-finances the purchase of a residential rental property (using their owner-occupied house as collateral). The principal investment is gradually paid back over time or is redeemed when the loan expires. Significant interest expenses are incurred in the first few years following purchase, with the consequent interest deductions more than fully offsetting the rental income earned. The operating losses are possibly offset against labour income that would otherwise be taxed at high marginal PIT rates.

In subsequent years interest payments fall and the operating loss approaches zero. However, at this point the taxpayer then fully debt-finances the purchase of another rental property. This process could continue as long as banks want to provide debt financing. On sale, the anticipated capital gain is made, and taxed at a concessionary rate, with the after-tax gain more than fully offsetting the operating losses incurred. A leverage-based profit is consequently made without any of the taxpayer's actual savings being used.

Depending on the tax system in a particular country, variants to the above scenario could include the carry-forward of losses to be utilised against capital gains once realised, additional losses being incurred up front due to depreciation deductions (potentially then "clawed back" on realisation of the capital gain, but with consequent timing benefits), and timed realisations to access age-based concessionary tax rates.

Such tax planning opportunities effectively require the after-tax expected return to be significant enough to (largely or fully) outweigh the mortgage interest costs and any other costs incurred. The tax rules illustrated above – deductibility of mortgage interest and concessionary treatment of capital gains – make such a possibility more likely and imply that investing in immovable property, even in the absence of equity, can be attractive. Such a scenario might in particular be attractive when housing markets are booming and investors are expecting a significant capital gain to make a positive return on investment. As noted in chapter 2, mortgage interest is indeed deductible in most countries on rental properties, while capital gains are also often taxed at concessionary rates.

These tax planning opportunities highlight how particular tax rules may lead to greater incentives to purchase residential rental property than the METRs presented in this chapter suggest is likely to occur. Analysing these types of investment within a METR framework is feasible, but would require major adjustments to the modelling underlying the calculations presented in this report, as the timing of repayment of the principal does not occur at the initial period (as currently is assumed) but gradually over time or at the moment when the loan is redeemed. This is left for future work.

Sensitivity analysis

Impact of inflation

The rate of inflation can have a significant impact on METRs. This is because, under nominal tax systems, inflationary gains will be taxed as well as real gains – so a higher rate of inflation will lead to a higher METR. Inflation rates in the five years to 1 July 2016 were low, averaging 1.59% across the OECD, although rates ranged from 8.14% in Turkey to -0.45 in Switzerland.

The impact of inflation on METRs is illustrated in Figure 3.7 which compares METRs faced by an average rate taxpayer on bank deposits calculated with the actual country inflation rate and with a zero inflation rate. The high inflation rate in Turkey can be seen to increase the METR on bank interest significantly from 15% (with no inflation) to 55.7%. However, even relatively low inflation rates can have a significant impact on METRs. For example, the METR on bank deposits for an average rate taxpayer in New Zealand is 41.0% when calculated using New Zealand's actual inflation rate (1.11%), but would be only 30.0% with no inflation.

Figure 3.7. **Marginal effective tax rates on bank interest: zero and actual inflation, 2016**

Personal tax rate: 100% of average wage case. Real return: 3%. Expected holding period: 5 years.

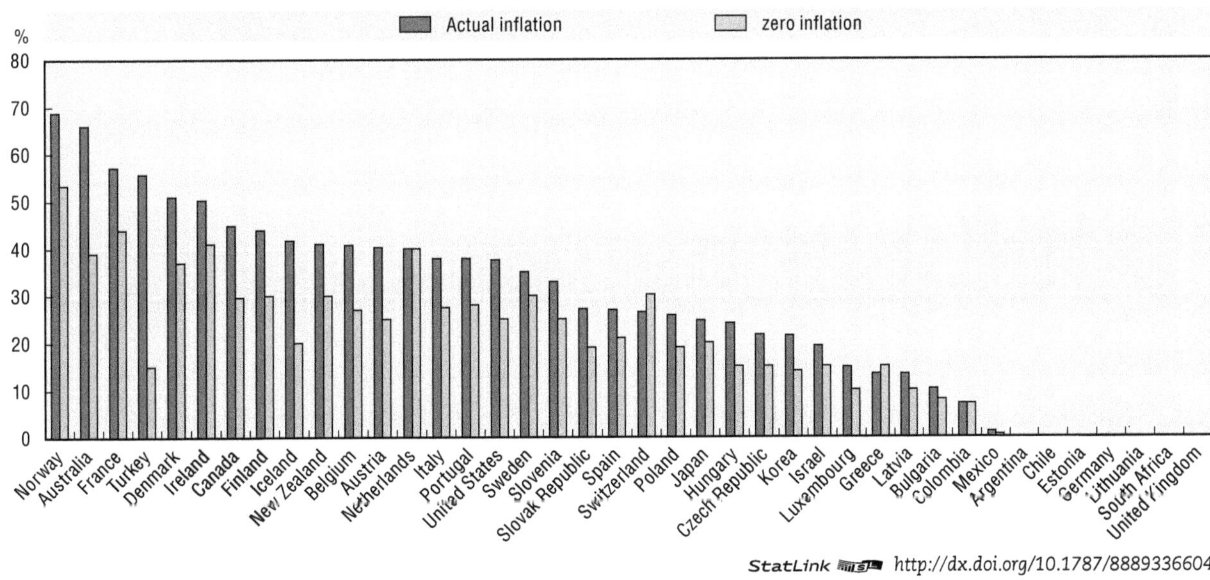

StatLink http://dx.doi.org/10.1787/888933660469

In contrast, the slightly negative actual inflation rates in Greece and Switzerland, decrease the METRs on bank accounts as compared to the no inflation case (e.g., from 30.2% to 26.5% in Switzerland). This highlights that negative inflation acts as a tax subsidy as less than the full real return is taxed.

In Colombia and the Netherlands, METR results in Figure 3.7 are the same both with and without inflation. In Colombia this is because real rather than nominal interest is taxed, whereas it is a result of the deemed return approach in the Netherlands. Meanwhile, in seven countries bank interest earned by the average rate taxpayer is untaxed, so METRs are zero irrespective of the inflation rate.

Zero inflation results for other assets are presented in Annex B.

Impact of expected holding period

METRs are also sensitive to the assumed expected holding period. There are several reasons for this. For assets producing capital gains, a longer expected holding period will mean the asset may be taxed on realisation at a lower – or even a zero – tax rate. Deferral effects on realised capital gains will also increase the longer the holding period. Meanwhile, one-off transaction taxes will effectively be spread over a longer period of time under a longer expected holding period, thereby lowering their effect on the METR.

The impact that the holding period can have on METRs is illustrated in Figure 3.8 which compares METRs faced by an average rate taxpayer on an equity investment (with 50% dividend distribution) for a six-month, five-year, and ten-year holding period. The impact of transaction taxes can be seen in the three countries with the highest METRs for a six-month holding period (Greece, Ireland and Korea). METRs in these countries fall markedly once the holding period increases and the transaction tax is spread over either five or ten years.

Figure 3.8. **Marginal effective tax rates on shares: varying holding periods, 2016**

Personal tax rate: 100% of average wage case. Real return: 3%. Inflation: country actual.

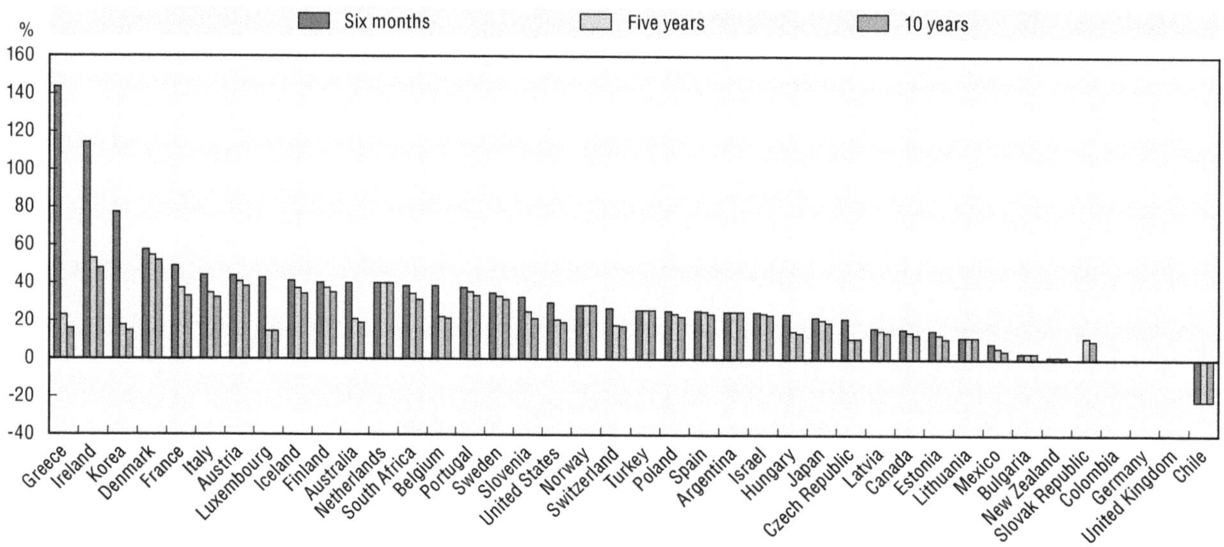

StatLink http://dx.doi.org/10.1787/888933660488

In most other countries, METRs fall as the holding period increases due to a reduced capital gains tax rate and/or deferral. For example, in the United States capital gains on equity are taxed at 25% if held for less than one year, but at 15% if held longer. This impact can be seen in the drop in the METR in Figure 3.8 from 29.7% for a six month holding period to 20.7% for a five year holding period. Deferral effects continue to lower the METR for longer holding periods, with a ten-year expected holding period producing a METR of 19.4%.

In seven countries, METRs are positive but stay constant across holding periods. In Bulgaria, Turkey and New Zealand this is because there is no taxation of capital gains even for shorter holding periods.[23, 24] In Lithuania, an average-rate taxpayer is assumed to receive less than an exempt amount of capital gains. In Argentina and Norway (given the modelling of the risk-free return allowance) only a wealth tax is applied to equity, which is not affected by the holding period. In the Netherlands, the deemed return approach similarly means METRs are not affected by the holding period. Meanwhile, METRs are zero in Colombia,

Germany and the United Kingdom as neither dividends nor capital gains are taxed for an average-rate taxpayer.

In the Slovak Republic, METRs increase between the six month and five-year holding period. This is because capital gains are assumed to be below a minimum threshold for the six-month holding period scenario, but above the threshold for a five-year holding period. Consistent with other countries, the results then show the impact of deferral lowering the METR between five- and ten-year holding periods.

Results for alternate expected holding periods for different assets are presented in Annex B.

Impact of pre-tax real rate of return

The choice of pre-tax real rate of return will also affect METRs. This is because, in almost all cases, the base of a tax is not solely the pre-tax real rate of return – it is either the nominal rate, or some other base such as the asset value or increase in asset value. Additionally, a wealth tax or a one-off transaction tax will be a smaller proportion of a higher return. As a consequence, an increase in the pre-tax real rate of return will result in a less than proportional increase in tax liability.

The impact that the real return can have on METRs is illustrated in Figure 3.9 which again focuses on an equity investment (with 50% dividend distribution), but this time for a high-rate taxpayer. METRs are compared for real returns of 2%, 3% and 4%. As expected, METRs fall as the real return increases in almost every country.

The greatest variation in METRs occurs in Argentina and the Netherlands. In the Netherlands, this is a logical consequence of the deemed return approach – which applies a 30% tax rate on a deemed 4% real return, irrespective of the actual return. The METR presented in Figure 3.9 is, by design, 30% when the real return is 4%. However, when the real return falls below 4%, the deemed rate, and hence the tax burden, does not change – and so METRs increase to 40% and 60%, for a 3% and 2% real return, respectively.

Figure 3.9. **Marginal effective tax rates on shares: varying real rates of return, 2016**

Personal tax rate: 500% of average wage case. Holding period: 5 years. Inflation: country actual.

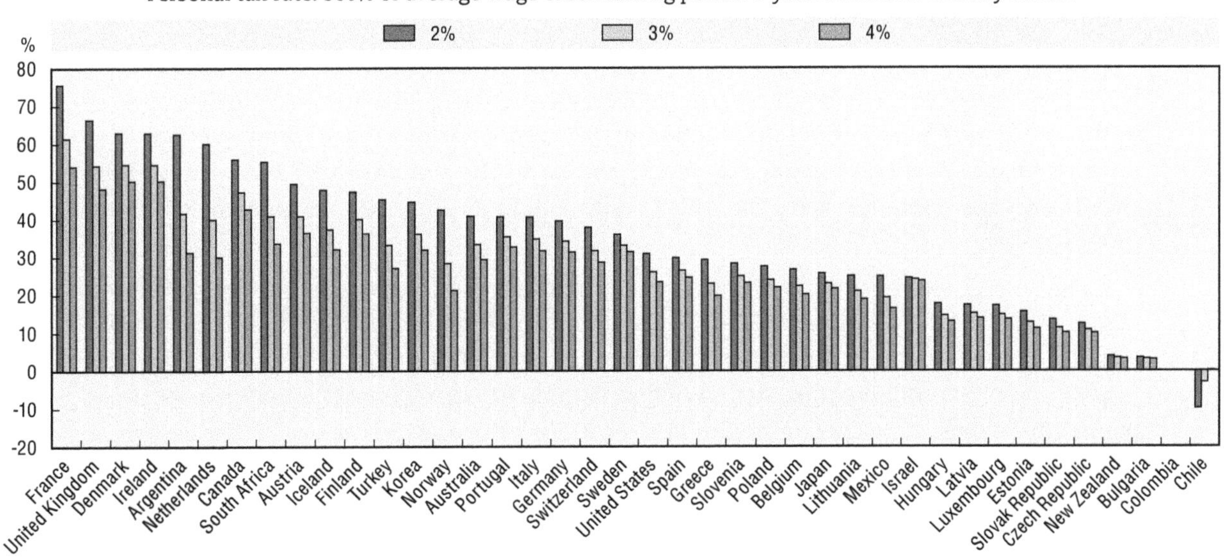

StatLink http://dx.doi.org/10.1787/888933660507

In Argentina, the wealth tax imposed on equity (and other asset holdings) has a similar effect on METRs as the Netherlands' deemed return approach (indeed a wealth tax can be thought of as equivalent to applying a fixed tax rate on an assumed rate of return). As the rate of return falls, the wealth tax burden does not change and hence METRs increase. A wealth tax has a similar impact in Norway and France, and to a lesser extent in Switzerland (and in Spain, though this is not captured in the modelling due to its high minimum threshold).

Results for alternate pre-tax real rates of return for different assets are presented in Annex B.

Residential property

METRs on residential property can be particularly affected by the assumptions made in the analysis. For example, the preponderance of property transaction taxes and recurrent property taxes can be expected to lead to significant variation in METRs depending on holding period and real return. This can be seen in Figure 3.10 which replicates Figure 3.9 but for debt-financed residential rental property and the average-rate taxpayer. Figure 3.10 shows METRs falling in all countries as the real return increases.

In addition to the basic assumptions regarding inflation, holding period and real return, an assumption regarding the split of return between (imputed or actual) rental income and capital gain is necessary. The METRs presented in the main results assume that the real return is split equally between rental income and capital gains. However, in some countries, and depending on market conditions, capital gains may be a far more significant component of the overall return from residential property investment. Given that capital gains are often taxed at lower rates as compared to rental income, this can significantly reduce the tax actually faced on a residential rental investment.

To illustrate the potentially large effect on METRs of a market generating substantial returns in the form of capital gains, Figure 3.11 compares the standard METR results (from Table 3.3) for debt-financed residential property with a high capital gain scenario. This scenario assumes a real return of 7% is generated entirely from capital gains.[25] Figure 3.11 shows returns significantly fall in such a scenario compared to the standard results. For example, in Australia the METR falls from 88% to just 25%, with similar reductions occurring in other countries under this scenario.

Another factor that can significantly affect METRs on debt-financed residential property is the presence of tax relief for mortgage interest payments. In 26 of the 40 countries covered in this study tax relief (either a deduction or tax credit) for mortgage interest is provided for debt-financed rental property. Figure 3.12 compares the standard METR results for these countries (from Table 3.3) with the METRs that would apply in the absence of mortgage interest relief.

Figure 3.12 shows that, in all but three countries, the presence of mortgage interest tax relief significantly reduces METRs. In Colombia and Korea the deductibility of mortgage interest against rental income does not impact the METRs as an average rate taxpayer faces no tax on rental income. Meanwhile in Estonia an average rate taxpayer is assumed to already be deducting the maximum EUR 1 200 per year, so receives no further benefit on the marginal euro of saved.

Figure 3.10. **Marginal effective tax rates on debt-financed rented residential property: varying real rates of return, 2016**

Personal tax rate: 100% of average wage case. Holding period: 20 years. Inflation: country actual.

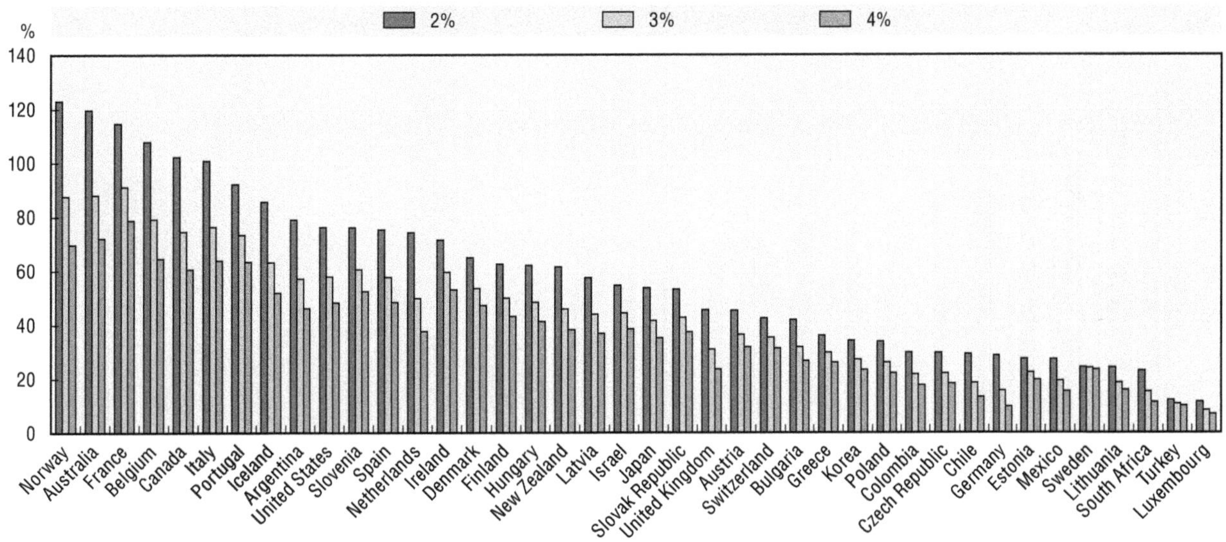

StatLink http://dx.doi.org/10.1787/888933660526

Figure 3.11. **Marginal effective tax rates on debt-financed rented residential property: high capital gain scenario, 2016**

Personal tax rate: 100% of average wage case. Holding period: 20 years. Inflation: country actual.

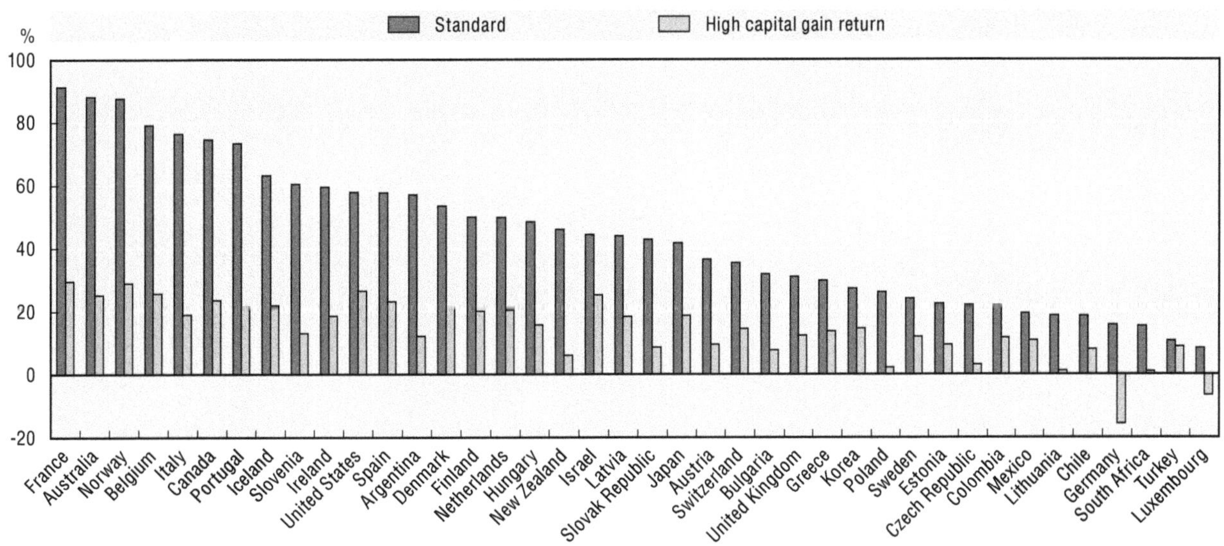

StatLink http://dx.doi.org/10.1787/888933660545

Figure 3.12. **Marginal effective tax rates on debt-financed rented residential property: with and without mortgage interest tax relief (selected countries), 2016**

Personal tax rate: 100% of average wage case. Holding period: 20 years. Inflation: country actual.

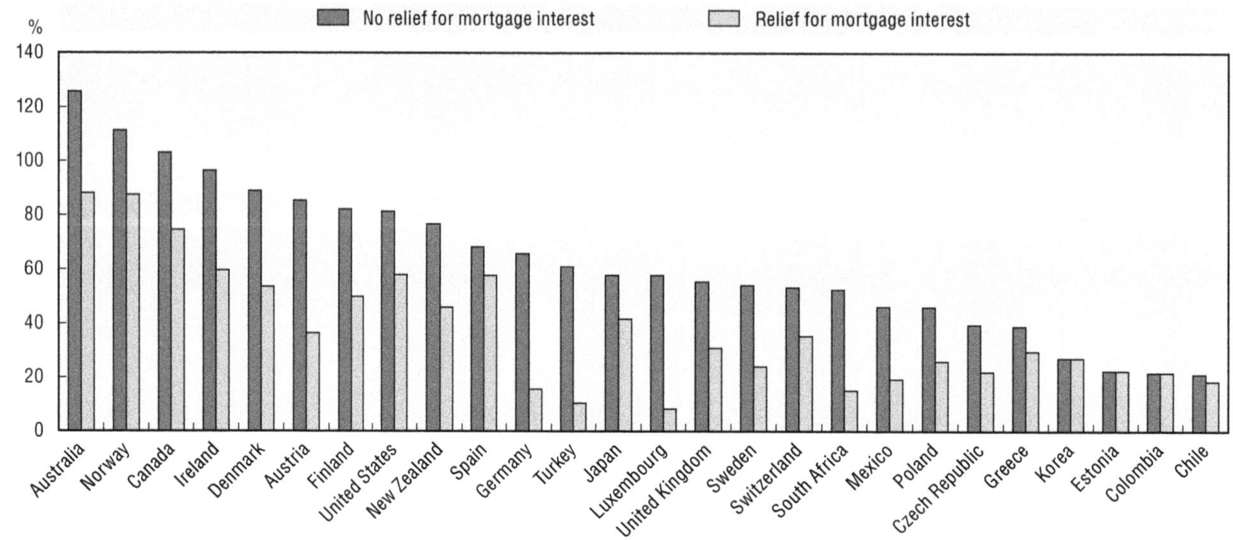

StatLink http://dx.doi.org/10.1787/888933660564

Individual country graphs

Figure 3.13. **Marginal effective tax rates: Argentina, 2016**

Actual inflation rate

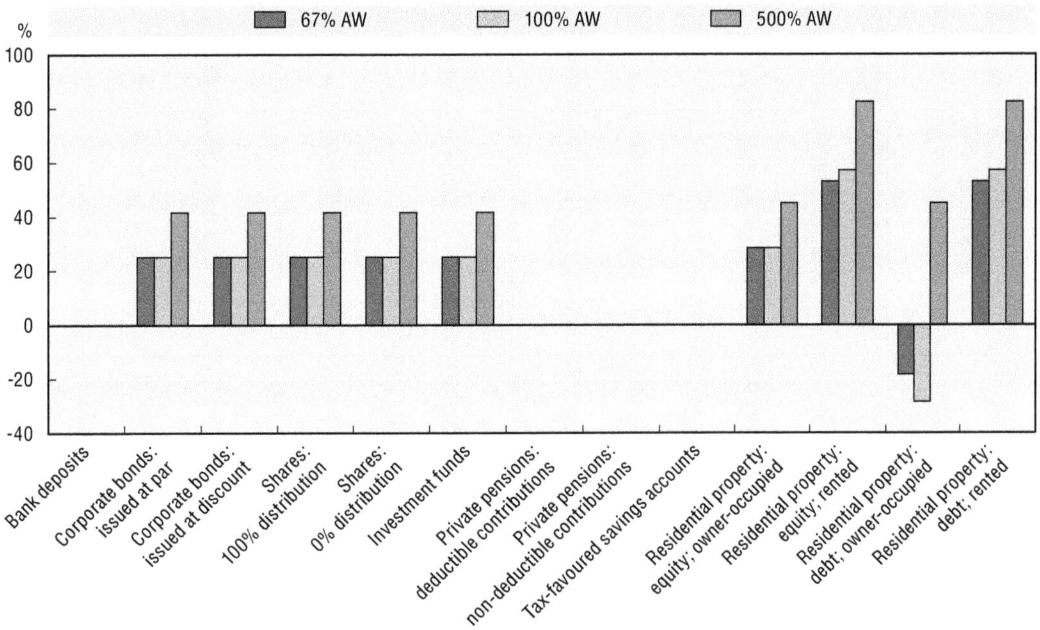

StatLink http://dx.doi.org/10.1787/888933660583

Figure 3.14. **Marginal effective tax rates: Australia, 2016**

Actual inflation rate

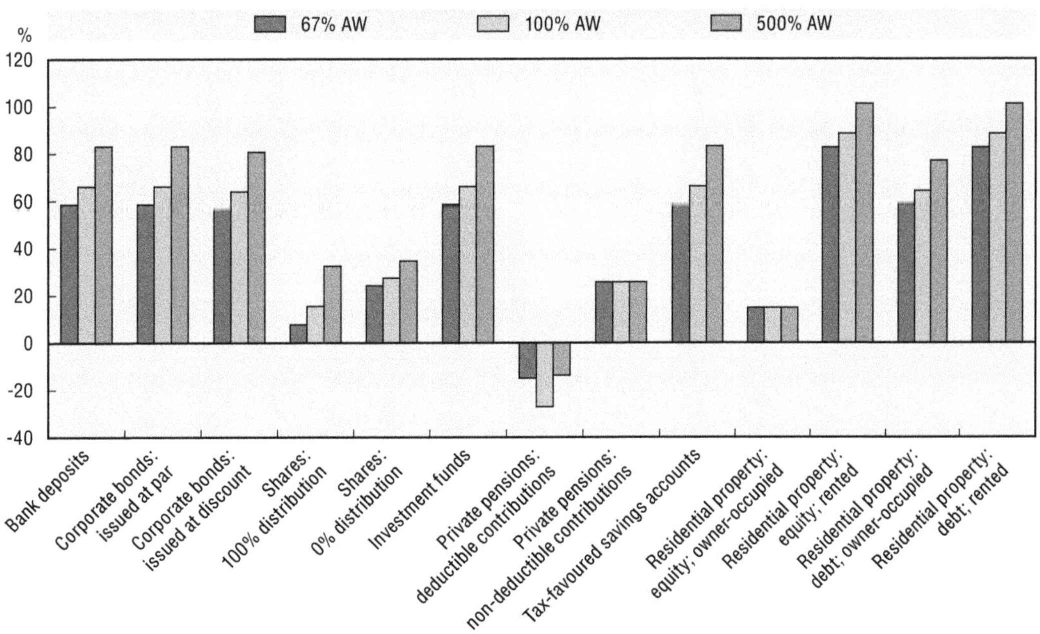

StatLink http://dx.doi.org/10.1787/888933660602

Figure 3.15. **Marginal effective tax rates: Austria, 2016**

Actual inflation rate

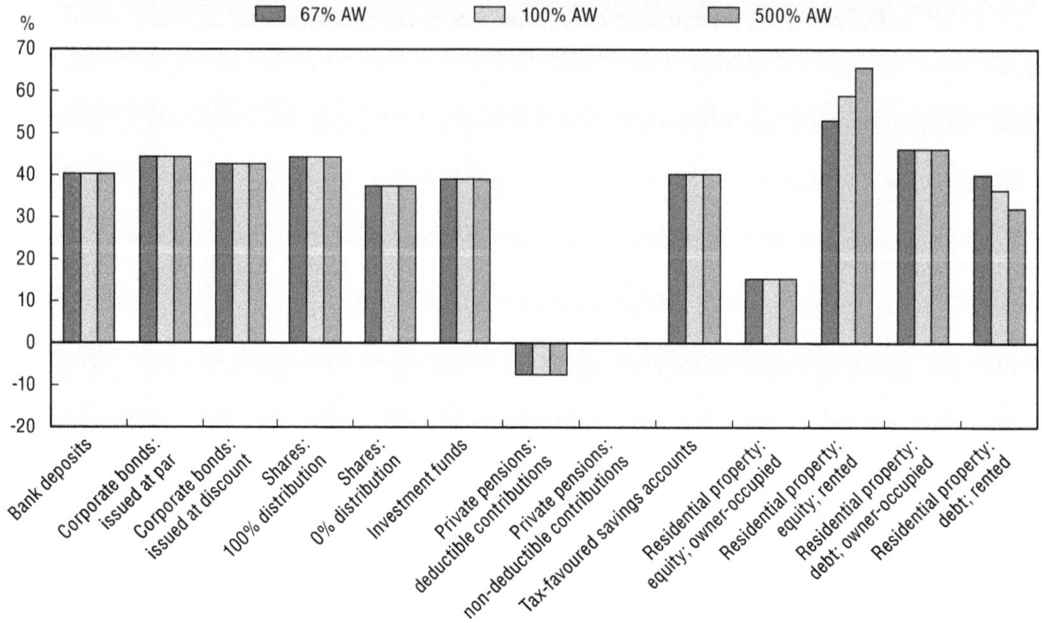

StatLink http://dx.doi.org/10.1787/888933660621

Figure 3.16. **Marginal effective tax rates: Belgium, 2016**

Actual inflation rate

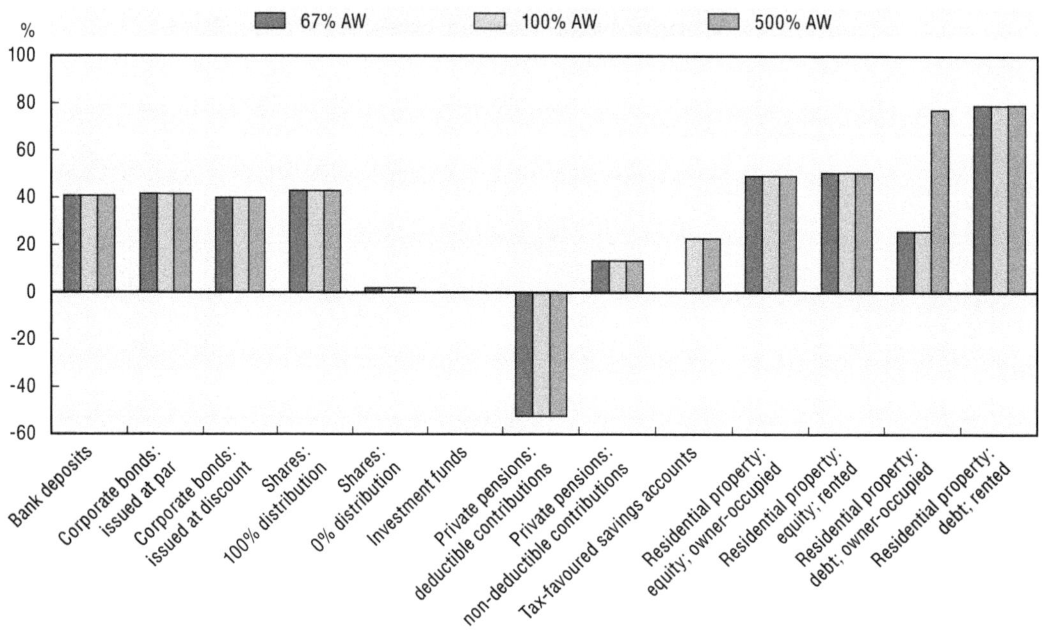

StatLink http://dx.doi.org/10.1787/888933660640

Figure 3.17. **Marginal effective tax rates: Bulgaria, 2016**

Actual inflation rate

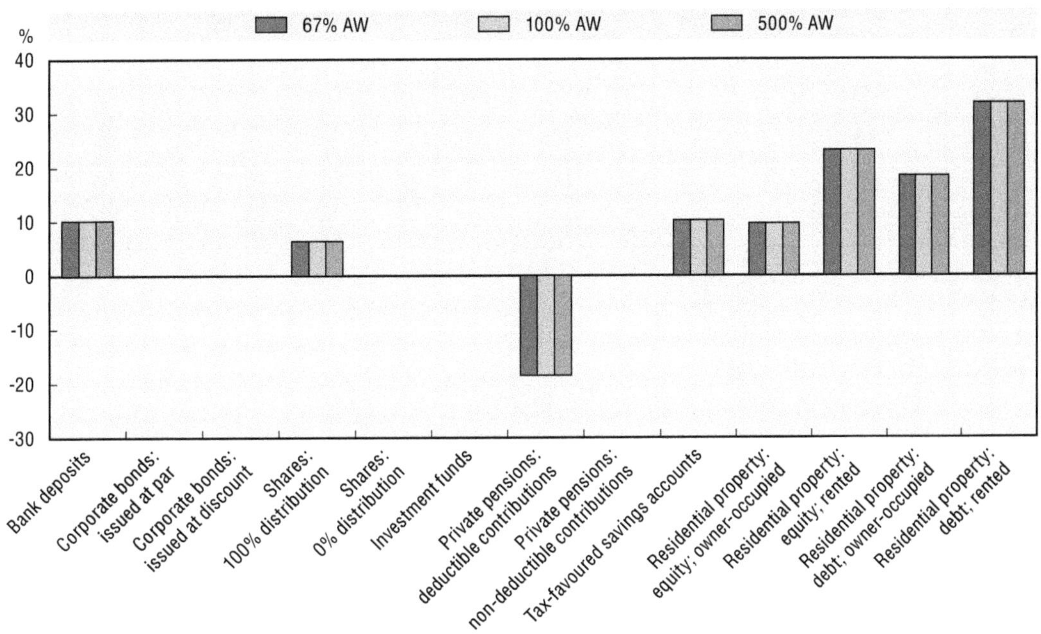

StatLink http://dx.doi.org/10.1787/888933660659

Figure 3.18. **Marginal effective tax rates: Canada, 2016**

Actual inflation rate

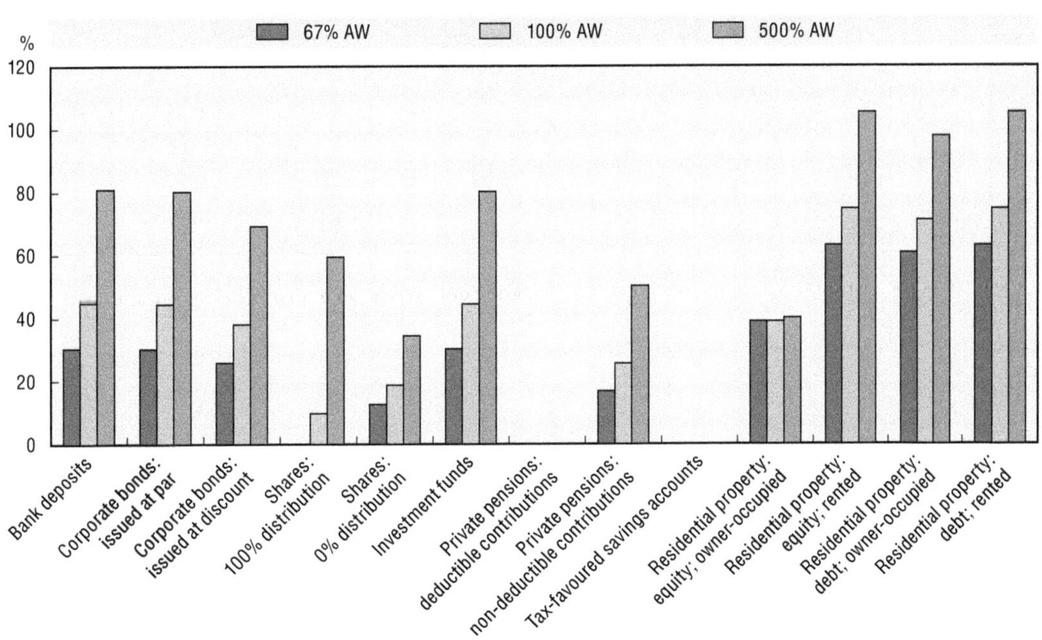

StatLink http://dx.doi.org/10.1787/888933660678

Figure 3.19. **Marginal effective tax rates: Chile, 2016**

Actual inflation rate

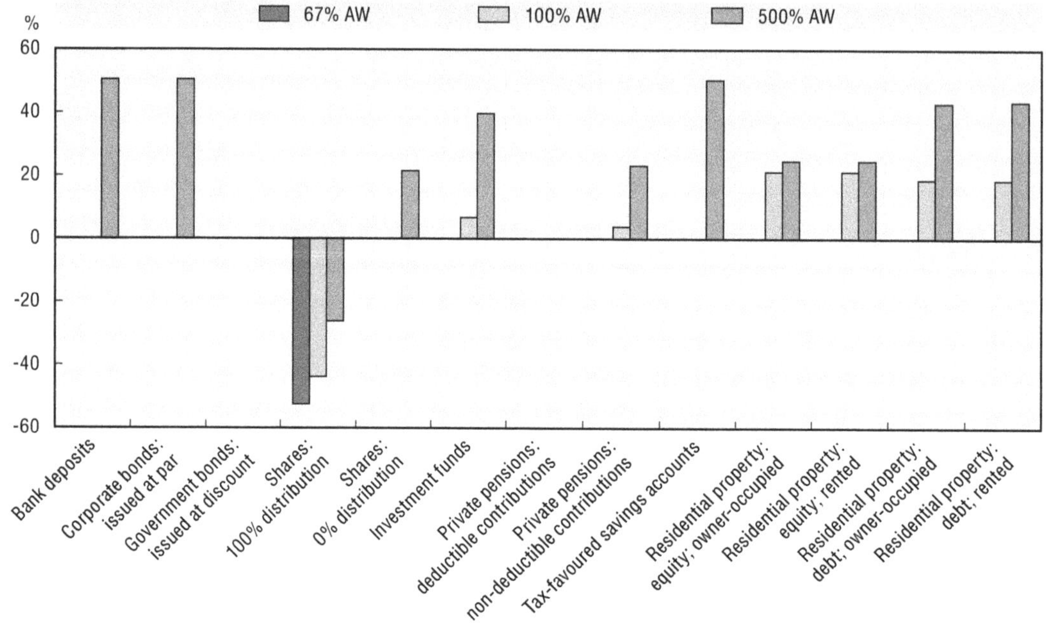

StatLink http://dx.doi.org/10.1787/888933660697

Figure 3.20. **Marginal effective tax rates: Colombia, 2016**

Actual inflation rate

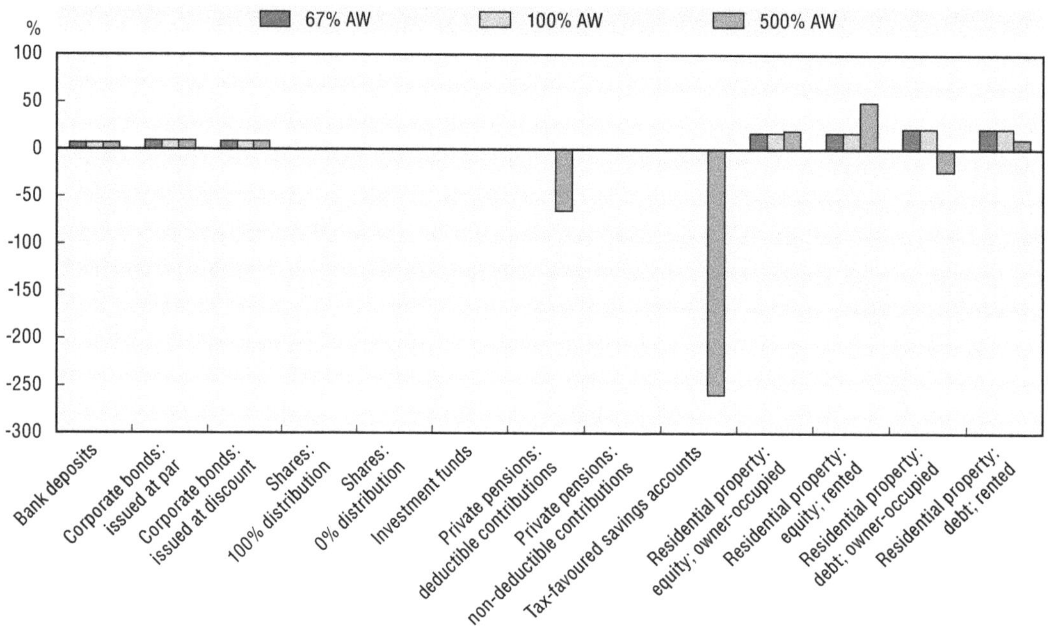

StatLink http://dx.doi.org/10.1787/888933660716

Figure 3.21. **Marginal effective tax rates: Czech Republic, 2016**

Actual inflation rate

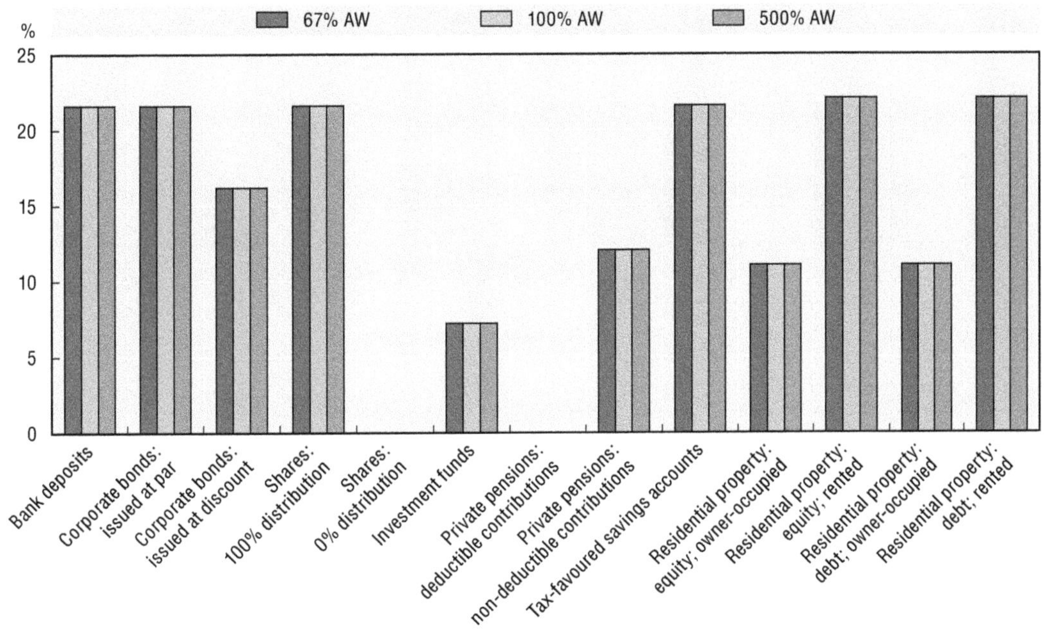

StatLink http://dx.doi.org/10.1787/888933660735

Figure 3.22. **Marginal effective tax rates: Denmark, 2016**

Actual inflation rate

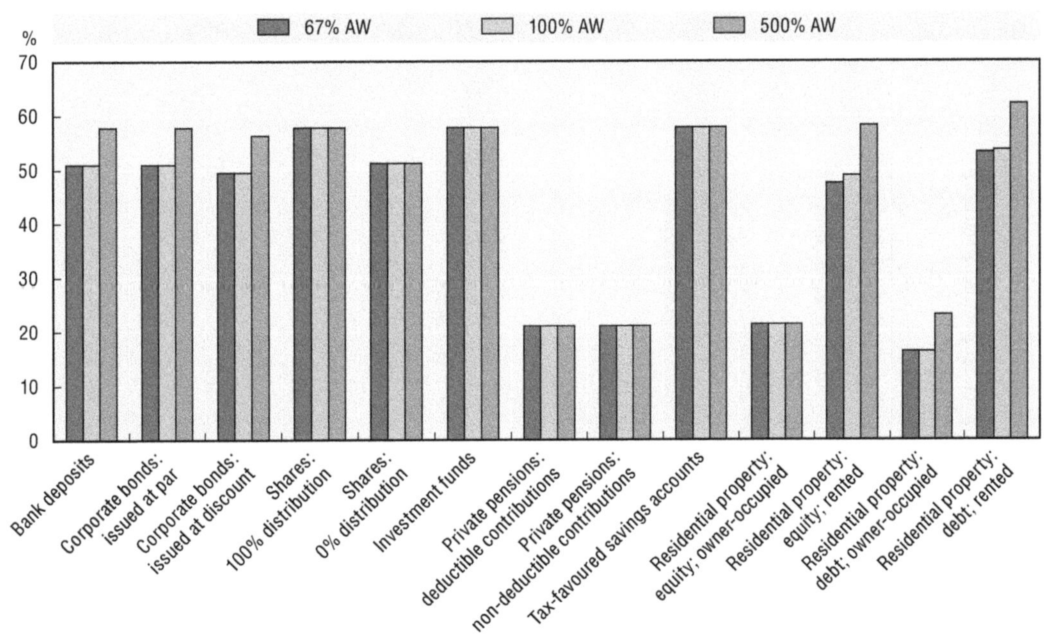

StatLink http://dx.doi.org/10.1787/888933660754

Figure 3.23. **Marginal effective tax rates: Estonia, 2016**

Actual inflation rate

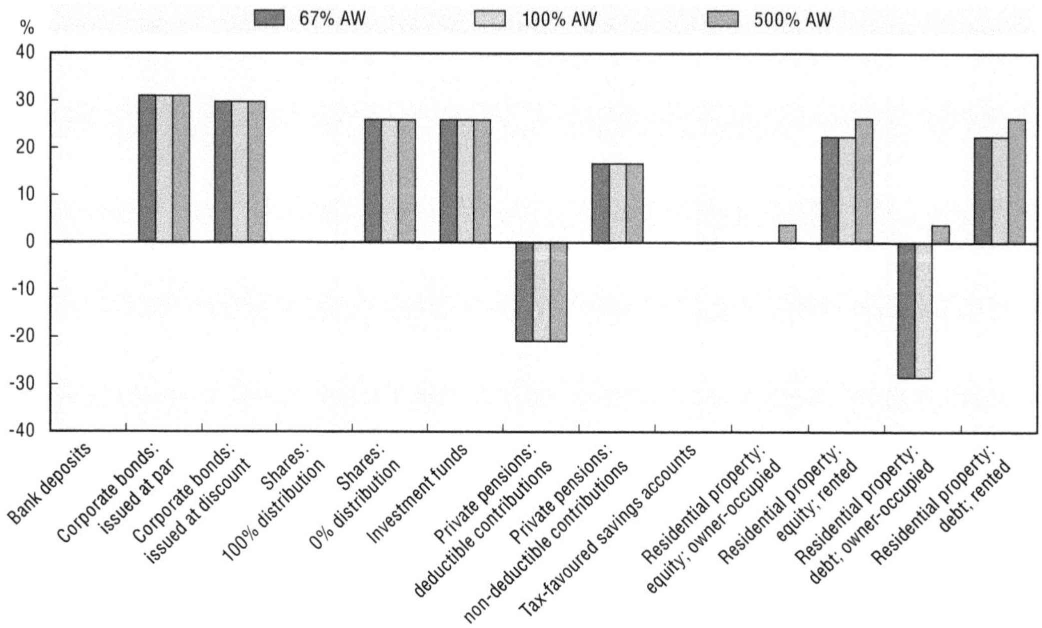

StatLink http://dx.doi.org/10.1787/888933660773

Figure 3.24. **Marginal effective tax rates: Finland, 2016**

Actual inflation rate

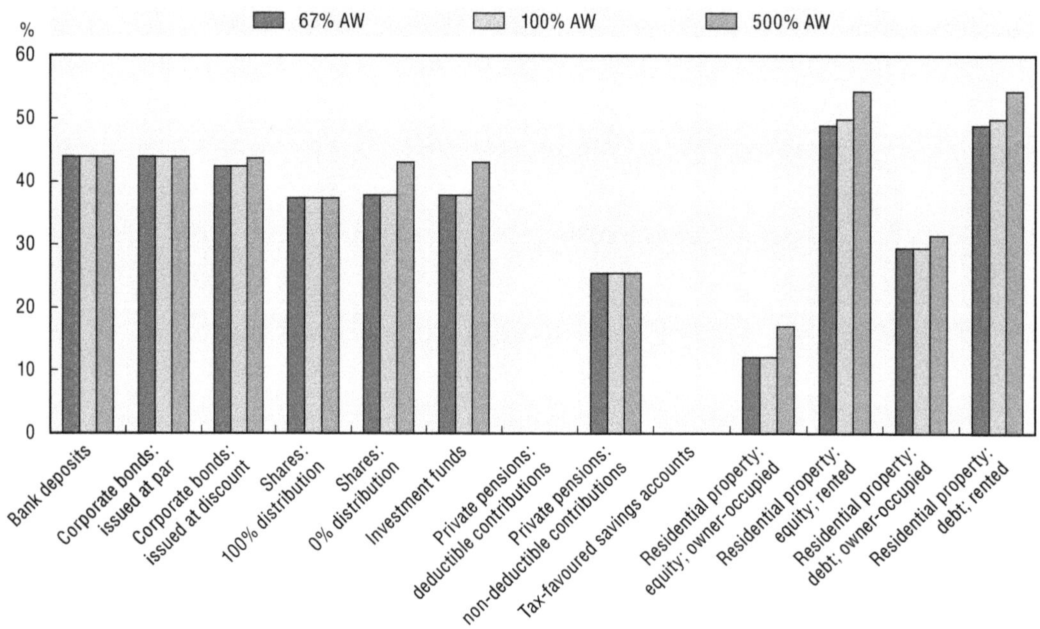

StatLink http://dx.doi.org/10.1787/888933660792

Figure 3.25. **Marginal effective tax rates: France, 2016**

Actual inflation rate

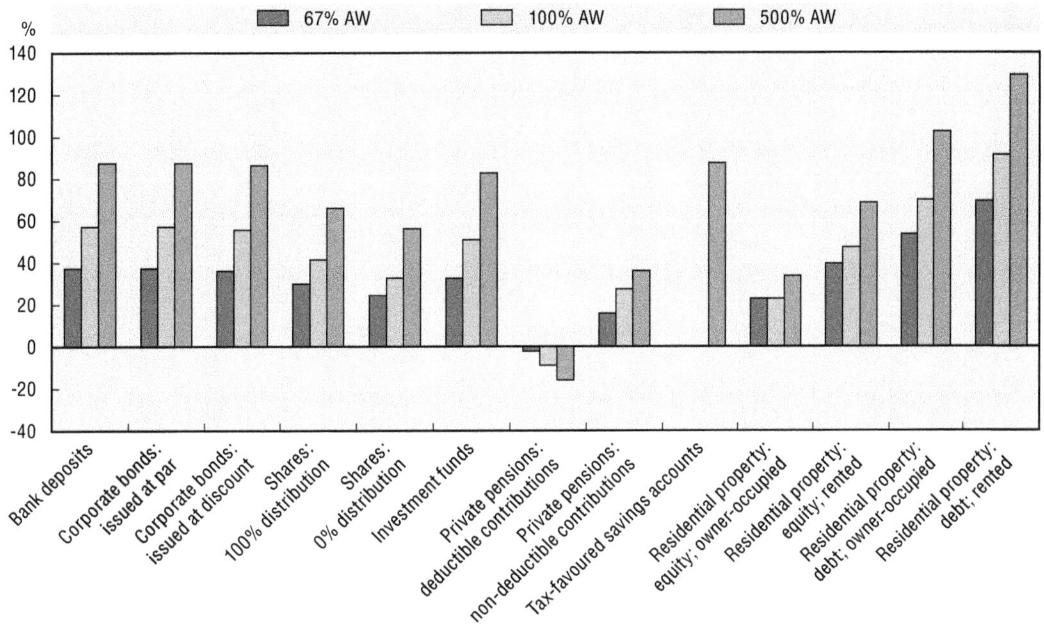

StatLink http://dx.doi.org/10.1787/888933660811

Figure 3.26. **Marginal effective tax rates: Germany, 2016**

Actual inflation rate

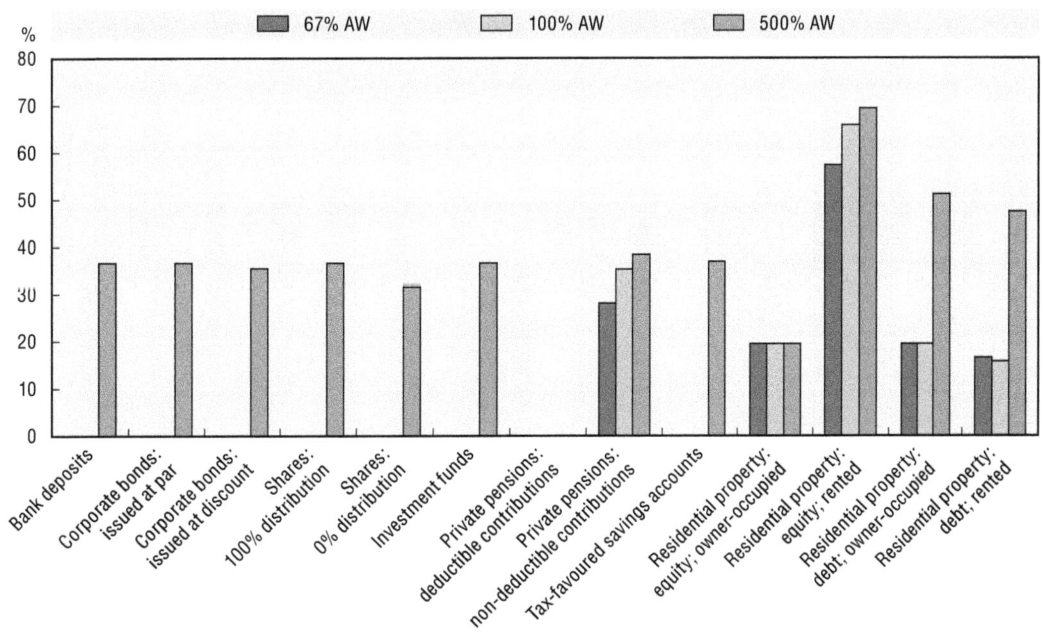

StatLink http://dx.doi.org/10.1787/888933660830

Figure 3.27. **Marginal effective tax rates: Greece, 2016**

Actual inflation rate

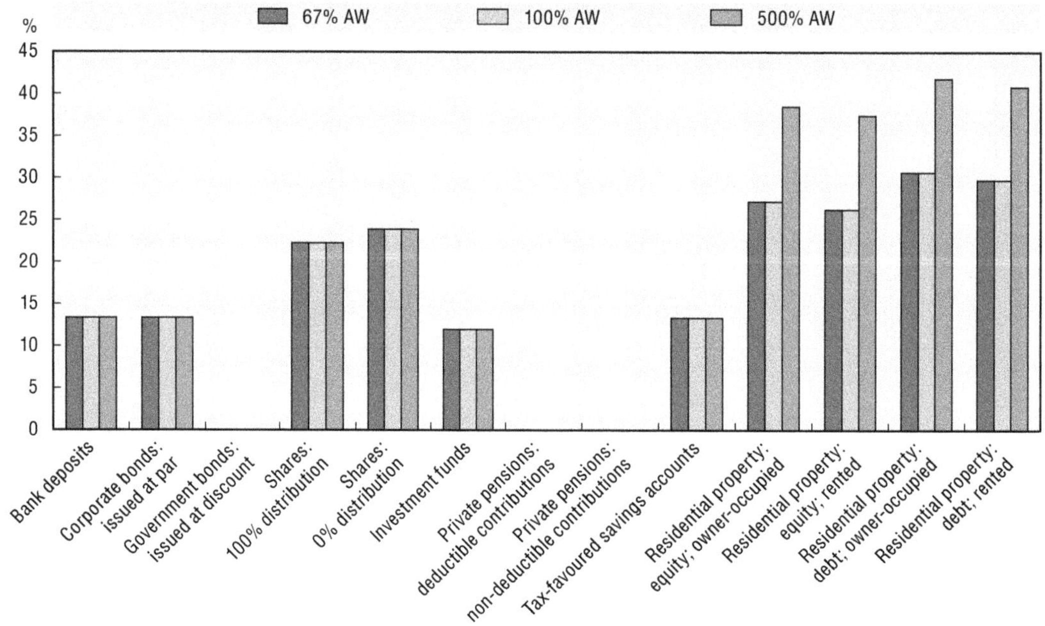

StatLink http://dx.doi.org/10.1787/888933660849

Figure 3.28. **Marginal effective tax rates: Hungary, 2016**

Actual inflation rate

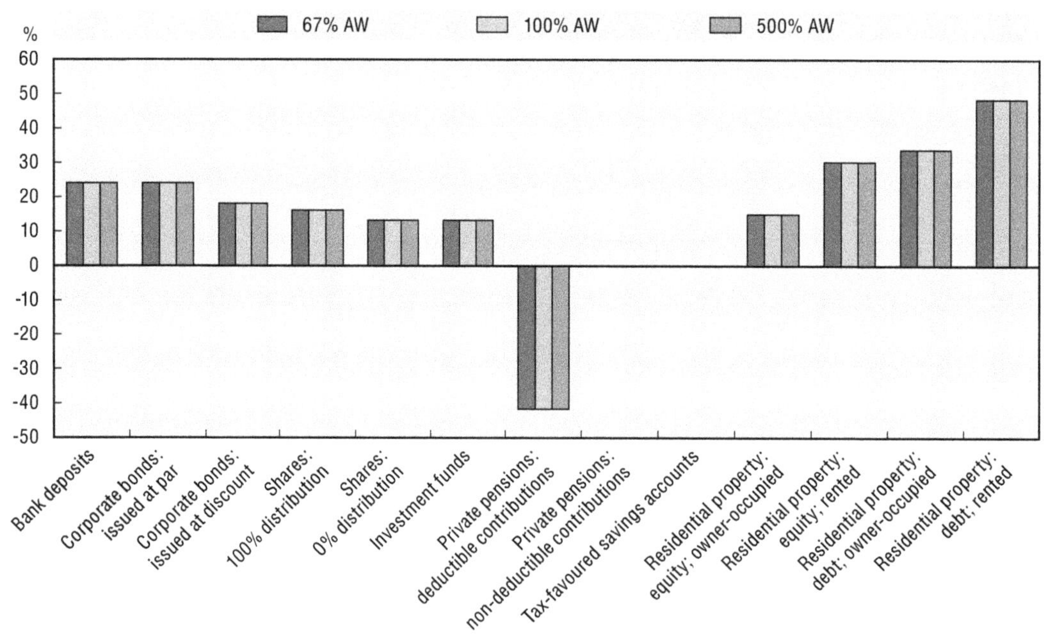

StatLink http://dx.doi.org/10.1787/888933660868

Figure 3.29. **Marginal effective tax rates: Iceland, 2016**

Actual inflation rate

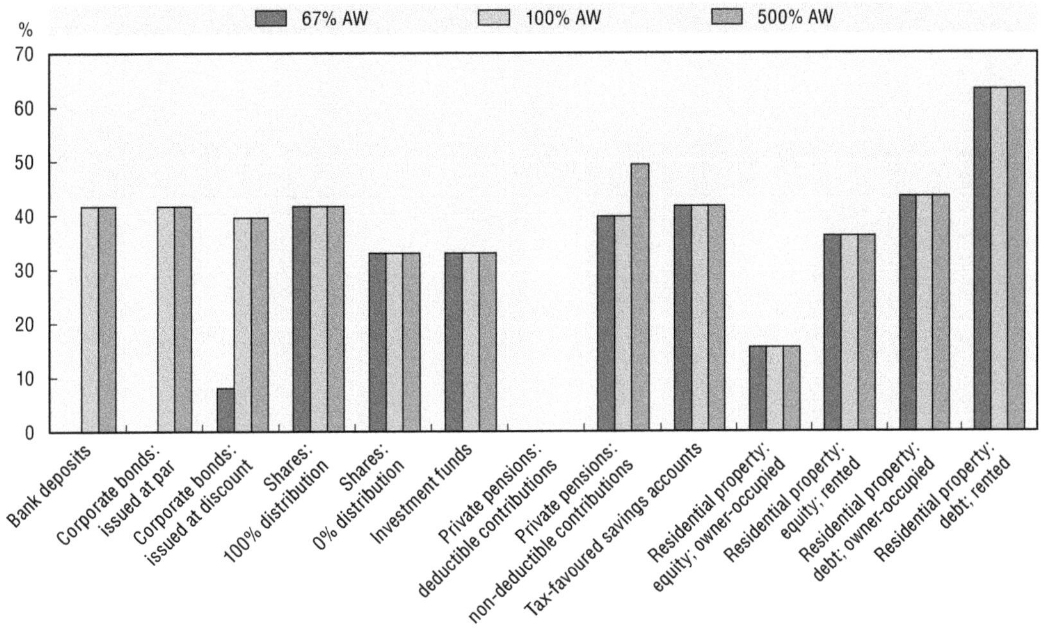

StatLink http://dx.doi.org/10.1787/888933660887

Figure 3.30. **Marginal effective tax rates: Ireland, 2016**

Actual inflation rate

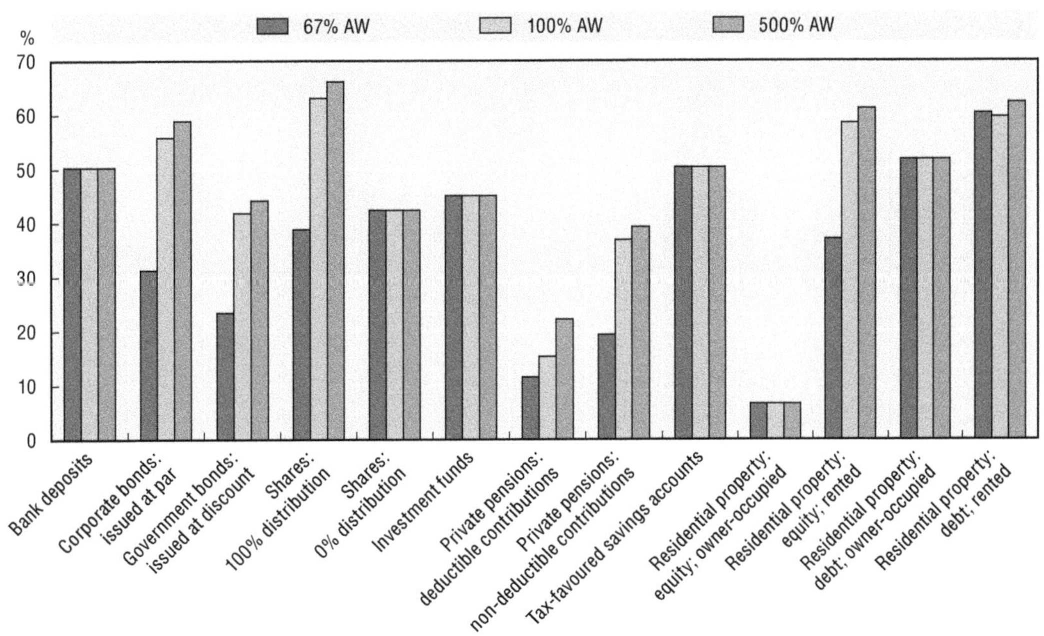

StatLink http://dx.doi.org/10.1787/888933660906

Figure 3.31. **Marginal effective tax rates: Israel, 2016**

Actual inflation rate

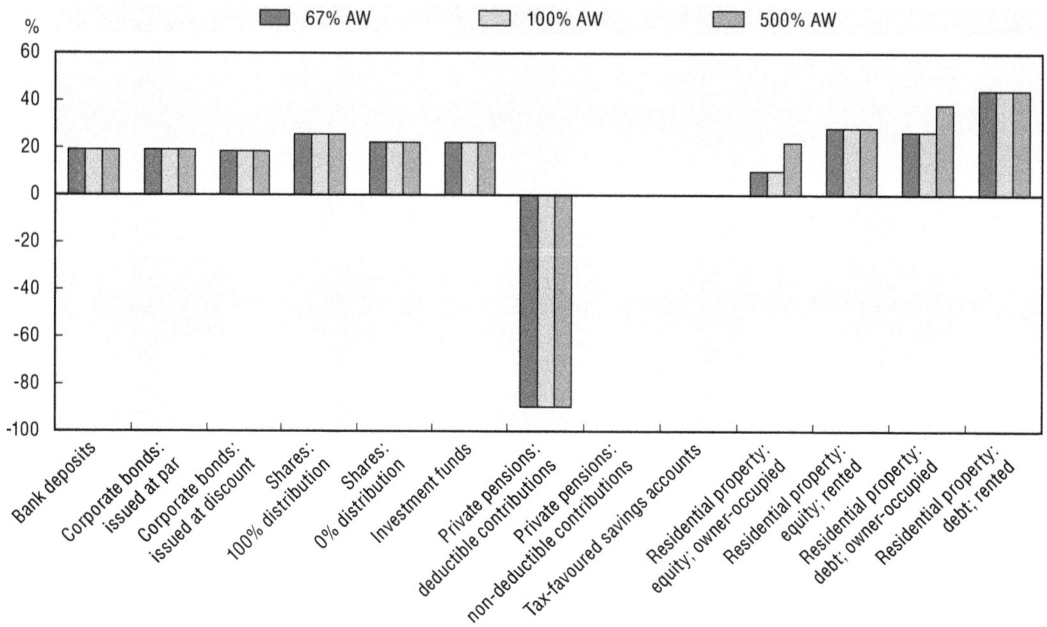

StatLink http://dx.doi.org/10.1787/888933660925

Figure 3.32. **Marginal effective tax rates: Italy, 2016**

Actual inflation rate

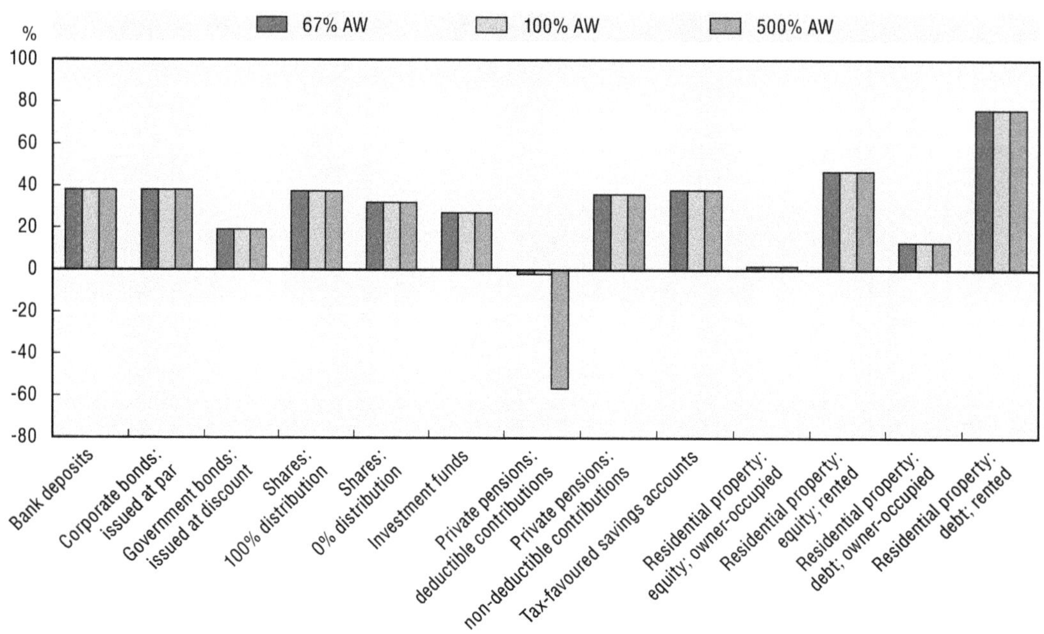

StatLink http://dx.doi.org/10.1787/888933660944

Figure 3.33. **Marginal effective tax rates: Japan, 2016**

Actual inflation rate

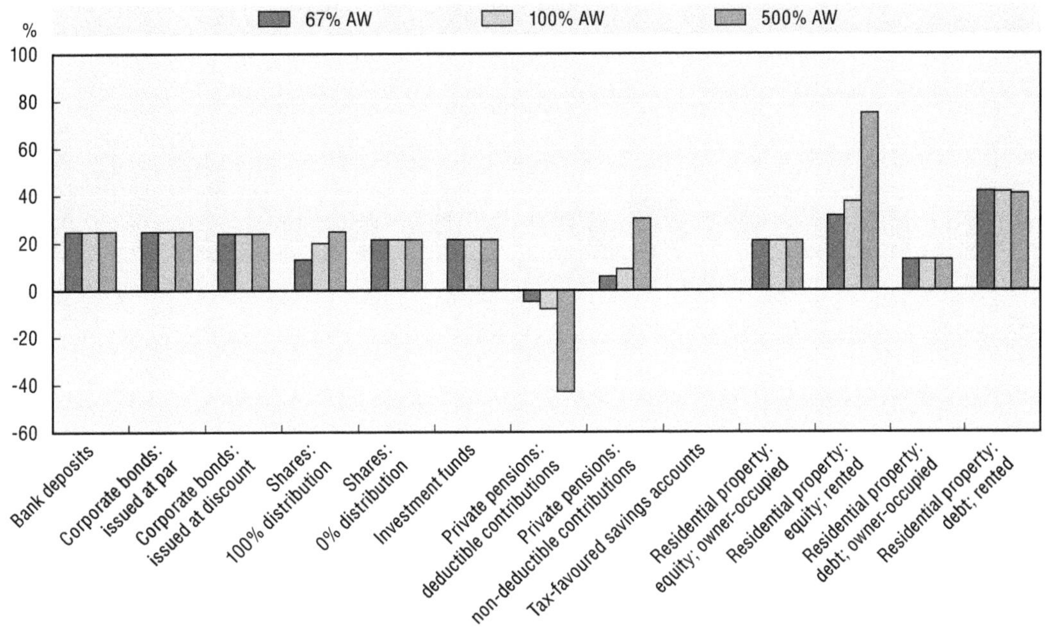

StatLink http://dx.doi.org/10.1787/888933660963

Figure 3.34. **Marginal effective tax rates: Korea, 2016**

Actual inflation rate

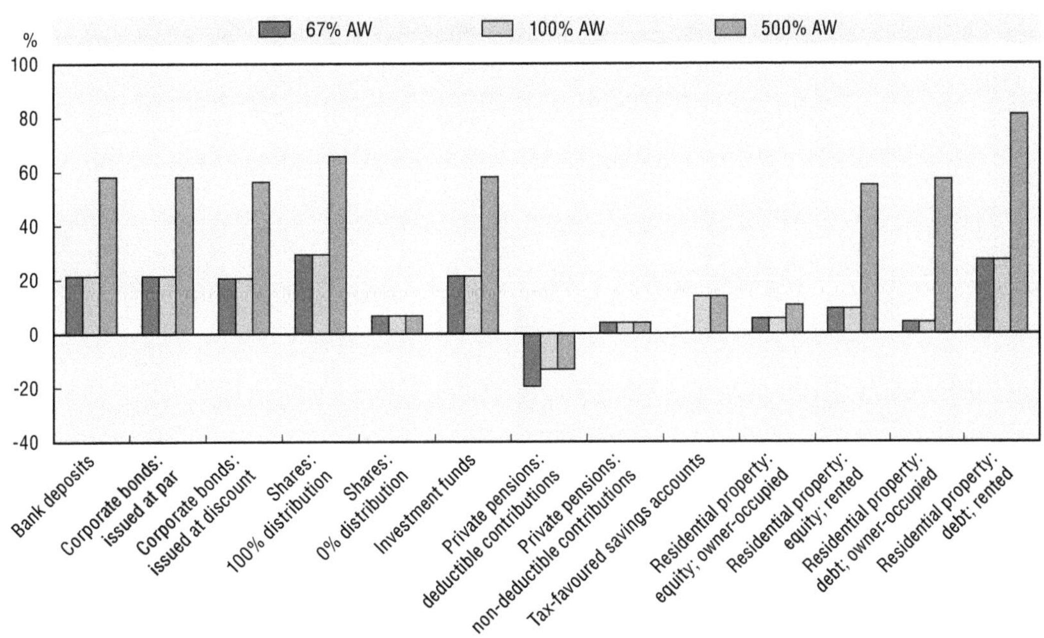

StatLink http://dx.doi.org/10.1787/888933660982

Figure 3.35. **Marginal effective tax rates: Latvia, 2016**

Actual inflation rate

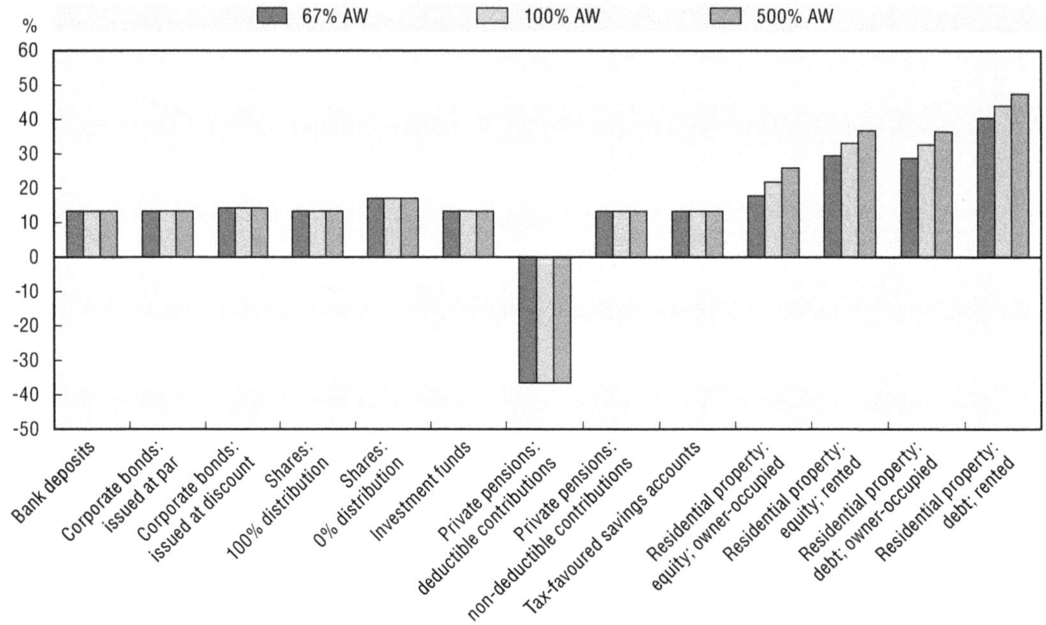

StatLink http://dx.doi.org/10.1787/888933661001

Figure 3.36. **Marginal effective tax rates: Lithuania, 2016**

Actual inflation rate

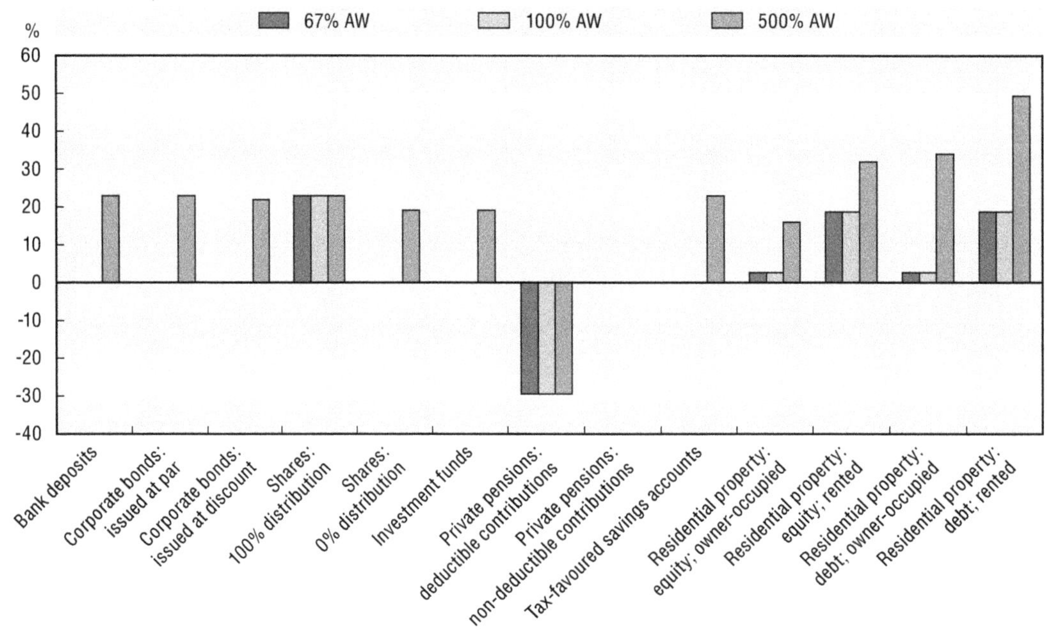

StatLink http://dx.doi.org/10.1787/888933661020

Figure 3.37. **Marginal effective tax rates: Luxembourg, 2016**

Actual inflation rate

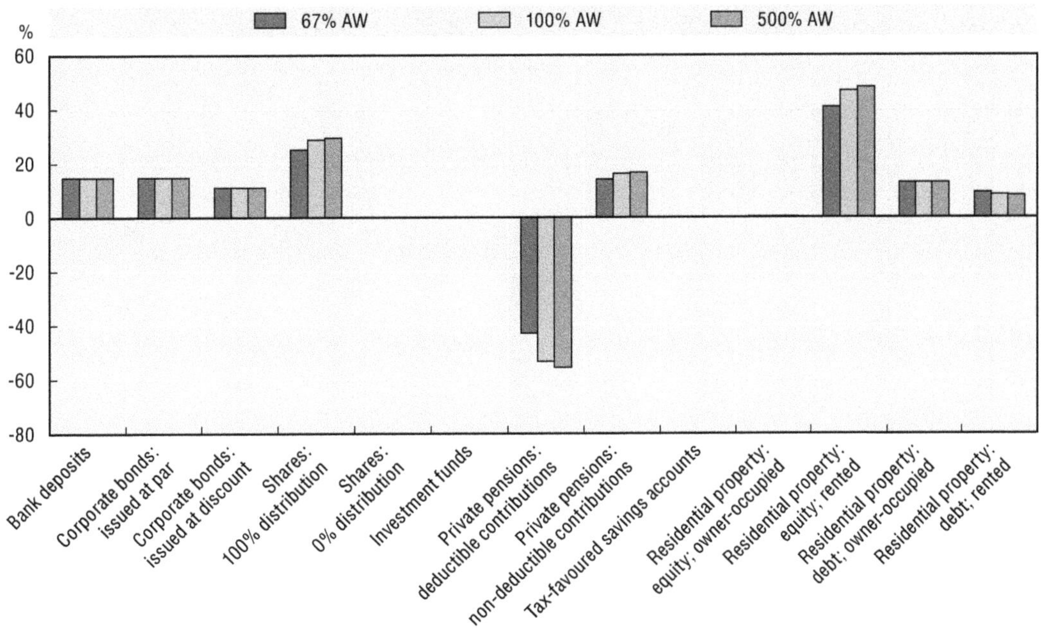

StatLink http://dx.doi.org/10.1787/888933661039

Figure 3.38. **Marginal effective tax rates: Mexico, 2016**

Actual inflation rate

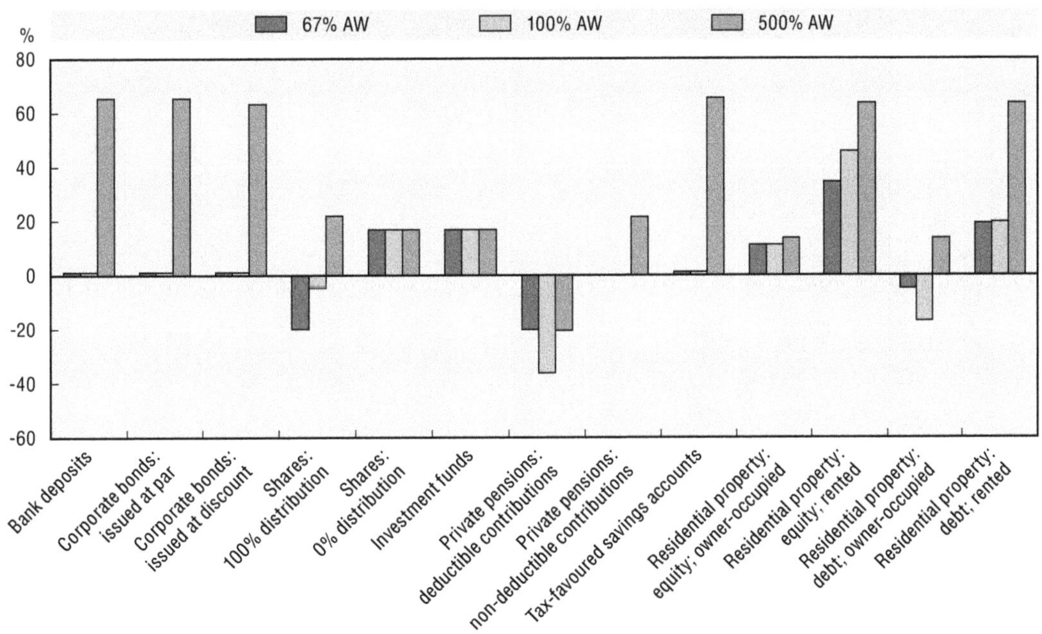

StatLink http://dx.doi.org/10.1787/888933661058

Figure 3.39. **Marginal effective tax rates: Netherlands, 2016**

Actual inflation rate

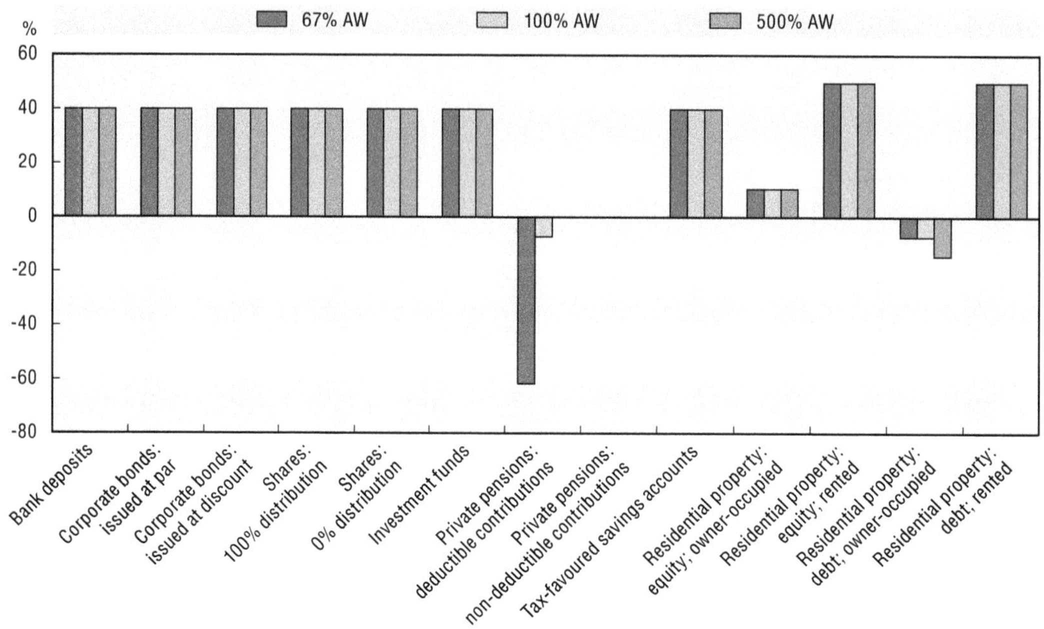

StatLink http://dx.doi.org/10.1787/888933661077

Figure 3.40. **Marginal effective tax rates: New Zealand, 2016**

Actual inflation rate

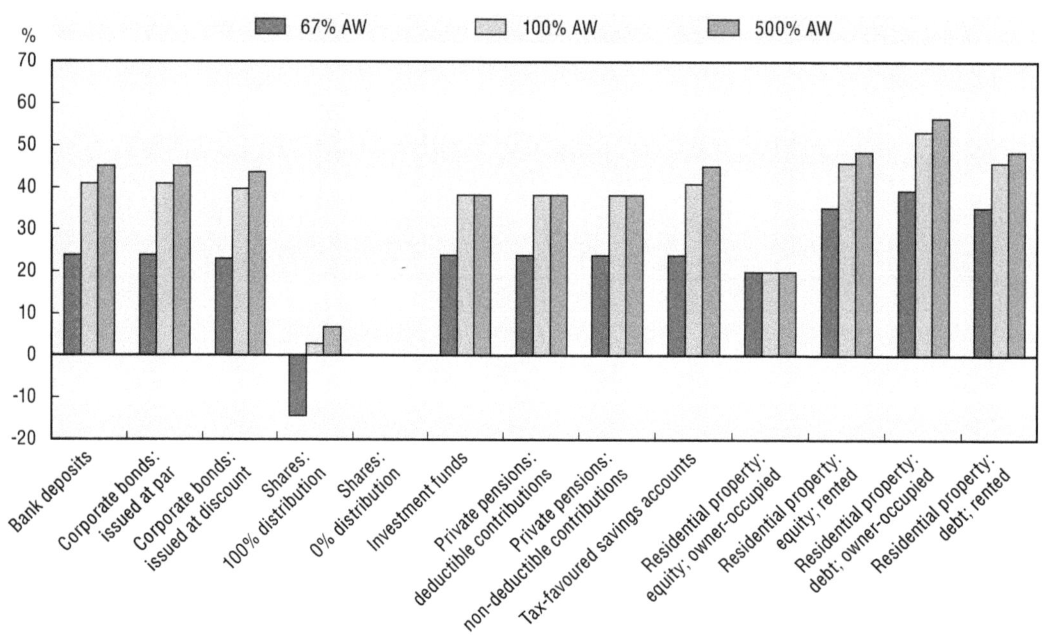

StatLink http://dx.doi.org/10.1787/888933661096

Figure 3.41. **Marginal effective tax rates: Norway, 2016**

Actual inflation rate

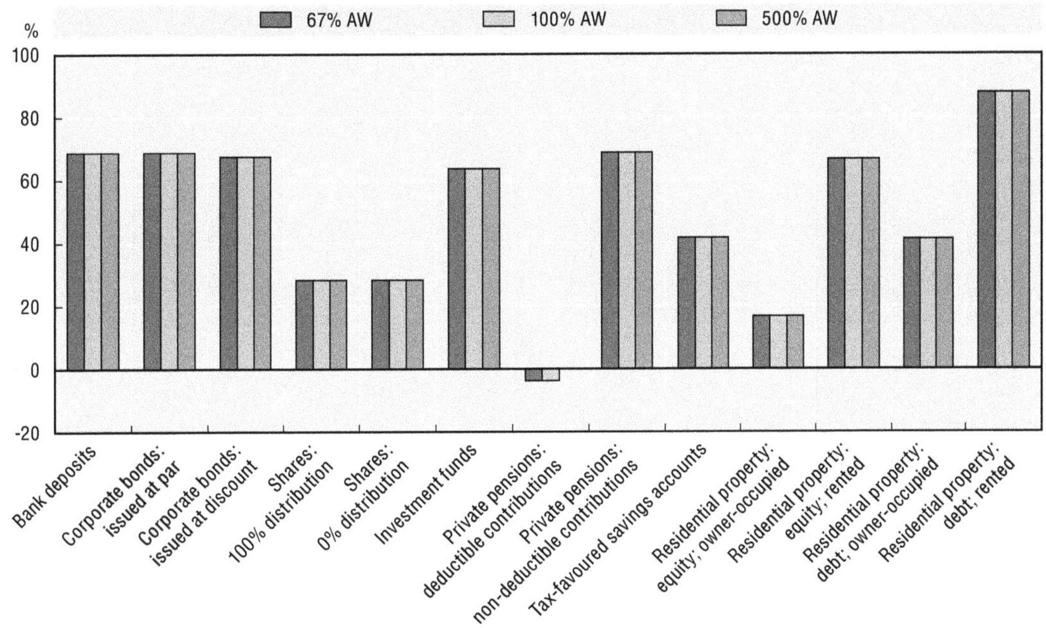

StatLink http://dx.doi.org/10.1787/888933661115

Figure 3.42. **Marginal effective tax rates: Poland, 2016**

Actual inflation rate

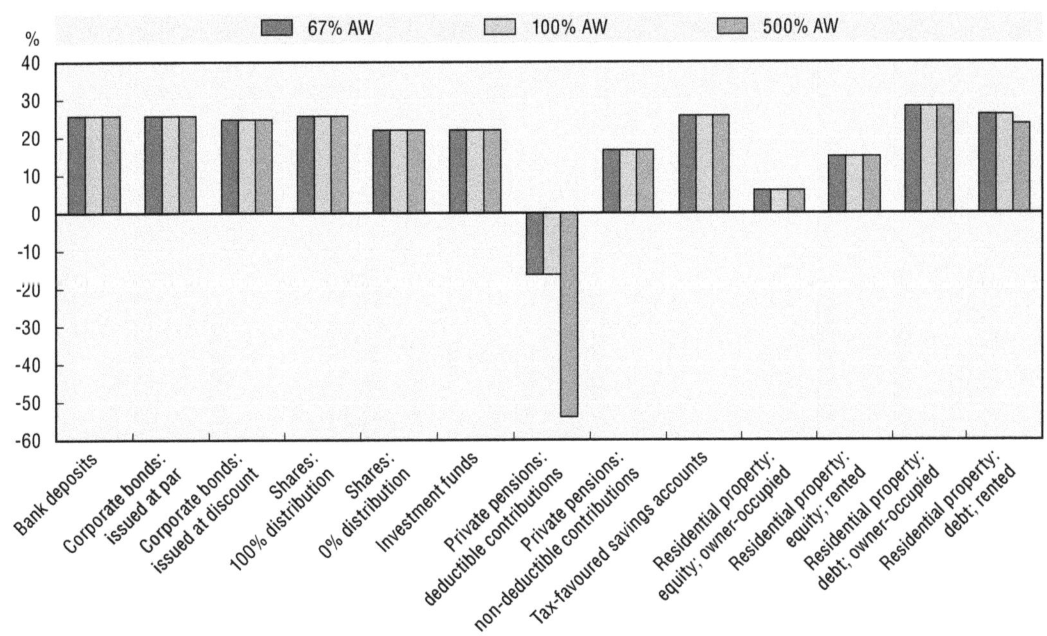

StatLink http://dx.doi.org/10.1787/888933661134

Figure 3.43. **Marginal effective tax rates: Portugal, 2016**

Actual inflation rate

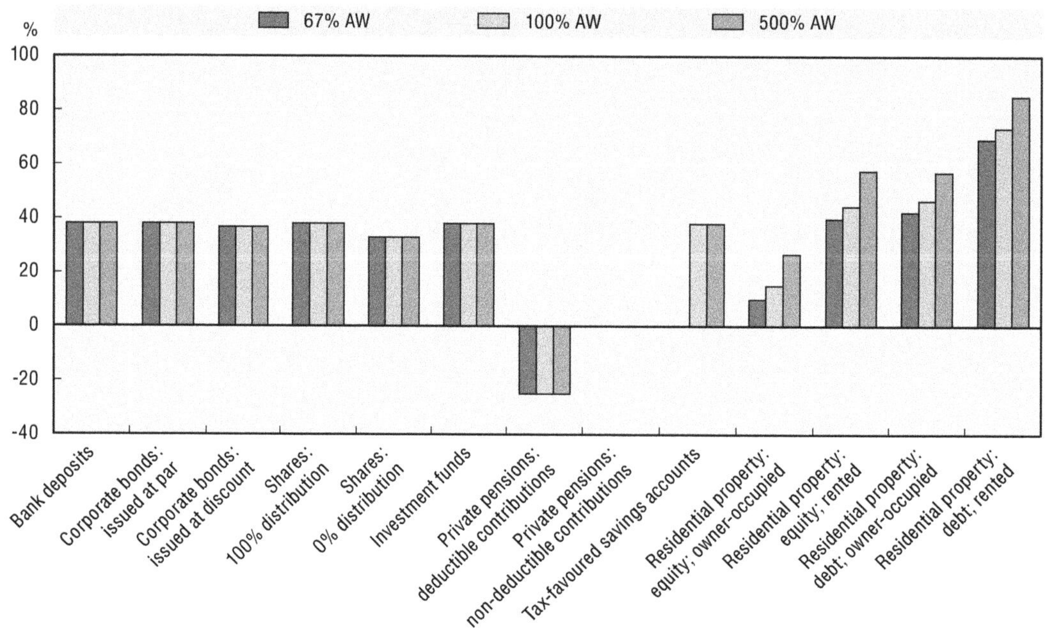

StatLink http://dx.doi.org/10.1787/888933661153

Figure 3.44. **Marginal effective tax rates: Slovak Republic, 2016**

Actual inflation rate

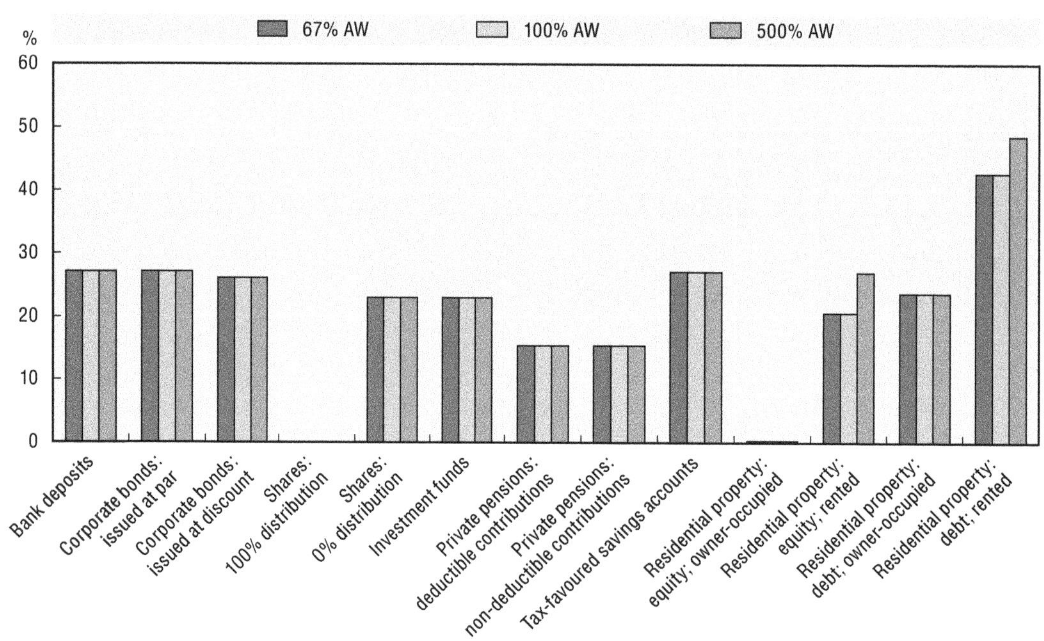

StatLink http://dx.doi.org/10.1787/888933661172

Figure 3.45. **Marginal effective tax rates: Slovenia, 2016**

Actual inflation rate

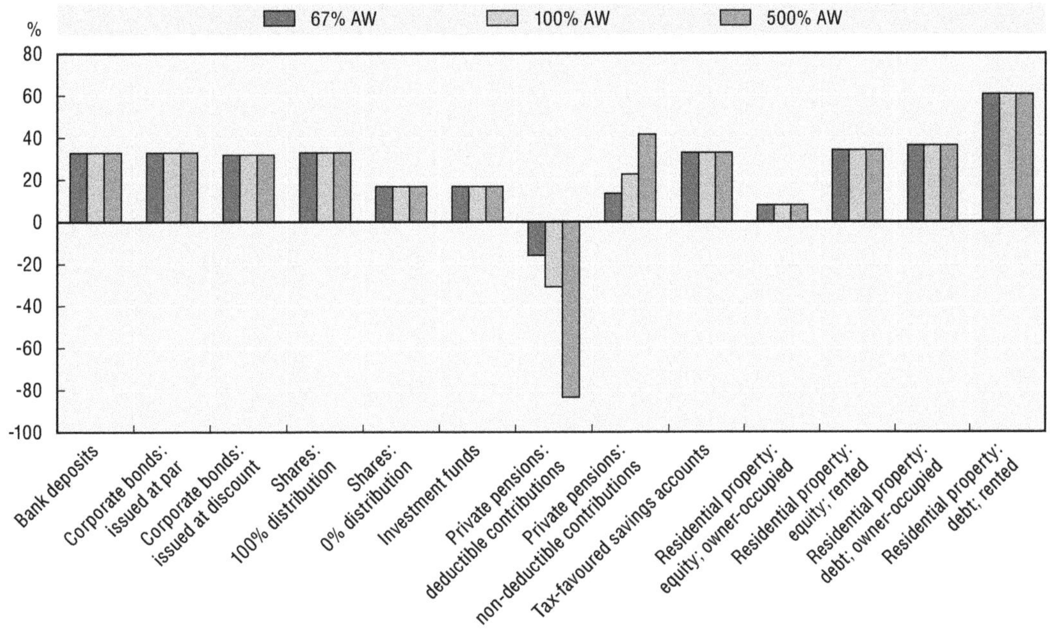

StatLink http://dx.doi.org/10.1787/888933661191

Figure 3.46. **Marginal effective tax rates: South Africa, 2016**

Actual inflation rate

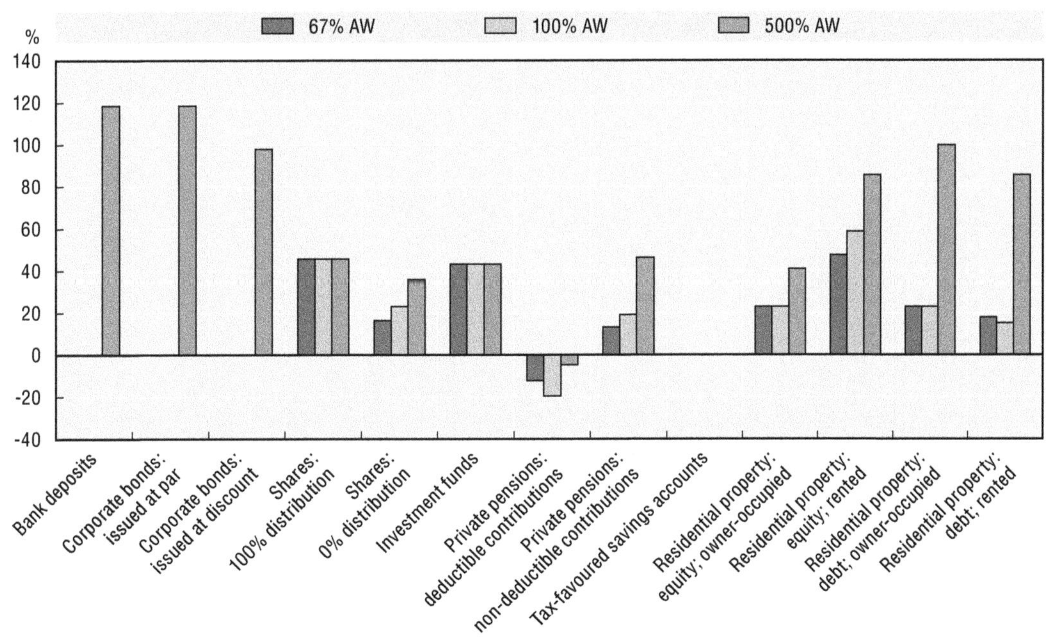

StatLink http://dx.doi.org/10.1787/888933661210

Figure 3.47. **Marginal effective tax rates: Spain, 2016**

Actual inflation rate

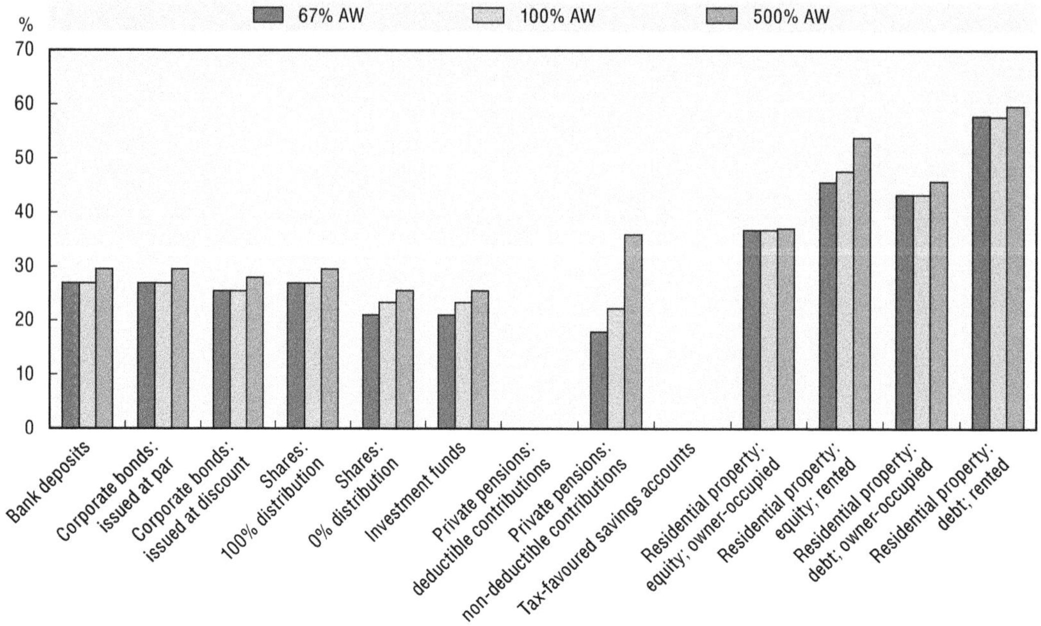

StatLink http://dx.doi.org/10.1787/888933661229

Figure 3.48. **Marginal effective tax rates: Sweden, 2016**

Actual inflation rate

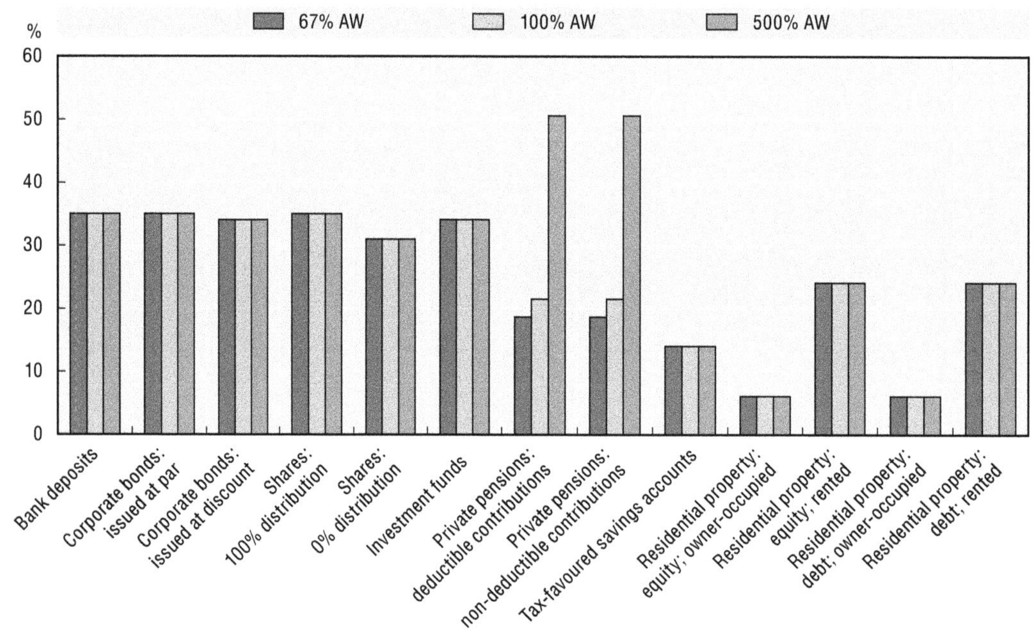

StatLink http://dx.doi.org/10.1787/888933661248

Figure 3.49. **Marginal effective tax rates: Switzerland, 2016**

Actual inflation rate

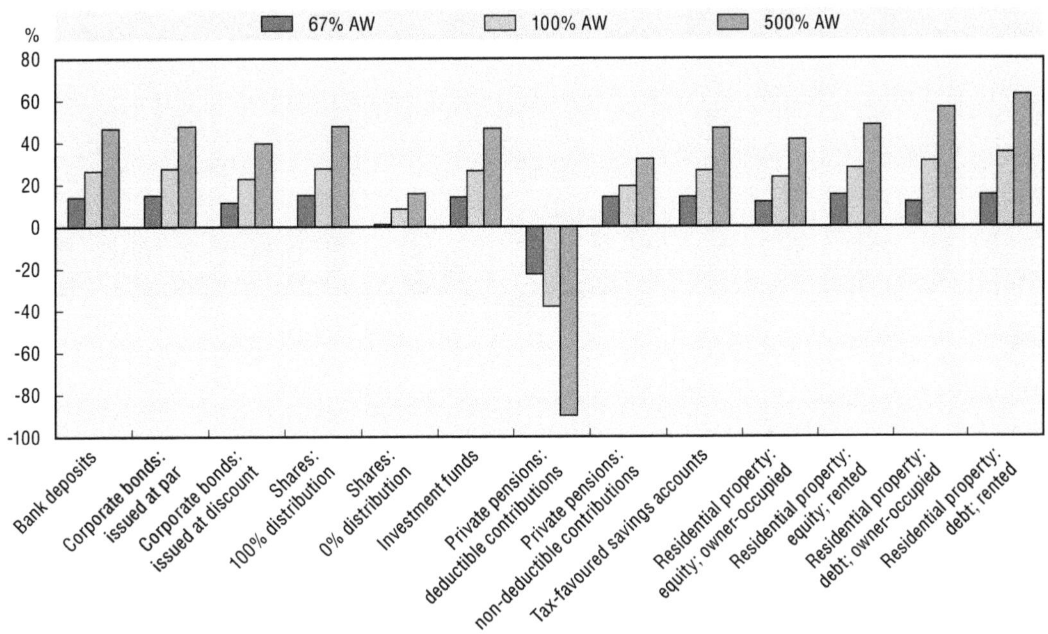

StatLink http://dx.doi.org/10.1787/888933661267

Figure 3.50. **Marginal effective tax rates: Turkey, 2016**

Actual inflation rate

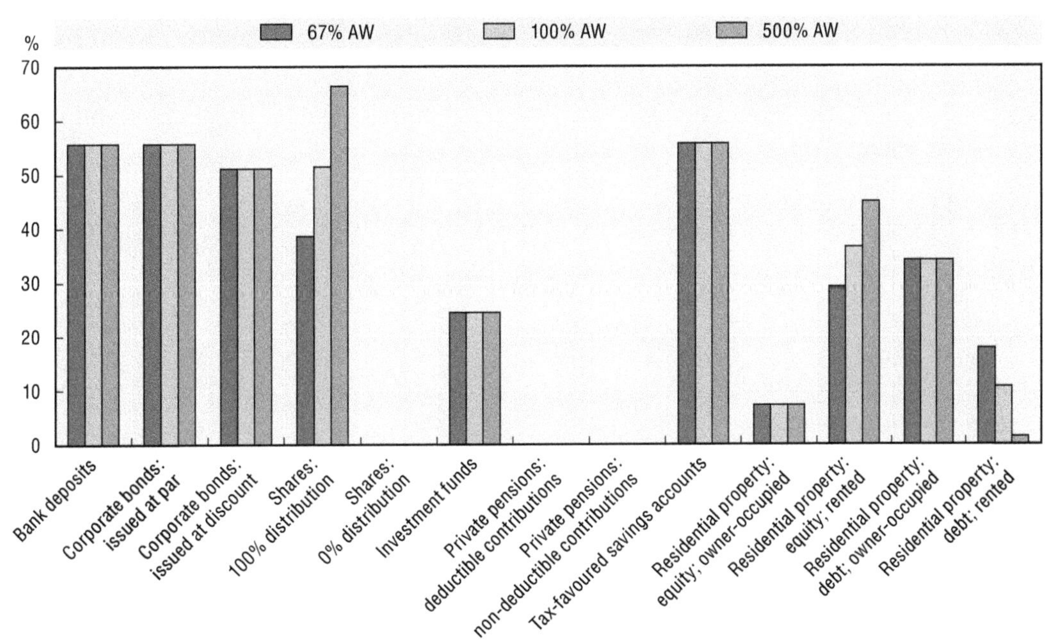

StatLink http://dx.doi.org/10.1787/888933661286

Figure 3.51. **Marginal effective tax rates: United Kingdom, 2016**

Actual inflation rate

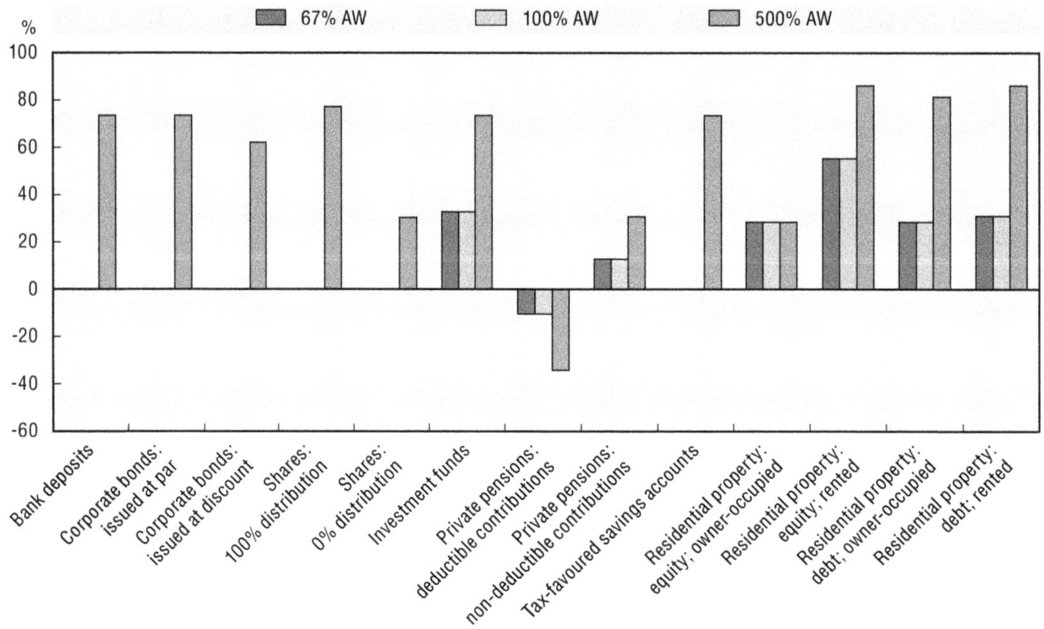

StatLink http://dx.doi.org/10.1787/888933661305

Figure 3.52. **Marginal effective tax rates: United States, 2016**

Actual inflation rate

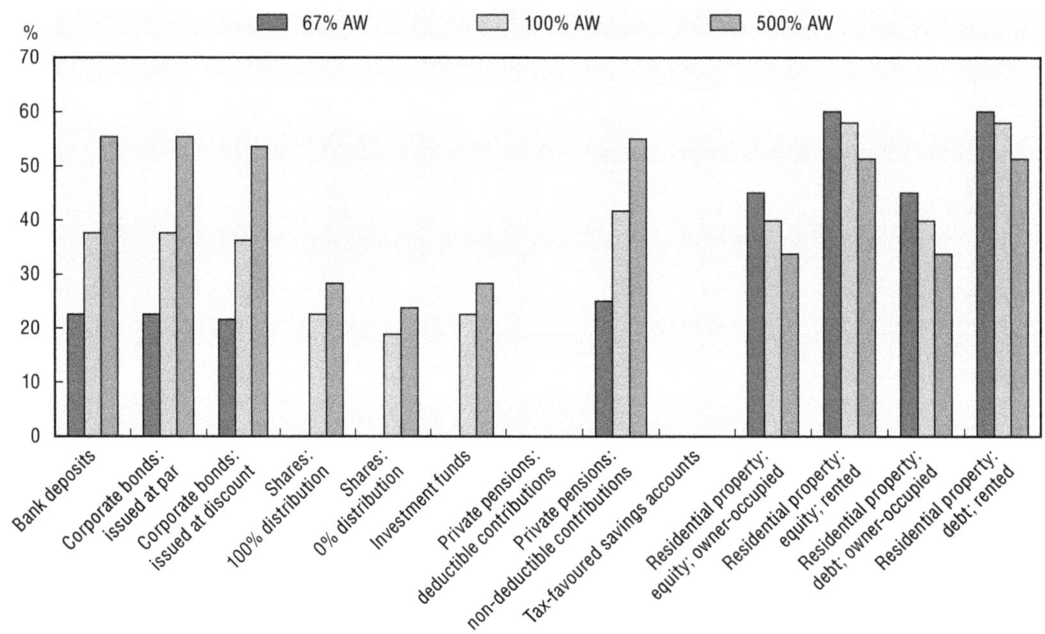

StatLink http://dx.doi.org/10.1787/888933661324

Notes

1. The *Taxation and Household Saving* study (OECD, 1994) calculated METRs for a group of five different assets: bank deposits, government bonds, equities, pensions and owner-occupied housing. The case of government bonds was subdivided into those issued at a discount and those issued and redeemable at par (in order to illustrate the effect of differential treatment of interest and capital gains). Different effective tax rates for pensions were calculated as well, focusing on the cases where pension premiums were deductible or non-deductible (if applicable) and on the cases where pension income was taxed at the standard tax schedule or at lower rates. Investment in owner-occupied housing was either fully financed with equity (own funds) or partly with equity (own funds) and borrowed funds.
2. With the exception of Argentina, where, due to recent inflation volatility, the five-year average from Q1 2008 to Q4 2013 has been used.
3. For example, Denmark has a semi-dual tax system where returns to household savings are mostly taxed separately from (and at different rates than) labor income, and where the (marginal) tax rates that apply to a given category of savings return will often depend on the size of this specific type of return – meaning the appropriate tax rate depends on the size and composition of the household's savings return – but not necessarily the size of the household's labour income and thus the household's overall level of income. METR results are consequently driven significantly by the assumptions made regarding capital income levels.
4. Assumptions for average- and high-rate taxpayers regarding wealth levels, and the mix between housing and non-housing wealth, are approximations based on unweighted averages of asset holdings for different income groups across eighteen European Union countries calculated from 2016 European Central Bank Household Finance and Consumption Survey (HFCS) microdata.
5. For the Netherlands, general scheme SSCs ("premies volksverzekeringen") are included in the modelling. The SSCs paid by employers and employees have not been included.
6. An outlier is defined as a result more than 1.5 times the inter-quartile range below the first quartile or above the third quartile. Where outliers are present, the upper and lower points of the box-and-whisker plot are set equal to this limit.
7. In a small number of countries a transaction tax is also applied to deposits in bank accounts. In Italy a reduced 0.2% transaction tax is applied under the assumption that the account is subject to some form of time constraint, in return for better interest rates.
8. All interest income from bank accounts is exempt in Argentina. In Estonia, interest income is exempt as long as it is received from deposits with a credit institution which is a resident of a Contracting State of the European Economic Area (EEA) or on account of a permanent establishment of a credit institution located in a Contracting State of the EEA Agreement, and the interest does not partially or completely depend on the value, or change in value, of a security, deposit, currency, other instrument or the underlying assets thereof.
9. In such cases, the level of interest income earned for each taxpayer type is determined by applying a 3% real return to the wealth levels for each taxpayer type specified in section 3.2.
10. Note that, as of 2017, the deemed return applied on net assets increases with the net value of the assets. The tax rate applied continues to be 30%.
11. A taxpayer does not have to return income from a financial arrangement on an accrual basis if they are a cash basis person. To be a cash basis person, the difference in the person's annual income on a cash basis and on an accrual basis must not exceed NZD 40 000; and either: the person's income and expenditure under all financial arrangements for the income year does not exceed NZD 100 000; or the value of the person's financial arrangements during the year does not exceed NZD 1 million.
12. The Estonian results provide an example of the limitation created by only modelling taxation at the personal level. In Estonia, tax is not paid at the corporate level until distribution of profits as dividends, with the dividends then exempt in the hands of the shareholder. Our modelling results consequently show a zero METR at the personal level for Estonia with 100% distribution. The results imply that there will be an incentive to distribute dividends to avoid paying the 20% capital gains tax, whereas there will in fact be an incentive to retain profits in the company to defer payment of the corporate income tax.
13. Effective 2006, Canada introduced an enhanced gross-up and dividend tax credit regime for dividends distributed by large corporations, which are subject to a higher statutory rate than small businesses. As a result, Canada operates a dual rate gross up and dividend tax credit system that provides full imputation at the federal level (a number of provinces responded to the federal initiative by adjusting their own dividend tax credit rates). Rates modelled are those applicable to large corporation dividends.

14. Note that thresholds can vary across asset types. For example, Spain provides a general threshold (which covers most assets including investment fund interests) and a specific threshold for property which is lower.
15. The statutory rate itself need not be reduced as long as there is some form of concessionary treatment on distribution. For example, distributions in the United Kingdom are taxed at the taxpayer's marginal PIT rate, but 25% may be distributed tax free immediately as a lump sum lowering the effective tax rate on distribution.
16. The "Riester-Rente" pension fund is modelled for Germany. Private cash-value life insurance plans are also available. Premiums paid for such life insurance plans are not tax deductible.
17. In the Netherlands, tax deductible contributions to private pension funds are limited to 13.8% of annual income (with a ceiling of EUR 101 519 in 2016) minus a threshold for the general state pension and taking into account accrued pensions rights in an occupational pension plan. Consequently, the marginal contribution by a high-rate taxpayer will not be deductible. The marginal contribution will instead be subject to a TEE regime, resulting in a zero METR.
18. A similar result occurs for low-rate and average-rate taxpayers in Australia. However, a top-rate taxpayer is assumed to be above the "untaxed plan cap amount" (AUD 1 395 000 in 2015-16) and, hence, liable to the top marginal tax rate on distributions which results in a large positive METR.
19. Given the requirement for retention in the account, full retention has been assumed in the modelling for Colombia, Hungary and Spain, whereas for other countries contributions to tax-favoured savings accounts are assumed to be distributed annually and reinvested.
20. This is likely to be the case for other countries. However, current limitations of the modelling, specifically the use of "average" property tax rates, may prevent their appearance in the current METR results. This modelling aspect could potentially be adjusted for the final project report.
21. It should be borne in mind that the choice of expected holding period can significantly affect METRs on residential property, particularly in countries that impose substantial transaction taxes as these fixed taxes are effectively apportioned across a larger or smaller number of years depending on the expected holding period modelled. The longer the expected holding period, the lower the METR will be.
22. METR calculations for saving in residential property when the household does not own the necessary funds would require a different modelling approach than the one followed in this report. Households who do not have savings, but want to purchase a house, will typically borrow from a financial institution with the commitment to pay for the principal investment in the house at a later point in time. The interest, net of mortgage interest relief, that has to be paid on the loan will then increase the cost of the investment. Instead of saving in the initial period (as assumed in this report), the saving event would arguably then occur in the future period when the household pays the financial institution for the principal. Such analysis is left for future work.
23. In the case of Chile, capital gains are untaxed as long as the taxpayer is not habitual in the trade of shares and the capital gains are less than approximately CLP 5.5 million (in 2016). In New Zealand, capital gains on shares are also untaxed as long as the taxpayer is not considered to be in the business of trading shares.
24. The higher METR for a holding period of six months in Belgium is due to a short-term capital gains tax that was in force at the reference date (1 July 2016). The tax has now been repealed, so there is no longer any differentiation of METRs across holding periods in Belgium.
25. For simplicity of modelling, it is also assumed that there is no economic depreciation.

References

Harding, M. and M. Marten (2018), "Statutory tax rates on dividends, interest and capital gains: the debt equity bias at the personal level", *OECD Taxation Working Papers*, No. 34, OECD Publishing, Paris.

IBFD Tax Research Platform, *www.ibfd.org*.

King, M. and D. Fullerton (1984), *Taxation of income from capital: a comparative study of the United States, United Kingdom, Sweden and West Germany*, Chicago University Press, Chicago.

OECD (1994), "Taxation and Household Saving", OECD Publishing, Paris.

OECD Tax Database, *www.oecd.org/tax/tax-policy/tax-database.htm*.

Chapter 4

The distribution of asset holdings

This chapter analyses patterns of asset holdings in selected OECD countries across both income and wealth distributions. The analysis draws on income and asset-holdings microdata for 18 countries from the Eurosystem Household Finance and Consumption Survey (HFCS). Patterns of asset holdings are found to vary substantially across both income and wealth distributions, with significant implications for the distributional effects of the taxation of household savings.

4.1. Introduction

A key consideration regarding the taxation of household savings is its impact on income and wealth inequality. This chapter provides an evidential base for examining the distributional effects of the taxation of household savings by analysing patterns of asset holdings in selected OECD countries across both income and wealth distributions. Detailed discussion of the tax policy implications of these patterns of asset holdings is left until Chapter 6.

The analysis draws on income and asset-holdings microdata for 18 countries from the second wave of the Eurosystem Household Finance and Consumption Survey (HFCS).[1] The HFCS is a survey carried out by the European Central Bank and national central banks in the European Union to gather micro-level information on households' assets and liabilities (European Central Bank, 2016). Further details on the HFCS are provided in Box 4.1.

The main findings of the chapter are as follows:

- Both income and net wealth inequality are substantial, although net wealth inequality is larger than income inequality. Most households at the bottom of the net wealth distribution have negative net wealth.
- The income and net wealth distributions are correlated, but not perfectly so. There are many households with limited net wealth and high incomes, and vice versa.
- Some asset holding patterns are the same across both the income and net wealth distributions.
  - Those with high levels of both income and net wealth hold a larger share of their assets in the form of second residences, shares, bonds, self-employed businesses, and mutual and other managed funds.
  - Those with low levels of both income and net wealth hold a larger share of their assets in the form of bank deposits, vehicles and valuables.
- Some patterns are not the same across the income and net wealth distributions, particularly with respect to housing and housing debt.
  - Those with higher levels of income hold a lower share of their assets in the form of their main residence. However, the share of the main residence in gross assets is high in the middle of the net wealth distribution, but not at the bottom or top. At the top, more wealth is held in financial assets, second residences and self-employed businesses. At the bottom, more wealth is held in bank deposits and vehicles.
  - The share of pensions in total assets is rising with income, though it is roughly constant with respect to net wealth.
  - Absolute debt levels are rising proportionately with income, but are roughly constant with net wealth. Most household debt is housing debt, and most housing debt is debt with regard to the main residence.
- Net wealth rises with age up to roughly the age of retirement, and broadly declines thereafter, though net wealth remains substantial amongst the elderly.
- For those households with self-employment wealth, this wealth is a substantial share of their total wealth.

These findings are summarised in Table 4.1.

The results present challenges for tax policymakers, and for those assessing the distributional impacts of capital taxes. Some taxes, such as those on bank deposits, bond interest income, dividend income, and capital gains on second residences, would seem to have straightforward distributional consequences. However, other policies such as property taxes, capital gains on main residences, and mortgage interest deductibility, would seem to have differing distributional consequences across the income and net wealth distributions. This is particularly challenging given the fact that the main residence makes up a large share of household assets in most of the countries discussed. Chapter 6 discusses the policy implications of these results, drawing also on the results of other chapters in this study.

The chapter presents patterns of asset holdings across both income deciles and net wealth deciles. When asset mixes are considered, the results are presented as a share of gross wealth rather than net wealth. This is because in many instances negative net wealth levels would complicate the exposition of asset mixes if asset mixes were displayed as a share of net wealth. The difference between net wealth and gross wealth (i.e. household debt) also forms a key aspect of the distributional burden of savings taxation. The distribution of household debt is considered at the end of the chapter.

The chapter proceeds as follows. Section 4.2 discusses income inequality and the mix of assets across the income distribution. Section 4.3 provides a similar discussion but focusses on wealth inequality instead of income inequality. Section 4.4 discusses the importance of the lifecycle in patterns of net wealth and asset holdings. Section 4.5 discusses differences between income and net wealth, and discusses the correlation between these two distributions. It also highlights the importance of housing in the net wealth distribution and of housing debt in particular.

Table 4.1. **Summary of stylised facts on asset mixes**

Higher Income

- Similar debt as a share of net wealth,
- More debt in absolute terms,
- More likely to own home.
- More gross housing wealth,
- More net financial wealth, as a share of total net wealth,
- More non-bank deposit financial wealth, as a share of total financial wealth.

More Net Wealth

- Less debt as a share of net wealth,
- More variation in absolute debt,
- More likely to own home,
- More net housing wealth,
- More financial wealth, as a share of total net wealth,
- More non-bank deposit financial wealth, as a share of total financial wealth

	High Income	Low Income
High Net Wealth	- More likely to own home, - Likely to own second home, - If a homeowner, insubstantial housing debt likely, - More financial wealth a share of total wealth, - Financial wealth that does exist more likely to be shares, bonds, mutual funds, less likely to be bank deposits.	- More likely to own home (than net wealth - less likely than high income counterparts), - Less likely to have substantial debt, - Debt likely to be housing debt, - Debt probably substantial relative to income, but may not be substantial relative to gross wealth.
Low Net Wealth	- More likely to own home (than low income counterpart) - less likely than high net wealth counterpart), - More likely to have substantial debt, - More likely to have debt likely to be housing debt, - Debt may not be substantial relative to income, but substantial relative to gross wealth.	- Less likely to own home - Unlikely to own second home - If a homeowner, substantial housing debt likely - Less financial wealth as a share of total wealth, - Financial wealth that does exist more likely to be bank deposits, less likely to be shares, bonds, mutual funds.

Box 4.1. **The Eurosystem Household Finance and Consumption Survey**

Data source

This chapter draws on microdata from the second wave of the Eurosystem Household Finance and Consumption Survey (HFCS). The HFCS provides household-level data on income, asset holdings and consumption (together with various demographic variables) for 20 European Union countries following a harmonised approach to facilitate cross-country comparability of results. It provides a sufficiently detailed breakdown of household wealth across different assets to enable a detailed analysis of patterns of household wealth.

The HFCS includes 18 OECD member countries, which are the focus of the analysis in this chapter: Austria, Belgium, Estonia, Finland, France, Germany, Greece, Hungary, Ireland, Italy, Latvia, Luxembourg, the Netherlands, Poland, Portugal, the Slovak Republic, Slovenia and Spain.

Asset holding data generally relates to the time of the underlying household interviews which occurred between March 2013 and January 2015. Income data typically relates to the year preceding the interview (most commonly 2013, with interviews having occurred in 2014). The main exception is Spain for which interviews occurred between October 2011 and April 2012, and income data relates to 2010.[1]

In total, the HFCS covers more than 84 000 households. As it is household data, the HFCS does not focus on the asset distribution at the individual level. However, the amount of wealth that a household can accumulate can depend heavily on whether a household is a single-earner household or a household with several earners. Sample sizes range between countries (from 1 202 households in Latvia to 12 035 households in France). In the majority of countries, the surveys are stratified to oversample wealthier households.

To account for missing variables, Ireland, Italy and Finland adopt single imputation. All other countries adopt multiple imputation. Multiple imputation is used to handle missing data in a way that increases the accuracy of standard errors as compared to single imputation by taking account of the uncertainty regarding the imputed values. Multiple imputation works by imputing five versions of any missing data point in the dataset (following the same imputation procedure each time). This means that the final dataset effectively contains five complete datasets (one with each of the five imputed values, but with the exact same values for all other non-missing data). Final parameter estimates are the mean of the estimates from the underlying analysis undertaken separately on the five datasets.

In this study, results are presented across both gross income and net wealth deciles. Neither are equivalised. Within both the income and net wealth distributions, results are presented for a variety of financial and non-financial assets. These are outlined in Table 4.2.

Table 4.2. **Main Asset Categories in the Household Finance and Consumption Survey**

Real Assets	Financial Assets
Value of household's main residence	Deposits in current and chequing accounts; deposits in saving accounts
Value of other real estate property	Bonds
Value of household's vehicles	Publicly traded shares
Value of household's other valuables	Mutual funds and managed accounts
Value of self-employed businesses	Occupational and private pensions
	Other assets (including value of money owed to households and value of non self-employment private business)

Note: Further detail is provided in ECB (2016).
Source: ECB (2016).

Data limitations

It is important to bear in mind the limitations of the results outlined in this chapter. First, only 18 European countries are covered as compared to the 40 countries considered in the effective tax rate (ETR) analysis contained elsewhere in this study. The results for these countries may not be representative of all OECD and G20 countries.

Box 4.1. **The Eurosystem Household Finance and Consumption Survey** *(cont.)*

The results may differ from the true distribution of income and wealth inequality due to the problems with estimating income inequality with survey data. This kind of data is usually biased downwards at the top of the income distribution. One reason for this bias is that household survey samples may not contain households from the top 1%, 0.1% or even 0.01% of the income distribution. Research using other data sources such as tax return data suggests that income and wealth are concentrated in these very high components of the income distribution, and so estimates of income and wealth inequality may be biased downwards due to the omission of these high-wealth and high-income households. These data issues mean that the results should be interpreted with caution.

A further reason why survey data estimates of asset holdings across income and net wealth distributions should be interpreted with caution concerns the fact that the results in these data only account for income and wealth that is declared by households to statistical agencies. These data may be biased due to poor recollection on the part of survey respondents, lack of effort in reporting accurately, or unwillingness to report accurate figures due to fear of non-confidentiality.

Individuals may also underreport income and wealth that they conceal from public authorities. There is a large and growing literature documenting tax evasion efforts by high income and high wealth households, some of which suggests that a larger percentage of total income and wealth go unreported at the top of the income and net wealth distribution than at the bottom (Zucman, 2013, 2014). This suggests that when concealed wealth and income is taken into account, income and wealth inequality is even greater than the estimates in this study may suggest. This may be particularly the case with respect to financial assets and the income from them, as these kinds of assets are particularly mobile and so may be easily moved offshore in an attempt to evade tax. This topic is discussed further in Chapter 5. Nonetheless, these issues suggest that the results concerning income and wealth inequality should be interpreted as a lower bound of the true levels.

In the HFCS, occupational pension wealth is only presented where there is a value to an account (i.e. as in defined-contribution pension schemes). In defined-benefit pension schemes, no data is provided in the HFCS. To address this, this study takes the following approach. The value of defined-benefit occupational pensions is set, where they are present, to be equal to the mean account value of defined-contribution accounts in the corresponding income or net wealth decile for each country. Given the generosity of defined-benefit schemes relative to defined-contribution schemes, this approach means that the estimate of occupational pension wealth in this study is likely to be an underestimate and may be interpreted as a lower bound occupational pension wealth figure.

1. Further detail is provided in ECB (2016).

4.2. Income inequality and the mix of assets across the income distribution

Income inequality in the Household Finance and Consumption Survey

Income inequality in OECD countries is at its highest level for the past half century (OECD, In It Together: Why Less Inequality Benefits All, 2015). Across the OECD, the average income of the richest 10% of the population is about nine times that of the poorest 10%, up from seven times 25 years ago, although there are wide differences across OECD countries. (OECD, 2015) (OECD, 2015). Figure 4.1 shows evidence of inequality across the sample of countries in the HFCS data. Households in the top income decile earn an average of 28% of total household income in the HFCS, while households in the bottom 90% earn 3.1% of total income on average.

Figure 4.1. **Distribution of market income by income decile, percentage of total national household market income**

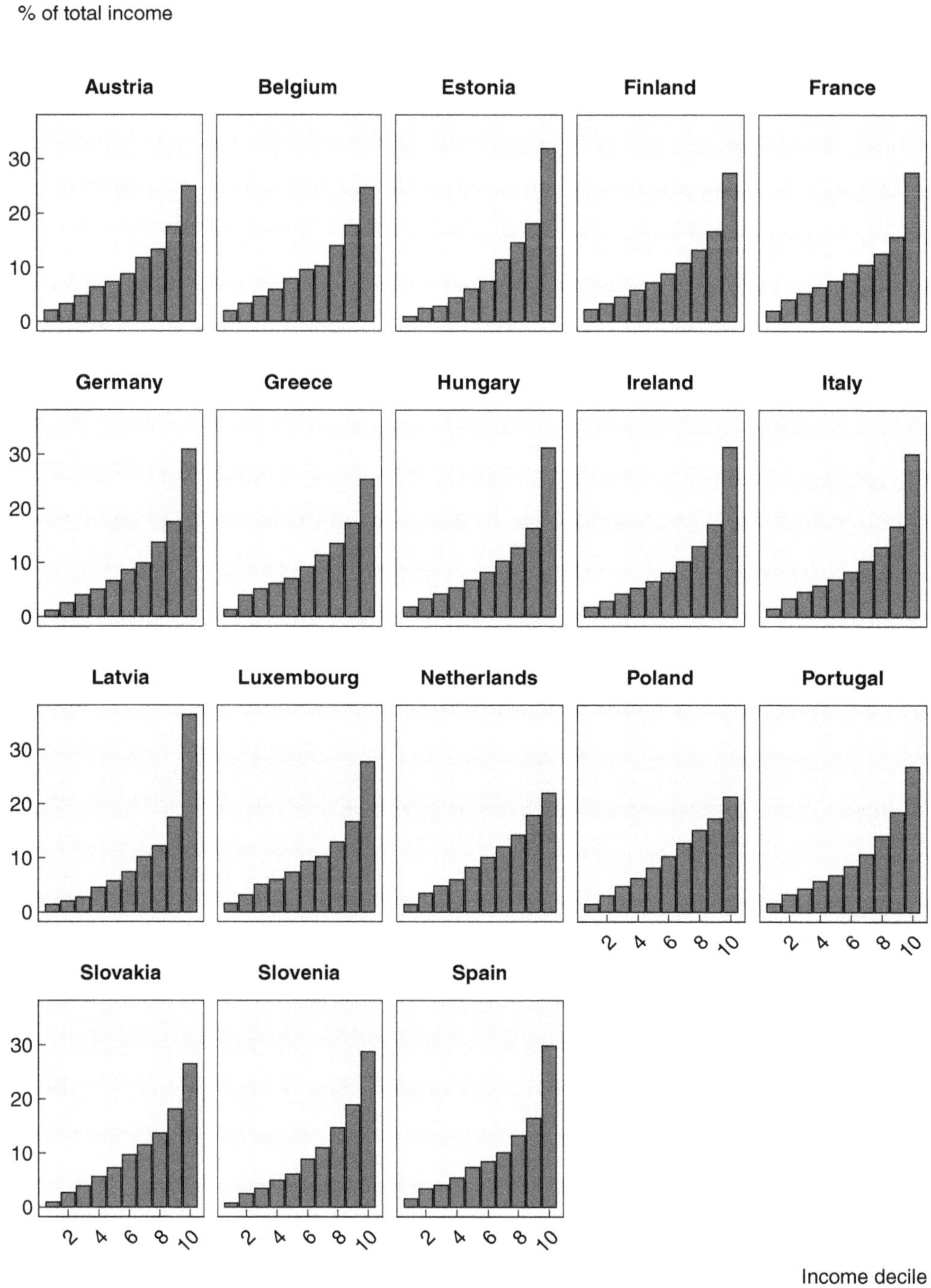

Note: Data are for 2013-4 (see Box 4.1). The distribution does not incorporate taxes and transfers.

Source: Authors' calculations based on Household Finance and Consumption Survey (2016).

StatLink http://dx.doi.org/10.1787/888933661343

Income inequality varies across countries. This variation can be due to differences in market incomes (i.e. incomes before taxes and transfers) and differences in disposable income (i.e. incomes after accounting for the tax and transfer system in reducing inequality.

OECD evidence suggests that the effectiveness of taxes and transfers has diminished in recent years.[2] There are many facets to the distribution of income in OECD economies.

The HFCS data shows that income inequality is particularly marked in Latvia where households in the top income decile earn 36.4% of total household income, and is relatively modest in Poland where households in the top income decile earn 21.3% of total household income.

Variation in inequality stems in part from the pre-tax and post-tax labour income distribution. One way in which these levels of income inequality are impacted by tax policy is through labour taxes. Research both within and outside the OECD suggests that labour income inequality is rising (OECD, 2015; Alvaredo, Chancel et al., 2018). Labour taxes, at the same time have become less progressive over the last several decades (OECD, 2018).

Disparities in capital income and assets are another driver of income inequality. Economic research has also highlighted the extent to which increasing income inequality is also driven by capital ownership (Saez, 2017). All households own assets of different forms. These can be real assets such as cars, houses, or other valuables such as jewellery and art, or financial assets such as pensions, shares, bonds, and bank deposits. Understanding the distribution of these assets is a key issue in understanding how capital taxes impact inequality. Where capital taxes are highest on income from the kinds of assets that are held mostly by those with higher incomes, the tax system is more likely to reduce income inequality than if capital taxes are highest on income from the kinds of assets that are held mostly by those with lower incomes.

Real and financial assets

Overall, households hold a greater share of total gross wealth in the form of real assets than financial assets, although this is less pronounced for higher-income households. This can be seen in Figure 4.2, which shows the distribution of overall household gross wealth between real and financial assets across countries and income deciles. On average, households in the HFCS hold 86.6% of total gross wealth in the form of real assets compared to 13.4% as financial assets.[3] Germany has the largest share of financial assets as a share of total assets (38.1% of total assets), while Latvia has the largest share of real assets (98% of total assets). Households in the top income decile hold a higher share of their gross wealth in financial assets than the average household, holding 18.1% of total gross wealth in the form of financial assets on average and 81.9% in the form of real assets on average. Financial asset holdings broadly form a larger share of total assets among those with higher levels of income and net wealth, although this is not the case for all countries.

Real asset holdings across the income distribution

Real assets form the majority of asset holdings for almost every income decile in almost every country covered by the HFCS. This means that the taxation of real assets is of crucial importance when considering the overall taxation of household savings. Figure 4.3 shows the distribution of real assets across income deciles, expressed as a share of total gross real assets. The relationship between household debt and net wealth is considered in Section 4.5.

Figure 4.2. **Holdings of real versus financial assets by income decile**

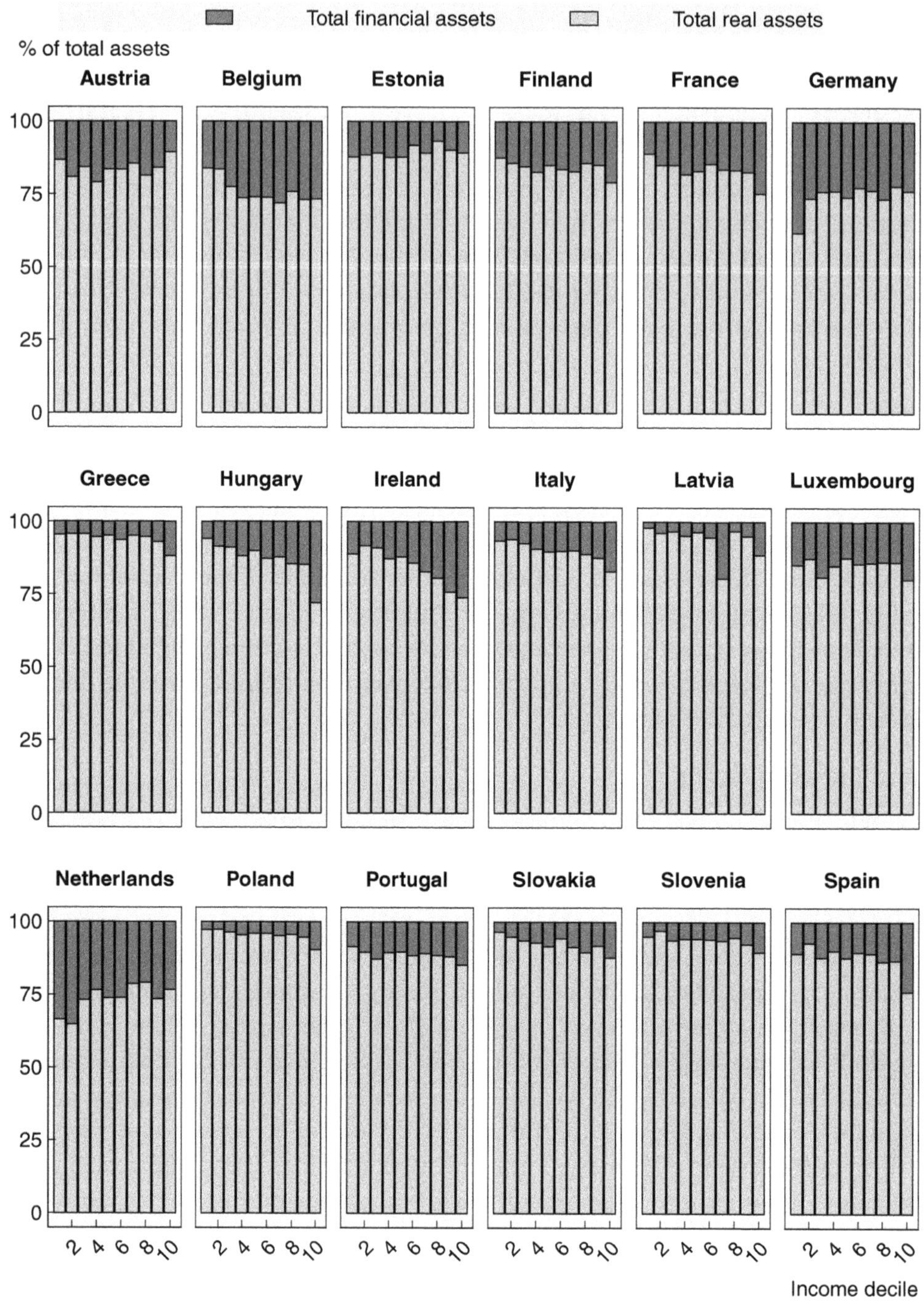

Note: Data are for 2013-4 (see Box 4.1). All income deciles are based on income gross of taxes and transfers. Holdings are expressed as a share of gross wealth.

Source: Authors' calculations based on Household Finance and Consumption Survey (2016).

StatLink http://dx.doi.org/10.1787/888933661362

Figure 4.3. **Breakdown of real assets, as a share of total real assets, by income deciles**

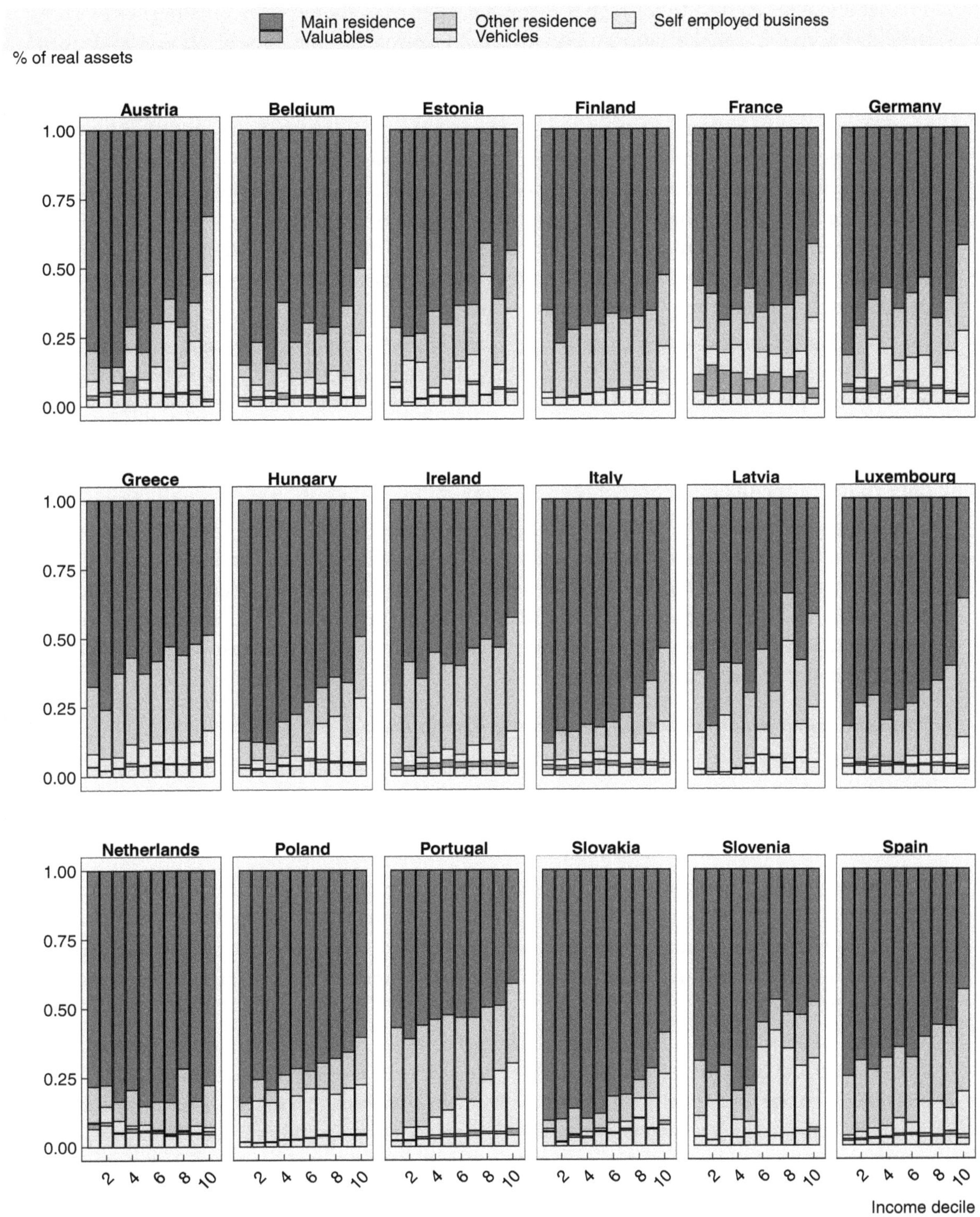

Note: Data are for 2013-4 (see Box 4.1). All income deciles are based on income gross of taxes and transfers. Holdings are expressed as a share of gross wealth

Source: Authors' calculations based on Household Finance and Consumption Survey (2016).

StatLink http://dx.doi.org/10.1787/888933661381

Main residences are by far the largest single asset category for most households, particularly for lower income deciles. Figure 4.3 shows that main residences make up a smaller share of net wealth for higher income deciles than for lower income deciles (with the exception of the Netherlands). In Austria and Luxembourg for example, households in the lowest income deciles hold 79.6% and 82.5% of their gross real wealth in the form of their main residence, while households in the highest income deciles hold 31.2% and 36.4% respectively. However there are exceptions. For example, in the Netherlands the distribution of gross housing wealth across the income distribution does not vary as substantially. In the Netherlands, 82.9 % of gross real wealth held by households in the bottom income decile is held in the form of housing, while the equivalent figure is 63.0% for the top income decile. However, while the percentage of total gross wealth held in the form of the main residence is lower, the absolute amount of wealth held in this form is still likely to be higher for higher income deciles due to their higher incomes overall.

The share of gross real wealth held in the form of a self-employed business is increasing with income (see Box 4.2). Assets in this category rise from an average of 4.4% for households in the bottom income decile (with a highest value of 17% in France and 13.2% in Latvia) to an average value of 5.5% for households in the fifth decile and 19.4% for households in top decile (with highest values of 45.3% in Austria and 13.2% in Estonia). This highlights the importance of the tax treatment of the self-employed.

In many countries the share of total gross real wealth held in the form of a second residence also rises with income. Gross real wealth held in the form of an additional residence rises from an average of 15.8% for households in the bottom income decile (with highest values of 38.4% in Portugal and 29.8% in Finland) to an average value of 17.7% for households in the fifth decile and 27.4% for households in the top decile (with highest values of 50.1% in Luxembourg and 41.1% in Ireland).

Financial asset holdings across the income distribution

The mix of financial assets varies substantially across countries. Figure 4.4 shows the breakdown of financial asset holdings – defined as a percentage of gross financial wealth – across income deciles for the countries in the HFCS sample. In this way it presents a more detailed breakdown of the financial assets presented in Figure 4.3.

Bank deposits (including deposit and savings or chequing accounts) are the most common form of financial asset for most households in the HFCS survey.[4] This asset class makes up 60% of gross financial wealth when averaged across all income deciles. They make up a particularly large share of total assets for those at the bottom of the income distribution.

Bank deposits make up a smaller share of the asset mix for those at the top of the income distribution. They comprise 40.6% of gross financial asset holdings on average for households in the top income decile, and 63.4% of gross financial asset holdings on average for households in the lowest income decile. This could mean that high levels of taxation of interest on bank deposits could have negative distributional consequences for those with low levels of income, although it should be noted that the absolute amounts of bank deposits in these very low income deciles are very small.

Figure 4.4. **Breakdown of financial assets, as a share of total financial assets, by income deciles**

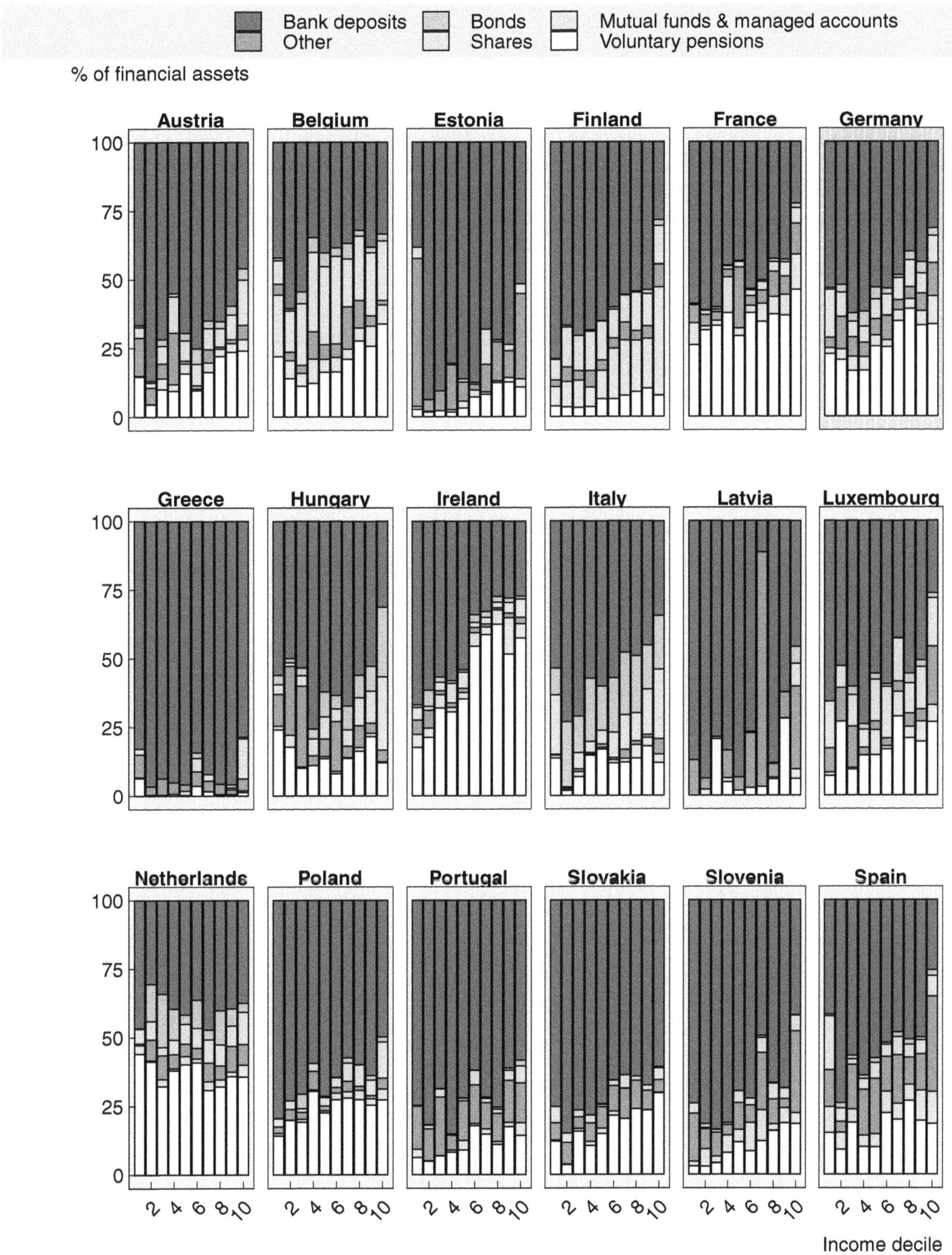

Note: Data are for 2013-4 (see Box 4.1). All income deciles are based on income gross of taxes and transfers. Holdings are expressed as a share of gross wealth

Source: Authors' calculations based on Household Finance and Consumption Survey (2016).

StatLink http://dx.doi.org/10.1787/888933661400

Box 4.2. **Household assets and the self-employed**

The distribution of real and financial assets is complicated for households where at least one individual is self-employed. For these individuals, a substantial amount of both net and gross wealth is held inside their business, regardless of whether the business is incorporated or not. Such assets may include financial assets such as business bank deposits, or other assets such as vehicles and equipment.

On average across all households, relatively little wealth is held inside self-employed businesses. However, for those who are self-employed, the amount held inside their businesses is substantial. Figure 4.5 shows this in more detail, dividing the HFCS sample into households where the head of household is self-employed and the overall sample. The blue bars show the average holdings of self-employment wealth across the entire population. The grey bars show the same data but for households with a self-employed head of household. In these households self-employment wealth is significantly higher than the population average.

On average, the households where the head of household is self-employed hold 33.9% of their total gross wealth inside their self-employed business, compared to 10.1% on average in the total population.

The taxation of the self-employed raises challenging issues from a tax policy perspective. Self-employment income is often taxed in a different way to other kinds of income such as wage income. Some self-employment income may not be immediately taxed under the personal income tax at all, but rather under the corporate income tax if businesses are incorporated.

Figure 4.5. **Self-employed wealth amongst the total population versus the employed, as a share of total gross wealth**

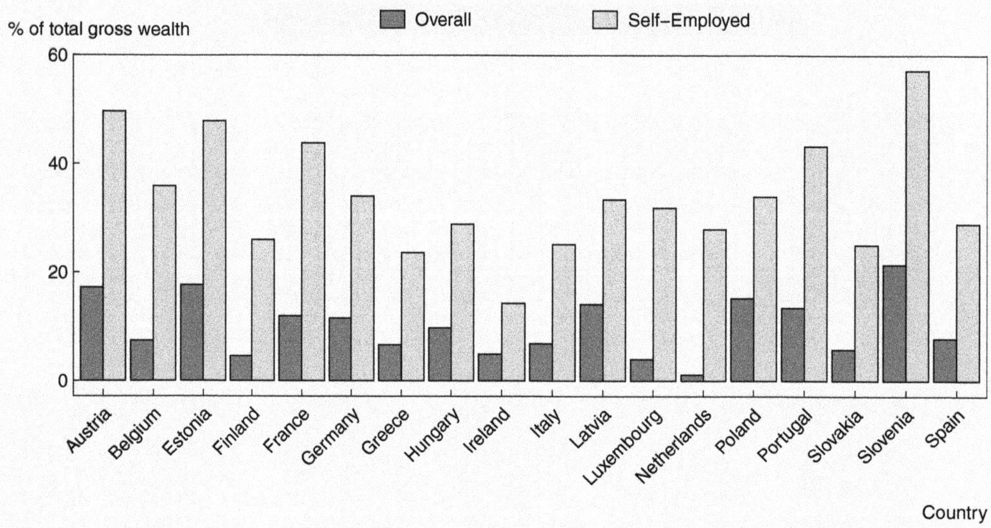

StatLink http://dx.doi.org/10.1787/888933661419

Note: Data are for 2013-4 (see Box 4.1).
Source: Authors' calculations based on Household Finance and Consumption Survey (2016).

4.3. Wealth inequality and the mix of assets across the wealth distribution

Wealth inequality in the Household Finance and Consumption Survey

While the distribution of incomes in society is of clear concern to policymakers, wealth inequality is another distributional dimension that is of particular interest to policymakers in the context of capital taxation. Results from the HFCS suggest that net wealth inequality is larger relative to income inequality. Figure 4.6 shows the distribution of net wealth by net wealth decile, expressed as a share of total household net wealth, for the 18 OECD countries in the HFCS. On average, households in the top decile hold 45.3% of total national household wealth, while the bottom 90% of households hold 54.7% on average. Wealth inequality is particularly marked in Latvia where households in the top decile hold 61.3% of total household wealth, and in Germany where households in the top decile hold 56.2%. Figure 4.7 ranks the value of the top deciles from Figure 4.6. Based on the HFCS data, the share of wealth held by the top decile is lowest in Poland and the Slovak Republic.

Those at the bottom of the net wealth distribution usually have negative net wealth. Households in the bottom decile have an average of -0.7% of total net wealth. In every country, the net wealth of the bottom decile in the country is negative, although in many countries the net wealth value is close to zero. Net wealth values in the lowest net wealth deciles are particularly low in the Netherlands and in Latvia, where the negative amount of net wealth is -3.1% and -2.3% of the total amount of national household wealth respectively. In the Netherlands, the second net wealth decile also has negative net wealth.

Real asset holdings across the net wealth distribution

Asset mixes across deciles vary more with respect to net wealth than with respect to income. As was shown in the discussion of assets across the income distribution, the main residence makes up a substantial share of assets. Figure 4.8 shows that on average across the countries in the HFCS sample, households' main residence makes up a substantial share of both gross wealth (71.1% averaged across all countries and deciles). In Figure 4.8, wealth held in the main residence dominates for middle net wealth deciles in most countries, but less so for high and low deciles. The average share of the main residence in gross wealth holdings of the 4th to 6th decile is 80.7%, compared to an average of 71.1% overall. This suggests that most households in the middle of the income distribution hold a significant part of their gross wealth in the form of their main residence. The importance of the main residence for middle deciles varies from 55.1% in Austria to 91.5% in Belgium.

The share of vehicles and valuables varies widely across net wealth deciles.[5] It makes up a substantial share of the gross wealth of those with low levels of net wealth overall, and a low share for those with higher levels of net wealth. The average share of vehicles amongst the lowest three deciles is 18.2% and the average share of valuables is 3.7%. On average, wealth held in vehicles and valuables makes up a small share of gross wealth for top deciles in all countries, with the highest value amongst the top decile being in the Slovak Republic at 3.7%. The highest overall value is in Austria at 13.5%. For most countries, the amount of wealth held in vehicles and valuables by the top decile is below 3%.

Main and other residences make up a large share of the total gross real wealth of those in lower deciles of the net wealth distribution. Among the lowest three deciles, this share is 65.7% of gross real wealth on average, varying between a lowest share of 34.4% in France and a highest of 85.6% in the Netherlands. Debt holdings are discussed further in Section 4.5 below.

Figure 4.6. **Distribution of net wealth by net wealth decile, percentage of total national household net wealth**

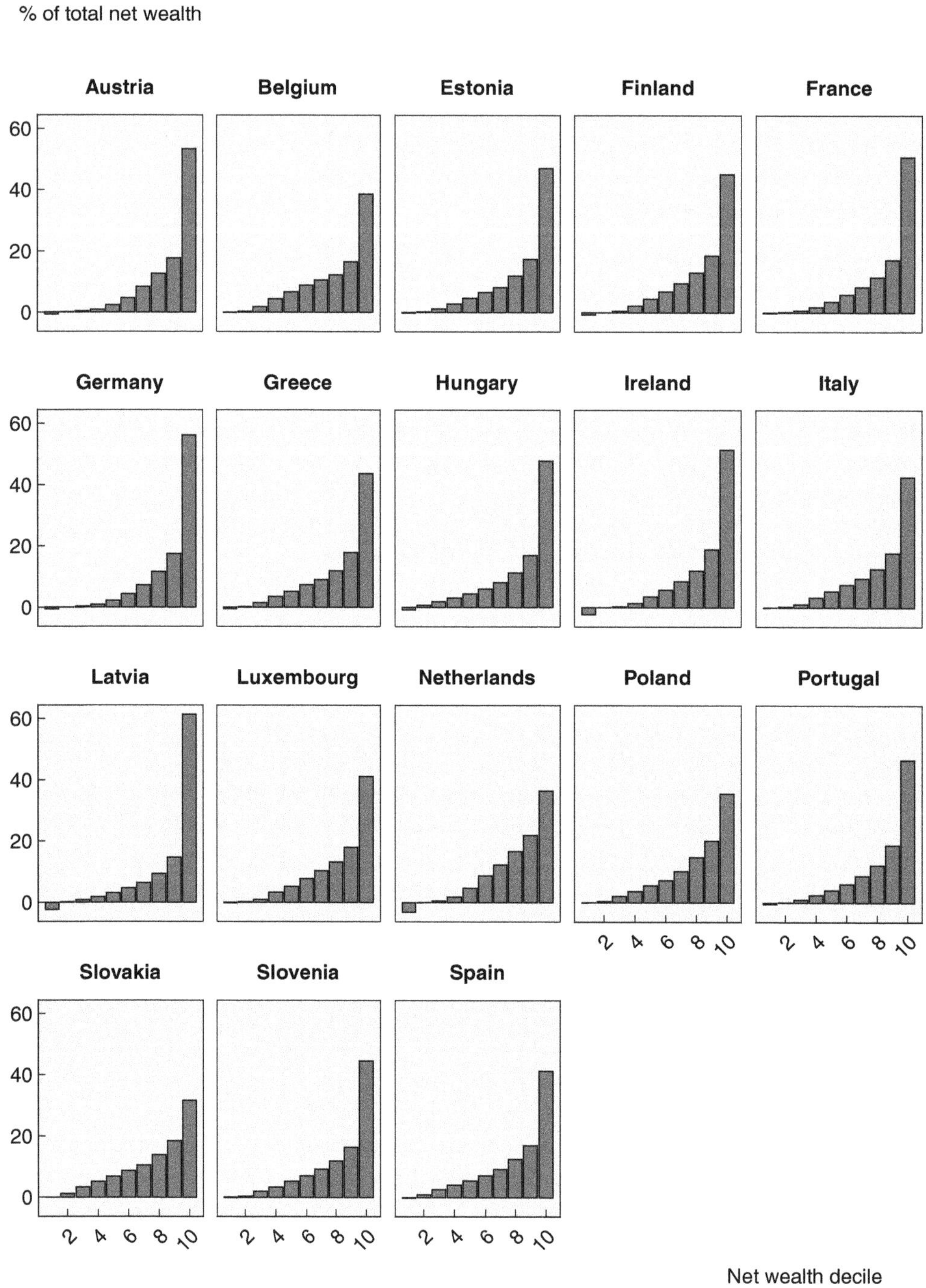

Note: Data are for 2013-4 (see Box 4.1).

Source: Authors' calculations based on Household Finance and Consumption Survey (2016).

StatLink http://dx.doi.org/10.1787/888933661438

Figure 4.7. **Net wealth holdings of top net wealth decile, percentage of total net wealth**

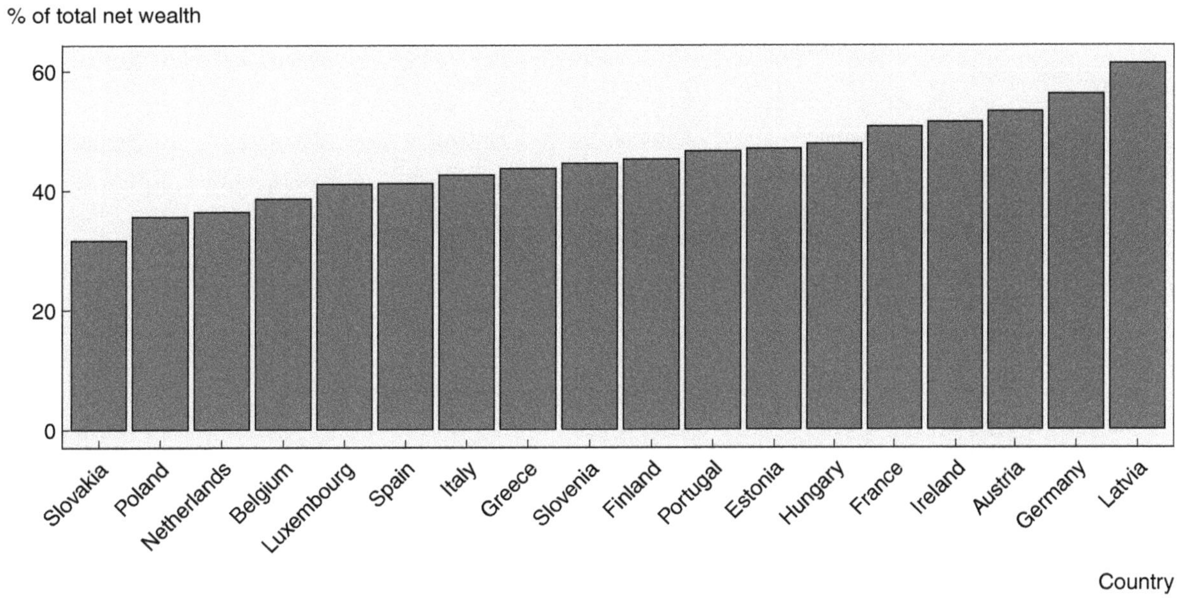

Note: Data are for 2013-4 (see Box 4.1).

Source: Authors' calculations based on Household Finance and Consumption Survey (2016).

StatLink http://dx.doi.org/10.1787/888933661457

Second residences form an increasing share of the gross wealth of those with higher net wealth levels. This share rises from a share of 14.9% of the gross real wealth of those in the bottom income decile on average to a share of 33% of the gross real wealth of those in the top income decile. These shares are highest in Ireland (60.3%) and Luxembourg (55.6%), and lowest in Poland (14.5%) and Slovenia (17.4%). This suggests that the taxation of second homes may be progressive with respect to net wealth as well as income. Other asset classes, including vehicles, valuables and wealth in the form of self-employed businesses also rise with income.

Households in top net wealth deciles also have high shares of gross wealth held in the form of self-employed businesses, and low shares of vehicles and valuables. Wealth held in self-employed business is particularly high in Slovenia, Austria and Estonia, where shares are 46.1%, 34%, and 33.3% respectively.

Financial asset holdings across the net wealth distribution

The variation in financial assets across countries and deciles is also substantial. Figure 4.9 shows this variation across the net wealth deciles. Bank deposits make up a much smaller share of the asset mix for those at the top of the net wealth distribution. They account for 42.4% of gross financial asset holdings on average for those in the highest net wealth decile. The highest share of bank deposits in the top net wealth decile is in Greece at 83.6% of total financial wealth, while the lowest share is in France at 20.3%. Households in these higher net wealth deciles are more likely to hold financial assets in other forms relative to those in lower net wealth deciles. Bank deposits comprise 52.4% of gross financial asset holdings on average for households in the lowest net wealth decile. The highest share of bank deposits in the lowest net wealth decile is in Latvia at 89.7% of total financial wealth, while the lowest share is in Ireland at 15.5%.

Figure 4.8. **Breakdown of real assets, as a share of total real assets, by net wealth deciles**

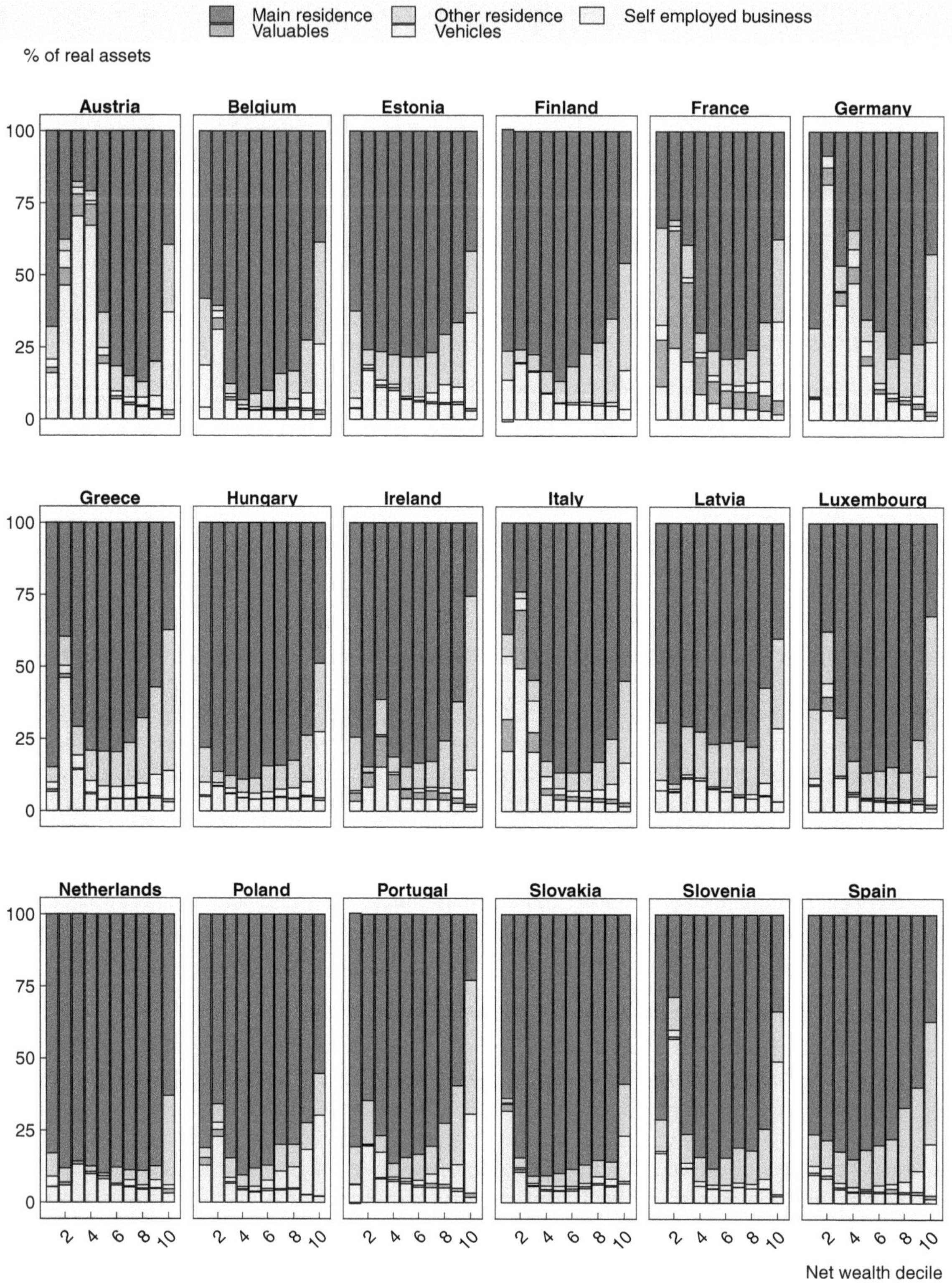

Note: Data are for 2013-4 (see Box 4.1).

Source: Authors' calculations based on Household Finance and Consumption Survey (2016).

StatLink http://dx.doi.org/10.1787/888933661476

Variation in bank deposits could be driven in part by financial sophistication (as discussed for example by Chetty et. al., 2013). Low income and low net wealth taxpayers could choose to save in bank deposits – which tend to have relatively low returns – due to lack of financial literacy and knowledge about savings opportunities with higher returns. Risk-averse households may also perceive bank deposits to be safer than other types of financial assets.

Holdings of shares and bonds are concentrated at the top of the net wealth distribution. Households in the top net wealth decile hold, on average, 7.4% of all financial assets in the form of shares, while households in the bottom net wealth decile hold only 1.3% on average. Households in the top net wealth decile hold 5.3% of all financial assets in the form of bonds, while households in the bottom net wealth decile hold 0.4%. The average across all net wealth deciles is 1.9%.

A key source of variation in net wealth over time relates to individuals' and households' saving for retirement. In many countries, individuals engage in substantial private pension provision, which is a source of variation in asset holdings across wealth levels and age levels, as reflected in the HFCS dataset. Pension saving is a widely-used form of saving across the entire income distribution, and usually forms the second-largest share of financial assets held in HFCS countries, after bank deposits.

Holdings of pension wealth decline across the net wealth distribution as a share of total holdings, although only modestly. In the top net wealth decile, households hold 16.9% of all financial assets in the form of pensions, while households in the bottom net wealth decile hold 31.8%. The average across all net wealth deciles is 22.8%.

The variation in private pension wealth across countries is substantial. As shown in Figure 4.9, there are relatively high shares of private pension wealth in Ireland (59% of total gross financial wealth on average), in Germany (38.7% on average), in the Netherlands (36.5% on average), and in Belgium (36.2% on average). By contrast, shares of pension wealth in total gross financial wealth are much more modest in some lower-income OECD countries such as Greece and Estonia, where even the highest net wealth decile holds no more than 1.3% and 8% respectively (averages across net wealth deciles are 2% and 8.6% respectively). However private pension wealth is also low in some countries that have higher levels of GDP per capita such as Finland and Austria, who have 8.6% and 21% respectively of total financial wealth held in the form of pensions. These results should be caveated by the fact that not all forms of pension saving are fully accounted for in the HFCS, and in particular, defined-benefit pension schemes are not fully reflected in these results.

Within those countries where pension wealth is substantial, there is some variation in the extent to which pension wealth varies with overall net wealth. In the Netherlands, even those with low levels of net wealth have a substantial portion of their financial wealth in the form of pensions. Households in the lowest net wealth decile hold 26.7% of total gross financial wealth in the form of pensions, while households in the top et wealth decile hold 23.5%. These households in low net wealth deciles may nonetheless have very low absolute amounts of pension wealth (as their total and financial wealth is low overall). The pattern in the Netherlands contrasts with France, for example. In France, 11.7% of total gross financial wealth is held among those in the lowest net wealth decile, 13.5% in the second net wealth decile, and 39% in the second-from-top net wealth decile, and 46.7% in the top net wealth decile.

Figure 4.9. **Breakdown of financial assets, as a share of total financial assets, by net wealth deciles**

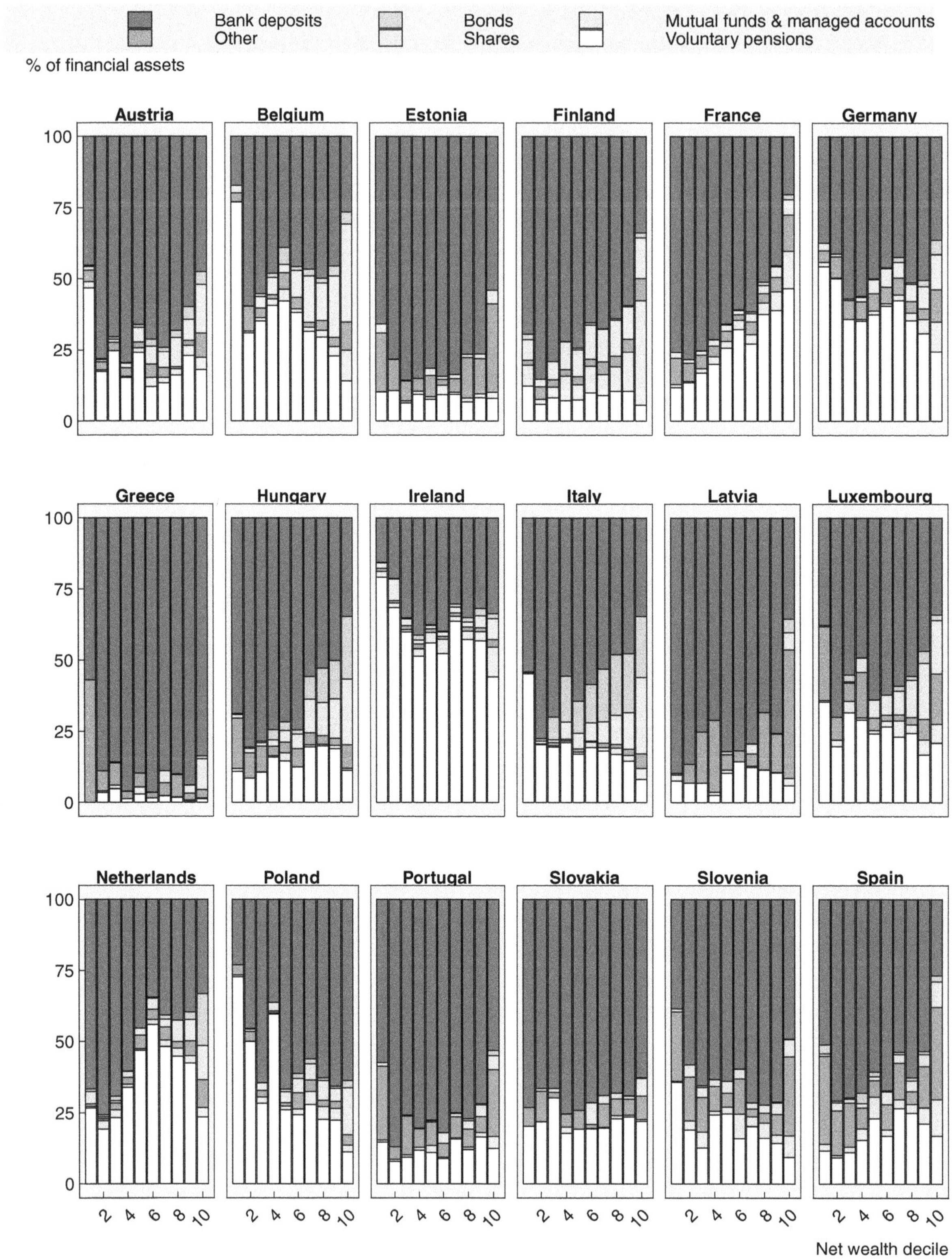

Note: Data are for 2013-4 (see Box 4.1).

Source: Authors' calculations based on Household Finance and Consumption Survey (2016).

StatLink http://dx.doi.org/10.1787/888933661495

There are similarities and contrasts between the results for net wealth deciles and the results for net income deciles. Pension wealth holdings are substantial across both income and net wealth deciles in Ireland, in Germany, in France, and in the Netherlands. Bond holdings are above average in Italy across income and net wealth deciles, as are equity holdings in Finland, and mutual fund holdings in Belgium and Germany. By contrast, bond holdings in Hungary and the Netherlands are concentrated amongst high net wealth deciles, while they are spread much more evenly across income deciles.

Tax factors could also drive various savings outcomes. Households may vary the asset composition of their savings depending on how the tax system treats different categories of assets (see Chapter 1 for a discussion of the literature on this subject). This may be particularly the case with respect to financial assets, which have comparatively low switching costs (compared to residences or other immovable property). The tax treatment of different asset classes is the subject of the next chapter.

4.4. Ageing and net wealth

The within-decile distribution of income and net wealth provides a snapshot in time, however, households' incomes and net wealth vary over time. As individuals enter the workforce, their income and net wealth are both likely to begin to rise compared to childhood. As individuals retire, their incomes often fall substantially, and their net wealth may decline as they dissave over their retirement years (although this dissaving may not apply to households with high levels of wealth). These trends may exist in each country independently of other tax and non-tax factors, but may be masked if the income and net wealth distributions are examined without taking age into account.

On average, household net wealth is highest in the years just prior to retirement. Figure 4.10 shows average and median net wealth across the age distribution. Overall, net wealth is highest amongst those from 50-59 years old, with an average net wealth level of EUR 205 501, and lowest amongst those from 20-29 years old, with an average net wealth level of EUR 68 600. The top three net wealth age groups are ages 50-59 years old, 40-49 years old and 60-69 years old, where the latter two groups have average net wealth levels of EUR 158 082 and EUR 222 938 respectively.

Median wealth across age groups is lower than average wealth across age group, which stems from the relatively high concentration of wealth at the top of the net wealth distribution. However, the stylised patterns across ages are similar to the patterns with respect to average wealth levels across age groups. Overall, net wealth is highest amongst those from 60-69 years old, with an median net wealth level of EUR 222 128, and lowest amongst those from 20-29 years old, with an average net wealth level of EUR 47 727.

The extent to which net wealth differs across age distributions varies across countries. In Austria and Belgium, for example, net wealth levels varies substantially, peaking at an average of EUR 506 811 and EUR 492 371 amongst those from 50 to 59 and 60 to 69 respectively (though this peak is not as pronounced with respect to median wealth levels). This compares to the lowest 10-year age bracket (ages 20 to 29) who have an average net wealth of EUR 282 329. By contrast, the Slovak Republic has a distribution of net wealth that is relatively flat in absolute terms across various age groups, with the wealthiest age group – those from 50 to 59 – having an average net wealth of EUR 76 772 (and a median level of EUR 61 474) compared to the age group with the lowest average net wealth - those from 20 to 29, who have a net wealth of EUR 22 165 (and a median level of EUR 8 777). This may suggest low levels of aggregate household saving for retirement. These results should be considered with caution however, given that the estimates of pension wealth in the NCFS are not comprehensive (see Box 4.1).

Figure 4.10. **Net wealth across the age distribution, EUR**

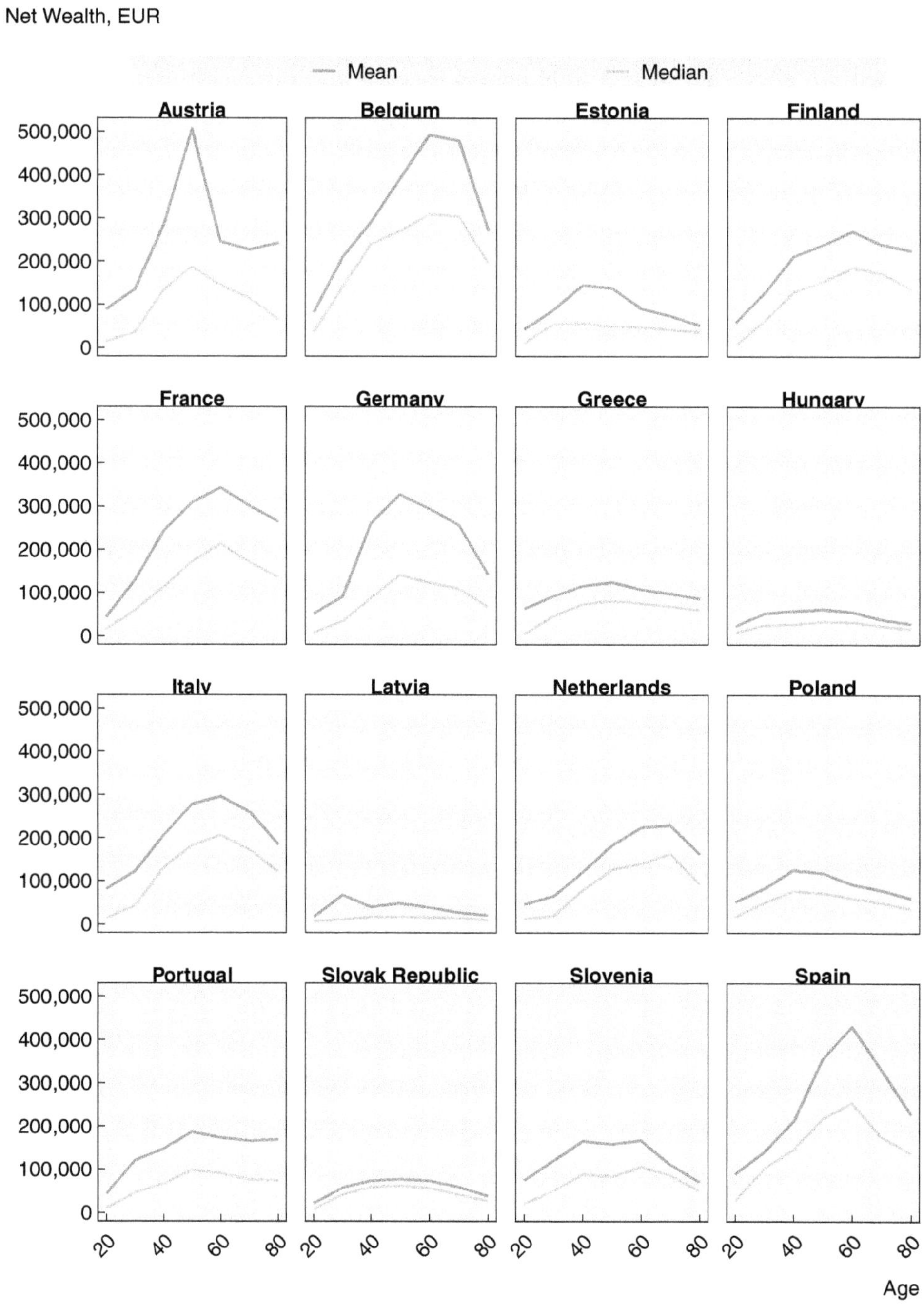

Note: Data are for 2013-4 (see Box 4.1).

Source: Authors' calculations based on Household Finance and Consumption Survey (2016).

StatLink http://dx.doi.org/10.1787/888933661514

4.5. Net wealth, debt and housing

Net wealth inequality and income inequality

A complicating factor for those assessing the impact of savings taxation is the fact that income and net wealth inequality present different policy challenges. Sections 4.2 and 4.3 of this chapter have highlighted differing patterns of income and net wealth inequality and the differing patterns of asset holding across different levels of income and net wealth. However those individuals and households with high incomes may not be same as those with high levels of net wealth, and vice versa. This is particularly the case because variation in net wealth across society results in substantial part from consumption smoothing over time.

Those who earn a high income are also more likely to be wealthy, and those who earn a low income are more likely to have low levels of net wealth. Figure 4.11 shows the share of each net wealth decile that is contained within each income decile. On average, the probability of a household from the highest income decile being in the highest net wealth decile is 43.2%, while the probability of a household from the lowest income decile being in the lowest net wealth decile is 22.2%.

However, the correlation between income and net wealth is not perfect. Indeed, the data suggest that there are some households in the highest net wealth deciles who earn among the lowest incomes in the sample. Conversely, some households in the lowest net wealth deciles who earn among the highest incomes in the sample.

Figure 4.11. **Correlations between net wealth deciles and income deciles**

Percentage of each net wealth decile in each income decile

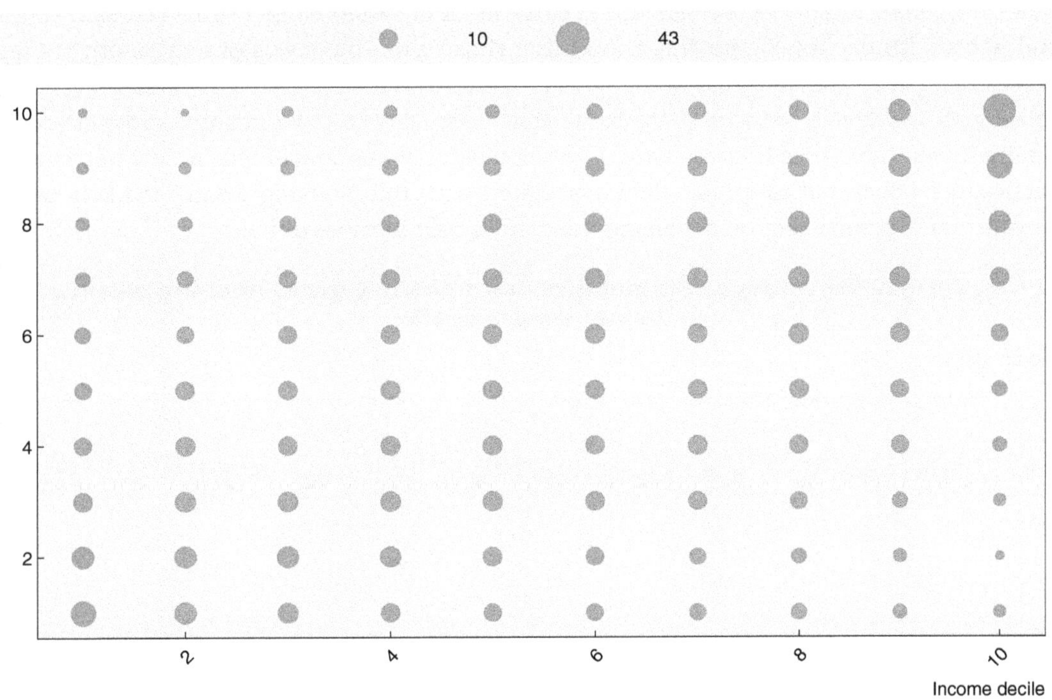

Note: Data are for 2013-4 (see Box 4.1). All income deciles are based on income gross of taxes and transfers.

Source: Authors' calculations based on Household Finance and Consumption Survey (2016).

StatLink http://dx.doi.org/10.1787/888933661533

The absence of perfect correlation between income and net wealth may present challenges for tax policymaking. Efforts to tax those with high levels of net wealth may encounter difficulties where those with high levels of net wealth may have low levels of income, and so may encounter liquidity problems when paying taxes levied. From an equity perspective, it is not obvious whether the most appropriate "ability-to-pay" criterion is income or net wealth, or whether progressive taxation should be progressive with respect to income, or net wealth, or both. These issues are discussed further in Chapter 6.

Net wealth vs gross wealth

The preceding analysis presented results as a percentage of gross wealth. As noted, this was to avoid interpretation difficulties. However, there are significant differences in asset mixes expressed as a percentage of net wealth and gross wealth, particularly regarding housing. This section examines this in more detail. The data in the HFCS suggests that many households that have significant gross assets may be indebted on many of those assets. This is particularly the case for households with low levels of net wealth. For example, many households may finance their principal residence with debt. This in turn means that while gross housing wealth is substantial, net housing wealth may be far lower or even negative.

Housing and housing debt are key drivers in the variation between gross and net wealth across income and net wealth deciles. The results presented in Sections 4.2, 4.3 and 4.4 have shown that housing is the predominant form of real asset holding across most income and net wealth deciles for most countries in the HFCS sample.

The probability of owning a home is positively correlated with both income and net wealth. Figure 4.12 and Figure 4.13 show patterns of gross housing wealth across income and net wealth deciles. Figure 4.12 shows that those with low levels of net wealth are far less likely to have positive gross housing wealth (i.e. to own a home). Figure 4.13 shows that those with low levels of income are somewhat less likely to have positive gross housing wealth. Given that gross housing wealth is positive for some households in low net wealth deciles, it follows that mortgage debt associated with this housing wealth is likely to be substantial. The next section discusses household debt in more detail.

Figure 4.12. **Percentage of population with positive gross housing wealth, by net wealth decile**

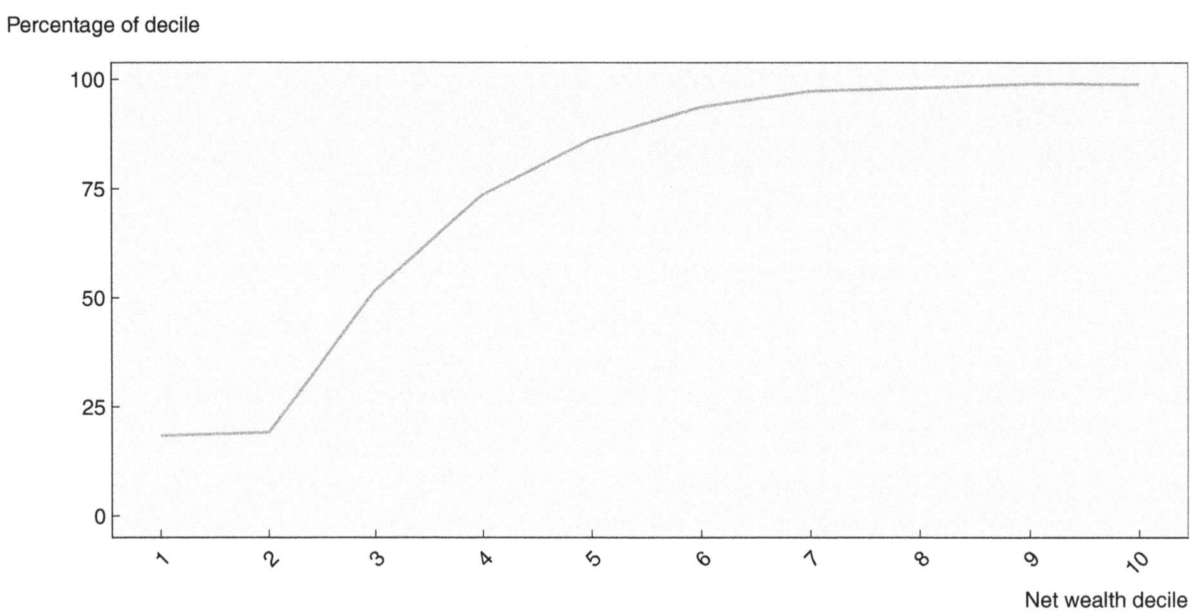

Note: Data are for 2013-4 (see Box 4.1).

Source: Authors' calculations based on Household Finance and Consumption Survey (2016).

StatLink http://dx.doi.org/10.1787/888933661552

Figure 4.13. **Percentage of population with positive gross housing wealth, by income decile**

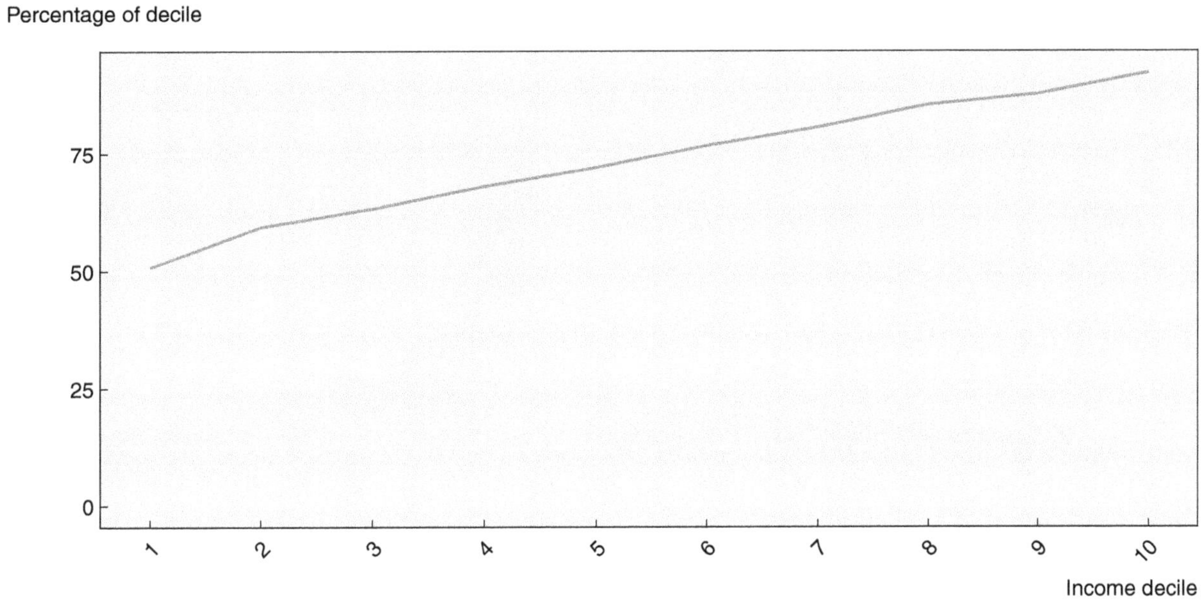

Note: Data are for 2013-4 (see Box 4.1). The distribution does not incorporate taxes and transfers.

Source: Authors' calculations based on Household Finance and Consumption Survey (2016).

StatLink http://dx.doi.org/10.1787/888933661571

Distribution of debt holdings

This section brings together several stylised facts on income, net wealth and debt in this chapter. Debt, and particularly mortgage debt, plays a crucial role in driving asset holdings and influencing the distributional effects of the taxation of household savings. Figure 4.12 and Figure 4.13 have shown that gross housing wealth increases with both income and net wealth. Figure 4.11 has highlighted substantial differences in the income and net wealth distribution, as there are many households with high incomes and low levels of net wealth, and also households with low incomes and high levels of net wealth.

Those with gross housing wealth who are in the lowest net wealth decile have low net wealth precisely because they have substantial housing debt. Gross housing wealth (i.e. home ownership) is spread more evenly across income deciles than across net wealth deciles. It follows that some part of the variation between income deciles and net wealth deciles shown in Figure 4.11 is a function of housing debt.

As a share of gross wealth, those in low net wealth deciles have much higher levels of debt relative to their wealth when compared to those in high net wealth deciles. Figure 4.14 shows that the average amount of household debt in the lowest net wealth decile is 141.8% of total gross wealth. For this decile, housing debt is 91.9% of gross wealth (75.2% on the main residence, 16.7% on other residences). Non-mortgage debt is 49.8% of gross wealth.

For higher net wealth deciles, the share of non-housing debt falls substantially. Mortgage debt on the main residence does fall as a share of net wealth at higher net wealth levels, but not by as much as non-mortgage debt. Mortgage debt is 25.4%, 9.6%, and 2.5% of gross wealth in the 4th, 7th, and top net wealth deciles respectively. High levels of debt in part explain the negative levels of net wealth seen in Figure 4.6.

Figure 4.14. **Household debt as a share of gross wealth, by income and net wealth deciles**

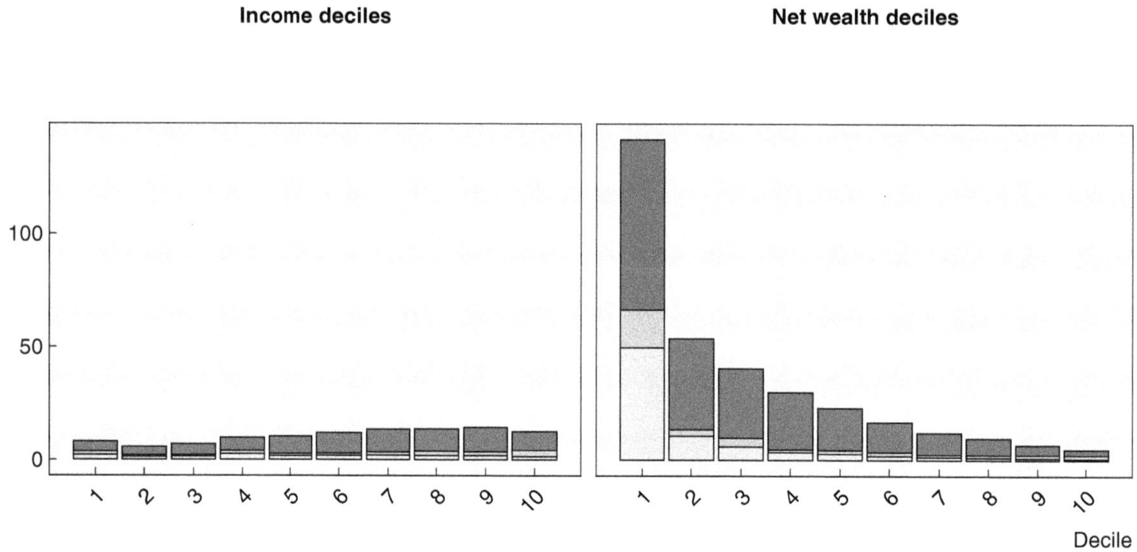

Note: Data are for 2013-4 (see Box 4.1). The distribution does not incorporate taxes and transfers.
Source: Authors' calculations based on Household Finance and Consumption Survey (2016).

StatLink http://dx.doi.org/10.1787/888933661590

As a share of gross wealth, debt levels are far less correlated with income than they are with net wealth. Figure 4.14 also shows that while households above the lowest income deciles do have higher debt as a share of gross wealth, these shares rise only modestly with income. Debt levels are is 8.1%, 9.9%, and 13.6% of gross wealth in the 1st, 4th, and 7th income deciles respectively. Moreover, debt levels in the top income decile are lower than those of the 9th decile (at 12.6%, compared to 14.4%).

The results in the left panel of Figure 4.14 mask substantial variation within income deciles that can be seen on the right panel. Figure 4.14 shows that those with low levels of net wealth may have low levels of net wealth not necessarily because they have low levels of gross wealth, but because they have high levels of debt.

The absolute level of debt is broadly constant across net wealth deciles, but rises with income, on average, across countries. This variation is explored in Figure 4.15. Figure 4.15 shows absolute debt levels (i.e. in euros) as opposed to as a percentage of gross wealth. These figures show that those with higher income levels have higher debt levels on average, but that these debt levels rise roughly proportionately with income. By contrast, absolute levels of gross debt are roughly constant across net wealth deciles. This means that debt falls substantially as a share of gross wealth across net wealth deciles.

These data provide important context for tax policymakers assessing savings tax policies from a distributional perspective. Debt levels rise with income in absolute terms, so deductions for interest (such as mortgage interest) provide a greater absolute benefit to those with higher incomes. However these same deductions provide higher proportional benefits to those with low levels of net wealth. This is because housing forms a greater part of their gross wealth, and because housing debt is also more substantial relative to their gross wealth.

Figure 4.15. **Household debt in EUR, by income and net wealth deciles**

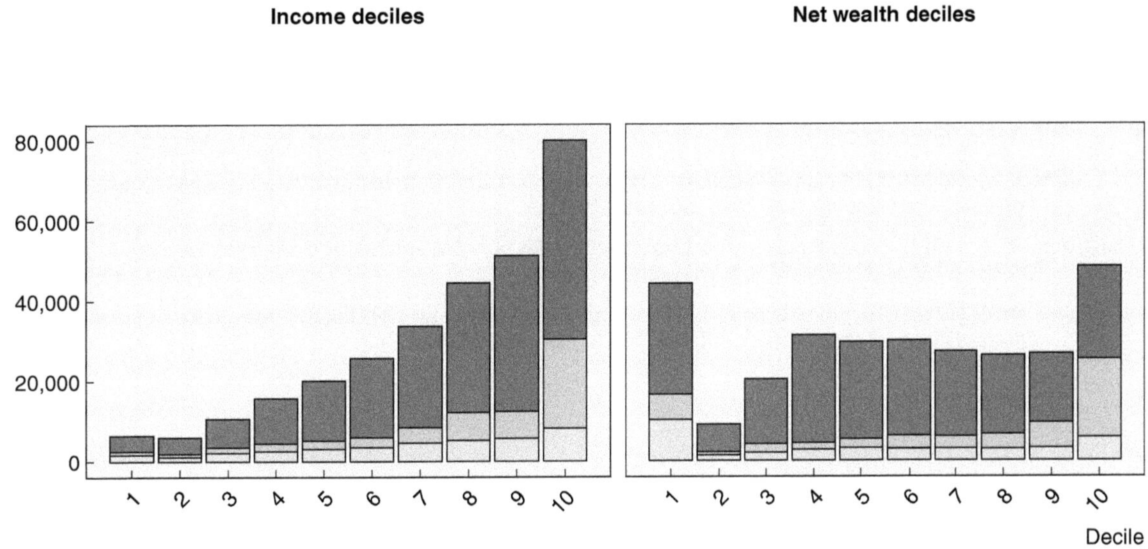

Note: Data are for 2013-4 (see Box 4.1). The distribution does not incorporate taxes and transfers.

Source: Authors' calculations based on Household Finance and Consumption Survey (2016).

StatLink http://dx.doi.org/10.1787/888933661609

Notes

1. The same analysis was replicated with data from the first wave of the HFCS, producing broadly consistent trends and results as those presented in this chapter for the second wave.
2. HFCS data contains information only about market income inequality. A discussion of the impact of the tax and transfer system is beyond the scope of this report. Recent OECD research has, however, considered these issues (Causa and Hermansen, n.d.).
3. Throughout, the results presented here are for the 18 OECD countries in the HFCS. When the text refers to HCFS average, it refers to 18-country averages, not 20-country averages.
4. This can include current accounts and savings accounts.
5. Valuables in this case refer to jewellery, works of art, antiques, etc.

References

Alvaredo, F. et al. (eds.) (2018), *The World Inequality Report*, Harvard University Press.

Atkinson, A. and J. Stiglitz (1976), "The design of the tax structure: direct versus indirect taxation", *Journal of Public Economics*, Vol. 6, pp. 55-75.

European Central Bank (2016), The Household Finance and Consumption Survey: Cross-country metadata information, Wave 2.

Brys, B., Perret, S., Thomas, A., and O'Reilly, P. (2016), "Tax Design for Inclusive Economic Growth", *OECD Tax Policy Working Papers, No. 26, OECD Publishing, Paris, http://dx.doi.org/10.1787/5jlv74ggk0g7-en.*

Causa, O. and M. Hermansen (n.d.), "The effectiveness of tax and transfer systems in reducing income inequality across OECD countries", *OECD Economics Department Working Papers* (forthcoming).

Chamley, C. (1986), "Optimal taxation of capital income in general equilibrium with infinite lives.", *Econometrica*, Vol. 54, pp. 607-622.

Golosov, M., Kocherlakota, N. and Tsyvinski, A. (2003), "Optimal Indirect and Capital Taxation", *Review of Economic Studies*, Vol. 70, No. 3, pp. 569-587.

Judd, K. (1985), "Redistributive taxation in a simple perfect foresight model", *Journal of Public Economics*, Vol. 29, pp. 59-83.

OECD (2018) *Gearing Tax Policy to Make Inclusive Growth Happen*, OECD, Paris (forthcoming).

OECD (2015), *In It Together: Why Less Inequality Benefits All*, OECD Publishing.

Saez, E. (2013), "Optimal progressive capital income taxes in the infinite horizon model", *Journal of Public Economics*, Vol. 97, pp. 61-74.

Saez, E. (2017), "Income and wealth inequality: Evidence and policy implications", Contemporary Economic Policy, Vol. 35, No.1, pp. 7-25.

Stantcheva, S. (2017), "Optimal Taxation and Human Capital Policies over the Life Cycle", Journal of Political Economy, Vol. 125, No.6, pp. 1931-1990.

Zucman, G. (2014), "Taxing across Borders: Tracking Personal Wealth and Corporate Profits", *Journal of Economic Perspectives*, Vol. 28, No.4, pp. 121-148.

Zucman, G. (2013), The missing wealth of nations: Are Europe and the U.S. net debtors or net creditors? *Quarterly Journal of Economics*, Vol. 128, No. 3, pp. 1321-1364.

Chapter 5

International aspects of the taxation of household savings

This chapter discusses the taxation of household savings from an international perspective, and considers the impact of exchange of financial account information between tax administrations on the taxation of capital income internationally. The chapter discusses the recent adoption and expansion of exchange of information in detail, highlighting the dramatic increase in the coverage of exchange of information networks. The automatic exchange of information is likely to make it harder for taxpayers to engage in tax evasion and may reduce the distortions involved in levying taxes on capital income. The chapter also highlights potential challenges that remain with respect to ensuring the coherent taxation of capital income on a residence basis in an international context.

5.1. Introduction

This chapter discusses the taxation of household savings from an international perspective, and considers the impact of exchange of information (EOI) on the taxation of capital income internationally. Previous chapters considered effective tax rates across asset types from the perspective of taxing a domestic saver. However, in an increasingly globalised economy a large share of total investment comes from abroad and, equally, a large share of domestic savings is invested abroad. This means that the returns to investment domestically often accrue to foreign investors. It also means that the capital income earned by domestic residents is often earned abroad.

This chapter focuses on the taxation of foreign-sourced capital income at the individual level levied in the taxpayer's tax residence. A crucial component of effectively implementing residence-based taxation of foreign income is the effective EOI between tax authorities. Without effective EOI, it is possible that some taxpayers may fail to declare their foreign-sourced income or assets and, through a lack of information in the hands of the tax authorities, avoid detection. This policy challenge has received widespread attention over recent years.

Effectively implementing international EOI has long been on the agenda of tax policymakers. However, some early efforts to exchange information have faced a number of challenges. In some instances, limited membership of countries in an EOI network has led to the shifting of assets to other countries not in the network (i.e. countries who have not signed an EOI agreement). In other instances, certain income or asset streams have been left out of information exchange agreements, leaving open some channels of evasion for taxpayers. Finally, information exchange on request has required tax authorities to already have some information prior to seeking information through formal information exchange channels from their foreign counterparts.

This chapter discusses the recent expansion and standardisation of EOI in detail. The implementation of the Common Reporting Standard (CRS) has allowed for EOI on an automatic and standardised basis across a rapidly expanding number of countries. This chapter highlights the dramatic change in the coverage of EOI networks, and the promulgation and monitoring of this new standard to improve the quality of information exchanged. It places these new initiatives in the context of previous EOI efforts, and highlights the potential impact of EOI for the taxation of capital income at the individual level overall.

This chapter also highlights potential challenges that remain with respect to ensuring the coherent taxation of capital income on a residence basis in an international context. These challenges are broadly twofold. The first relates to ensuring that information exchange is effectively implemented. This chapter highlights the importance of ensuring a comprehensive EOI network amongst all relevant jurisdictions. This is necessary to prevent assets from flowing to jurisdictions that remain outside the global EOI network. It is also important that the CRS is implemented consistently across all jurisdictions that adhere to its principles. These tasks have been assigned to the Global Forum on Transparency and Exchange of Information for Tax Purposes or "Global Forum"[1] and highlight the need not only for a robust Global Forum peer review process but also for technical support, particularly for countries and jurisdictions with limited administrative capacity. It is also important to ensure that persons, assets, and institutions not covered under existing EOI standards do not offer opportunities for continued tax evasion and therefore that the standards remain fit for purpose.

The second challenge relates to coherently taxing capital income in a world where EOI is effectively implemented. First, the impact of EOI will be limited unless tax authorities have the administrative means and methods to effectively use the information exchanged. Tax authorities should take advantage of new analytical tools and technological advances. Second, the expansion and effectiveness of EOI may also induce taxpayers to shift their wealth to assets not covered by EOI, such as real property. This increases the importance of the tax treatment of these assets. Third, taxation at the personal level in a world of falling corporate tax rates may lead taxpayers to shift income from the personal level to the corporate level, and may also exacerbate lock-in problems as taxpayers postpone the realisation of capital gains. This suggests that a key policy priority is ensuring that the corporate income tax functions effectively as a "withholding" tax for what is in effect personal capital income. Taxpayers may also "vote with their feet" as a result of countries' efforts to strengthen the taxation of capital income in their tax residence, although these mobility responses, which are worthy of more detailed analysis, are not considered in this chapter.

The chapter proceeds as follows. Section 5.2 discusses key choices available to international tax policymakers and considers the development of the international tax system over recent years. Section 5.3 discusses recent developments in exchanging information between tax authorities in more detail, focusing on the development of the Exchange of Information on Request (EOIR) networks in recent years as well as the expansion of Automatic Exchange of Information (AEOI) through the development of the CRS. Section 5.4 considers the impacts of the expansion of EOI between tax authorities. Section 5.5 concludes with some potential priorities for policymakers following the advent of widespread EOI.

5.2. Capital taxation and globalisation

Globalisation presents a wide variety of policy challenges, not least in the area of savings taxation (OECD, 2017a). Many of the key tax policy insights that can be drawn from the optimal taxation literature about the design of capital income taxation in a social welfare maximising setting have been developed from the perspective of a closed economy.[2] However, continuing expansion of global trade in goods and services as well as expansion of cross-border investment and financial flows mean that national tax policies cannot be designed in isolation from one another.

This globalisation of the world economy has been intensifying over recent decades. For the purposes of capital taxation, the key trend brought about by globalisation has been the increase in cross-border financial and investment flows. Foreign investment is an increasingly large share of total investment in any given economy and forms a larger share of the capital tax base in any given economy. Savings and ownership are now, more often than not, cross national; a taxpayer does not need to be tax resident in a country to invest there. In addition, a taxpayer may invest in the country where they are tax resident, but mediated through foreign companies or structures.

Strong tax policy rationales exist for the taxation of capital income at source. Source-based taxation implies that the returns to capital are taxed only in the country where value is created. Source-based taxation allows countries to tax location-specific economic rents and compensates the source jurisdiction for the public services that it provides to investors. Source-based taxation also contributes to the coherent functioning of the domestic tax system in that it provides for a withholding function of the taxes on capital income at the individual level.

However, as countries tax the income earned by the capital being used in their countries at source, the cost of capital will rise and domestic investment will fall. It may negatively impact the inflow of FDI and will stimulate the outflow of domestic savings. This in turn will reduce labour productivity and so will reduce wages. It is widely documented that source-based taxes are partially borne by immobile factors (such as land or labour) in that country. The academic literature estimates that between 30% and 55% of international corporate income taxation is borne by labour (Milanez, 2017; Fuest, Peichl and Siegloch, 2018; Arulampalam, Devereux and Maffini, 2012). This raises the question of how and on what basis internationally mobile capital is best taxed.

The challenges of taxing mobile capital in an internationally competitive tax environment are evident in the trends in both the average combined corporate income tax (CIT) rate, and the average combined statutory rate on dividends in recent years. The total tax burden on dividend income has increased slightly since the crisis, in contrast with the pre-crisis period during which the tax burden on dividend income generally decreased. The post-crisis rise in dividend taxation has been the result of increased taxation at the shareholder level while corporate tax rates continued to decrease modestly, as shown in Figure 5.1. The figure shows the continuous fall of the average standard CIT rate in OECD countries from 32.5% in 2000 to 24.7% in 2016. This trend towards lower CIT rates has continued in the aftermath of the OECD/G20 BEPS project, which has levelled the playing field by preventing harmful tax competition in relation to the tax base. These reductions in taxation at the corporate level highlight the importance of taxation through the PIT system, which is the focus of this study.

Figure 5.1. **Trends in Corporate Income Tax Rates**

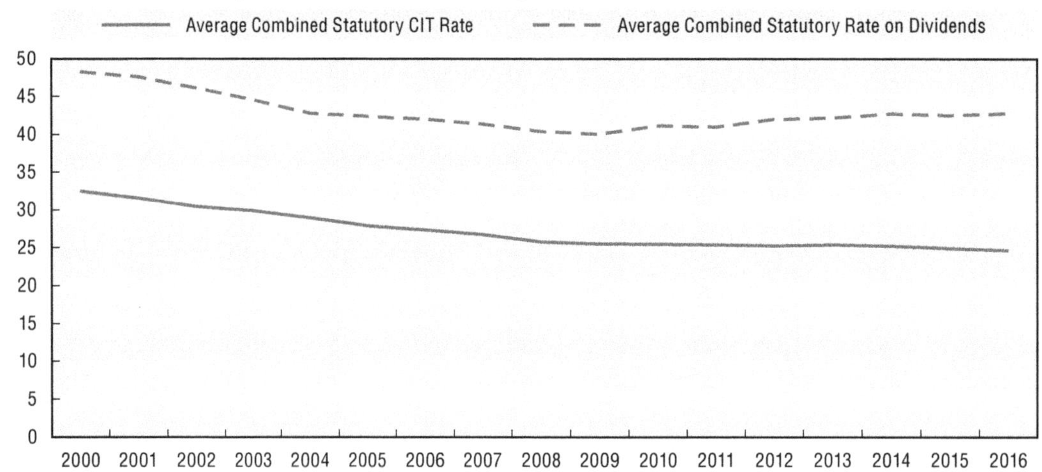

Source: OECD Tax Database

StatLink http://dx.doi.org/10.1787/888933661628

Discussions about the optimal design of capital income taxes often focuses on efficiency issues, but equity considerations are equally important. From an equity perspective, it is the overall tax burden on capital income that matters, irrespective of whether capital income is taxed at source or residence. Residence-based taxation implies that the returns to capital taxes are levied where the investor is tax resident. These taxes are in theory levied whether the income is earned on capital invested at home or abroad. It ensures that tax residents who earn their income in the form of labour or capital income are taxed on a relatively equal footing, thereby strengthening the fairness of the tax system.

However, taxing foreign source income on a residence basis is complicated by the challenge of tax evasion. Individuals who do not report their foreign source income or assets to their domestic tax authority can evade paying taxes on this income if the domestic tax authority cannot access information about this income or these assets. Estimates of the size of offshore wealth are challenging to construct and maintain, and are subject to considerable uncertainty. However, recent estimates in the literature have varied from USD 6-7 trillion to USD 22 trillion (Alstadsaeter et al., 2017). The general order of magnitude of these estimates suggests that levying residence-based personal taxes is a considerable policy challenge.

Information exchange is a key aspect of the solution to international tax evasion, and, therefore, information exchange provisions have been a key aspect of tax treaties, as is discussed below. Effective information exchange involving foreign-source income is crucial for the maintenance of residence-based taxation and potentially for capital taxation in general. Without adequate information about cross-border income and wealth, it is all too easy for taxpayers to conceal wealth from the tax authorities of their residence jurisdiction and avoid detection. Moreover, as the combination of source and residence taxation may imply that capital income is unintendedly taxed twice, effective information exchange is also crucial in order to prevent double taxation.

5.3. Exchange of information

Background

This section outlines recent progress made towards effective EOI between countries. Key initiatives discussed include the application of a common international standard on EOIR, and more recently AEOI. The development of these EOI mechanisms allows countries to better cooperate with one another to detect and identify capital assets and income that could otherwise be hidden.

The key forum for promoting the widespread implementation of EOI internationally is the Global Forum on Transparency and Exchange of Information (The Global Forum). The Global Forum was created in the early 2000s to address the risks to tax compliance posed by non-cooperative jurisdictions. On 2 April 2009, following a call from the G20 to “end bank secrecy”, the Global Forum moved to strengthen and expand EOI on a world-wide basis (G20, 2009). Today, with over 147 member countries and jurisdictions, it is the key global body ensuring international tax co-operation through the effective implementation of the international standards of tax transparency and exchange of information (i.e. EOIR and AEOI).[3]

EOIR and AEOI are complementary tools in the fight against tax evasion. Effective AEOI will provide tax administrations with information needed not only to tax the foreign source income and capital of their tax residents that is located abroad, but also with the necessary information to effectively use the OECD standard on EOIR. As discussed, tax administrations need specific information (e.g. information identifying the taxpayer and the jurisdiction where assets may be located) in order to file a request for information (see Section 3.3 above). With the information obtained from the AEOI, tax administrations will have details to file a request. As a result, both standards are interdependent, working together to enhance the effectiveness of tax administrations' efforts in addressing international tax evasion.

Multilateral approaches to EOI

Two key instruments promulgated by the Global Forum to facilitate information exchange include the Convention on Mutual Administrative Assistance in Tax Matters (the Convention) and the OECD's Model Agreement on Exchange of Information for Tax Matters. The Convention is the most comprehensive multilateral instrument available for AEOI.[4] In 1988, the Council of Europe and the OECD jointly developed the Convention as a multilateral instrument among OECD member countries, allowing all forms of tax co-operation including AEOI. In 2010, the Convention was amended to allow it to become open to non-OECD countries. It allows for administrative assistance across all types of taxes, facilitates AEOI and EOIR, as well as spontaneous exchange, provides for the possibility of running cross-border and simultaneous tax audits, and allows states to assist each other in tax collection. The Convention also has the advantage that signature of the Convention creates EOI relationships with every other signatory, obviating the need for separate bilateral agreements in each instance.

The OECD's Model Agreement on Exchange of Information for Tax Matters (OECD Model TIEA) may also be used for AEOI purposes. The TIEA was developed by the OECD in 2002 to promote international co-operation in tax matters. In its first version, it included the possibility of EOI considered "foreseeably relevant" to the determination, assessment, collection, recovery and enforcement, or the investigation or prosecution of tax matters under the EOIR. In 2015, the model TIEA was amended to include AEOI and spontaneous EOI. Even though a TIEA can either be bilateral or multilateral, only the bilateral version is currently being used in practice. In this instance, both countries exchanging information on an automatic basis must sign a TIEA containing provisions relating to AEOI with each other.

A key difference between the Convention and a bilateral Double Tax Convention (DTC) or TIEA is that countries signing the Convention provide the basis for AEOI with every other Convention signatory. By contrast, bilateral TIEAs require separate agreements with each country.

The scope of the Convention is broader than that of the model TIEA. One of the main differences between the model TIEA and the Convention is that the former looks to promote international co-operation in tax matters through EOI only, while the latter also includes other types of international co-operation such as assistance in recovery and simultaneous tax audits. Similarly, the Convention provides for assistance with respect to taxes like social security contributions (SSCs) which are not covered by the model TIEA. However, AEOI can take place under either the Convention or a bilateral TIEA following the OECD Model TIEA.

Exchange of Information on Request

Overview

EOIR refers to a situation where the tax authority of one jurisdiction asks for particular information from the authority of another jurisdiction (with which it has signed a tax treaty and/or a tax information exchange agreement) in connection with a tax inquiry or investigation (OECD, 2016). The requesting jurisdiction must provide specific details on the information it needs, and show that the requested information is "foreseeably relevant" to the tax affairs of a given taxpayer or a group of taxpayers in order for the other tax administration to answer the request.

The Global Forum's EOIR standard is the most widely-implemented standard on EOI for tax purposes. The EOIR standard is primarily drawn from the 2002 OECD Model Agreement on Exchange of Information on Tax Matters (OECD Model TIEA) and its commentary, Article 26 of the OECD Model Tax Convention on Income and on Capital and its commentary, as updated in 2012 (OECD, 2016), and Article 26 of the UN Model Double Tax Convention.

EOIR is possible because there are domestic laws enabling availability of information, and there are international agreements allowing the exchange of that information between countries and jurisdictions.[5] Jurisdictions implementing the standard are expected to introduce all necessary domestic regulation ensuring availability of the requested information as well as access to that information by tax/competent authorities of the requested jurisdiction. They are also expected to have international instruments in place that enable them to exchange information with all relevant partners.

Different mechanisms exist enabling EOI between jurisdictions. Some agreements are bilateral (i.e. an agreement taking place between two jurisdictions), while there is also an increasing use of multilateral agreements (i.e. agreements under which jurisdictions agree with many countries to exchange information). The various types of agreements that can allow for EOI are outlined in Table 5.1. Most double tax treaties include provisions which require EOI. For example, article 26 of the OECD Model Tax Convention provides the most widely accepted legal basis for bilateral EOI for tax purposes (OECD, 2016). Similar provisions can be found in other instruments such as the Convention and the OECD Model TIEA.

Table 5.1. **Kinds of agreements providing for EOIR**

Bilateral Instruments
OECD Tax Model (article 26)
OECD's model agreement on EOI for tax matters (TIEA)
Tax treaties not based on the OECD model
Multilateral Instruments
The Convention on Mutual Administrative Assistance in Tax Matters (The Convention)
Other Multilateral Agreements (e.g. Multilateral TIEA)
EU Council Directive 2011/16

The development of the network of EOIR agreements

There has been a substantial increase in the number of agreements facilitating EOIR worldwide in the period since the 2009 G20 declaration. Figure 5.2 shows the development of the network of relationships for EOIR over this period. The panel (a) shows the network of information exchange relationships in 2009 amongst OECD and G20 countries. Blue areas have active EOIR relationships, grey areas do not. It is clear from the first figure that many gaps existed in the network of EOIR relationships amongst OECD and G20 countries in 2009.

Panel (b) of Figure 5.2 shows the position of information exchange relationships in 2018. Here it can be seen that all OECD/G20 countries now participate in EOIR with each other. In large part, this change has come about not through increased numbers of bilateral relationships, but rather due to an increase in the number of countries that have signed the Convention.

Figure 5.3 shows a similar picture to Figure 5.2, but shows the network of EOIR relationships between OECD/G20 countries and a set of International Financial Centres (IFCs).[6] It can immediately be seen from panel (a) that the network of EOIR relationships was far less comprehensive than was the case amongst the OECD/G20 countries in 2009.

Figure 5.2. **The EOIR Network among OECD/G20 Countries, 2009 and 2018**

(a) 2009

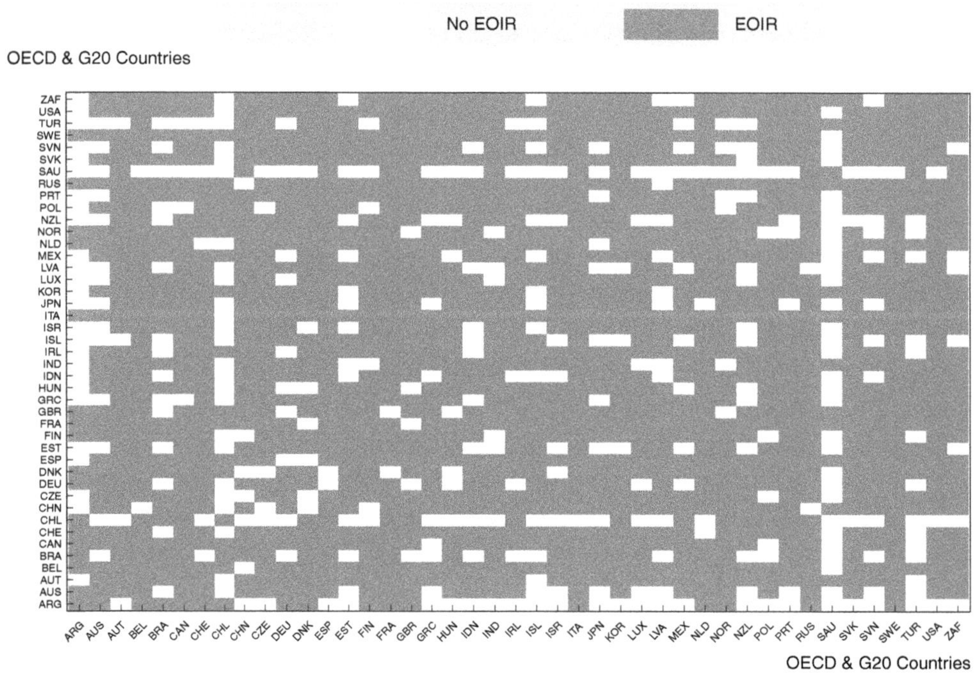

(b) 2018

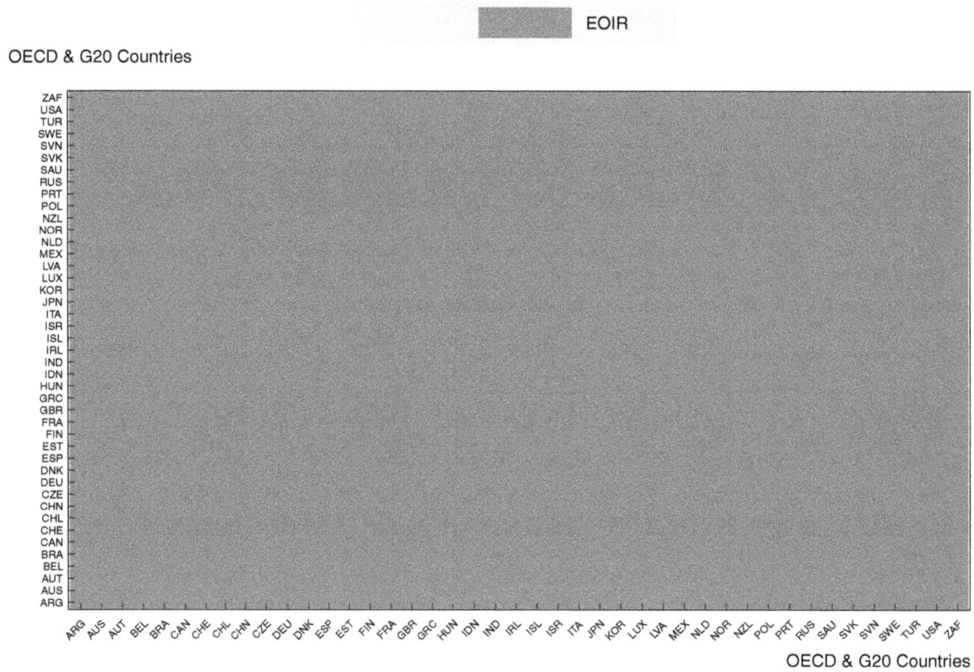

Note: This graph includes EOIR relationships that may not meet Global Forum standards. Agreements are shown based on the earliest date of signature, ratification, or entry into force that is available from the Global Forum.

StatLink *http://dx.doi.org/10.1787/888933661647*

Figure 5.3. **The EOIR Network between OECD/G20 and OFCs, 2009 and 2018**

(a) 2009

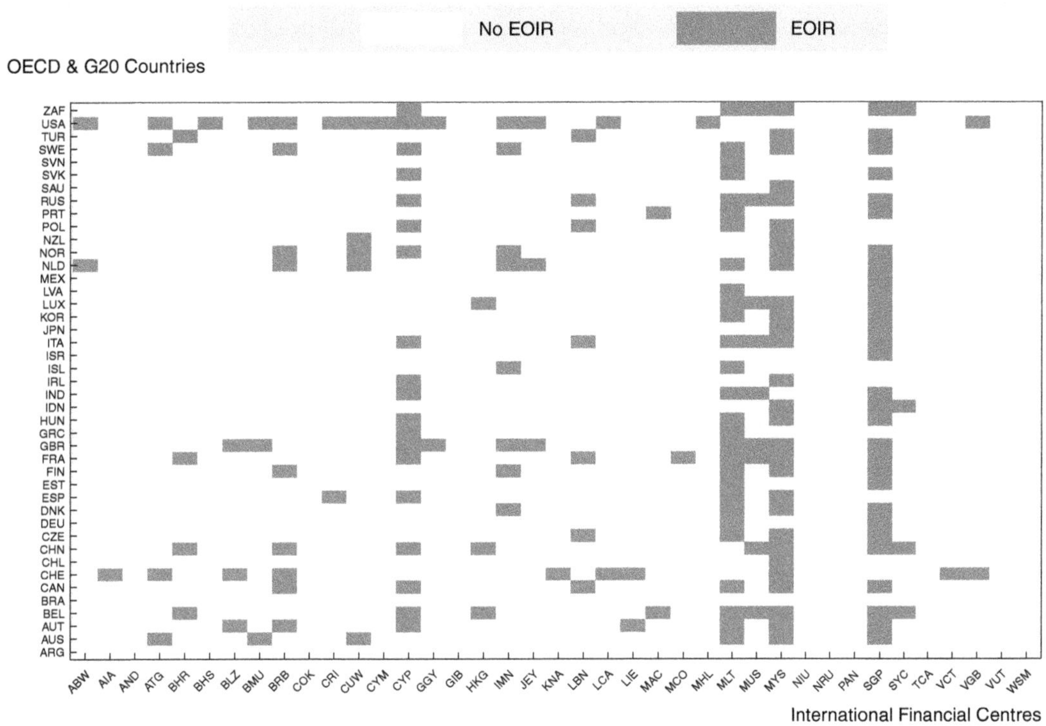

(b) 2018

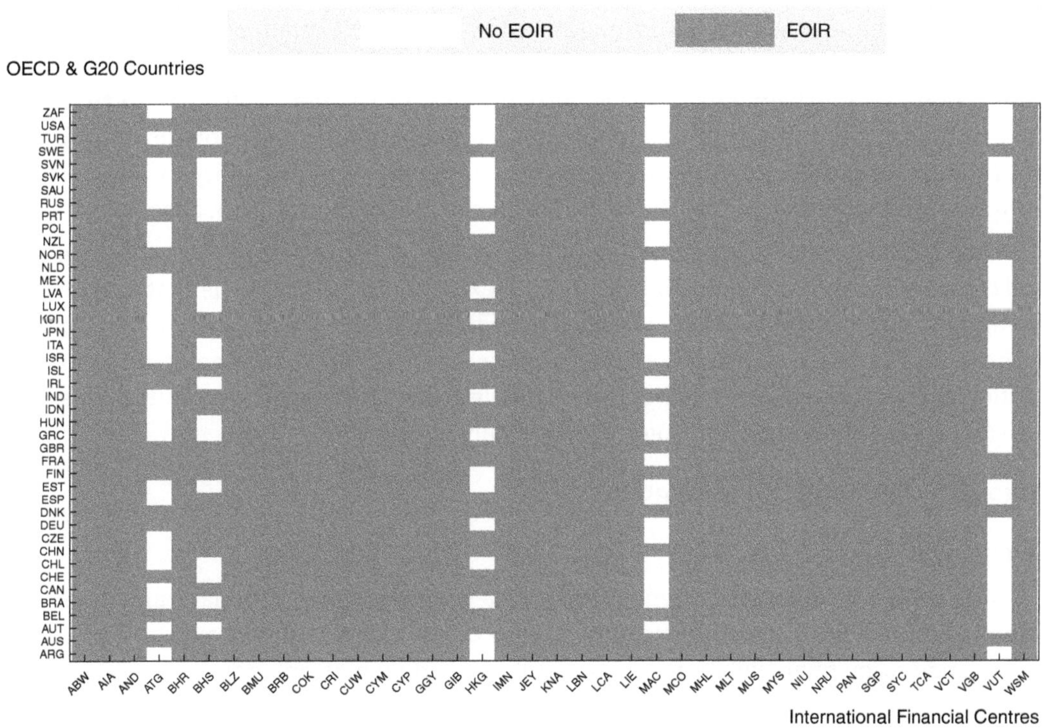

Note: This graph includes EOIR relationships that may not meet Global Forum standards. Agreements are shown based on the earliest date of signature, ratification, or entry into force that is available from the Global Forum. Data on International Financial Centres are based on IMF (2004).

StatLink http://dx.doi.org/10.1787/888933661666

EOIR peer review process

The Global Forum seeks to ensure that its members fully implement the international standards of transparency on EOIR and AEOI through in-depth peer review and monitoring processes. The peer reviews of EOIR, which have taken place since 2009, involve a two-phase process under which an assessment team made up of peers and a member of the Global Forum Secretariat analyses the compliance of jurisdictions with the international standard of EOIR. The reviews are then adopted by the Global Forum's Peer Review group before being adopted by all members of the Global Forum operating on an equal footing. Phase one reviews cover the legal and regulatory framework, while phase two looks into the implementation of the framework in practice. At the end of the process, each jurisdiction receives an overall rating of compliance, consisting of either: compliant, largely compliant, partially compliant, or non-compliant. A first cycle of EOIR reviews took place from 2010 until 2016.

The second round of EOIR reviews will assess both the legal and regulatory framework as well as the working of the standard in practice (i.e. the two phases of the reviews have been combined). This round has already been launched with the first ten reports being published in August 2017. This round is scheduled to run from 2016 until 2020 and reviews will be carried out against an enhanced EOIR standard which now includes requirements relating to the access to and exchange of beneficial ownership information (OECD, 2016). The ultimate goal of these reviews is to ensure jurisdictions effectively implement the international EOIR standard (OECD, 2016).

The peer-review process focuses on three main aspects: first, availability of information; second, access to information; and third, exchange of information. For EOIR to be effective, each jurisdiction must make sure that information (ownership information of legal entities and arrangements, accounting information and banking information) should be available and accessible to its competent authority.[7] Finally, each jurisdiction should have appropriate international EOI instruments in place with all relevant partners. Information that is not available or cannot be accessed cannot be exchanged. Even if a jurisdiction never exchanges information, implementing the Global Forum's standards on availability of and access to information is vital to ensuring that it can protect its own domestic tax base.[8]

The standard on EOIR provides for the exchange of foreseeably relevant information and does not allow for the possibility of "fishing expeditions". This means that a jurisdiction looking for information must know which jurisdiction to ask for the information, provide sufficient information to identify the tax payer(s) and establish foreseeable relevance to a particular tax investigation. Furthermore, knowledge of the financial institution in a given jurisdiction that holds the information is typically required.

Automatic Exchange of Information

Overview

The OECD and G20 have also more recently developed an international standard on AEOI relating to financial accounts (consisting largely of the CRS which sets out the information to be reported by financial institutions and the due diligence obligations to ensure those financial institutions properly identify RFAs). This allows for international tax co-operation beyond what was possible under the EOIR. Based on an automatic and standardised methodology explained further below, AEOI provides for jurisdictions to periodically and automatically exchange information and obtain data about tax residents with financial assets abroad. Instead of jurisdictions requesting information on specific details about a specific taxpayer or establishing foreseeable relevance to a specific ongoing case, the scope and content of the information exchange is agreed in advance and the information is automatically exchanged each year. By the end of 2017, 49 member jurisdictions should have commenced exchanging information automatically under the CRS. A further 53 jurisdictions are due to commence in 2018.

A variety of mechanisms exist enabling AEOI between jurisdictions. As with EOIR, these can be either bilateral (e.g. a bilateral TIEA or a DTC) or multilateral (e.g. the Convention) (see Figure 5.4).[9] The kinds of international agreements that can allow for AEOI are outlined in Table 5.2. Most AEOI takes place under the Convention, but other forms also exist.

Table 5.2. **Primary Authoritative Sources – Agreements providing for AEOI**

Bilateral Instruments
Foreign account tax compliance act intergovernmental agreement (FATCA IGA)
OECD Tax Model (article 26)
OECD's model agreement on EOI for tax matters (TIEA)
Tax treaties not based on the OECD model (e.g. UN Tax Model Article 26)
Multilateral Instruments
Multilateral Instruments
The Convention on Mutual Administrative Assistance in Tax Matters (The Convention)
Other Multilateral Agreements (e.g. Multilateral TIEA)
EU Directive 2011/2016

Figure 5.4. **International Instruments for EOI**

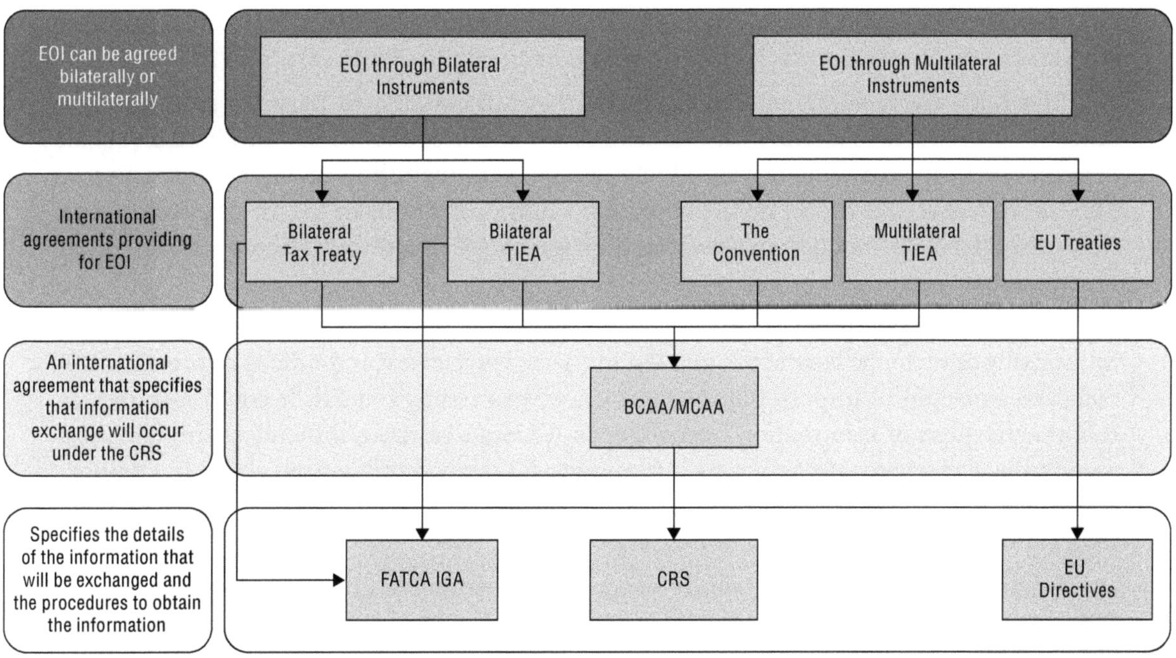

Note: This chart only refers to forms of EOI that pertain to personal taxation. Other forms of information exchange such as country by country reporting may also exist. Abbreviations are as follows: FATCA IGA: Foreign Account Tax Compliance Act Intergovernmental Agreement; TIEA: OECD Model Agreement on Exchange of Information on Tax Matters; The Convention: The Convention on Mutual Administrative Assistance in Tax Matters; MCAA: The Model Competent Authority Agreement that specifies that information will be exchanged under the CRS which can be bilateral (BCAA) or multilateral (MCAA); CRS: The Common Reporting Standard.

Other forms of AEOI

Under the auspices of the European Union, AEOI has also been taking place since the early 2000s. In 2003, under the EU Savings Directive, Member States agreed to exchange information on interest payments derived from savings schemes (EU Council Directive 2003/48/EU).[10] In 2011, under the Directive on Enhanced Administrative Co-operation in the Field of (Direct) Taxation, Member States agreed to EOIR, AEOI (later including the international AEOI Standard), spontaneous EOI and participation in administrative inquiries (EU Council Directive 2011/16/EU).[11]

Other initiatives have also been implemented allowing for AEOI. In 2010, the United States enacted the Foreign Account Tax Compliance Act (FATCA) requiring foreign financial institutions to perform specified due diligence procedures to identify and report information on foreign assets held by United States account holders, or be subject to a withholding tax of 30% of the gross amount of certain payments made from the United States to these institutions. Many countries and jurisdictions have implemented FATCA by entering into intergovernmental agreements (referred to as FATCA Intergovernmental Agreements, or IGAs) with the United States offering a bilateral approach to FATCA implementation under which the United States also provides certain (albeit more limited) information in return (OECD, 2014).[12]

A variety of legal means, therefore, exist to facilitate AEOI and many countries have engaged in AEOI with each other for a relatively long period of time. However, a key challenge has been standardising the information exchange across jurisdictions. In 2014 the OECD finalised the AEOI Standard for the automatic exchange of financial account information, developed in close co-operation with the G20, the EU and other stakeholders. This standard builds on the FATCA IGA to maximise efficiency and minimise costs. It is now a new global standard on tax transparency, having been endorsed by the Global Forum in 2014.

The AEOI framework requires Financial Institutions (FIs) to perform specified due diligence procedures to identify the financial assets and accounts which they hold on behalf of taxpayers from jurisdictions with which their tax administration exchanges information. The FIs are required to report information to tax administrations in the jurisdictions where they are located. The tax administrations then exchange that information with each other on an annual basis.

The CRS is seen as an effective way to tackle tax evasion and bank secrecy while minimising costs for governments and FIs. In the absence of a standardised approach, AEOI could be expected to impose higher costs on governments and FIs. It could also reduce the effectiveness of information exchange, as it would be more difficult to implement a standardised method of utilising the information for tax compliance purposes. In addition, the absence of a standard may create uncertainty among interested stakeholders on what information should be collected or exchanged.

International instruments require a separate agreement to operationalise AEOI. This is the case due to the fact that most international instruments, either bilateral or multilateral, only include a general provision enabling governments to exchange information without providing details on how the exchange will take place and exactly what information will be exchanged. In other words, signing the Convention or the TIEA does not allow for AEOI to take place by itself. Governments must agree on the distinctive features of the exchange through a separate agreement, such as the details as to what exactly is to be exchanged and the form in which the AEOI will take place. An example of such an agreement is the Multilateral Competent Authority Agreement on Automatic Exchange of Financial Account Information (CRS MCAA).[13] The CRS MCAA includes the specific details of the information that will be exchanged between countries, and provides details on how the AEOI can happen. In other words, the CRS MCAA activates and operationalises the AEOI between jurisdictions by referring them to the CRS. To date 97 jurisdictions have signed the MCAA to implement AEOI.[14]

The implementation of AEOI in detail

The network of AEOI relationships amongst OECD/G20 has also expanded substantially in recent years. Most AEOI relationships between OECD/G20 countries and IFCs exist under the CRS, though there are also other AEOI relationships in the form of FACTA IGAs. While many countries began exchanging in 2017, a further large part of the expansion of AEOI will only commence by September 2018. The network will continue to expand in 2019 and 2020.

The implementation of AEOI requires a series of steps and agreements to ensure that the nature of information exchange and the means by which it is exchanged are consistent across all countries. This requires: rules on the collection and reporting of financial information by FIs; IT and administrative capabilities in order to receive and exchange the information; a legal instrument providing for information exchange between the jurisdictions; and measures to ensure the standards of confidentiality and data safeguards are met. The AEOI Standard therefore incorporates requirements in relation to each of these areas.

In 2014 the Global Forum adopted the AEOI Standard and put in place a commitment process to ensure its rapid implementation to create a level playing field. Following this commitment process more than 100 jurisdictions including almost all financial centres have committed to implement the CRS with exchanges starting in 2017 or 2018. To ensure completeness in coverage, the commitment includes a commitment to exchange information with "all interested appropriate partners", which are all those partners wishing to receive information and which meet the expected standards on the confidentiality and proper use of the data. The Global Forum is now monitoring, assessing and assisting in the delivery of the commitments.

For AEOI to be effective there are four core requirements that must be met. These are:

- Translating the due diligence and reporting rules into domestic law; as discussed, the detailed due diligence and reporting rules contained in the CRS must be translated into domestic law to ensure FIs perform the due diligence procedures and obtain and report the required information;
- Selecting a legal basis for the AEOI to take place; countries will need to agree with other countries on the international instrument (bilateral or multilateral) under which the EOI will take place – in practice almost all jurisdictions have favoured the multilateral approach;
- Putting in place IT and administrative infrastructure and resources; and
- Protecting confidentiality and safeguarding data to guarantee that all collected and exchanged information will be kept confidential and that there are proper remedies that will be implemented in case of a breach.

Non-fulfilment of any of the requirements makes it impossible for AEOI under the CRS to take place.

Overview of the CRS

The CRS is the main part of the AEOI Standard as it contains the detailed rules and procedures that FIs must follow to ensure the relevant information is collected and reported. It provides for a standard on the due diligence procedures needed to identify who is a reportable person (RP), what are reportable financial accounts (RFAs), and what information needs to be reported. As has been mentioned, the benefit of adopting a common approach is to tackle tax evasion and bank secrecy with greater efficiency while minimising costs for governments and FIs.

Only Reporting Financial Institutions (RFIs) are required to perform the due diligence procedures outlined in the CRS. That is, only RFIs are required to report information in relation to certain individuals and entities to tax authorities if those individuals or entities hold a financial account with the RFI. The CRS defines RFIs as FIs located in a participating jurisdiction. The term FI includes depository institutions, custodial institutions, investment entities and specified insurance companies (see Annex C for more details).

Only entities can be considered RFIs.[15] In other words, individuals directly engaging in any of the activities described above are not considered entities. Only entities can be considered to be FIs, and only those located in participating jurisdictions, may be a RFI provided they are not specifically exempted.

Some FIs are specifically excluded from these requirements because they pose a low risk of being used to evade taxes. The CRS includes a list of FIs that are specifically excluded. The list includes certain governmental entities, international organisations or central banks, broad and narrow participation retirement funds, pension funds of a governmental entity, qualified credit card issuers, exempt collective investment vehicles, certain trusts, and any other entity that presents a low risk of being used to evade taxes in the view of the signatory jurisdiction (see Annex C for further details).

RFIs must review the financial accounts they maintain to determine whether they are RFAs or not. A reportable account means an account maintained by FIs, and includes a depository account, a custodial account, equity and debt interests in certain investment entities, cash value insurance contracts, and annuity contracts (see Annex C for further details). The CRS specifically excludes certain retirement and pension accounts, non-retirement tax-favoured accounts, term life insurance contracts, estate accounts, escrow accounts, depository accounts due to unreturned overpayments, accounts established by court orders, accounts created for the sale, exchange or lease of real or personal property, and other low-risk accounts (see Annex C for further details). For financial accounts to be reportable accounts, they must be held by RPs.

1. Only information about RFAs held by RPs will be subject to AEOI. Therefore, RFIs must identify whether the account holder is a RP. According to the CRS, a RP is any account holder who is a tax resident in a participating jurisdiction with which the jurisdiction where the RFA is located is exchanging information under the AEOI Standard. The following account holders, however, are not considered RPs:
2. A corporation, the stock of which is regularly traded on one or more established securities markets, and any corporation that is related to this entity;
3. A governmental entity;
4. An international organisation;
5. A central bank,
6. A financial institution.

Table 5.3 lists the asset types that will be covered by the CRS.

Implementation of EOI

Exchange of information represents a "step-change" in transparency in the international tax environment, first with more widespread EOIR and then more recently with AEOI. As discussed above, the development of EOI, and in particular the advent of the CRS as a means to standardise EOI, is a significant new tool in the fight against tax evasion.[16] However, continued efforts are required to ensure that the implementation of the CRS is as effective as possible. This section discusses these challenges and the efforts of the Global Forum and the OECD in this regard.

Administrative capacity

Collecting CRS information from FIs and exchanging it with participating tax administrations is only part of the implementation challenge. And while the deterrent effect in relation to the move to AEOI may be substantial, tax administrations also need to develop the capacity to use the information received in an efficient way to combat tax evasion. In this regard, work is ongoing within the Forum on Tax Administration to share knowledge and experience amongst tax administrations (see, for example, OECD (2016)) and the Global Forum is providing associated technical assistance.

Table 5.3. **Asset types that will be covered by EOIR/AEOI**

Type of Asset	Comments
Bank Deposits	Information will be exchanged as regards of commercial accounts, checking accounts, and, savings accounts.
Bonds	An entity that owns bonds for the account of others is considered a custodial institution and thus, a reporting financial institution.
Equities (shares)	An entity that holds shares of stock in a corporation or partnership for the account of others is considered a custodial institution and thus, a reporting financial institution.
Interests in investment entities (including collective investment vehicles)	Entities that primarily conduct as a business investment activities or operations on behalf of other persons, and those that are managed by other financial institutions are considered investment entities and thus are potentially reporting financial institutions. Any debt or equity interest an individual or entity has in one of these vehicles may need to be reported.
Cash-value insurance contracts.	Information will be exchanged as regards cash value insurance contracts. These are insurance contracts that have a cash value. The term "cash value" is defined by the CRS as the greater of the amount that the policy holder is entitled to receive upon surrender or termination of the contract, and the amount the policyholder can borrow under or with regards to the contract.

Non-participating jurisdictions

Countries and jurisdictions not yet committed to exchanging information automatically under the CRS or any other standards will neither collect nor share any financial information as part of AEOI process. It is crucial that as many relevant jurisdictions as possible commit to AEOI to achieve effective EOI coverage and optimal international tax transparency. To address this, through the Global Forum members can identify "jurisdictions of relevance" for tax transparency. On identification by the Global Forum as a jurisdiction of relevance, countries can be asked to be members of the Global Forum or peer reviewed in absentia. Empirical evidence of the importance of the coverage of the EOI network is outlined in Section 5.4 below.

Non-reportable persons, accounts and assets

The potential for lack of coverage of non-reportable persons may generate challenges for the effective implementation of EOI. Only financial accounts held by RPs at a reporting financial institution will be reported under the CRS. In legal terms, a RP is any person (whether an individual, entity or legal arrangement) who is a tax resident in a reportable jurisdiction. However in some instances it may be challenging to ensure that the person who is in fact the beneficial owner of certain assets is identified. However, the current round of peer reviews with respect to EOIR now includes requirements relating to the access to and exchange of beneficial ownership information (OECD, 2016) and the future peer reviews in relation to AEOI will also need to incorporate these aspects.

Taxpayers may respond to more effective taxation of an asset by shifting savings to other forms of assets. Under the CRS, most financial accounts maintained by a financial institution are reportable (see Section 5.3). However, the CRS was always designed to focus on financial accounts, which is a particularly high-risk area. This therefore excludes a variety of kinds of assets which may include real assets as well as certain kinds of accounts that are non-reportable accounts. Example of real assets that are not currently reportable include:

- Jewellery, art, cars and horses, although establishing effective AEOI over some of these assets might face additional challenges due to the difficulties in valuing and taxing these items, although EOIR regarding these assets is covered under the EOIR standard.
- The direct ownership of commodities such as gold and silver, or less long-lasting ones such as rubber, live cattle and wheat, etc.
- Real immovable property.

Continued vigilance will be required to ensure that these assets do not become an obstacle to effective international tax transparency as taxpayers may shift their assets held in financial products to these other types of assets.

In addition to some forms of assets that are not covered under the CRS, some financial accounts are also specifically treated as low risk accounts and excluded from reporting by the CRS. These include certain retirement and pension accounts, non-retirement tax-favoured accounts, term life insurance contracts, estate accounts, escrow accounts, depository accounts due to non-returned overpayments, accounts established by court orders, accounts created for the sale, exchange or lease of real or personal property, and other low-risk accounts (see Annex C for further details).

The Global Forum is reviewing all non-reportable accounts to make sure they are low risk. Jurisdictions themselves are also required to monitor low risk accounts to ensure they remain low risk. In addition, any scheme found to be used to hinder effective EOI can be disclosed through the CRS disclosure facility. This will allow these schemes to be systematically analysed by the OECD with a view to assessing the risk they present to the overall integrity and effectiveness of the CRS and to reach an agreement on appropriate courses of action (see Box 5.1).

Ensuring effective implementation

In order to maximise the effectiveness of the AEOI Standard and minimise the implementation challenges the Global Forum is responsible for monitoring the effective implementation of the AEOI Standard and ensuring any failings are addressed in order to deliver a level-playing field. This includes all aspects of AEOI implementation. Almost all jurisdictions have already been assessed in relation to the confidentiality and data safeguard standards they apply and the Global Forum is part-way through assessing the domestic legislative provisions implementing the AEOI Standard in each jurisdiction to ensure they properly reflect the detailed rules in the CRS and the associated Commentaries. There is also a process in place to identify and address any gaps in international exchange networks. A Common Transmission System has also been put in place to overcome some of the operational challenges and extensive technical assistance is being provided as necessary.

Given that exchanges have only just commenced amongst a subset of the jurisdictions it is not possible to assess effectiveness in implementation at this stage, although the Global Forum is currently developing a detailed framework for the peer reviews of the implementation of the AEOI Standard which are due to commence in 2019-2020. A major component of this will be ensuring FIs comply with their obligations under the AEOI Standard. The next important step will be the development of a robust Terms of Reference and methodology for the peer reviews of the effectiveness of the implementation of the AEOI Standard to ensure the AEOI Standard works as intended as a tool to tackle tax evasion.

Box 5.1. **CRS Disclosure Facility**

The CRS was designed with a broad scope in terms of the financial information to be reported, the Account Holders subject to reporting and the FIs required to report, in order to limit the opportunities for taxpayers to circumvent reporting. It also requires that jurisdictions, as part of their effective implementation of the Standard, put in place anti-abuse rules to prevent any practices intended to circumvent the reporting and due diligence procedures.

On 5 May 2017, the OECD launched a public disclosure facility for information on schemes designed to circumvent the application of the CRS.[1] This online facility provides practitioners, financial advisers, and civil society with the means to disclose schemes that purport to circumvent the application of the CRS. Those with knowledge of such schemes are strongly encouraged to come forward and make use of this facility, including on an anonymous basis.

Using the Common Reporting Standard Disclosure Facility, interested parties are invited to describe the identified loophole, scheme, product, or arrangement that may be used for circumventing the CRS, and to provide as much supporting information as possible. Those who come forward are also allowed, if desired, to specify the countries or regions in which the scheme is being used, and to share any publicly available documents in which the scheme/product/arrangement is described/promoted.

1. The facility can be accessed through the Automatic Exchange Portal in the following link: *https://survey.oecd.org/Survey.aspx?s=9b9dbd31c73e4b888753a8de3d222214&&forceNew=true&test=true*

Source: OECD (2017c), *The fight against offshore tax evasion continues: CRS disclosure facility delivers first results, http://www.oecd.org/tax/the-fight-against-offshore-tax-evasion-continues-crs-disclosure-facility-delivers-first-results.htm.*

5.4. The impacts of tax transparency

There have been substantial changes in the EOI environment over recent years. This means that a key policy question becomes how taxpayers will respond to these changes? Assessing what the taxation of foreign source income will look like is subject to considerable uncertainty. This section provides some preliminary evidence that EOI results in a reduction in incentives to hold wealth offshore. This section also identifies some of the potential limitations of current approaches to assessing the impact of more effective EOI.

Offshore wealth and the international capital environment have been a source of increased public debate in recent years. As a consequence, there is a small but expanding amount of empirical literature on this subject. This section will concentrate on those studies that specifically attempt to assess the impact of international information exchange on tax compliance and collections. There are, however, a wide variety of other papers attempting to characterise the size of hidden wealth as well as to assess taxpayer responses to international tax and to other international tax policies such as withholding taxes and blacklisting.

Efforts to evaluate the effectiveness of EOI rely on estimating the size of tax evasion in the first place, which by its nature is challenging and subject to significant uncertainty. For this reason many studies in this area do not focus on estimating the impact of EOI on tax evasion (which is difficult to estimate), but rather focus on a proxy for tax evasion: e.g. financial investments and bank liabilities in international financial centres. The assessment of the impact of EOI is uncertain, in part, because there are many reasons apart from tax evasion that may explain why assets may be held in foreign jurisdictions. Moreover, what constitutes an international financial centre is itself difficult to define. Much more research in this area is needed to effectively estimate the impact of EOI on international tax evasion and to develop tax policy recommendations for the future. In addition, because this literature is growing quickly, some of the papers cited in this section are unpublished. For all these reasons, the estimates cited in this section should be interpreted with caution.

Huizinga and Nicodème (2004) wrote one of the first papers to analyse the impact of information exchange. This paper uses data on bank liabilities from the Bank for International Settlements (BIS) to investigate the tax and non-tax factors that impact the holdings of bank liabilities by non-residents in a sample of 25 countries ending in 1999 (the year the Global Forum was set up). While they analyse a wide variety of explanatory variables from typical gravity models of trade and investment, the tax factors they investigate include withholding taxes and wealth taxes. They also examine whether international EOI impacts bank liabilities, although they do not make a distinction in their analysis between EOIR and AEOI. Most of the effects in the study likely stem from the impacts of EOIR, as the network of AEOI agreements was very limited at the time.

They find that information exchange has little impact on deposit holdings. However, their paper is hampered by two factors. First, while the paper relies on a time-series of data regarding bank liabilities, only one year of data is available on the information exchange network. This means that when analysing the impact of information exchange, it is not possible to control for country-specific factors such as withholding tax rates or GDP. Moreover, the information exchange data are for 1999. Out of 288 potential country-pair information exchange relationships in their dataset, only 67 entries show the presence of international information exchange. One-way exchanges are reciprocated in only 30 cases. As highlighted in Section 5.3, information exchange networks have expanded substantially since then following the G20's call for an end to bank secrecy and the creation of the Global Forum to ensure the effective implementation of EOI worldwide. Moreover, as there was very little AEOI in 1999 it is difficult for the analysis to distinguish between the impact of EOIR and AEOI.

Huizinga and Nicodème argue that the limited impact of information exchange on bank liabilities in their sample could be a result of "the haphazard pattern of international information exchange at present". They also suggest that "for [information exchange] to become more effective, the quality of the information exchanged may need to be improved, for instance through the adoption of a common protocol regarding tax identification numbers. Also, the international exchange of information has to cover most industrialized countries and other financial centres to be truly effective." These two goals have largely been accomplished by the advent of the CRS and the work of the Global Forum in recent years.

Johannesen and Zucman (2014) study an expanded dataset from the BIS. This study incorporates data on foreign bank liabilities in 41 countries, and the time series runs from the fourth quarter of 2003 to the second quarter of 2011. This is a substantially larger dataset than Huizinga and Nicodème. Unlike Huizinga and Nicodème, they use a time-series dataset of EOI treaties which allows them to analyse the impact of the development of the EOI network over time, controlling for country-pair fixed effects, as well as time fixed effects. This can facilitate controls for events such as the financial crisis that impact bank liabilities in many countries at the same time.

Unlike the Huizinga and Nicodème paper, the Johannesen and Zucman study examines EOIR specifically. They suggest that EOIR does reduce bank liabilities in IFCs, by between 11% and 16% depending on the analytical specification. However, Johannesen and Zucman suggest that EOIR does not result in repatriation of foreign wealth to taxpayers' countries of residence. They suggest that assets are shifted from country to country in response to the expansion of the EOIR network. This finding is based on the fact that in their estimation total global liabilities in IFCs have not fallen over the period they study. They argue that the lack of repatriation is evidence that tax is still being evaded on foreign wealth (though foreign wealth could remain in a foreign jurisdiction after having been declared to tax authorities). Based on this, these authors argue that "the G20 tax crackdown" had been ineffective.[17] Although their data captures time series variation in EOI, in contrast to that of Huizinga and Nicodème, these authors do not analyse: (1) the impact of the expansion of the EOIR network after 2011; (2) the continued impact of the Global Forum's peer review process which was a key driver in the increasing EOI networks; or (3) the widespread introduction of AEOI which began in 2017. This is because BIS data for this period was not available at that time.

Like Huizinga and Nicodème, Johannesen and Zucman highlight the fact that the EOI network is incomplete. They suggest that this means that when any given IFC signs and EOI agreement, tax evaders simply transfer funds from that jurisdiction to another jurisdiction that has not signed an EOI agreement. They say that "[a] comprehensive multilateral agreement would prevent tax evaders from transferring their funds from haven to haven", alhough they also suggest that "even in the presence of a complete network of EOIR treaties, there may remain scope for improved tax collection by making treaties more demanding."

In an unpublished paper, Gorea (2017) assesses the impact of tax treaties using equity and debt holdings of United States residents only.[18] He uses data from 2002 to 2013, with the sample size of 43 IFCs. He finds that tax treaty signature has no effect on inflows in the sample. He does, however, find that treaty signature has a statistically significant positive impact on flows to IFCs that have not signed treaties with the United States. He supports the argument in Johannesen and Zucman that EOIR signature results in asset-shifting, and this highlights the importance of a securing a comprehensive network of agreements. He also finds larger effects for treaties that override bank secrecy laws; suggesting that this aspect of the development of EOI is an important factor in successful implementation.

The Gorea paper is different from both the Huizinga and Nicodème and Johannesen and Zucman papers in that he focuses on overall portfolio investment and not simply on bank liabilities. This means that he accounts for forms of tax evasion that may not be mediated through banks (for example investment in companies that hold immovable property). Like the Huizinga and Nicodème and Johannesen and Zucman papers, the analysis focuses on

EOIR and not on AEOI – it does not account for the presence or absence of FATCA IGAs. The paper attempts to separately assess the impact of treaties that override bank secrecy provisions and those that do not. This highlights the importance of overriding bank secrecy in ensuring the EOIR instruments are as effective as possible.

Gorea focuses only on the impact of tax treaties on investment flows from the United States to IFCs. This means that he may miss a large amount of cross-national variation available with a larger data sample. He suggests that the incomplete nature of the United States tax treaty network could be a source of the statistically insignificant impact of tax treaties on investment flows, writing that rather than repatriating funds, investors simply choose to "relocate funds to other tax havens". He also argues that "this study provides empirical support for the theory that ... a multilateral treaty would have much greater effect on curtailing tax evasion, because it would limit asset relocations to jurisdictions with fewer information exchange agreements".

In another unpublished paper, Omartian (2016) analyses the impact of signature of TIEA and commitment to implement the CRS on incorporation of companies in IFCs by foreign residents. His data sources include files released as part of the Panama Papers leak. He notes a decline in incorporation activity of the clients of the Panamanian law firm Mossack Fonseca in the years from 2012 to 2015. He also notes an increase in the terminations (i.e. liquidations and dissolutions) of companies held by Mossack Fonseca clients over this period, and that "terminations ... accelerate at the tail end of the sample, eclipsing incorporations in 2014." He suggests that the terminiations are evidence of the impact of EOI.

Analysing the impact of TIEA signature, he finds that "the number of incorporations per month for an investor country-jurisdiction pair falls roughly 12%" in the aftermath of a TIEA signature. When analysing the effects of the CRS on incorporation activity, he finds that incorporation activity occurring from investors in a country that publicly commited to exchange information fell by roughly 6 percentage points after the commitment.

Overall, the Omartian paper finds that commitments to the CRS and having TIEAs in place did have negative impacts on incorporations facilitated by Mossack Fonseca. However, it may not be the case that all of these incorporations were for the purpose of tax evasion, or that reducing incorporation levels are a good indicator of the EOI successfully tackling tax evasion and allowing for better taxation at the residence level. Nor does the paper assign a nominal figure to the tax revenue impact of the EOI. It is, however, one of the first papers to analyse the impact of commitments to the CRS, as opposed to information exchange efforts more broadly. He does not, however, test the impact of the implementation of the CRS itself, as the first exchanges under the CRS did not take place until September 2017.

A recently produced (and also unpublished) paper, Menkhoff and Miethe (2017), also considers these issues with new data. They use an expanded set of bilateral BIS data relative to the dataset used by Huizinga and Nicodème and by Johannesen and Zucman. This dataset contains data from 46 countries between 2003 to 2016. These authors use a more up-to-date set of EOI agreements than Johannsen and Zucman, and find a larger impact of EOIR agreements, which are found to reduce liabilities held by non-IFC residents in IFCs by 36%. This contrasts to the 11-16% found by Johannsen and Zucman.

In addition, Menkhoff and Miethe not only analyse inflows to IFCs but also outflows from these centres, based on the argument that investments in IFCs are subsequently "round-tripped" to other investment locations (Hanlon, Maydew, and Thornock, 2015). They find that EOI signature also reduces outflows from IFCs to non-IFCs in addition to inflows to IFCs from non-IFCs.

Overall, the literature provides suggestive evidence that EOI can be effective in reducing tax evasion through offshore locations. However, the literature is hampered by lack of data on offshore activity which is difficult to measure. The literature also provides evidence of factors that may limit the effectiveness of EOI. Huizinga and Nicodème suggest that EOI in 1999 has limited effects on bank liabilities due to the relatively incomplete nature of the EOI network at that time. Johannesen and Zucman find that EOIR is effective, but only in terms of reducing bank liabilities bilaterally, not in terms of reducing offshore bank liabilities overall. This highlights the extent to which early EOI efforts have been hampered by their patchwork nature. Given that the EOI network is continuing to expand, it is therefore likely that the impact of EOI has strengthened as the network has continued to expand. To assess this, it is important that the impact of EOIR and AEOI be regularly evaluated.

5.5. The implications of the expansion of EOI

In the last decade international progress in the field of tax transparency and EOI for tax purposes has been unprecedented. Co-operation between tax authorities has rapidly expanded and jurisdictions have been able to increase the effectiveness with which they tax their residents, especially on income resulting from assets held offshore.

Forecasting the impact of the expansion of the EOI network and the introduction of the CRS is challenging, in part because of the complex nature of estimating the size of global tax evasion to begin with (see for example, Pellegrini et. al. (2016) and Zucman (2013)). Existing studies suggest that EOI does reduce offshore liabilities, which means that it should enable more effective residence-based taxation.

It is also clear that the CRS substantially increases the chances of tax evasion being detected by authorities, which increases the risks that individuals engaging in tax evasion will be subjected to serious penalties and even possible prosecution. It also raises the legal, accounting and administrative costs of those wishing to persist with tax evasion. It does so by increasing the complexity of the schemes required to attempt to circumvent the CRS, and by increasing the likelihood that such attempts will fail. There is evidence to suggest that these increased costs can have a positive impact on compliance, as taxpayers tend to respond by reducing evasion and avoidance (Slemrod and Yitzhaki, 2002).

Many taxpayers will change their behaviour as the costs of attempting to continue to evade taxes become even higher and the risks of detection also increase. In addition, as most participating jurisdictions have put in place voluntary-disclosure programs, taxpayers have been provided with a strong incentive to come forward and start reporting their assets. Indeed, the evidence suggests that many have already done so: the most recent data suggest that countries have already received close to EUR 80 billion in unplanned additional revenue as a result of voluntary disclosure programmes and other similar initiatives in the lead-up to the first exchanges under the CRS (OECD, 2017b). Such voluntary disclosure programs are an integral part of a strategy to strengthen residence based taxation.

However, some taxpayers may accept a higher degree of risk as they assess the risks of their tax evasion activities becoming detected. In cases where the costs of implementing arrangements to remain outside the scope of the CRS/AEOI are lower than the taxes they would otherwise be liable to pay and where the complexity of the legal and administrative arrangements necessary to evade the tax are relatively small given the tax savings, taxpayers will have incentives to use mechanisms that ensure they remain outside the scope of AEOI.

As the costs and complexity associated with implementing arrangements to circumvent the CRS increase, it is likely that only those individuals that have the largest amounts of potential tax liability at stake and those that have a very high appetite for risk will be prepared to continue to arrange their affairs in ways that may conceal their assets with a view towards evading taxes.

The effectiveness of the CRS as a tool to enable more efficient taxation of capital income and assets will be limited by the extent to which taxpayers can and are willing to shift holdings of income and wealth to asset classes not covered by the CRS. Direct investment in real property is one such class. While, it may be possible that non-financial assets could be brought under the scope of an expanded AEOI standard at some future point, it should be noted that real-estate investments would still be subject to property taxes in the jurisdictions where the property is located. This raises the issue of the taxation of property covered elsewhere in this study, particularly given the relatively benign impacts of property taxation on economic growth (OECD, 2010).

Seminal papers in taxation have argued that the efficiency consequences of income taxation can be measured through the summary statistic of the elasticity of taxable income (Feldstein, 1999). If taxable income falls too much in response to taxation, then taxation becomes more costly. In respect of taxation of foreign source income and taxation on a residence basis, this elasticity has been high for many years. However, the core impact of the CRS from an economic perspective is that the strengthened EOI standards are likely to play an important role in reducing the elasticity of taxable income - especially capital income - with respect to the tax rate.

Recent papers have also highlighted the extent to which the elasticity is not a fixed factor for policymakers but rather itself an instrument of government policy that policymakers can reduce to varying degrees with the right policy mix (Slemrod and Kopczuk, 2002). By making it harder for taxpayers to conceal income and wealth in foreign jurisdictions, the expansion of EOI does exactly this. By making tax evasion more costly, it reduces one of the key elasticities pertaining to the taxation of top incomes (Piketty, Saez and Stantcheva, 2011). Holding other factors constant, the optimal response to a reduced elasticity from a policymakers' perspective is an increase in the tax rate; in this case, with respect to capital income. These issues will be discussed further in Chapter 6.

Notes

1. *http://www.oecd.org/tax/transparency/*
2. See for example Chamley (1986), Judd (1985) and Atkinson and Stiglitz (1976).
3. This data is current as of January 2018.
4. As of July 2017, the Convention has been signed by 112 jurisdictions. Other instruments that are used to enable cross-border EOI between tax authorities include double tax treaties and bilateral tax information exchange agreements. The number of these instruments has also been steadily growing.

5. Different procedures may be required under the domestic laws of each country for an international agreement to be executed and implemented. In either case, international agreements are required for countries to have the legal grounds under which to exchange information among each other.
6. This list is based on that found in IMF (2004) and includes: Andorra, Anguilla, Antigua and Barbuda, Aruba, Bahamas, Bahrain, Barbados, Belize, Bermuda, Cayman Islands, Cook Islands, Costa Rica, Curaçao, Cyprus, Gibraltar, Guernsey, Hong Kong, Isle of Man, Jersey, Lebanon, Liechtenstein, Macao, Malaysia, Malta, Marshall Islands, Mauritius, Monaco, Nauru, Niue, Panama, Sint Maarten, Saint Kitts and Nevis, Saint Lucia, Saint Vincent and the Grenadines, Samoa, Seychelles, Singapore, Turks and Caicos Islands, Vanuatu, and the British Virgin Islands.
7. The term competent authority is the authority designated by each jurisdiction in charge of collecting and providing the requested information to the requesting jurisdiction.
8. Global Forum on Transparency and Exchange of Information for Tax Purposes, Exchange of Information on Request, *www.oecd.org/tax/transparency/exchange-of-information-on-request/* (accessed 19 September 2017).
9. These are considered primary authoritative sources of AEOI which must be complemented by a number of secondary documents, such as a competent authority agreement, which give elements of context for the understanding, interpretation and implementation of AEOI.
10. The Directive was repealed on 10 November 2015 by the European Council as part of a tax transparency package presented by the European Commission to avoid a significant overlap that had developed with other European legislation.
11. In December 2014, the European Council adopted the Directive 2014/107/EU extending the scope of the EOI to include interest, dividends, and other types of income requiring Member States to implement reporting and due diligence rules fully consistent with those set out in the OECD CRS.
12. In 2012 the five largest European countries (France, Germany, Italy, Spain, and the United Kingdom) agreed with the United States on a reciprocal exchange of FATCA information under Intergovernmental Agreements (IGAs) concluded between the United States and each of the five countries.
13. Other MCAA agreements also exist, such as the Multilateral Competent Authority Agreement on Country by Country Reporting (CbC MCAA). Bilateral Competent Authority Agreements also exist.
14. This data is current as of 13 December 2017; *http://www.oecd.org/tax/automatic-exchange/international-framework-for-the-crs/MCAA-Signatories.pdf*
15. The term 'entities' being used throughout this document corresponds to the definition provided by the CRS, which includes only legal entities and legal arrangements.
16. While other forms and legal bases for EOI exist and are effective, the discussion in this section will focus on the CRS as it is the central multilateral mechanism to exchange information.
17. The renewed efforts to end bank secrecy and expand EOI after the April 2009 G20 meeting in London, UK.
18. The data used in this paper come from the Treasury International Capital (TIC) reporting system maintained by the U.S. Department of the Treasury (Gorea, 2015).

References

Alstadsaeter, A., Johannesen, N., and Zucman, G. (2017), "Who owns the wealth in tax havens? Macro evidence and implications for global inequality", NBER Working Paper, (23805), Cambridge, *http://www.nber.org/papers/w23805*.

Arulampalam, W., Devereux, M., and Maffini, G. (2012), "The Direct Incidence of Corporate Income Tax on Wages", *European Economic Review*, Vol. 56/6, pp. 1038-1054.

Brys, B., Perret, S., Thomas, A. and O'Reilly, P. (2016), "Tax Design for Inclusive Economic Growth", *OECD Taxation Working Papers*, No. 26, OECD Publishing, Paris, *http://dx.doi.org/10.1787/5jlv74ggk0g7-en*.

Diamond, P., and Mirrlees, J. (1971), "Optimal Taxation and Public Production I: Production Efficiency", *The American Economic Review*, Vol. 61/1, American Economic Association, pp. 8-27.

Feldstein, M. (1999), "Tax avoidance and the deadweight loss of the income tax", *Review of Economics and Statistics*, Vol. 81/4, The MIT Press, pp. 674-680.

Financial Action Task Force (2017), FATF website, *www.fatf-gafi.org/*.

Fuest, C., Peichl, A., and Siegloch, S. (2018), "Do Higher Corporate Taxes Reduce Wages ? Micro Evidence from Germany", *TheAmerican Economic Review*. (forthcoming)

G20 (2009), London Summit Leader's Statement ,OECD and the G20, *http://www.oecd.org/g20/summits/london/G20-Action-Plan-Recovery-Reform.pdf*.

Global Forum on Transparency and Exchange of Information for Tax Purposes (2014), *Final Report to the G20 Development Working Group Automatic Exchange of Information: A roadmap for developing country participation*, , Paris, *http://www.oecd.org/tax/exchange-of-tax-information/global-forum-AEOI-roadmap-for-developing-countries.pdf*.

Gorea, D. (2017), "Catch Me If You Can: U. S. Tax Treaties and Shifts in Offshore Investments". *Working Paper*, European University Institute.

Hanlon, M., Maydew, E., and Thornock, J. (2015), "Taking the long way home: US tax evasion and offshore investments in US equity and debt markets", The *Journal of Finance*, Vol. 70/1, The Journal of the American Finance Association, pp. 257-287.

Huizinga, H., and Nicodème, G. (2004), "Are international deposits tax-driven", *Journal of Public Economics*, Vol. 88/6, Elsevier, pp. 1093-1118.

Johannesen, N., and Zucman, G. (2014), "The end of bank secrecy? An evaluation of the G20 tax haven crackdown", *American Economic Journal: Economic Policy*, Vol. 6/1 B, American Economic Association, pp. 65-91.

Keen, M., and Ligthart, J. (2006), "Information sharing and international taxation: A primer", *International Tax and Public Finance*, Vol. 13/1, pp. 81-110

Menkhoff, L., and Miethe, J. (2017), "Dirty money coming home: Capital flows into and out of tax havens", *Discussion Papers*, No. 1711, DIW, Berlin.

Milanez, A. (2017), "Legal tax liability,legal remittance responsibilityand tax incidence: Three dimensions of business taxation", *OECD Taxation Working Papers*, No. 32, OECD Publishing, Paris, *http://dx.doi.org/10.1787/e7ced3ea-en*.

OECD (2017a), *Fixing Globalisation: Time to Make it Work for All*,OECD Publishing, Paris, *http://dx.doi.org/10.1787/9789264275096-en*.

OECD (2017b), *OECD Secretary-General's Report to G20 Finane Ministers*, Baden-Baden, Germany, *http://www.oecd.org/tax/oecd-secretary-general-tax-report-g20-finance-ministers-march-2017.pdf*.

OECD (2017c), The fight against offshore tax evasion continues: CRS disclosure facility delivers first results, *www.oecd.org/tax/the-fight-against-offshore-tax-evasion-continues-crs-disclosure-facility-delivers-first-results.htm*

OECD (2017d), *Standard for Automatic Exchange of Financial Account Information in Tax Matters, Second Edition*, OECD Publishing, Paris, *http://dx.doi.org/10.1787/9789264267992-en*.

OECD (2016), *Exchange of information on request: handbook for peer reviews 2016-2020*, OECD Publishing, Paris.

OECD (2014), "Commentaries on the Common Reporting Standard", in *Standard for Automatic Exchange of Financial Account Information in Tax Matters*, OECD Publishing, Paris, *http://dx.doi.org/10.1787/9789264216525-7-en*.

OECD (2014), *Standard for Automatic Exchange of Financial Information in Tax Matters*, OECD Publishing, Paris, *http://dx.doi.org/10.1787/9789264216525-en*.

OECD (2010), *Tax Policy Reform and Economic Growth*, OECD Publishing, Paris, *http://dx.doi.org/10.1787/9789264091085-en*.

OECD (2006*), Taxation of Capital Gains of Individuals: Policy Considerations and Approaches*, OECD Publishing, Paris, *http://dx.doi.org/10.1787/9789264029507-en*.

Omartian, J. (2016), "Tax Information Exchange and Offshore Entities: Evidence from the Panama Papers", *SSRN Electronic Journal*, 10/2139.

Pellegrini, V., Sanelli, A., and Tosti, E. (2016), "What do external statistics tell us about undeclared assets held abroad and tax evasion?", *Questioni de Economia e Finanza Occasional Papers*, No. 367, Banca d'Italia.

Piketty, T., Saez, E., and Stantcheva, S. (2011), "Optimal Taxation of Top Labor Incomes: A Tale of Three Elasticities", *American Economic Journal: Economic Policy*, Vol. 6/1, The National Bureau of Economic Research, pp. 230-271.

Sheppard, Lee A. (2017), "Is bitcoin going out of style?", *Tax Notes International*, *www.taxnotes.com*, (accessed 11 September 2017).

Slemrod, J., and Kopczuk, W. (2002), "The Optimal Elasticity of Taxable Income", *Journal of Public Economics*, Vol. 84/1, Elsevier, pp. 91-112.

Slemrod, J., and Yitzhaki, S. (2002), "Tax Avoidance, Evasion, and Administration", in *Handbook of Public Economics*, Vol. 3, Elsevier, pp. 1423-1470.

Zucman, G. (2013), "The missing wealth of nations: Are Europe and the U.S. net debtors or net creditors?", The *Quarterly Journal of Economics*, Vol. 128/3, Oxford Academic, pp.1321-1364.

Chapter 6

Conclusions and policy options

This chapter presents the conclusions of the Taxation of Houshold Savings report and discusses potential tax policy options. It concludes that, while countries do not necessarily need to tax household savings more, there is significant scope to improve the way countries tax household savings. Most significantly, there are opportunities for countries to increase neutrality in taxation across assets and thereby improve both the efficiency and fairness of their tax systems. There may also be opportunities for many countries to increase progressivity in their taxation of savings. At the same time, there remains a case for well-designed preferential tax treatment of private pensions in order to encourage retirement savings. The chapter also highlights opportunities for improvement in tax design regarding private pensions and in a number of other areas such as residential property, in particular to improve the equity of the tax system.

6.1. Introduction

Countries take a wide range of approaches to taxing household savings. Historically, most OECD countries tended to tax capital income on a comprehensive basis together with labour income at progressive rates. While many countries still follow this broad approach, a significant number of countries reformed their tax systems in the 1980s and 1990s to tax capital income separately from labour income, at lower flat rates. At the same time, many countries also introduced specific tax-favoured regimes for certain forms of capital income. These reforms were generally motivated by two factors: concern about low levels of savings, and difficulty in imposing high progressive tax rates on mobile capital income due to the ability of some taxpayers to hide wealth offshore.

Since this period of major reform, a number of factors have changed that make a review of the taxation of household savings timely. Inequality has continued to increase. This has been brought into particular focus as a result of the 2008 global financial and economic crisis, and has led to strong calls for greater taxation of savings and wealth in many countries. Furthermore, recent changes in the international tax environment regarding the exchange of financial account information between tax administrations can be expected to significantly alter the ability of countries to tax capital income. Meanwhile, concern about low levels of retirement savings persist, particularly in light of continued population ageing.

This report has undertaken a detailed review of the taxation of household savings in OECD and key partner countries in light of these and other developments. It has examined the different approaches that countries take to tax savings and quantified the incentives created by these approaches; examined the distribution of asset holdings in a range of OECD countries; and examined the ground-breaking changes in the international tax environment. This final chapter brings together the insights from this analysis and discusses their implications for savings tax policy.

The chapter is structured as follows: Sections 6.2 and 6.3 summarise the key messages from the preceding chapters of the report; Section 6.4 then presents the resulting conclusions and discusses policy options. Finally, Section 6.5 points towards future research.

6.2. The taxation of household savings

The focus of this study has been on assessing the efficiency and equity consequences of savings taxation in OECD and key partner countries. There are a wide variety of approaches taken by countries to the taxation of household savings. Details of these approaches have been outlined in Chapter 2.

Most countries tax the majority of savings vehicles broadly following either a comprehensive income tax or flat rate capital income tax approach. Under these approaches, no tax relief is provided on acquisition of the asset, income is taxed as it is earned at either progressive or flat rates, and distributions are untaxed (see Box 6.1 for a summary of various stylised tax systems). However, even within these two broad approaches there can be significant differences in taxation, particularly in relation to the size of statutory tax rates on income and regarding the tax treatment of capital gains. Meanwhile, some assets – e.g. private pensions – are typically taxed on an entirely different basis. The addition of transaction, wealth and recurrent property taxes on some, but not all, assets adds further complexity to any comparative analysis.

Box 6.1. **Stylised approaches to taxing savings**

Based on the approaches currently taken by countries (as summarised in Chapter 2), it is possible to distinguish several "stylised approaches" to how OECD countries tax savings: a comprehensive income tax, a flat rate capital income tax; an expenditure tax, a tax exempt savings approach; a tax deferral approach; a rate of return allowance approach; and a deemed return approach. Most countries implement a combination of these approaches.

- Under a **comprehensive income tax (CT)** approach, labour and capital income are taxed together at progressive rates. No tax relief is provided when the saving is made. A pure CT approach is based on the Schanz-Haig-Simons comprehensive definition of income, and would require all income and gains to be taxed on an accrual basis. However, in practise this is extremely rare with capital gains being taxed instead on realisation. As such we refer to such systems, where they are in place, as "broadly comprehensive".
- Under a **flat rate capital income tax** approach, labour and capital income are taxed separately, with capital income taxed at a flat statutory rate. Like a CT approach, no tax relief is provided when the saving is made. Two subsets of this system are a dual income tax system and a final withholding tax system.
- Under an **expenditure tax** approach, taxes are levied only when income is spent. An expenditure tax approach is often taken in relation to private pension savings. In such cases, upfront relief against income tax is given for amounts saved, returns from savings are untaxed as they accrue, but both savings and returns are taxed when a pension is paid.
- Under a **tax exempt savings** approach, no relief is provided when savings are made. However, returns are untaxed as they accrue, and both savings and accrued returns are untaxed on distribution.
- Under a **tax deferral** approach, no tax relief is provided when the saving is made, returns from savings are untaxed as they accrue, but the accrued returns are taxed on distribution (either at flat rates, or together with labour income at progressive rates). This approach is typically applied when intermediaries manage the household savings on behalf of the individual.
- Under a **rate of return allowance** (RRA) approach, taxation occurs as with a CT approach or a flat rate capital income tax approach except that an allowance is provided for the normal return on savings. As such only economic rents from savings are taxed at the individual level. Any unutilised allowance amount would be carried forward to future years.
- Under a **deemed return** approach, the actual return on savings is not taxed but a presumptive return is taxed instead. No tax relief is provided when the saving is made, and there is also no taxation on distribution or when capital gains are realised. A single or multiple deemed return can be applied and can be taxed at a flat or progressive rates.

Given the variation in approaches, an assessment of the magnitude of the taxes on capital income at the individual level and their impact on the incentives individuals face to save in different forms requires a methodology which goes beyond a mere focus on statutory tax rates. A focus on statutory tax rates, for example, would not capture the impact of multiple taxes on a particular savings vehicle, of deductions and variations in the tax base, of different holding periods and the potential build-up of untaxed or tax-deferred returns, and of variation in the type of return generated (e.g. interest, dividends, or capital gains). In addition, statutory tax rates do not take account of inflation which can result in a significant increase in the effective tax burden on the return to savings.

Consideration of all aspects of taxation is therefore crucial to properly assess the overall coherence of savings tax systems. Chapter 3 achieves this by calculating marginal effective tax rates (METRs) which enable the impact of a wide range of taxes and tax design features to be incorporated into the one indicator. The METR methodology applied in this report builds on and extends the methodology applied in OECD (1994). The results for the 40 countries examined in Chapter 3 highlight significant variation in METRs across savings vehicles. Tax systems create significant incentives to alter portfolio allocation away from that which would be optimal in the absence of taxes, with some assets tending to be particularly tax-favoured as compared to others.

The variation in the taxation of savings has efficiency and equity consequences. Chapter 4 provided an evidential base for examining the distributional effects of the taxation of household savings by analysing patterns of asset holdings in selected OECD countries across both income and wealth distributions. The analysis draws on income and asset-holdings microdata for 18 countries from the Eurosystem Household Finance and Consumption Survey (HFCS).

General trends

The METR results from Chapter 3 are broadly summarised in Figure 6.1 which presents the distribution of METRs across the 40 countries considered for a range of savings vehicles for an average-income, average-wealth taxpayer. Pension funds tend to be the most tax-favoured asset class, with owner-occupied residential property, and tax-favoured savings accounts also significantly tax-favoured. Perhaps surprisingly, rental property is often subject to relatively high METRs due to the application of progressive marginal personal income tax (PIT) rates, capital gains taxes and significant property taxes.

Variation in the progressivity of savings taxation is not observed in Figure 6.1, but stems from different aspects of the tax system. For example, the distinction already highlighted between progressive rates in some countries and flat rate approaches in others is clearly seen in the METR results presented in Chapter 3, with countries either applying constant METRs across income levels or progressive METRs. Variation in progressivity can also stem from deductions and exemptions. Countries providing deductions for contributions to pension funds provide greater support to higher income taxpayers than lower income taxpayers. Similarly, countries allowing mortgage interest deductibility provide greater support to higher income than lower income households.

Bank accounts, bonds and equities

The majority of countries broadly follow either a comprehensive income tax or flat rate capital income tax approach to the taxation of bank accounts, bonds, and equities. Eleven countries apply broadly comprehensive approaches, with progressive rates applying to capital income, though not necessarily to capital gains – which are often taxed at lower or even flat rates. Capital gains are also taxed on a realisation rather than accrual basis, which tends to significantly lower METRs on equity when income is retained within the company and to a lesser extent for bonds when issued below par.

Figure 6.1. **Distribution of marginal effective tax rates across countries for each asset type: average income and wealth taxpayer case, 2016**

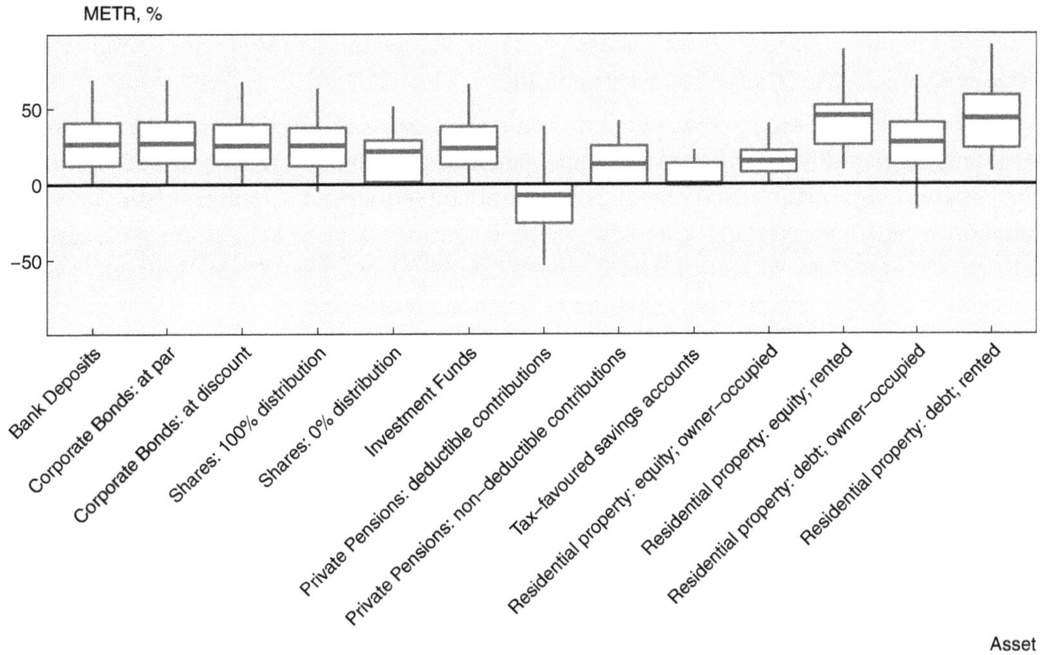

Explanatory note: The bold horizontal line within each "box" represents the median METR for that asset type, while the box itself reflects the inter-quartile range. The extreme points of each "whisker" show the minimum and maximum METR values for each asset type, excluding outliers. An outlier is defined as a result more than 1.5 times the inter-quartile range below the first quartile or above the third quartile.

StatLink http://dx.doi.org/10.1787/888933661685

In 21 countries, flat rates are applied to all capital income either as part of a dual income tax or a final withholding tax system. Rates are almost always at a significantly lower level than the top marginal rates on labour income. Capital gains are again taxed on a realisation rather than accrual basis.

In the remaining countries, a mixed approach is common – with low income taxpayers subject to withholding rates, and higher income taxpayers subject to progressive rates. Finally, there are a range of less common approaches, such as the deemed return approach in the Netherlands, and the rate of return allowance approach applied on equities in Norway.

As outlined in Chapter 4, bank deposits are the most common form of financial asset held by those with low levels of income and net wealth. By contrast, equities and bonds are much more likely to be held by those with higher levels of income and wealth.

Private pension funds

There is broad consistency across countries in the tax treatment of private pension funds, which are taxed on an expenditure basis in 32 out of 40 countries. That is, tax relief is provided for contributions made to an approved private pension scheme (though all countries have some limitation on the amount of eligible contributions); there is no taxation of the income accrued within the pension fund, but distributions are taxed (though to differing degrees). Countries that follow a comprehensive income tax approach for other assets generally apply progressive rates to distributions, though often at concessionary rates as compared to labour income. Other countries tend to tax distributions at flat rates.

A small number of countries tax pensions on a comprehensive income tax basis, while a few adopt other variants (such as taxing income accrued within a pension fund). Tax relief for contributions is provided as a deduction in many countries, but via a tax credit in a smaller number. Several countries with flat rate PIT systems provide deductions that are effectively equivalent to applying a tax credit.

As will be discussed below, pension funds are a key source of household savings, and encouraging pension saving is a key policy goal in the context of ageing societies. However, the taxation of pensions also has distributional consequences. Chapter 4 has shown that pension wealth, on average, rises with income and net wealth as a share gross financial wealth (though there is substantial between-country variation). Thus, the concessionary treatment of pensions generally favours richer households more.

Investment funds

There is considerable variation in the taxation of investment funds across countries, with the approaches applied in each country not necessarily consistent with the broad approach taken to most other assets. In some countries, a broadly comprehensive income tax approach is taken with income taxed as it accrues in the fund, but in many others tax is deferred until distribution of the income occurs. Countries that apply progressive rates on other assets typically do the same for investment funds, and likewise with flat rate countries. In some cases, potentially depending on the form of the return, income from an investment fund can effectively be tax exempt.

Chapter 4 highlights that investment funds are generally held by those with higher levels of income and wealth, so preferential tax treatment of these funds can be regressive.

Tax-favoured savings accounts

A number of countries have tax-favoured savings accounts, typically following a tax exempt pure labour tax approach, but with a limit on contributions. In some cases a comprehensive income tax approach is applied but at concessionary tax rates. Unfortunately, no distributional information is available on tax-favoured savings accounts in the HFCS data.

Residential property

The tax treatment of residential property varies depending on whether the property is rented or owner-occupied. Residential rental property is typically taxed on a comprehensive basis, in a similar way to interest income. No tax relief is provided upfront and returns are taxed as they are earned, but no further taxation is due on disposal. Both interest and capital gains tend to be taxed, and capital gains are taxed upon realisation. Recurrent property taxes are almost always applicable and often transaction taxes. The combination of taxes often leads to considerable METRs relative to other assets.

Unlike rental property, income from owner-occupied property, whether in the form of the imputed rental income or capital gains, is typically untaxed. That said, recurrent property taxes, and in many cases transaction taxes, are applied. Nevertheless METRs tend to be low for owner-occupied property.

The taxation of residential property raises complex distributional questions. The main residence makes up a larger share of household assets of poorer households in most of the countries discussed in Chapter 4. That said, the very poorest of households tend not to own a home. This means that concessionary taxation of owner-occupied property relative to other forms of assets could provide a greater tax benefit to those in the middle and top of the income distribution compared to those at the very bottom.

Providing tax relief for mortgage interest is common and also raises challenging distributional questions. Chapter 4 has shown that housing debt levels rise with income in absolute terms, so deductions for mortgage interest provide a greater benefit to those with higher incomes in absolute terms. However, deductions for mortgage interest also provide higher proportional benefits to those with low levels of net wealth. This is because housing forms a greater part of their gross wealth, and because housing debt is also more substantial relative to their gross wealth.

Second homes (which are often, but not always, rented) make up a greater proportion of gross wealth of higher income and wealth households, suggesting higher METRs on rental property aid progressivity. However, it should be borne in mind that debt financing can often enable tax planning opportunities that lower METRs on debt financed rental property.

6.3. The changing international tax environment

Chapter 5 highlighted the substantial changes in the international tax environment in the period since the 2008 global financial and economic crisis. Historically, a key barrier to the effective and efficient taxation of savings has been the ability of taxpayers to hide wealth offshore. In the absence of effective exchange of information (EOI) between tax authorities, it has been possible for some taxpayers to fail to declare their foreign-sourced income or assets and, through a lack of information in the hands of the tax authorities, avoid detection. Estimates of the size of offshore holdings have varied from USD 6-7 trillion to USD 22 trillion (Alstadsaeter, Johannesen and Zucman, 2017).

However, as a result of the work of the Global Forum on Transparency and Exchange of Information for Tax Purposes (Global Forum), the coverage of the network of exchange of information agreements has expanded substantially, both in relation to the exchange of information on request (EOIR) and the automatic exchange of information (AEOI). Furthermore, the promulgation of the Common Reporting Standard (CRS) means that AEOI will be standardised across a wider variety of countries. More than 100 countries have committed to automatically exchange financial account information by 2018. More than 110 jurisdictions have signed the Multilateral Convention on Mutual Administrative Assistance in Tax Matters – one of the key instruments promoted by the Global Forum to facilitate information exchange.

These various initiatives suggest that in the future it will be more difficult for taxpayers to engage in tax evasion by hiding their wealth offshore, and as a result these developments will make it easier for countries to levy taxes on capital with a much reduced risk that taxpayers will shift their income and assets offshore in response. Additionally, individuals who have been hiding financial assets offshore now have greater incentives than ever before to come forward and start reporting their financial assets to tax authorities. Indeed, there is evidence that the expansion of EOI has caused a substantial increase in the disclosure of offshore assets, and thus an expansion in the capital tax base.

Continued work will be needed to ensure that exchange of information is effective in reducing tax evasion. Chapter 5 has highlighted statistical evidence that the effectiveness of information exchange is increasing in the number of countries participating in EOI. The coverage of the EOI network, which has grown rapidly over recent years, has been a key ingredient of this success.

Beyond ensuring the effectiveness of EOI, continued efforts and constant vigilance will be needed to ensure that capital income can be effectively taxed internationally. The risk remains that some taxpayers will seek to use elaborate structures and mechanisms to frustrate the effectiveness of the EOI. Equally, some taxpayers may also attempt to shift their wealth into assets not covered by the most common EOI agreements or to jurisdictions not participating in the EOI.

6.4. Policy challenges for the taxation of household savings

Capital taxation is an issue that is high on the policy agenda for governments and citizens. There are widespread calls for higher levels of capital taxation both domestically and internationally in response to increasing levels of income and wealth inequality. This has been brought into particular focus as a result of the 2008 global financial and economic crisis. Meanwhile, continued population ageing is placing significant pressure on public pension systems, with many countries therefore looking to further encourage private pension savings.

While countries do not necessarily need to tax savings more, the analysis in this study shows that there is significant scope to improve the way countries tax savings. Most significantly, there are opportunities for countries to increase coherency and consistency in taxation across assets and thereby improve both the efficiency and fairness of their tax systems. There may also be opportunities for many countries to increase progressivity in their taxation of savings. At the same time, there remains a case for preferential tax treatment of private pensions in order to encourage retirement savings. However, there are also opportunities for improvement in tax design regarding private pensions and in a number of other areas such as residential property. This section discusses these policy challenges in more detail.

Increasing coherency in the taxation of savings

How a country taxes household savings can have significant effects on both the efficiency and fairness of the tax system. However, economic theory does not provide a definitive picture of how savings should optimally be taxed.[1] In the absence of such guidance, the concept of tax neutrality is generally relied on, at least as a starting point, in assessing how savings should be taxed (OECD, 1994; Mirrlees et al., 2011).

There are two main aspects of tax neutrality relevant from a savings perspective: neutrality regarding the allocation of savings over the lifecycle; and neutrality regarding the allocation of savings across different assets. To achieve neutrality regarding savings over the lifecycle, a tax should not distort the decision between consumption tomorrow as compared to consumption today. Theoretically, this suggests that the 'normal' return to savings – defined as the return required to make a taxpayer ambivalent between consuming today and consuming in the next period – should not to be taxed.[2] Meanwhile, to achieve neutrality across different assets, the tax system should impose the same effective tax rate on all assets.

Almost all tax systems breach these neutrality principles in some way, and so create incentives to consume now rather than later and to save in certain assets over others. However, these tax-induced incentives are only of concern if taxpayers actually alter their behaviour in response to them. As highlighted in Chapter 1, empirical evidence is mixed regarding the former, but clear regarding the latter: while taxes may affect consumption choices over the lifecycle (and hence the total level of savings in an economy), they clearly do affect decisions regarding which assets to save in. Tax differentials across assets are therefore likely to result in significant distortions to the allocation of savings. This suggests that, at least as a starting point, ensuring neutrality as regards the allocation of savings should be of primary concern in tax policy development.

There are also arguments in favour of taxing the normal return to savings, despite its potential distortion of lifecycle savings. For example, recent papers in capital taxation have highlighted the extent to which the absence of taxation of even normal returns on capital investment may distort the mix of assets between physical and human capital (Golosov, Kocherlakota and Tsyvinski, 2003; Stantcheva, 2017). This is particularly the case given that returns to human capital may be taxed at higher rates than physical capital – i.e. at labour income tax rates (OECD, 2017).

Neutrality in the allocation of savings

To assess the degree of neutrality in the allocation of savings in countries' tax systems, a major focus of this study has been on the calculation of marginal effective tax rates (METRs) on different assets / savings vehicles. The METR results presented in Chapter 3 clearly highlight the lack of neutrality across assets in almost all 40 countries examined. METRs vary significantly across assets, creating strong incentives at the margin for taxpayers to save in some assets over others, thereby distorting the allocation of savings. There is consequently a clear case for countries to look to adjust their tax systems to increase the consistency of METRs across assets.

Not only will enhanced neutrality in the taxation of savings increase efficiency, it will also increase the fairness of the system. A key finding from Chapter 4 of this report is that the allocation of asset holdings varies across the income and wealth distributions. In particular:

- Poorer households hold a significantly greater proportion of their wealth in typically highly-taxed bank accounts than richer households;
- Richer households hold a greater proportion of their wealth in investment funds, pension funds and shares, which are all often taxed relatively lightly, than poorer households.
- The very poorest households do not own residential property, which at least in the owner-occupied case is significantly tax favoured.
- Where they are able to own their own home, poorer households hold a greater share of their wealth in owner-occupied property than richer households. Richer households tend to hold a greater amount of aggregate wealth in owner-occupied property.
- Richer households hold a far greater share of their wealth in second properties than poorer households. While these tend to be taxed relatively heavily when equity financed, when debt financed there are significant tax planning opportunities that can reduce the effective tax burden to concessionary levels.

These distributions of asset holdings mean that tax systems often favour the savings of households that are financially better-off, thereby strengthening the case for a move towards neutrality.

Neutrality will also limit other tax planning incentives to structure savings in a way that lowers taxation, such as by retaining income within a corporate structure to defer taxation.

Achieving neutrality across assets

Part of the reason for the lack of neutrality across assets exhibited in many tax systems is the inherent difficulty in achieving it. Most countries adopt a broadly comprehensive or flat rate capital tax approach to taxing savings which involve taxing returns as they are earned. However, part of the return from many assets comes in the form of capital gains. To achieve neutrality, capital gains should be taxed identically to interest, dividends and other forms of income – i.e. as they accrue. However, gains are almost always taxed on a realisation basis due to the difficulty, particularly in thin markets, of determining and taxing gains as they accrue, as well as liquidity concerns. This deferral reduces the net present value of the tax as compared to accrual taxation so that an asset earning interest or dividends at the same rate will face a higher METR than an asset producing the same return as a capital gain.

Furthermore, the deferral benefit actually creates incentives for taxpayers not to sell assets (a 'lock-in' effect), discouraging the efficient sale of assets that would have occurred in the absence of taxation. Concern over potential lock-in effects has led many countries to apply reduced rates on capital gains or to even exempt, for example, long-term capital gains. However, this pushes tax systems even further from achieving neutrality. Additionally, some countries do not impose a capital gains tax at all on the basis that these gains are different in nature to 'ordinary' income.

Fundamental reform to the tax system – such as moving to a pure expenditure tax system (with no taxation of savings) – could eliminate the difficulty created by realisation-based capital gains taxation in achieving neutrality. However, an alternative option compatible with the broadly comprehensive and flat rate capital tax approaches adopted by most countries currently is to apply an interest adjustment to capital gains. Taxation would still occur on a realisation basis alleviating asset pricing difficulties and liquidity concerns, but interest would also be charged on realisation to approximate the net present value of accrual taxation. This would reduce deferral benefits and consequent lock-in effects, and move systems closer to neutrality.

Practical implementation issues would need to be considered further regarding the introduction of an interest charge. For example, while the timing of gains across the total holding period is likely to be variable, it may be most practical to assume a smooth increase in asset value – resulting in some inaccuracy in net present value calculations. Additional issues, such as how to prevent incentives to defer dividend payments, would also need to be considered.

Beyond the taxation of capital gains, there are other aspects of tax design highlighted in Chapter 3 that impede neutrality. In particular, some countries will apply additional taxes to some assets but not others. For example, a transaction tax may be applied to the purchase of some assets (e.g. bonds, shares, residential property) but not others. This differential treatment unsurprisingly exacerbates the variation in METRs across assets. It also creates variation across holding periods, so that distortions across briefly held assets will be greater than across longer held assets as the one-off transaction tax can effectively be spread over a longer time period.

Transaction taxes are historically popular due to the easily identifiable base, but in addition to the impact of their sporadic application on neutrality, they are highly inefficient in another way as they discourage transactions. For example, a property transaction tax will discourage efficient labour mobility as they increase the costs associated with relocation.

Net wealth taxes are applied in a small number of countries, but often with a number of exclusions and exemptions that potentially also exacerbate differences in METRs across assets. Caution also needs to be taken with wealth taxes more generally as when combined with already high personal tax rates on capital income they can result in extremely high METRs being imposed on certain assets. In general, there is a weaker case for implementing a net wealth tax where a country already has a broad-based capital income tax, including a tax on capital gains, and a well-designed inheritance tax (OECD, 2018a).

Recurrent property taxes are often also levied on residential property, but not on other bases. However, there is more justification here. In particular, these taxes can partially make up for the non-taxation of imputed rental income and capital gains on owner-occupied property. As land is in fixed supply, they are also likely to be amongst the least distortionary of taxes (Johansson et al., 2008), although their distributional effects are less clear.

The impact of inflation may also prevent tax neutrality. As nominal rather than real returns are typically taxed, assets that produce higher real returns will face lower effective tax rates than those producing lower real returns (as the inflationary component makes up a smaller part of the total tax base). Not only can this prevent neutrality, it may also have a regressive impact as wealthier individuals tend to invest in assets that generate higher returns.[3] A small number of countries provide tax relief for the inflationary components of some, but not all, income or capital gains but such non-uniform treatment could further exacerbate non-neutrality. Instead, adjustments should be provided uniformly if full neutrality across assets is to be achieved.

Neutrality across the lifecycle

In addition to neutrality across assets, there is merit in countries also considering options to achieve neutrality across the lifecycle. Fundamental reform such as a pure expenditure tax will achieve this, as will non-taxation of savings. However, the provision of an allowance for the normal return on savings (a "rate of return allowance" or "RRA") is an option worth consideration that fits within the broadly comprehensive and flat rate approaches currently taken by most OECD countries in relation to the taxation of savings. Although only one country (Norway) currently adopts such an approach, it has received significant recent support in the academic literature (see, in particular, Mirrlees et al., 2011).

While increasing compliance and administrative costs, there are a number of factors in favour of the adoption of an RRA. In addition to mitigating potential distortions to lifecycle savings decisions, an RRA will also help mitigate distortions with respect to the allocation of savings across assets by partly removing the deferral advantage attached to capital gains (as any unutilised allowance would be carried forward until realisation of the capital gain). Furthermore, it is likely to be consistent with equity goals as economic rents are still taxed. Indeed, there is no clear equity case for taxing the normal return as this simply taxes more heavily those who prefer consumption in the future over those that prefer consumption today.

An important point to note though is that concern from an efficiency perspective only relates to the distortion of lifecycle savings decisions. There is consequently no clear case to exempt the normal return from inherited wealth. Taxing the total return (normal return plus rents) on non-lifecycle savings can effectively be achieved by the combination of an estate tax (or approximated by an inheritance tax) and an RRA. In the absence of an estate or inheritance tax, a net wealth tax levied on the part of the wealth which will not be consumed across the lifecycle might be an alternative (OECD, 2018a).

In practice, an RRA could be approximated by providing a fixed basic allowance or exempt amount of savings (or preferably a tax credit in order to fix the tax benefit) – as currently provided in a number of countries. If restricted to assets such as bank accounts and bonds – that are unlikely to return significantly more than the normal return – this approach will have largely the same effect as an RRA, but with less compliance and administrative costs. An RRA could then be applied to assets expected to produce economic rents.

There are also arguments in favour of taxing the normal return to savings, despite its potential distortion of lifecycle savings. Recent papers in capital taxation have highlighted the extent to which the absence of taxation of even normal returns on capital investment may distort the mix of assets between physical and human capital (Golosov, Kocherlakota and Tsyvinski, 2003; Stantcheva, 2017). This is particularly the case given that the returns to human capital are taxed at higher rates than physical capital (i.e. at labour income tax rates). (OECD, 2017). Such concerns may be particularly relevant given the increases in capital share of national income in many OECD countries.

Increasing progressivity in the taxation of savings

While a significant number of the countries considered in this report tax savings progressively, a large number of countries tax most savings at flat rates. In relation to this latter group, two factors highlight the case for these countries to reassess the merits of applying a degree of progressivity to their taxation of savings:

- First, inequality has continued to increase in most OECD countries since the late 1980s/early 1990s when most flat rate reforms took place. This has been brought into particular focus as a result of the 2008 global financial and economic crisis, and has led to strong calls for greater taxation of savings and wealth in many countries (see, e.g., Piketty, 2014).
- Second, the ground-breaking changes in the international tax environment regarding the move to the automatic exchange of taxpayer information (AEOI) should decrease the ability of many taxpayers to hide income and wealth offshore.

The ability to implement such reform and the degree to which progressivity should be increased will depend on a range of country-specific factors, including existing levels of inequality and preferences for redistribution. Whilst the reform could involve a shift back to the comprehensive taxation of labour and capital income together at progressive rates, it could also involve implementing a schedular system with progressive rates applied to capital income. Such a "dual progressive income tax" approach could increase progressivity while taking into account that capital income has been taxed already at the corporate level with the corporate income tax rate.

Increased progressivity does not necessarily require increased tax revenue from savings. Although, doing so may provide an opportunity to raise additional revenues where necessary or to fund reductions in other tax bases likely to be more damaging to growth such as labour and corporate income (Johansson et al., 2008).

The introduction of an RRA would also introduce some capital income tax progressivity given that, as already noted, wealthier individuals tend to invest in assets that generate higher returns (Fagereng et al., 2016). Nevertheless, richer households would gain a lot more than poorer households from an RRA.

As noted above, an RRA could be approximated for certain assets – e.g. bank accounts – by a basic allowance, exempt amount or tax credit. Given the evidence from Chapter 4 that bank accounts are predominantly held by poorer households, a basic tax credit for bank accounts can further aid overall progressivity.

The analysis in the report also highlights that distributional objectives can also be achieved by removing certain provisions that favour the rich. As discussed further below, tax deductions provided for pension contributions and mortgage interest could be turned into tax credits so that richer taxpayers do not benefit disproportionately from these concessions as compared to poorer taxpayers.

As already noted, moving towards neutrality in tax treatment across assets will also aid distributional goals by eliminating any regressivity arising from variation in asset holdings between rich and poor.

Additionally, more progressive taxation of savings will reduce incentives for taxpayers to re-characterise labour income as capital income to reduce their marginal rate. This may occur through incorporation by the self-employed. Such re-characterisation is often available to those with higher levels of income and wealth and consequently may have a regressive effect.

In any reform, policymakers also need to bear in mind the mobility of high-income and high-skilled labour in response to increased taxation. This can be the case with respect to both labour and capital income. Recent studies have suggested that high-income and high-wealth individuals will respond by shifting location in response to both personal and corporate income taxes (Kleven, Landais, and Saez, 2013; Kleven, Landais, Saez and Schultz, 2013; Moretti and Wilson, 2017). Some countries are putting in place schemes to target highly-mobile taxpayers, signalling growing competition not just for capital, but also for highly-skilled labour (OECD, 2017). To some extent, this may limit the scope for higher income taxes on those with high levels of income and wealth, even in the context of expanded information exchange on tax matters.

Encouraging retirement savings

While the main conclusion of this report is the need for greater consistency and neutrality in the tax treatment of savings, there are some notable exceptions. Encouraging retirement savings is the clearest example. Most countries attempt to encourage retirement savings by providing highly concessionary expenditure tax regimes for private pensions that often result in negative METRs.

As noted in Chapter 1, there is clear evidence that incentives to save for retirement do increase the overall level of retirement savings, and there is some evidence that this does not entirely crowd out other savings. However, even if they do not increase total savings, there might remain merit in encouraging a shift of some household savings into long-term retirement focused savings vehicles over shorter term vehicles. As societies in most OECD countries continue to age, public pension systems are coming under increasing strain. This means that it might be important to provide sufficient incentives for private savings, and hence the case to continue with these incentives, in breach of tax neutrality, is strong.

That said, the particular tax treatment of voluntary private pension savings in each country should be considered in a coordinated way with the financial advantages and generosity of public pension systems. For example, where public pension provision is substantial, there may be less need to incentivise the use of private pensions. However, where public pension provision is less expansive, it may be increasingly important to provide larger incentives for private savings.

As noted above, the design of pension systems can be improved in many countries by replacing tax deductions for private pension contributions with tax credits so that richer taxpayers do not benefit disproportionately from these concessions. Ideally tax credits would be refundable to ensure that low-income taxpayers without sufficient tax liability in a particular year still receive the full benefit of the tax credit. Alternatively, pension contributions could be matched by government contributions to ensure that the support is provided immediately rather than at year end – which may potentially increase pension savings (OECD, 2018b). Limits on the size of the tax incentive available should also be utilised to manage both fiscal cost and the distributional effects.

A number of countries have also attempted to encourage savings through the introduction of tax-favoured savings accounts that often provide exemptions for the income earned. Where the policy goal is to encourage long-term savings, there may be merit in imposing minimum holding period requirements on these accounts (as some countries do).

Improving the taxation of residential property

Owner-occupied property

After private pensions, this report has highlighted that owner-occupied residential property is typically the next most tax favoured savings option for households. This stems chiefly from the absence of a capital income tax on the imputed rental income and of a capital gains tax. However, the presence of recurrent property taxes and, in many cases, transaction taxes ensure some positive degree of taxation.

In addition to the non-taxation of imputed rental income and capital gains, many countries have other tax policies that result in favourable treatment of home ownership over other forms of saving. As discussed in Chapter 2, 19 out of 40 countries allow tax relief for mortgage interest paid on owner-occupied properties, either as a tax credit or a deduction against labour and/or other income.

While, from a neutrality perspective, this tax relief is difficult to justify – especially in light of the non-taxation of the income generated, this position reflects the fact that a large number of countries place considerable importance on the policy objective of supporting home ownership. There are various reasons why governments may wish to support home ownership. For example, home ownership may be seen as a way to encourage long-term savings similar to tax relief for private pensions. There may also be a range of perceived social benefits from increased home ownership (see, for example, Engelhardt et al., 2010).

Tax support for home ownership may also be seen as a means to support middle income households who – as shown in Chapter 4 – hold a large proportion of their wealth in housing. However, it will not support the poorest of households as these households do not own residential property; meanwhile higher income households are likely to purchase more expensive homes and thereby benefit even more with greater deductions in aggregate terms (Fatica and Prammer, 2017). A number of countries provide caps on relief for mortgage interest which may ameliorate these negative distributional consequences.

Furthermore, when mortgage interest relief is provided as a deduction against income taxed at progressive rates it will have a regressive impact. As noted previously, this is because it allows those paying tax at higher marginal rates to deduct their mortgage at a higher rate than those paying tax at lower marginal rates. Consequently, countries should consider providing tax credits rather than deductions.

Reform of housing tax policy and reform of mortgage interest deductibility in particular, is complicated by the fact that those households that have very low or negative levels of net wealth often have substantial housing debt. While these low net wealth households may not have low incomes, reducing support for mortgage debt in a sudden way may place substantial burdens on highly indebted households. Furthermore, the tax advantage from mortgage interest deductibility may be capitalised into the value of a property, so that its removal would act as an implicit tax on current homeowners.

One approach worth consideration in addressing the non-taxation of imputed income and capital gains is through increases in recurrent property taxes beyond the level that reflects the benefits received from local public series (such as waste disposal, fire brigade, etc.). There is also a broader case for increasing recurrent property taxes as they are likely to be less damaging to economic growth than most other taxes (Johansson et al., 2008), although the distributional effects are less clear.

However, political economy issues once again arise. Local property taxes are one of the least popular taxes of all major tax categories according to some studies (OECD, 2010). Property taxes also require regular property valuations to maximise their efficiency and fairness, which can be administratively burdensome. Recurrent property taxes may also be considered a payment for local government services, so that the tax liability might have to be presented as a payment for government services and the pure tax component which is levied on the imputed income. Further complexity arises as this would also require property tax rates to vary between owner-occupied property and rental property where actual rental income is subject to income taxation.

Another potential policy reform option would involve imposing a limit on the value of owner-occupied housing that benefits from an exemption from taxation on capital gains. Given that higher income households are likely to purchase more expensive homes and have more of their savings directed towards owner-occupied housing, one way of mitigating the adverse distributional effects of an open-ended exemption would be to cap this benefit. This cap could be imposed at a relatively high level to ensure that only those properties and the high end of the residential housing market are affected.

Rental property

Chapter 3 of this report has shown that rental property is generally taxed far more significantly than owner-occupied property. Nevertheless, there may be opportunities to improve tax design in many countries.

In almost all countries rental income is taxed, and in all but seven countries capital gains on rental properties are taxed – although sometimes at concessionary rates. From a political economy perspective it should be significantly easier to justify taxing the capital gains from residential rental property and hence efforts could be made by countries to increase the taxation of capital gains where concessionary rates, or exemptions for long-term gains, are currently applied. As noted earlier, countries could consider implementing an interest charge to minimise lock-in effects and allow increased taxation of capital gains.

The case for allowing mortgage interest deductibility is stronger for rental property than owner-occupied property given that income is generally subject to comparable levels of taxation as alternative savings options. Even in this case, mortgage interest deductibility for rental property might still distort saving decisions if interest paid on debt which is incurred to buy other assets is not deductible from taxable income. Moreover, the same distributional concerns arise as with owner-occupied property and should be addressed accordingly.

As noted in Chapter 3, debt financing can create opportunities for tax planning when mortgage interest is deductible and capital gains are taxed at concessionary rates, or there are other means of reducing tax on sale of a property (e.g. age-based exemptions). In such countries, the importance of removing concessionary treatment of capital gains becomes even more pertinent. Again, lock-in concerns can be mitigated by applying an interest charge. Alternatively, if concessionary rates continue for capital gains then there is merit in considering removing the deductibility of mortgage interest, as a number of countries do. In contrast, when rental income and capital gains are fully taxed, removing mortgage interest deductibility would be more difficult to justify.

As noted earlier, there is a strong case to remove transaction taxes on at least owner-occupied residential property. These discourage efficient relocation reducing labour mobility. That said, there may be a case to retain transaction taxes where there are concerns about asset bubbles. Finally, consideration should be given to the merits of imposing wealth taxes where significant taxation of rental income and capital gains already applies.

6.5. Further research

This study has highlighted many patterns in the taxation of household savings across OECD countries. It has highlighted areas where the taxation of savings is distortive, particularly between different asset classes. It has also placed the taxation of household savings within the context of continuing changes in OECD and other countries, including: rising inequality, increasing globalisation, and increasing global co-operation on tax. However, there remains considerable scope for further research. Some possibilities are highlighted below.

- Chapter 5 has highlighted the changing nature of the **international tax environment**. The network of EOI agreements continues to expand in scope, and the various standards promulgated by the OECD and other actors continue to be strengthened and enforced. However, more needs to be done to improve our understanding of the impact of these standards on tax evasion and the nature of taxpayer responses to the increased risk of evasion being detected.
- This study has also discussed the **taxation of residential property** and has noted that a wide variety of taxes impact on the overall tax burden on housing. The taxation of residential property in particular often interacts with house prices in complex ways – and has been subject to strong assumptions in the METRs presented in Chapter 3. Further analysis is warranted. In addition, Chapter 4 has highlighted the centrality of residential property and debt in determining the interaction of the net wealth and income distributions. Further analysis of the taxation of residential property from an inclusive growth perspective is therefore warranted.
- A key issue, which has not been the focus of this study, is the **taxation of inherited wealth**. Taxation of this form of asset acquisition may have different consequences for the distribution of wealth and the effectiveness of capital use in the economy than the taxation of non-inherited capital. However, the distributional consequences – and economic incidence of the taxation of estates and inheritances are so far relatively poorly understood.

- This study has considered the taxation of capital income at the personal level. However, capital income is also often subject to **corporate income tax**. As discussed in Chapter 5, globalisation and increased international mobility of international capital raise the challenges of effectively taxing corporate income at source. For this reason, many countries shift the taxation of this income to the personal level. Thus the interaction of the personal and corporate income tax systems is of key concern for capital taxation overall. The METR modelling presented in Chapter 3 in particular could be expanded to incorporate effective corporate tax rates.
- Consideration of the taxation of capital income from a **life-cycle perspective** also warrants further attention. Tax systems are typically designed from a static perspective which may lead to unfair outcomes as taxpayers whose incomes vary considerably over time may pay considerably more taxes than taxpayers who have a more constant stream of earnings.
- The case for **fundamental reform** to the taxation of savings has also been briefly raised in this Chapter. In particular, the case for shifting from comprehensive to pure expenditure taxation merits further consideration. Expenditure taxation is often criticised for its inability to achieve distributional goals, however, the merits of an expenditure tax in a lifecycle context may be very different from a single-year perspective and warrant further investigation. The possibility of pure comprehensive taxation on an accrual basis also warrants consideration. In particular, the increased digitalisation of the economy and new technology and improved tax administration tools may make accrual taxation more feasible than has previously been the case.
- This Chapter has also discussed the provision of a **rate of return allowance**. Further work assessing the merits of such an allowance, including its impacts on efficiency and equity and practical implementation issues is warranted, as well as its interactions with inheritance and net wealth taxes.
- Chapter 4 has used data on wealth to examine distributional aspects of the taxation of household savings. The potential **use of information on household wealth to aid tax design** warrants much greater attention. In particular, wealth information may be able to be used to more accurately target support to certain taxpayer groups to achieve distributional objectives. In the past, targeting of support has had a much greater focus on incomes rather than wealth, although it is clear that better policy outcomes should involve consideration of the position of the taxpayer across both of these dimensions.

Notes

1. Early papers on optimal capital taxation (e.g. Chamley,1986; Judd, 1985; Atkinson and Stiglitz, 1976), concluded that the optimal tax rate on capital income was zero. However, recent papers (e.g. Golosov, Kocherlakota and Tsyvinski, 2003; Piketty and Saez, 2012; Gordon and Kopczuk, 2014; Stantcheva, 2017) do find a role for capital income taxation. See, e.g., Broadway (2012) or Banks and Diamond (2010) for detailed reviews of the optimal capital taxation literature.
2. The 'normal' return to savings may vary across taxpayers as preferences vary, but is typically approximated by the risk free return (which itself is typically approximated by the return on a short-term government bond).
3. This is potentially explained by wealthy investors' lower risk aversion and better access to financial education, financial expertise and more lucrative investment opportunities (Fagereng et al., 2016).

References

Alstadsaeter, A., Johannesen, N. and Zucman, G. (2017), "Who owns the wealth in tax havens? Macro evidence and implications for global inequality", *NBER Working Paper*, No. 23805.

Atkinson, A. and J. Stiglitz (1976), "The design of the tax structure: direct versus indirect taxation", *Journal of Public Economics*, Vol. 6, Elsevier, pp. 55-75.

Banks, J. and P. Diamond (2010), "The base for direct taxation", in J. Mirrlees, S. Adam, T. Besley, R. Blundell, S. Bond, R. Chote, M. Gammie, P. Johnson, G. Myles and J. Poterba (eds), *Dimensions of Tax Design: The Mirrlees Review*, Oxford University Press for Institute for Fiscal Studies, Oxford.

Broadway, R. (2012), *From Optimal Tax Theory to Tax Policy*, MIT Press, Cambridge.

Chamley, C. (1986), "Optimal taxation of capital income in general equilibrium with infinite lives", *Econometrica*, Vol. 54, No. 3, JSTOR, pp. 607-622.

Engelhardt, G., M. Eriksen, W. Gale and G. Mills (2010), "What Are the Social Benefits of Homeownership? Experimental Evidence for Low-Income Households", *Journal of Urban Economics*, Vol. 67, No. 3, pp. 249-258.

Fagereng, A. Guiso, L. and Malacrino, D. and L., Pistaferri (2016), "Heterogeneity and Persistence in Returns to Wealth", *NBER Working Paper,* No. w22822.

Fatica, S., and Prammer, D. (2017), "Housing and the tax system: how large are the distortions in the euro area?", *European Central Bank Working Paper Series*, No. 2087, European Central Bank.

Golosov, M., N. Kocherlakota and A. Tsyvinski (2003), "Optimal Indirect and Capital Taxation", The *Review of Economic Studies*, Vol. 70, No. 3, JSTOR, pp. 569-587.

Gordon, R. and W. Kopczuk (2014), "The choice of the personal income tax base", *Journal of Public Economics*, Vol. 118, Elsevier, pp. 97-110.

Johansson et al. (2008), "Taxation and Economic Growth", *OECD Economics Department Working Papers*, No. 620, OECD Publishing, Paris, *http://dx.doi.org/10.1787/241216205486.*

Judd, K. (1985), "Redistributive taxation in a simple perfect foresight model", *Journal of Public Economics*, Vol. 28, No. 1, Elsevier, pp. 59-83.

Kleven, H., Landais, C., and Saez, E. (2013), "Taxation and International Migration of Superstars: Evidence from the European Football Market". *The American Economic Review*, Vol. 103, No. 5, pp. 1892-1924.

Kleven, H., Landais, C., Saez, E. and Schultz, E. (2013), "Migration and Wage Effects of Taxing Top Earners: Evidence from the Foreigners' Tax Scheme in Denmark", *NBER Working Paper*, No. 18885.

Mirrlees, J., S. Adam, T. Besley, R. Blundell, S. Bond, R. Chote, M. Gammie, P. Johnson, G. Myles and J. Poterba (2011), *Tax by Design: The Mirrlees Review*, Oxford University Press for Institute for Fiscal Studies, Oxford.

Moretti, E., and Wilson, D. (2017), "The Effect of State Taxes on the Geographical Location of Top Earners: Evidence from Star Scientists", *American Economic Review*, Vol. 107, No. 7, pp. 1858-1903.

OECD (2018a), *The Role and Design of Net Wealth Taxes in the OECD,* OECD Tax Policy Studies, No. 26, OECD Publishing, Paris (forthcoming).

OECD (2018b), *Pensions Outlook*, OECD Publishing, Paris. (forthcoming).

OECD (2017), *Taxation and Skills*, OECD Publishing, Paris, *http://dx.doi.org/10.1787/9789264269385-en.*

OECD (2010), *Tax Policy Reform and Economic Growth*, OECD Publishing, Paris, *http://dx.doi.org/10.1787/9789264091085-en.*

OECD (1994), "Taxation and Household Saving", OECD Publishing, Paris.

Piketty, T. (2014), *Capital in the twenty-first century*. Cambridge: The Belknap Press of Harvard University Press.

Piketty, T. and E. Saez (2012), "A Theory of Optimal Capital Taxation", *NBER Working Paper*, No. 17989.

Stantcheva, S. (2017), "Optimal Taxation and Human Capital Policies over the Life Cycle", *Journal of Political Economy*, Vol. 125/6, Harvard University and National Bureau of Economic Research.

Zucman G. (2014),"Taxing across Borders: Tracking Personal Wealth and Corporate Profits", *The Journal of Economic Perspectives*, Vol. 28, No. 4, pp. 121-148.

ANNEX A

Methodology for calculating marginal effective tax rates on household savings

Introduction

This annex outlines in detail the underlying methodology for calculating the marginal effective tax rates (METRs) presented in Chapter 3. The methodology follows broadly the approach of the OECD (1994) *Taxation and Household Savings* study, which itself drew on the methods used by King and Fullerton (1984).

The analysis considers a saver who is contemplating investing an additional currency unit in one of a range of assets. The investment is a marginal investment, both in terms of being an incremental purchase of the asset, and in terms of generating net returns just sufficient to make the purchase worthwhile (as compared to the next best savings opportunity). The approach assumes a fixed pre-tax real rate of return and calculates the minimum post-tax real rate of return that will, at the margin, make the savings worthwhile. The METR can then be calculated as the difference between the pre- and post-tax rates of return divided by the pre-tax rate of return.

The pre-tax rate of return is determined by explicitly modelling the stream of returns and taxes associated with a marginal investment over time. The modelling incorporates the impact of a wide range of taxes in the one indicator, including taxes on cash income (at the personal level as well as the level of the savings intermediary), taxes on realised capital gains (with or without indexation), taxes on asset purchases and/or sales, transaction taxes and wealth taxes. The tax gain as a result of the deductibility of savings from taxable income as well as of interest payments which have to be paid if the investment is financed with borrowed funds are modelled as well.

METRs are calculated for the following types of savings vehicles:

- Bank deposits
- Corporate and Government bonds
- Equities (purchase of corporate shares)
- Investment fund assets (marketable, collective investment vehicles)
- Private pensions
- Individual tax-favoured savings accounts
- Equity-financed owner-occupied and rented residential property
- Debt-financed owner-occupied and rented residential property

The overall methodological approach is first detailed, before METR equations for each savings vehicle are explicitly derived.

Overall approach

Consider a saver contemplating investing one currency unit in a particular savings vehicle. The present value of the returns and costs (taxes) of investing in that savings vehicle over time can be expressed as:

$$V = -1 + \int_{t=0}^{n} (R_t - T_t) e^{-\rho_H t} dt \qquad (1)$$

where R_t is the stream of returns and T_t the stream of taxes on those returns (which will vary depending on the particular savings vehicle and the way in which it is taxed). The returns and costs are discounted at a rate ρ_H.

The length of time for which an asset is held is often crucial in determining tax liabilities. The approach taken here (and in the OECD, 1994 study) is to assign a probability to each possible holding period. The expected return is then calculated in each case, on the basis of risk neutrality. It is assumed that the probability of sale in each period is fixed, so that there is, for example, a 10 per cent chance of sale in the first period; if the asset is not sold, there is a 10 per cent chance of sale in the second period, and so on.

The time of sale of asset 't' may be thought of as a random variable, which follows an exponential probability density function with rate parameter λ:

$$p(t) = \lambda e^{-\lambda t} \qquad (2)$$

This setup implies that the investment will earn a return in period 0 with full certainty while the probability that the investment yields a return in the following periods decreases over time until n reaches infinity, when the probability that the investment earns a return is zero.[1]

This endogenous asset holding period approach has a number of advantages. First, it allows focusing on different holding periods while avoiding time-related variables in the analytical solution of the derived effective tax rates. Second, where tax rates vary with the holding period, the method implicitly weights the different tax rates (avoiding the need to calculate different METRs for each holding period). It therefore gives a reasonable summary of the overall tax treatment where incentive effects vary with the holding period.

Incorporating the endogenous holding period into equation 1 gives:

$$V = -1 + \int_{n=0}^{\infty} \lambda e^{-\lambda n} \left[\int_{t=0}^{n} (R_t - T_t) e^{-\rho_H t} dt \right] dn \qquad (3)$$

Setting V = 0 and solving for ρ_H will yield an expression for the investor's after-tax nominal rate of return on the particular savings vehicle. The after-tax real rate of return of investing in a particular savings vehicle, s, given an inflation rate of π, is then:

$$s = \rho_H - \pi \qquad (4)$$

The investment is assumed to earn a fixed real return, r. Consequently, the METR, t_e, is:

$$t_e = \frac{r - s}{r} \qquad (5)$$

Explicit equations for each savings vehicle

In this section we derive explicit METR equations for each of the savings vehicles considered in the study. A basic form of the equations is first derived for each savings vehicle (representing a "typical country" approach). A number of potential extensions are then presented to illustrate how a wide range of different taxes and tax designs can be incorporated into the METR modelling for each savings vehicle. Where countries rules vary from the possibilities presented here, the modelling is altered accordingly.

Bank deposits

Basic case

The net present value of an investment of one currency unit in a bank account equals:

$$V = -(1+t_p) + \int_{n=0}^{\infty} \lambda e^{-\lambda n} \left[\int_{t=0}^{n} \left((1-t_y)(r+\pi) - t_w \right) e^{-\rho_H t} dt + (1-t_s) e^{-\rho_H n} \right] dn$$

where:

r = real interest rate

π = inflation rate

t_p = tax on purchase of the asset

t_s = tax on sale of the asset

t_y = tax on income / return that the asset generates in every period

t_w = tax on wealth (levied on the principal); to some extent, it is assumed that the after-tax interest is consumed)

$1/\lambda$ = expected holding period of the asset

ρ_H = discount rate/ the after-tax nominal return the household realises on a marginal investment

V = present value of the investment

A transaction tax, t_p, has to be paid as a result of the one currency unit of savings in a bank deposit. The cost of the savings is therefore equal to one plus the transaction tax. The investment earns a nominal return, $r+\pi$, which is taxed at the rate t_y. A yearly wealth tax on the value of the deposit, t_w, has to be paid as well. This recurrent after-tax return is discounted at the rate ρ_H. The probability that the household keeps the one currency unit as a bank deposit for n periods is assumed to decrease exponentially as n increases, as implied by the integral of the term $\lambda e^{-\lambda n}$. The inverse of λ is the expected holding period of the savings. The one currency unit is withdrawn from the bank account after n years, after which a tax on the sale of the asset t_s has to be paid.

Setting V = 0 allows us to solve for ρ_H:

$$\rho_H = \frac{(1-t_y)(r+\pi) - t_w}{1+t_p} - \frac{\lambda(t_s+t_p)}{1+t_p}$$

The marginal effective tax rate equals:

$$t_e = \frac{(t_y+t_p)}{(1+t_p)} + \frac{(t_y+t_p)\pi + t_w + \lambda(t_s+t_p)}{(1+t_p)r}$$

Extension 1: x% of return is tax-exempt

If x% of the return is tax-exempt, then:

$$\rho_H = \frac{(1-x)(1-t_y)(r+\pi)+x(r+\pi)-t_w}{1+t_p} - \frac{\lambda(t_s+t_p)}{1+t_p}$$

Extension 2: a savings subsidy is paid by government for each currency unit saved

In some countries, the government may provide a (tax or other type of) subsidy "su" for each currency unit of savings. This may function as a negative transaction tax, reducing the cost of the savings (in case the subsidy is given up-front when the savings are made):

The net present value of an investment of 1 currency unit in a bank account equals:

$$V = -(1+t_p-su) + \int_{n=0}^{\infty} \lambda e^{-\lambda n}\left[\int_{t=0}^{n} \left((1-t_y)(r+\pi)-t_w\right)e^{-\rho_H t}dt + (1-t_s)e^{-\rho_H n}\right]dn$$

Setting V = 0 and solving for ρ_H gives:

$$\rho_H = \frac{(1-t_y)(r+\pi)-t_w}{1+t_p-su} - \frac{\lambda(t_s+t_p-su)}{1+t_p-su}$$

Corporate and Government bonds

Issued at par

Corporate and Government bonds issued at par will be taxed in the same manner as bank interest.

Issued at a discount

Instead of offering the nominal interest rate, the bond only pays the interest rate $(1-x)(r+\pi)$. As a result, the price that will have to be paid for the bond will not be 1 but $(1-c)$ instead (where $c<1$). The bondholder will recover the full face value of the bond when it is sold and a capital gains tax will have to be paid on the gain.

First note that the discount c equals the net present value of the interest foregone:

$$c = \int_{n=0}^{\infty} \lambda e^{-\lambda n}\left[\int_{t=0}^{n} x(r+\pi)e^{-\rho_H t}dt\right]dn = \frac{x(r+\pi)}{\lambda+\rho_H}$$

The net present value of an investment in a bond issued at a discount where $x\%$ of the return is in the form of a capital gain equals:

$$V = -(1-c)(1+t_p) + \int_{n=0}^{\infty} \lambda e^{-\lambda n}\left[\int_{t=0}^{n} \left((1-t_y)(1-x)(r+\pi)-t_w\right)e^{-\rho_H t}dt + (1-t_s-t_c c)e^{-\rho_H n}\right]dn$$

Setting V = 0 and solving for ρ_H gives:

$$\rho_H = \frac{(1-t_y)(1-x)(r+\pi)-t_w}{(1-c)(1+t_p)} - \frac{\lambda(t_s+t_p(1-c))}{(1-c)(1+t_p)} + \frac{\lambda c(1-t_c)}{(1-c)(1+t_p)}$$

where:

$$c = \frac{x(r+\pi)}{\lambda+\rho_H}$$

Equities (purchase of corporate shares)

Basic case

The net present value of an investment of one currency unit in a share of a business equals (first assuming no tax on purchase and sale):

$$V=-1+\int_{n=0}^{\infty}\lambda e^{-\lambda n}\begin{bmatrix}\int_{t=0}^{n}(1-t_d)c(r+\pi)\left(e^{(1-c)(r+\pi)t}\right)e^{-\rho_H t}dt\\ +\\ \left(e^{(1-c)(r+\pi)n}-1\right)(1-t_c)e^{-\rho_H n}\\ +\\ e^{-\rho_H n}\\ -\\ \int_{t=0}^{n}t_w\left(e^{(1-c)(r+\pi)t}\right)e^{-\rho_H t}dt\end{bmatrix}dn$$

where (in addition to the previously defined parameters):

c = fraction of return that is distributed as dividends

t_d = tax on dividends

t_c = capital gains tax (capital gains are taxed upon realization)

The household buys a share at a price of one currency unit; the investment yields a nominal return, $r+\pi$, which is partly $(c\%)$ distributed (and taxed) as dividends, and partly $((1-c)\%)$ retained and reinvested. It is assumed that the reinvested earnings yield a nominal return of $r+\pi$ as well. At time t, the value of the share is $e^{(1-c)(r+\pi)t}$. The first term within the square brackets reflects the present value of the after-tax dividends. The household sells the share in period n; a capital gains tax has to be paid on the increase in value of the share; the second term within the square brackets reflects the after-tax capital gain. The household recovers the original one currency unit of savings tax-free (third term). A yearly wealth tax is also paid on the value of the share (fourth term).

Setting V = 0 and solving for ρ_H gives:

$$\rho_H=\left\{c(1-t_d)+(1-c)\left[1-\frac{\lambda t_c}{\lambda+\rho_H}\right]\right\}(r+\pi)-t_w$$

The marginal effective tax rate then equals:

$$t_e=ct_d+(1-c)\frac{\lambda t_c}{\lambda+\rho_H}+\frac{\left[ct_d+(1-c)\frac{\lambda t_c}{\lambda+\rho_H}\right]\pi}{r}+\frac{t_w}{r}$$

Extension 1: tax on purchase of the share

Incorporating a tax on the purchase of the share changes the first term to $-(1+t_p)$. Setting V = 0 and solving for ρ_H gives:

$$\rho_H=\frac{\left\{c(1-t_d)+(1-c)\left[1+t_p-\frac{\lambda t_c}{\lambda+\rho_H}\right]\right\}(r+\pi)-\lambda t_p-t_w}{(1+t_p)}$$

Extension 2: (partly or fully) indexing the capital gains for inflation

If the capital gains tax is levied only on the real capital gains (and not the nominal gains), the after-tax nominal rate of return amounts to (in the absence of sales taxes and if x and y are 0):

$$\rho_H = \frac{\left\{c(1-t_d)+(1-c)\left[1+t_p-\frac{\lambda t_c}{\lambda+\rho_H-d\pi}\right]\right\}(r+\pi)-\lambda t_p+\left[\frac{\lambda t_c}{\lambda+\rho_H-d\pi}\right]d\pi - t_w}{(1+t_p)}$$

where d is the degree to which capital gains are indexed for inflation.

The indexation appears twice. First, the capital gains tax, which is levied on the nominal interest rate, is now discounted at a real instead of nominal rate. Second, the after-tax nominal return increases with the term $\left[\frac{\lambda t_c}{\lambda+\rho_H-d\pi}\right]d\pi$.

Investment fund assets (marketable, collective investment vehicles, where 100% of the return is retained and reinvested)

Basic case

The net present value of an investment of one currency unit in a share of an investment fund equals:

$$V = -1 + \int_{n=0}^{\infty} \lambda e^{-\lambda n} \begin{bmatrix} \left(1.e^{(1-t_{if})(r+\pi)n} - 1\right)(1-t_c)e^{-\rho_H n} \\ + \\ e^{-\rho_H n} \\ - \\ \int_{t=0}^{n} t_w \left(1.e^{(1-t_{if})(r+\pi)t}\right) e^{-\rho_H t} dt \end{bmatrix} dn$$

where t_{if} = the tax on the investment fund's earnings.

In the first period, the household buys a share of the investment fund at price of one currency unit. The investment fund invests these funds in saving opportunities which earn a nominal return, $r+\pi$. The tax t_{if} is due on the investment fund's earnings. Consequently, the fund will reinvest in every period the return $(1-t_{if})(r+\pi)$. After n periods, the household sells its share in the investment fund. It realises the capital gains and recovers the original investment. The increase in value of the asset is taxed under the capital gains tax at rate t_c. Additionally, in every period the tax authorities levy a wealth tax, t_w, on the value of the asset in that particular period.

Setting V = 0 and solving for ρ_H gives:

$$\rho_H = \left[1-\frac{\lambda t_c}{\lambda+\rho_H}\right]\left[1-t_{if}\right](r+\pi)-t_w$$

The marginal effective tax rate then equals:

$$t_e = t_{if} + (1-t_{if})\frac{\lambda t_c}{\lambda+\rho_H} + \frac{\left[t_{if}+(1-t_{if})\frac{\lambda t_c}{\lambda+\rho_H}\right]\pi}{r} + \frac{t_w}{r}$$

Extension 1: purchase tax + sales (exit) tax on the value of the share at the moment of sale

The net present value of an investment of one currency unit in a share of an investment fund becomes:

$$V = -(1+t_p) + \int_{n=0}^{\infty} \lambda e^{-\lambda n} \begin{bmatrix} \left(1.e^{(1-t_{if})(r+\pi)n} - 1\right)(1-t_c)e^{-\rho_H n} \\ + \\ e^{-\rho_H n} \\ - \\ t_s^* \left(1.e^{(1-t_{if})(r+\pi)n}\right) e^{-\rho_H n} \\ - \\ \int_{t=0}^{n} t_w \left(1.e^{(1-t_{if})(r+\pi)t}\right) e^{-\rho_H t} dt \end{bmatrix} dn$$

The household's after-tax nominal rate of return then amounts to:

$$\rho_H = \frac{\left[1 + t_p - \dfrac{\lambda t_c}{\lambda + \rho_H}\right]\left[1 - t_{if}\right](r+\pi) - \lambda(t_s^* + t_p) - t_w}{1 + t_p}$$

Private pensions

Basic case

The net present value of a household investment of 1 currency unit in a pension fund amounts to:

$$V = -(1-t_{ded}) + \int_{n=0}^{\infty} \lambda e^{-\lambda n} \begin{bmatrix} \left(1.e^{(1-t_{pf})(r+\pi)n}\right)(1-t_y)e^{-\rho_H n} \\ - \\ \int_{t=0}^{n} t_w \left(1.e^{(1-t_{pf})(r+\pi)t}\right) e^{-\rho_H t} dt \end{bmatrix} dn$$

where:

t_{pf} = the tax on the pension fund's earnings

t_{ded} = income tax rate at which pension savings can be deducted from taxable personal income

t_y = income tax rate at which the pension is taxed (note that this excludes employee social security contributions)

The household has one currency unit which it saves for a pension through a pension fund. Even though the pension fund receives savings of one currency unit, the cost to the household is only $(1-t_{ded})$ because pension savings can be deducted from taxable personal income at rate t_{ded}, which will typically be the household's marginal income tax rate at the time of saving. The pension fund invests the funds in savings opportunities that earn a nominal return, $r+\pi$. A tax, t_{pf}, is due on the fund's earnings. The fund then reinvests in every period the return, $(1-t_{pf})(r+\pi)$. After n years, the total return, which equals the original contributions plus the return on the investment, is distributed and entirely taxed at the rate t_y, typically the household's personal income tax rate. In addition, wealth taxes are due yearly on the value of the pension savings in that particular year.

Setting V = 0 and solving for ρ_H gives:

$$\rho_H = \left(1-t_{pf}\right)\left(r+\pi\right)+\frac{\lambda(t_{ded}-t_y)}{(1-t_{ded})}-\frac{t_w}{(1-t_{ded})}$$

The marginal effective tax rate then equals:

$$t_e = t_{pf}+\frac{t_{pf}\pi}{r}-\frac{\lambda(t_{ded}-t_y)}{(1-t_{ded})r}+\frac{t_w}{(1-t_{ded})r}$$

Extension 1: purchase tax on the contributions paid to the pension fund

The household may have to pay a purchase tax on the contributions paid to the pension fund, which may be either deductible (in which case d=1) or not (d=0) from personal income tax. The cost of the investment then amounts to: $(1+t_p-t_{ded}(1+dt_p)$.

The household's nominal after-tax rate of return amounts to:

$$\rho_H = \left(1-t_{pf}\right)\left(r+\pi\right)+\frac{\lambda\left(t_{ded}\left(1+dt_p\right)-t_y\right)-\lambda t_p-t_w}{(1+t_p-t_{ded}(1+dt_p))}$$

Individual tax-favoured savings accounts

Basic case

The net present value of an investment of one currency unit in a tax-favoured savings account (assuming that 100% of the return is paid out each year) equals:

$$V=-\left(1-g.t_{ded}\right)+\int_{n=0}^{\infty}\lambda e^{-\lambda n}\left[\int_{t=0}^{n}\left\{\left[x+(1-x)\left(1-t_y\right)\right]\left(r+\pi\right)-t_w\right\}e^{-\rho_H t}dt+e^{-\rho_H n}\right]dn$$

where *g*% of the savings are tax-deductible at a rate t_{ded}; *x*% of the return is tax-exempt; and *(1-x)*% is taxed at rate t_y. There is also a wealth tax, t_w.

Setting V = 0 and solving for ρ_H gives:

$$\rho_H=\frac{\left[x+(1-x)\left(1-t_y\right)\right]\left(r+\pi\right)-t_w+\lambda g t_{ded}}{1-gt_{ded}}$$

The marginal effective tax rate amounts to:

$$t_e=\frac{t_y(1-x)-gt_{ded}}{1-gt_{ded}}+\left[\frac{t_y(1-x)-gt_{ded}}{(1-gt_{ded})r}\right]\pi+\frac{t_w-\lambda g t_{ded}}{(1-gt_{ded})r}$$

Extension 1: purchase tax, sale tax, and tax on principal

There may be a tax on purchase t_p, which may be deductible (if d=1) or not (if d=0), and a tax on sale, t_s, on the principal investment. Part of the principal (w%) when recovered (i.e. when the asset is sold) may also be taxed at a rate, t_υ. The net present value of an investment of one currency unit in a tax-favoured savings account would then equal (assuming that 100% of the return is paid out each year):

$$V=-\left(1+t_p-g(1+dt_p)t_{ded}\right)+\int_{n=0}^{\infty}\lambda e^{-\lambda n}\left[\int_{t=0}^{n}\left\{\left[x+(1-x)\left(1-t_y\right)\right]\left(r+\pi\right)-t_w\right\}e^{-\rho_H t}dt+\left((1-w)+w(1-t_\upsilon)\right).e^{-\rho_H n}-t_s.e^{-\rho_H n}\right]dn$$

The household's after-tax nominal rate of return then amounts to:

$$\rho_H = \frac{\left[x+(1-x)\left(1-t_y\right)\right]\left(r+\pi\right)-t_w+\lambda\left[g(1+dt_p)t_{ded}-wt_v\right]-\lambda(t_p+t_s)}{\left(1+t_p-g(1+dt_p)t_{ded}\right)}$$

Equity-financed owner-occupied and rented residential property

Basic case

The net present value of a one currency unit equity-financed investment in owner-occupied housing equals:

$$V=-\left(1+t_p\right)+\int_{n=0}^{\infty}\lambda e^{-\lambda n}\left[\begin{array}{c}\int_{t=0}^{n}\left\{\begin{array}{c}\left[x+(1-x)\left(1-t_y\right)\right]\left(r+\delta\right)\\ -irv.t_{irv}-t_l-t_w\end{array}\right\}e^{-(\rho_H+\delta-\pi)t}dt\\ +\\ e^{-(\rho_H+\delta-\pi)n}\end{array}\right]dn$$

Equity-financed investment in housing costs the household one currency unit plus a transaction tax (property transfer tax), t_p. The investment yields a pre-tax real return (imputed or actual rental income), r, and a return to pay for the depreciation of the house, δ. The value of the house is increasing in the inflation rate, π, and decreasing in δ. Earnings are discounted at the nominal rate ρ_H. *x%* of the return is tax-exempt; *(1-x)%* of the return is taxed under an income tax, t_y. The imputed rental income (*irv*) may be taxed instead at a rate t_{irv}. Additionally, the value of the house is taxed under a local property tax, t_l, and may be subject to a wealth tax, t_w. After n years, the household sells the house and recovers the value of one currency unit.

The household's after-tax nominal rate of return is:

$$\rho_H = \frac{\left\{\begin{array}{c}\left[x+(1-x)\left(1-t_y\right)\right]\left(r+\delta\right)\\ -irv.t_{irv}-t_l-t_w\end{array}\right\}-\lambda t_p}{1+t_p}-(\delta-\pi)$$

The marginal effective tax rate then equals:

$$t_e = \frac{t_y(1-x)+t_p}{1+t_p}+\left[\frac{t_y(1-x)+t_p}{\left(1+t_p\right)r}\right]\delta+\frac{irv.t_{irv}+t_l+t_w+\lambda t_p}{\left(1+t_p\right)r}$$

Extension 1: capital gains, and depreciation provisions

Instead of deriving the return entirely each year (from imputed or actual rental income) part of the return, pr, is now earned each year and the rest of the return, $(1-p)r$, is earned in the form of capital gains. The house depreciates in value due to wear and tear and the owner receives a return δ to pay for the economic depreciation of the asset; this return may be taxed, and the taxpayer may be able to claim tax depreciation allowances, A. The value of the house, which is used for tax purposes, is updated yearly (and increases with the inflation rate, the economic return $(1-p)r$ and decreases with the economic depreciation rate, δ). The tax depreciation allowances equal:

- Straight line tax depreciation allowances:

$$A=\int_{n=0}^{\infty}\lambda e^{-\lambda n}\left[\int_{t=0}^{n}t_y.\left[\frac{1}{L}\right]e^{-\rho_H t}dt\right]dn=\frac{t_y}{L(\lambda+\rho_H)}$$

where t_y is the income tax rate; L is the number of years over which the house has to be depreciated.

- Declining balance tax depreciation allowances:

$$A = \int_{n=0}^{\infty} \lambda e^{-\lambda n} \left[\int_{t=0}^{n} t_y.a.e^{-(a+\rho_H)t} dt \right] dn = \frac{t_y.a}{\lambda + a + \rho_H}$$

where a is the tax depreciation rate.

The net present value of an equity-financed investment in owner-occupied housing equals:

$$V = -\left(1+t_p-A\right) + \int_{n=0}^{\infty} \lambda e^{-\lambda n} \left[\begin{array}{c} \int_{t=0}^{n} \left\{ \begin{array}{c} \left[x+(1-x)\left(1-t_y\right)\right](pr+\delta) \\ -irv.t_{irv} - t_l - t_w \end{array} \right\} e^{-(\rho_H+\delta-\pi-(1-p)r)t} dt \\ + \\ e^{-(\rho_H+\delta-\pi-(1-p)r)n} \\ - \\ t_c\left[e^{-(\delta-\pi-(1-p)r)n} - e^{i\pi n}\right].e^{-\rho_H n} \end{array} \right] dn$$

where i takes the value 1 if the capital gains are indexed for inflation and 0 if they are not.

Setting V=0 and solving for ρ_H gives:

$$\rho_H = \frac{\left[\begin{array}{c} \left\{ \begin{array}{c} \left[x+(1-x)\left(1-t_y\right)\right](pr+\delta) \\ -irv.t_{irv} - t_l - t_w \end{array} \right\} \\ + \\ (1-p)r\left(1 - \frac{\lambda t_c}{\lambda + \rho_H - i\pi}\right) \\ + \\ (1-p)r\left(t_p - A\right) \\ + \\ \left(\frac{\lambda t_c}{\lambda + \rho_H - i\pi}\right)(i\pi + \delta - \pi) \\ - \\ \lambda\left(t_p - A\right) \end{array} \right]}{\left(1+t_p-A\right)} - (\delta - \pi)$$

Debt-financed owner-occupied and rented residential property

Basic case

Instead of buying residential property with own funds (equity), households may decide to borrow money to finance the investment and invest their own funds in an alternative savings opportunity. In some countries, mortgage interest payments are deductible from taxable personal income. As a result, the after-tax borrowing cost may be lower than the return which the household can realise on an alternative savings opportunity. This will reduce the financing, FC, below the equity-financed cost of investing in residential property (i.e. $(1 + t_p)$).

The net present value of a debt-financed investment in owner-occupied housing then equals:

$$V = -FC + \int_{n=0}^{\infty} \lambda e^{-\lambda n} \left[\begin{array}{c} \int_{t=0}^{n} \left\{ \begin{array}{c} \left[x + (1-x)(1-t_y)\right](r+\delta) \\ -irv.t_{irv} - t_l - t_w \end{array} \right\} e^{-(\rho_H + \delta - \pi)t} dt \\ + \\ e^{-(\rho_H + \delta - \pi)n} \end{array} \right] dn$$

The financing cost amounts to:

$$FC = (1+t_p) \cdot \int_{n=0}^{\infty} \lambda e^{-\lambda n} \left[\int_{t=0}^{n} \left((1-t_{ded})(r+\pi) - t_{ded}^{w} \right) e^{-\rho_H^* t} dt + e^{-\rho_H^* n} \right] dn$$

The household borrows $(1+t_p)$ currency units. Interest payments have to be paid, but may be deductible from the household's personal income, thereby reducing the cost to $(1-t_{ded})(r+\pi)$. Moreover, the debt may be deducted from the household's taxable wealth, which reduces the yearly cost by t_{ded}^{w}. After *n* years, the originally borrowed funds must be paid back. The discount rate is the opportunity return, ρ_H^*, which is assumed to be the after-tax return on savings in a bank deposit.

The financing costs can be written as $FC = (1+t_p)(1-F)$, where $F = \dfrac{\rho_H^* - \left((1-t_{ded})(r+\pi) - t_{ded}^{w}\right)}{\lambda + \rho_H^*}$ denotes the financing gains (or losses) and depends on the difference between the household's opportunity return on an alternative savings opportunity and the borrowing costs. The opportunity return ρ_H^* is assumed to be the after-tax return on savings in a bank deposit. If this is not tax favoured (i.e is taxed at t_y), then F will likely be equal to zero. If it is tax-favoured, or if an alternative tax-favoured savings vehicle was chosen as the opportunity return, F will be positive (and the effective tax rate would be lower).

The household's after-tax nominal rate of return then amounts to:

$$\rho_H = \frac{\left\{ \begin{array}{c} \left[x + (1-x)(1-t_y)\right](r+\delta) \\ -irv.t_{irv} - t_l - t_w \end{array} \right\} + \lambda(F - t_p(1-F))}{(1+t_p)(1-F)} - (\delta - \pi)$$

Extension 1: capital gains, and depreciation provisions

Instead of deriving the return entirely each year (from imputed or actual rental income) part of the return, *pr*, is now earned each year and the rest of the return, $(1-p)r$, is earned in the form of capital gains. The household now borrows $1+t_p-A$. The house depreciates in value due to wear and tear and the owner receives a return δ to pay for the economic depreciation of the asset; this return may be taxed, and the taxpayer may be able to claim tax depreciation allowances, A. The value of the house, which is used for tax purposes, is updated yearly (and increases with the inflation rate, the economic return $(1-p)r$ and decreases with the economic depreciation rate, δ). The tax depreciation allowances are as detailed for an equity financed investment.

The net present value of a debt-financed investment in owner-occupied housing equals:

$$V = -FC + \int_{n=0}^{\infty} \lambda e^{-\lambda n} \left[\begin{array}{c} \int_{t=0}^{n} \left\{ \begin{array}{c} \left[x + (1-x)\left(1-t_y\right)\right](pr+\delta) \\ -irv.t_{irv} - t_l - t_w \end{array} \right\} e^{-(\rho_H+\delta-\pi-(1-p)r)t} dt \\ + \\ e^{-(\rho_H+\delta-\pi-(1-p)r)n} \\ - \\ t_c \left[e^{-(\delta-\pi-(1-p)r)n} - e^{d\pi n} \right] . e^{-\rho_H n} \end{array} \right] dn$$

The financing cost amounts to:

$$FC = \left(1 + t_p - A\right) . \int_{n=0}^{\infty} \lambda e^{-\lambda n} \left[\int_{t=0}^{n} \left(\left(1-t_y\right)(r+\pi) - t_w^d\right) e^{-\rho_H^* t} dt + e^{-\rho_H^* n} \right] dn$$

$$FC = \left(1 + t_p - A\right)(1-F) \text{ where } F = \frac{\rho_H^* - \left(\left(1-t_{ded}\right)(r+\pi) - t_{ded}^w\right)}{\lambda + \rho_H^*}$$

Setting V = 0 and solving for ρ_H gives:

$$\rho_H = \frac{\left[\begin{array}{c} \left\{ \begin{array}{c} \left[x + (1-x)\left(1-t_y\right)\right](pr+\delta) \\ -irv.t_{irv} - t_l - t_w \end{array} \right\} \\ + \\ (1-p)r\left(1 - \frac{\lambda t_c}{\lambda + \rho_H - i\pi}\right) \\ + \\ (1-p)r\left[(1-F)\left(t_p - A\right) - F\right] \\ + \\ \left(\frac{\lambda t_c}{\lambda + \rho_H - i\pi}\right)(i\pi + \delta - \pi) \\ - \\ \lambda\left[(1-F)\left(t_p - A\right) - F\right] \end{array} \right]}{\left(1 + t_p - A\right)^{(1-F)}} - (\delta - \pi)$$

Note

1. The expected holding period of the asset (i.e. the expected period when the asset will be sold) is the inverse of the rate parameter λ (i.e. $1/\lambda$), and is calculated as the expected value of the exponential distribution: $E(t) = \int_0^{\infty} t \lambda e^{-\lambda t} dt = \frac{1}{\lambda}$

References

King, M. and D. Fullerton (1984), *Taxation of income from capital: a comparative study of the United States, United Kingdom, Sweden and West Germany*, Chicago University Press, Chicago.

OECD (1994), "Taxation and Household Saving", OECD Publishing, Paris.

ANNEX B

Additional marginal effective tax rate results

This annex presents additional marginal effective tax rate (METR) results for variations to the basic modelling assumptions presented in Chapter 3 regarding the inflation rate, real rate of return and expected holding period.

Tables B.1-B.3 provide results for sensitivity analysis regarding the inflation rate by providing results for a zero inflation rate, while holding constant the real rate of return (3%) and expected holding period (20 years for private pensions and residential property; 5 years for all other assets). Results were presented in the main text using the country actual and OECD average inflation rates.

Tables B.4-B.9 provide results for sensitivity analysis regarding the real rate of return by providing results for a lower (2%) and higher (4%) real rate of return, while holding constant the inflation rate (country actual) and expected holding period (20 years for private pensions and residential property; 5 years for all other assets).

Tables B.10-B.15 provide sensitivity analysis regarding the expected holding period by providing results for a short (10 years for private pensions and residential property; 6 months for all other assets) and long (30 years for private pensions and residential property; 10 years for all other assets) expected holding period, while holding constant the inflation rate (country actual) and real rate of return (3%).

Table B.1. **Marginal effective tax rates by asset: zero inflation, 67% of average wage, 2016**

Standard assumptions: 3% real return, 5 years expected holding period (20 years for pensions and property)

Country	Bank deposits	Corporate bonds		Government bonds		Shares		
		Issued at par	Issued at discount	Issued at par	Issued at discount	100% distribution	50% distribution	0% distribution
Australia	34.5%	34.5%	33.7%	34.5%	33.7%	4.5%	9.8%	15.3%
Austria	25.0%	27.5%	26.8%	27.5%	26.8%	27.5%	26.1%	24.7%
Belgium	27.0%	27.7%	27.0%	27.7%	27.0%	29.0%	15.4%	1.8%
Canada	20.1%	20.1%	17.3%	20.1%	17.3%	0.0%	4.4%	8.8%
Chile	0.0%	0.0%	0.0%	0.0%	0.0%	-24.0%	-12.0%	0.0%
Czech Republic	15.0%	15.0%	11.3%	15.0%	11.3%	15.0%	7.5%	0.0%
Denmark	37.0%	37.0%	36.2%	37.0%	36.2%	42.0%	40.3%	38.5%
Estonia	0.0%	20.0%	19.5%	20.0%	19.5%	0.0%	8.8%	17.8%
Finland	30.0%	30.0%	29.3%	30.0%	29.3%	25.5%	26.3%	27.0%
France	28.8%	28.8%	28.1%	28.8%	28.1%	23.2%	21.3%	19.4%
Germany	0.0%	0.0%	0.0%	0.0%	0.0%	0.0%	0.0%	0.0%
Greece	15.0%	15.0%	14.6%	0.0%	0.0%	23.3%	24.2%	25.0%
Hungary	15.0%	15.0%	11.3%	15.0%	11.3%	10.0%	9.4%	8.8%
Iceland	0.0%	0.0%	4.4%	0.0%	4.4%	20.0%	18.9%	17.8%
Ireland	41.0%	25.5%	26.6%	25.5%	19.1%	32.8%	34.6%	36.4%
Israel	15.0%	15.0%	14.6%	15.0%	14.6%	25.0%	23.7%	22.4%
Italy	27.5%	27.5%	26.8%	14.0%	13.6%	26.9%	25.5%	24.1%
Japan	20.0%	20.0%	19.5%	20.0%	19.5%	10.6%	14.2%	17.8%
Korea	14.0%	14.0%	13.6%	14.0%	13.6%	21.5%	14.0%	6.6%
Latvia	10.0%	10.0%	10.8%	10.0%	10.8%	10.0%	11.6%	13.3%
Luxembourg	10.0%	10.0%	7.5%	10.0%	7.5%	17.0%	8.5%	0.0%
Mexico	0.5%	0.5%	0.5%	0.5%	0.5%	-9.2%	-0.2%	8.8%
Netherlands	40.0%	40.0%	40.0%	40.0%	40.0%	40.0%	40.0%	40.0%
New Zealand	17.5%	17.5%	17.2%	17.5%	17.2%	-10.5%	-5.3%	0.0%
Norway	53.3%	53.3%	52.9%	53.3%	52.9%	28.3%	28.3%	28.3%
Poland	19.0%	19.0%	18.5%	19.0%	18.5%	19.0%	18.0%	16.9%
Portugal	28.0%	28.0%	27.3%	28.0%	27.3%	28.0%	26.6%	25.2%
Slovak Republic	19.0%	19.0%	18.5%	19.0%	18.5%	0.0%	8.4%	16.9%
Slovenia	25.0%	25.0%	24.4%	25.0%	24.4%	25.0%	19.2%	13.3%
Spain	21.0%	21.0%	20.0%	21.0%	20.0%	21.0%	19.0%	16.9%
Sweden	30.0%	30.0%	29.3%	30.0%	29.3%	30.0%	28.5%	27.0%
Switzerland	16.6%	17.7%	13.5%	17.7%	13.5%	17.7%	9.4%	1.0%
Turkey	15.0%	15.0%	14.6%	15.0%	14.6%	10.4%	5.2%	0.0%
United Kingdom	0.0%	0.0%	0.0%	0.0%	0.0%	0.0%	0.0%	0.0%
United States	15.0%	15.0%	14.6%	15.0%	14.6%	0.0%	0.0%	0.0%
Argentina	0.0%	25.0%	25.0%	0.0%	0.0%	25.0%	25.0%	25.0%
Bulgaria	8.0%	0.0%	0.0%	0.0%	0.0%	5.0%	2.5%	0.0%
Colombia	7.0%	4.0%	3.9%	4.0%	3.9%	0.0%	0.0%	0.0%
Lithuania	0.0%	0.0%	0.0%	0.0%	0.0%	15.0%	7.5%	0.0%
South Africa	0.0%	0.0%	0.0%	0.0%	0.0%	16.9%	9.3%	8.0%

Table B.1. **Marginal effective tax rates by asset: zero inflation, 67% of average wage, 2016** *(cont.)*

Standard assumptions: 3% real return, 5 years expected holding period (20 years for pensions and property)

Country	Investment funds	Pension funds		Tax-favoured savings accounts	Residential property			
		Deductible contributions	Non-deductible contributions		Equity-financed		Debt-financed	
					Owner-occupied	Rented	Owner-occupied	Rented
Australia	34.5%	-25.4%	15.0%	34.5%	14.7%	74.7%	47.3%	74.7%
Austria	24.8%	-7.4%	0.0%	25.0%	15.5%	39.9%	39.0%	30.3%
Belgium	0.0%	-52.4%	13.3%	0.0%	49.3%	50.6%	31.7%	73.1%
Canada	20.1%	0.0%	13.2%	0.0%	38.9%	59.5%	56.0%	59.5%
Chile	0.0%	0.0%	0.0%	0.0%	0.0%	0.0%	0.0%	0.0%
Czech Republic	5.0%	0.0%	9.7%	15.0%	11.1%	22.1%	11.1%	22.1%
Denmark	42.0%	15.3%	15.3%	42.0%	21.3%	38.9%	17.7%	43.8%
Estonia	17.8%	-20.8%	16.7%	0.0%	0.0%	16.2%	-21.6%	16.2%
Finland	27.0%	0.0%	20.3%	0.0%	12.1%	40.1%	26.0%	40.1%
France	25.9%	-2.3%	13.4%	0.0%	22.8%	37.1%	49.2%	62.5%
Germany	0.0%	0.0%	23.1%	0.0%	19.4%	57.4%	19.4%	24.7%
Greece	13.3%	0.0%	0.0%	15.0%	27.2%	27.4%	30.9%	31.3%
Hungary	8.8%	-41.7%	0.0%	0.0%	10.3%	25.2%	24.7%	39.2%
Iceland	17.8%	0.0%	26.6%	20.0%	15.5%	25.2%	34.3%	43.8%
Ireland	37.5%	11.5%	17.0%	41.0%	6.6%	32.0%	46.6%	52.4%
Israel	22.4%	-89.7%	0.0%	0.0%	10.0%	28.4%	24.4%	42.1%
Italy	20.2%	-9.3%	26.7%	27.5%	1.8%	47.2%	11.4%	71.5%
Japan	17.8%	-4.9%	5.1%	0.0%	17.7%	28.1%	3.5%	37.1%
Korea	14.0%	-19.6%	3.2%	0.0%	5.6%	5.1%	4.6%	19.1%
Latvia	10.0%	-39.8%	10.0%	10.0%	17.8%	26.4%	27.1%	35.7%
Luxembourg	0.0%	-42.9%	11.1%	0.0%	0.3%	35.7%	10.3%	11.3%
Mexico	8.8%	-20.3%	0.0%	0.5%	11.0%	21.4%	0.7%	11.3%
Netherlands	40.0%	-61.6%	0.0%	40.0%	10.5%	49.8%	15.8%	49.8%
New Zealand	17.5%	17.5%	17.5%	17.5%	20.0%	35.2%	36.2%	35.2%
Norway	51.6%	-3.9%	53.3%	41.7%	16.7%	56.8%	46.0%	82.0%
Poland	16.9%	-16.3%	16.7%	19.0%	5.9%	15.0%	24.5%	25.9%
Portugal	28.0%	-25.0%	0.0%	0.0%	10.0%	36.4%	37.0%	61.2%
Slovak Republic	16.9%	12.5%	12.5%	19.0%	0.4%	20.6%	19.3%	38.6%
Slovenia	13.3%	-15.9%	13.3%	25.0%	7.9%	34.2%	32.1%	56.6%
Spain	16.9%	0.0%	15.4%	0.0%	33.2%	41.9%	38.8%	52.4%
Sweden	30.1%	17.3%	17.3%	14.0%	3.9%	20.7%	3.9%	20.7%
Switzerland	16.6%	-22.6%	16.6%	16.6%	11.6%	17.0%	11.6%	17.0%
Turkey	8.8%	0.0%	0.0%	15.0%	7.2%	29.1%	21.8%	23.4%
United Kingdom	20.0%	-10.4%	9.7%	0.0%	28.4%	48.5%	28.4%	30.4%
United States	0.0%	0.0%	25.0%	0.0%	45.0%	56.4%	45.0%	56.4%
Argentina	25.0%	0.0%	0.0%	0.0%	28.3%	52.9%	5.8%	52.9%
Bulgaria	0.0%	-18.5%	0.0%	8.0%	9.6%	23.2%	17.2%	30.7%
Colombia	0.0%	0.0%	0.0%	0.0%	11.9%	11.5%	18.6%	18.4%
Lithuania	0.0%	-29.4%	0.0%	0.0%	2.7%	18.7%	2.7%	18.7%
South Africa	15.0%	-12.2%	7.7%	0.0%	22.9%	41.8%	22.9%	25.0%

StatLink http://dx.doi.org/10.1787/888933661932

Table B.2. **Marginal effective tax rates by asset: zero inflation, 100% of average wage, 2016**

Standard assumptions: 3% real return, 5 years expected holding period (20 years for pensions and property)

Country	Bank deposits	Corporate bonds		Government bonds		Shares		
		Issued at par	Issued at discount	Issued at par	Issued at discount	100% distribution	50% distribution	0% distribution
Australia	39.0%	39.0%	38.2%	39.0%	38.2%	9.0%	13.1%	17.3%
Austria	25.0%	27.5%	26.8%	27.5%	26.8%	27.5%	26.1%	24.7%
Belgium	27.0%	27.7%	27.0%	27.7%	27.0%	29.0%	15.4%	1.8%
Canada	29.7%	29.7%	25.6%	29.7%	25.6%	6.4%	9.7%	13.1%
Chile	0.0%	0.0%	0.0%	0.0%	0.0%	-20.0%	-10.0%	0.0%
Czech Republic	15.0%	15.0%	11.3%	15.0%	11.3%	15.0%	7.5%	0.0%
Denmark	37.0%	37.0%	36.2%	37.0%	36.2%	42.0%	40.3%	38.5%
Estonia	0.0%	20.0%	19.5%	20.0%	19.5%	0.0%	8.8%	17.8%
Finland	30.0%	30.0%	29.3%	30.0%	29.3%	25.5%	26.3%	27.0%
France	44.0%	44.0%	43.1%	44.0%	43.1%	32.0%	29.1%	26.1%
Germany	0.0%	0.0%	0.0%	0.0%	0.0%	0.0%	0.0%	0.0%
Greece	15.0%	15.0%	14.6%	0.0%	0.0%	23.3%	24.2%	25.0%
Hungary	15.0%	15.0%	11.3%	15.0%	11.3%	10.0%	9.4%	8.8%
Iceland	20.0%	20.0%	19.5%	20.0%	19.5%	20.0%	18.9%	17.8%
Ireland	41.0%	45.5%	41.7%	45.5%	34.1%	52.6%	44.7%	36.4%
Israel	15.0%	15.0%	14.6%	15.0%	14.6%	25.0%	23.7%	22.4%
Italy	27.5%	27.5%	26.8%	14.0%	13.6%	26.9%	25.5%	24.1%
Japan	20.0%	20.0%	19.5%	20.0%	19.5%	16.2%	17.0%	17.8%
Korea	14.0%	14.0%	13.6%	14.0%	13.6%	21.5%	14.0%	6.6%
Latvia	10.0%	10.0%	10.8%	10.0%	10.8%	10.0%	11.6%	13.3%
Luxembourg	10.0%	10.0%	7.5%	10.0%	7.5%	19.5%	9.8%	0.0%
Mexico	0.5%	0.5%	0.5%	0.5%	0.5%	-2.2%	3.3%	8.8%
Netherlands	40.0%	40.0%	40.0%	40.0%	40.0%	40.0%	40.0%	40.0%
New Zealand	30.0%	30.0%	29.3%	30.0%	29.3%	2.0%	1.0%	0.0%
Norway	53.3%	53.3%	52.9%	53.3%	52.9%	28.3%	28.3%	28.3%
Poland	19.0%	19.0%	18.5%	19.0%	18.5%	19.0%	18.0%	16.9%
Portugal	28.0%	28.0%	27.3%	28.0%	27.3%	28.0%	26.6%	25.2%
Slovak Republic	19.0%	19.0%	18.5%	19.0%	18.5%	0.0%	8.4%	16.9%
Slovenia	25.0%	25.0%	24.4%	25.0%	24.4%	25.0%	19.2%	13.3%
Spain	21.0%	21.0%	20.0%	21.0%	20.4%	21.0%	19.9%	18.7%
Sweden	30.0%	30.0%	29.3%	30.0%	29.3%	30.0%	28.5%	27.0%
Switzerland	30.2%	31.3%	25.5%	31.3%	25.5%	31.3%	19.8%	8.3%
Turkey	15.0%	15.0%	14.6%	15.0%	14.6%	13.9%	6.9%	0.0%
United Kingdom	0.0%	0.0%	0.0%	0.0%	0.0%	0.0%	0.0%	0.0%
United States	25.0%	25.0%	24.4%	25.0%	24.4%	15.0%	14.1%	13.3%
Argentina	0.0%	25.0%	25.0%	0.0%	0.0%	25.0%	25.0%	25.0%
Bulgaria	8.0%	0.0%	0.0%	0.0%	0.0%	5.0%	2.5%	0.0%
Colombia	7.0%	4.0%	3.9%	4.0%	3.9%	0.0%	0.0%	0.0%
Lithuania	0.0%	0.0%	0.0%	0.0%	0.0%	15.0%	7.5%	0.0%
South Africa	0.0%	0.0%	0.0%	0.0%	0.0%	16.9%	13.9%	10.8%

Table B.2. **Marginal effective tax rates by asset: zero inflation, 100% of average wage, 2016** *(cont.)*

Standard assumptions: 3% real return, 5 years expected holding period (20 years for pensions and property)

Country	Investment funds	Pension funds		Tax-favoured savings accounts	Residential property			
					Equity-financed		Debt-financed	
		Deductible contributions	Non-deductible contributions		Owner-occupied	Rented	Owner-occupied	Rented
Australia	39.0%	-37.6%	15.0%	39.0%	14.7%	79.2%	51.5%	79.2%
Austria	24.8%	-7.4%	0.0%	25.0%	15.5%	45.0%	39.0%	28.8%
Belgium	0.0%	-52.4%	13.3%	15.0%	49.3%	50.6%	31.7%	73.1%
Canada	29.7%	0.0%	20.0%	0.0%	38.9%	69.3%	64.2%	69.3%
Chile	3.5%	0.0%	2.5%	0.0%	21.2%	21.2%	17.5%	17.4%
Czech Republic	5.0%	0.0%	9.7%	15.0%	11.1%	22.1%	11.1%	22.1%
Denmark	42.0%	15.3%	15.3%	42.0%	21.3%	39.6%	17.7%	43.7%
Estonia	17.8%	-20.8%	16.7%	0.0%	0.0%	16.2%	-21.6%	16.2%
Finland	27.0%	0.0%	20.3%	0.0%	12.1%	39.9%	26.0%	39.9%
France	40.4%	-9.0%	23.4%	0.0%	22.8%	44.7%	63.0%	82.3%
Germany	0.0%	0.0%	28.9%	0.0%	19.4%	65.8%	19.4%	26.1%
Greece	13.3%	0.0%	0.0%	15.0%	27.2%	27.4%	30.9%	31.3%
Hungary	8.8%	-41.7%	0.0%	0.0%	10.3%	25.2%	24.7%	39.2%
Iceland	17.8%	0.0%	26.6%	20.0%	15.5%	25.2%	34.3%	43.8%
Ireland	37.5%	15.3%	32.4%	41.0%	6.6%	53.0%	46.6%	54.0%
Israel	22.4%	-89.7%	0.0%	0.0%	10.0%	28.4%	24.4%	42.1%
Italy	20.2%	-9.3%	26.7%	27.5%	1.8%	47.2%	11.4%	71.5%
Japan	17.8%	-8.1%	7.8%	0.0%	17.7%	34.1%	3.5%	37.7%
Korea	14.0%	-13.3%	3.2%	9.0%	5.6%	5.1%	4.6%	19.1%
Latvia	10.0%	-39.8%	10.0%	10.0%	21.8%	30.0%	31.0%	39.1%
Luxembourg	0.0%	-53.3%	12.8%	0.0%	0.3%	40.9%	10.3%	11.4%
Mexico	8.8%	-36.2%	0.0%	0.5%	11.1%	28.4%	-6.8%	11.4%
Netherlands	40.0%	-7.2%	0.0%	40.0%	10.5%	49.8%	15.8%	49.8%
New Zealand	28.0%	28.0%	28.0%	30.0%	20.0%	46.0%	47.8%	46.0%
Norway	51.6%	-3.9%	53.3%	41.7%	16.7%	56.8%	46.0%	82.0%
Poland	16.9%	-16.3%	16.7%	19.0%	5.9%	15.0%	24.5%	25.9%
Portugal	20.0%	25.0%	0.0%	28.0%	15.0%	41.0%	41.5%	65.3%
Slovak Republic	16.9%	12.5%	12.5%	19.0%	0.4%	20.6%	19.3%	38.6%
Slovenia	13.3%	-30.8%	22.5%	25.0%	7.9%	34.2%	32.1%	56.6%
Spain	18.7%	0.0%	19.0%	0.0%	33.2%	43.8%	38.8%	52.5%
Sweden	30.1%	19.9%	19.9%	14.0%	3.9%	20.7%	3.9%	20.7%
Switzerland	30.2%	-38.1%	22.9%	30.2%	23.3%	30.6%	30.6%	37.9%
Turkey	8.8%	0.0%	0.0%	15.0%	7.2%	36.5%	21.8%	23.8%
United Kingdom	20.0%	-10.4%	9.7%	0.0%	28.4%	48.5%	28.4%	30.4%
United States	15.0%	0.0%	41.7%	0.0%	39.8%	47.0%	39.8%	47.0%
Argentina	25.0%	0.0%	0.0%	0.0%	28.3%	57.1%	1.5%	57.1%
Bulgaria	0.0%	-18.5%	0.0%	8.0%	9.6%	23.2%	17.2%	30.7%
Colombia	0.0%	0.0%	0.0%	0.0%	11.9%	11.5%	18.6%	18.4%
Lithuania	0.0%	-29.4%	0.0%	0.0%	2.7%	18.7%	2.7%	18.7%
South Africa	15.0%	-19.5%	11.3%	0.0%	22.9%	50.1%	22.9%	26.1%

StatLink http://dx.doi.org/10.1787/888933661951

Table B.3. Marginal effective tax rates by asset: zero inflation, 500% of average wage, 2016

Standard assumptions: 3% real return, 5 years expected holding period (20 years for pensions and property)

Country	Bank deposits	Corporate bonds		Government bonds		Shares		
		Issued at par	Issued at discount	Issued at par	Issued at discount	100% distribution	50% distribution	0% distribution
Australia	49.0%	49.0%	48.1%	49.0%	48.1%	19.0%	20.4%	21.9%
Austria	25.0%	27.5%	26.8%	27.5%	26.8%	27.5%	26.1%	24.7%
Belgium	27.0%	27.7%	27.0%	27.7%	27.0%	29.0%	15.4%	1.8%
Canada	53.5%	53.5%	46.3%	53.5%	46.3%	39.3%	31.8%	24.0%
Chile	23.0%	23.0%	22.6%	23.0%	17.3%	-1.0%	10.1%	21.5%
Czech Republic	15.0%	15.0%	11.3%	15.0%	11.3%	15.0%	7.5%	0.0%
Denmark	42.0%	42.0%	41.1%	42.0%	41.1%	42.0%	40.3%	38.5%
Estonia	0.0%	20.0%	19.5%	20.0%	19.5%	0.0%	8.8%	17.8%
Finland	30.0%	30.0%	30.2%	30.0%	30.2%	25.5%	28.1%	30.8%
France	71.1%	71.1%	70.5%	71.1%	70.5%	54.7%	51.5%	48.1%
Germany	26.4%	26.4%	25.7%	26.4%	25.7%	26.4%	25.0%	23.7%
Greece	15.0%	15.0%	14.6%	0.0%	0.0%	23.3%	24.2%	25.0%
Hungary	15.0%	15.0%	11.3%	15.0%	11.3%	10.0%	9.4%	8.8%
Iceland	20.0%	20.0%	19.5%	20.0%	19.5%	20.0%	18.9%	17.8%
Ireland	41.0%	48.0%	43.6%	48.0%	36.0%	55.1%	46.0%	36.4%
Israel	15.0%	15.0%	14.6%	15.0%	14.6%	25.0%	23.7%	22.4%
Italy	27.5%	27.5%	26.8%	14.0%	13.6%	26.9%	25.5%	24.1%
Japan	20.0%	20.0%	19.5%	20.0%	19.5%	20.0%	18.9%	17.8%
Korea	38.0%	38.0%	37.2%	38.0%	37.2%	45.2%	25.9%	6.6%
Latvia	10.0%	10.0%	10.8%	10.0%	10.8%	10.0%	11.6%	13.3%
Luxembourg	10.0%	10.0%	7.5%	10.0%	7.5%	20.0%	10.0%	0.0%
Mexico	30.0%	30.0%	29.7%	30.0%	29.7%	10.0%	9.4%	8.8%
Netherlands	40.0%	40.0%	40.0%	40.0%	40.0%	40.0%	40.0%	40.0%
New Zealand	33.0%	33.0%	31.4%	33.0%	31.4%	5.0%	2.5%	0.0%
Norway	53.3%	53.3%	52.9%	53.3%	52.9%	28.3%	28.3%	28.3%
Poland	19.0%	19.0%	18.5%	19.0%	18.5%	19.0%	18.0%	16.9%
Portugal	28.0%	28.0%	27.3%	28.0%	27.3%	28.0%	26.6%	25.2%
Slovak Republic	19.0%	19.0%	18.5%	19.0%	18.5%	0.0%	8.4%	16.9%
Slovenia	25.0%	25.0%	24.4%	25.0%	24.4%	25.0%	19.2%	13.3%
Spain	23.0%	23.0%	21.9%	23.0%	21.9%	23.0%	20.9%	20.6%
Sweden	30.0%	30.0%	29.3%	30.0%	29.3%	30.0%	28.5%	27.0%
Switzerland	53.0%	54.1%	44.4%	54.1%	44.4%	54.1%	34.8%	15.6%
Turkey	15.0%	15.0%	14.6%	15.0%	14.6%	17.9%	8.9%	0.0%
United Kingdom	45.0%	45.0%	38.3%	45.0%	38.3%	48.6%	35.0%	21.1%
United States	36.8%	36.8%	36.0%	36.8%	36.0%	18.8%	17.8%	16.7%
Argentina	0.0%	41.7%	41.7%	0.0%	0.0%	41.7%	41.7%	41.7%
Bulgaria	8.0%	0.0%	0.0%	0.0%	0.0%	5.0%	2.5%	0.0%
Colombia	7.0%	4.0%	3.9%	4.0%	3.9%	0.0%	0.0%	0.0%
Lithuania	15.0%	15.0%	14.6%	15.0%	14.6%	15.0%	14.1%	13.3%
South Africa	41.0%	41.0%	34.5%	41.0%	34.5%	16.9%	16.5%	16.2%

Table B.3. **Marginal effective tax rates by asset: zero inflation, 500% of average wage, 2016** *(cont.)*

Standard assumptions: 3% real return, 5 years expected holding period (20 years for pensions and property)

Country	Investment funds	Pension funds		Tax-favoured savings accounts	Residential property			
					Equity-financed		Debt-financed	
		Deductible contributions	Non-deductible contributions		Owner-occupied	Rented	Owner-occupied	Rented
Australia	49.0%	-24.1%	15.0%	49.0%	14.7%	89.0%	61.0%	89.0%
Austria	24.8%	-7.4%	0.0%	25.0%	15.5%	50.8%	39.0%	27.0%
Belgium	0.0%	-52.4%	13.3%	15.0%	49.3%	50.6%	71.3%	73.2%
Canada	53.5%	0.0%	39.2%	0.0%	40.0%	94.4%	85.5%	94.4%
Chile	20.6%	0.0%	15.2%	23.0%	24.8%	24.8%	24.8%	24.8%
Czech Republic	5.0%	0.0%	9.7%	15.0%	11.1%	22.1%	11.1%	22.1%
Denmark	42.0%	15.3%	15.3%	42.0%	21.3%	44.7%	23.1%	48.2%
Estonia	17.8%	-20.8%	16.7%	0.0%	3.8%	20.0%	3.8%	20.0%
Finland	30.8%	0.0%	20.3%	0.0%	17.0%	44.4%	28.4%	44.4%
France	68.6%	-15.9%	30.8%	71.1%	33.9%	65.7%	95.9%	120.8%
Germany	26.4%	0.0%	31.4%	26.4%	19.4%	69.3%	45.5%	52.1%
Greece	13.3%	0.0%	0.0%	15.0%	38.5%	38.7%	42.1%	42.4%
Hungary	8.8%	-41.7%	0.0%	0.0%	10.3%	25.2%	24.7%	39.2%
Iceland	17.8%	0.0%	33.0%	20.0%	15.5%	25.2%	34.3%	43.8%
Ireland	37.5%	22.2%	34.5%	41.0%	6.6%	55.6%	46.6%	56.6%
Israel	22.4%	-89.7%	0.0%	0.0%	22.2%	28.4%	36.0%	42.1%
Italy	20.2%	-63.7%	26.7%	27.5%	1.8%	47.2%	11.4%	71.5%
Japan	17.8%	-43.0%	26.4%	0.0%	17.7%	70.8%	3.5%	42.1%
Korea	38.0%	-13.3%	3.2%	9.0%	10.6%	50.0%	47.1%	70.2%
Latvia	10.0%	-39.8%	10.0%	10.0%	25.8%	33.7%	34.9%	42.6%
Luxembourg	0.0%	-55.6%	13.1%	0.0%	0.3%	42.0%	10.3%	11.5%
Mexico	8.8%	-20.6%	14.1%	30.0%	13.6%	43.0%	13.6%	43.0%
Netherlands	40.0%	0.0%	0.0%	40.0%	10.5%	49.8%	11.4%	49.8%
New Zealand	28.0%	28.0%	28.0%	33.0%	20.0%	48.6%	50.5%	48.6%
Norway	51.6%	0.0%	53.3%	41.7%	16.7%	56.8%	46.0%	82.0%
Poland	16.9%	-53.9%	16.7%	19.0%	5.9%	15.0%	24.5%	26.6%
Portugal	28.0%	-25.0%	0.0%	28.0%	20.8%	61.2%	52.0%	74.4%
Slovak Republic	16.9%	12.5%	12.5%	19.0%	0.4%	27.0%	19.3%	44.6%
Slovenia	13.3%	-83.3%	41.7%	25.0%	7.9%	34.2%	32.1%	56.6%
Spain	20.6%	0.0%	30.7%	0.0%	33.2%	49.6%	40.6%	54.6%
Sweden	30.1%	46.0%	46.0%	14.0%	3.9%	20.7%	3.9%	20.7%
Switzerland	53.0%	-90.0%	38.4%	53.0%	41.5%	53.6%	55.9%	67.5%
Turkey	8.8%	0.0%	0.0%	15.0%	7.2%	44.9%	21.8%	24.4%
United Kingdom	45.0%	-34.1%	23.1%	45.0%	28.4%	74.0%	68.6%	74.0%
United States	18.8%	0.0%	55.0%	0.0%	33.7%	36.7%	33.7%	36.7%
Argentina	41.7%	0.0%	0.0%	0.0%	45.0%	82.3%	45.0%	82.3%
Bulgaria	0.0%	-18.5%	0.0%	8.0%	9.6%	23.2%	17.2%	30.7%
Colombia	0.0%	-64.8%	0.0%	-259.3%	14.0%	43.1%	-8.2%	22.9%
Lithuania	13.3%	-29.4%	0.0%	15.0%	16.0%	32.0%	30.1%	45.6%
South Africa	15.0%	-4.7%	27.4%	0.0%	41.0%	72.4%	75.7%	72.4%

StatLink http://dx.doi.org/10.1787/888933661970

Table B.4. **Marginal effective tax rates by asset: 2% real return, 67% of average wage, 2016**

Standard assumptions: country actual inflation, 5 years expected holding period (20 years for pensions and property)

Country	Bank deposits	Corporate bonds		Government bonds		Shares		
		Issued at par	Issued at discount	Issued at par	Issued at discount	100% distribution	50% distribution	0% distribution
Australia	70.4%	70.4%	68.3%	70.4%	68.3%	9.2%	19.4%	30.0%
Austria	47.9%	52.7%	51.0%	52.7%	51.0%	52.7%	49.4%	46.0%
Belgium	47.7%	48.7%	47.3%	48.7%	47.3%	50.7%	26.7%	2.7%
Canada	35.5%	35.1%	30.1%	35.1%	30.1%	0.0%	7.6%	15.3%
Chile	0.0%	0.0%	0.0%	0.0%	0.0%	-66.8%	-33.4%	0.0%
Czech Republic	24.9%	24.9%	18.7%	24.9%	18.7%	24.9%	12.5%	0.0%
Denmark	57.9%	57.9%	56.6%	57.9%	56.6%	65.7%	62.9%	59.9%
Estonia	0.0%	36.4%	35.2%	36.4%	35.2%	0.0%	15.6%	31.6%
Finland	50.9%	50.9%	49.5%	50.9%	49.5%	43.2%	44.2%	45.2%
France	41.7%	41.7%	40.8%	41.7%	40.8%	33.6%	31.0%	28.3%
Germany	0.0%	0.0%	0.0%	0.0%	0.0%	0.0%	0.0%	0.0%
Greece	12.5%	12.5%	12.3%	0.0%	0.0%	28.4%	29.3%	30.3%
Hungary	28.6%	28.6%	21.4%	28.6%	21.4%	19.1%	17.6%	16.2%
Iceland	0.0%	0.0%	10.5%	0.0%	10.5%	52.5%	47.9%	43.1%
Ireland	54.9%	34.2%	35.7%	34.2%	25.6%	45.1%	47.6%	50.3%
Israel	21.4%	21.4%	20.8%	21.4%	20.8%	25.7%	24.5%	23.2%
Italy	43.8%	43.8%	42.7%	22.3%	21.6%	42.9%	40.6%	38.2%
Japan	27.0%	27.0%	26.3%	27.0%	26.3%	14.3%	19.3%	24.3%
Korea	25.1%	25.1%	24.3%	25.1%	24.3%	36.6%	23.2%	9.9%
Latvia	15.0%	15.0%	16.2%	15.0%	16.2%	15.0%	17.4%	19.9%
Luxembourg	17.2%	17.2%	12.9%	17.2%	12.9%	29.2%	14.6%	0.0%
Mexico	1.4%	1.4%	1.3%	1.4%	1.3%	-25.4%	-1.9%	22.1%
Netherlands	60.0%	60.0%	60.0%	60.0%	60.0%	60.0%	60.0%	60.0%
New Zealand	27.1%	27.1%	26.4%	27.1%	26.4%	-16.3%	-8.1%	0.0%
Norway	90.6%	90.6%	89.5%	90.6%	89.5%	42.5%	42.5%	42.5%
Poland	29.2%	29.2%	28.4%	29.2%	28.4%	29.2%	27.5%	25.9%
Portugal	42.8%	42.8%	41.8%	42.8%	41.8%	42.8%	40.7%	38.4%
Slovak Republic	31.2%	31.2%	30.2%	31.2%	30.2%	0.0%	13.5%	27.4%
Slovenia	36.9%	36.9%	35.9%	36.9%	35.9%	36.9%	28.3%	19.6%
Spain	29.9%	29.9%	28.5%	29.9%	28.5%	29.9%	27.1%	24.2%
Sweden	37.5%	37.5%	36.7%	37.5%	36.7%	37.5%	36.0%	34.4%
Switzerland	12.5%	14.1%	11.0%	14.1%	11.0%	14.1%	7.8%	1.5%
Turkey	76.1%	76.1%	70.3%	76.1%	70.3%	52.6%	26.3%	0.0%
United Kingdom	0.0%	0.0%	0.0%	0.0%	0.0%	0.0%	0.0%	0.0%
United States	26.3%	26.3%	25.5%	26.3%	25.5%	0.0%	0.0%	0.0%
Argentina	0.0%	37.5%	37.5%	0.0%	0.0%	37.5%	37.5%	37.5%
Bulgaria	11.3%	0.0%	0.0%	0.0%	0.0%	7.0%	3.5%	0.0%
Colombia	7.0%	11.6%	10.9%	11.6%	10.9%	0.0%	0.0%	0.0%
Lithuania	0.0%	0.0%	0.0%	0.0%	0.0%	26.8%	13.4%	0.0%
South Africa	0.0%	0.0%	0.0%	0.0%	0.0%	60.8%	31.7%	22.7%

Table B.4. **Marginal effective tax rates by asset: 2% real return, 67% of average wage, 2016** *(cont.)*

Standard assumptions: country actual inflation, 5 years expected holding period (20 years for pensions and property)

Country	Investment funds	Pension funds		Tax-favoured savings accounts	Residential property			
					Equity-financed		Debt-financed	
		Deductible contributions	Non-deductible contributions		Owner-occupied	Rented	Owner-occupied	Rented
Australia	70.4%	-30.0%	30.6%	n.a.	20.9%	112.5%	75.8%	112.5%
Austria	47.0%	-11.1%	0.0%	47.9%	22.3%	66.3%	60.6%	50.1%
Belgium	0.0%	-78.6%	20.0%	0.0%	71.2%	73.0%	43.4%	107.8%
Canada	35.1%	0.0%	21.8%	0.0%	57.9%	87.8%	84.3%	87.8%
Chile	0.0%	0.0%	0.0%	n.a.	0.0%	0.0%	0.0%	0.0%
Czech Republic	8.3%	0.0%	15.5%	n.a.	15.6%	29.6%	15.6%	29.6%
Denmark	65.7%	23.9%	23.9%	n.a.	31.8%	57.6%	26.5%	64.8%
Estonia	31.6%	-31.3%	25.0%	n.a.	0.0%	27.4%	-34.5%	27.4%
Finland	45.2%	0.0%	32.9%	0.0%	17.6%	61.5%	38.5%	61.5%
France	37.7%	-3.5%	19.7%	0.0%	32.9%	52.7%	69.0%	87.9%
Germany	0.0%	0.0%	35.8%	n.a.	28.3%	77.1%	28.3%	28.5%
Greece	11.7%	0.0%	0.0%	n.a.	37.4%	32.5%	40.9%	36.1%
Hungary	16.2%	-62.5%	0.0%	0.0%	20.0%	39.3%	43.4%	62.0%
Iceland	43.1%	0.0%	55.0%	n.a.	23.2%	50.4%	59.2%	85.7%
Ireland	50.7%	17.2%	23.7%	n.a.	9.6%	43.6%	61.9%	70.4%
Israel	23.2%	-134.6%	0.0%	0.0%	15.0%	36.0%	34.6%	54.6%
Italy	32.1%	-12.1%	42.4%	n.a.	2.5%	65.0%	16.6%	100.8%
Japan	24.3%	-7.4%	7.1%	0.0%	28.3%	41.3%	5.1%	53.2%
Korea	25.1%	-29.4%	5.3%	0.0%	8.2%	12.2%	6.5%	34.2%
Latvia	15.0%	-59.7%	15.0%	n.a.	26.2%	39.2%	39.2%	52.2%
Luxembourg	0.0%	-64.4%	18.1%	0.0%	0.4%	50.6%	15.7%	12.1%
Mexico	22.1%	-30.4%	0.0%	n.a.	15.7%	47.0%	-5.0%	26.8%
Netherlands	60.0%	-92.5%	0.0%	n.a.	15.2%	74.2%	10.6%	74.2%
New Zealand	27.1%	27.1%	27.1%	n.a.	30.0%	48.4%	53.1%	48.4%
Norway	86.0%	-5.8%	90.6%	62.5%	24.4%	90.3%	62.2%	123.0%
Poland	25.9%	-24.4%	25.0%	n.a.	8.4%	19.9%	34.9%	33.9%
Portugal	42.8%	-37.5%	0.0%	n.a.	15.0%	50.5%	53.3%	86.2%
Slovak Republic	27.4%	19.8%	19.8%	n.a.	0.5%	26.2%	28.7%	53.2%
Slovenia	19.6%	-23.8%	20.0%	n.a.	11.3%	44.6%	45.1%	76.2%
Spain	24.2%	0.0%	22.3%	0.0%	50.0%	60.9%	57.5%	75.2%
Sweden	38.9%	23.5%	23.5%	21.0%	5.5%	24.4%	5.5%	24.4%
Switzerland	12.5%	-34.0%	12.5%	n.a.	14.5%	14.5%	14.5%	14.5%
Turkey	34.4%	0.0%	0.0%	n.a.	10.5%	38.2%	47.1%	22.7%
United Kingdom	39.0%	-15.6%	17.1%	0.0%	42.0%	75.9%	42.0%	45.6%
United States	0.0%	0.0%	37.5%	0.0%	67.4%	84.8%	67.4%	84.8%
Argentina	37.5%	0.0%	0.0%	n.a.	42.5%	73.6%	-20.8%	73.6%
Bulgaria	0.0%	-27.8%	0.0%	n.a.	13.7%	31.7%	24.0%	41.9%
Colombia	0.0%	0.0%	0.0%	0.0%	25.5%	25.1%	30.1%	29.8%
Lithuania	0.0%	-44.1%	0.0%	n.a.	4.0%	24.3%	4.0%	24.3%
South Africa	57.5%	-18.3%	18.7%	0.0%	34.4%	66.6%	34.4%	27.1%

StatLink http://dx.doi.org/10.1787/888933661989

Table B.5. **Marginal effective tax rates by asset: 2% real return, 100% of average wage, 2016**

Standard assumptions: country actual inflation, 5 years expected holding period (20 years for pensions and property)

Country	Bank deposits	Corporate bonds		Government bonds		Shares		
		Issued at par	Issued at discount	Issued at par	Issued at discount	100% distribution	50% distribution	0% distribution
Australia	79.6%	79.6%	77.3%	79.6%	77.3%	18.4%	26.1%	34.0%
Austria	47.9%	52.7%	51.0%	52.7%	51.0%	52.7%	49.4%	46.0%
Belgium	47.7%	48.7%	47.3%	48.7%	47.3%	50.7%	26.7%	2.7%
Canada	52.5%	51.9%	44.7%	51.9%	44.7%	11.3%	17.0%	22.7%
Chile	0.0%	0.0%	0.0%	0.0%	0.0%	-55.7%	-27.9%	0.0%
Czech Republic	24.9%	24.9%	18.7%	24.9%	18.7%	24.9%	12.5%	0.0%
Denmark	57.9%	57.9%	56.6%	57.9%	56.6%	65.7%	62.9%	59.9%
Estonia	0.0%	36.4%	35.2%	36.4%	35.2%	0.0%	15.6%	31.6%
Finland	50.9%	50.9%	49.5%	50.9%	49.5%	43.2%	44.2%	45.2%
France	63.8%	63.8%	62.5%	63.8%	62.5%	46.4%	42.2%	37.9%
Germany	0.0%	0.0%	0.0%	0.0%	0.0%	0.0%	0.0%	0.0%
Greece	12.5%	12.5%	12.3%	0.0%	0.0%	28.4%	29.3%	30.3%
Hungary	28.6%	28.6%	21.4%	28.6%	21.4%	19.1%	17.6%	16.2%
Iceland	52.5%	52.5%	50.2%	52.5%	50.2%	52.5%	47.9%	43.1%
Ireland	54.9%	61.0%	56.0%	61.0%	45.7%	71.6%	61.2%	50.3%
Israel	21.4%	21.4%	20.8%	21.4%	20.8%	25.7%	24.5%	23.2%
Italy	43.8%	43.8%	42.7%	22.3%	21.6%	42.9%	40.6%	38.2%
Japan	27.0%	27.0%	26.3%	27.0%	26.3%	21.9%	23.1%	24.3%
Korea	25.1%	25.1%	24.3%	25.1%	24.3%	36.6%	23.2%	9.9%
Latvia	15.0%	15.0%	16.2%	15.0%	16.2%	15.0%	17.4%	19.9%
Luxembourg	17.2%	17.2%	12.9%	17.2%	12.9%	33.5%	16.8%	0.0%
Mexico	1.4%	1.4%	1.3%	1.4%	1.3%	-6.0%	7.9%	22.1%
Netherlands	60.0%	60.0%	60.0%	60.0%	60.0%	60.0%	60.0%	60.0%
New Zealand	46.5%	46.5%	45.4%	46.5%	45.4%	3.1%	1.6%	0.0%
Norway	90.6%	90.6%	89.5%	90.6%	89.5%	42.5%	42.5%	42.5%
Poland	29.2%	29.2%	28.4%	29.2%	28.4%	29.2%	27.5%	25.9%
Portugal	42.8%	42.8%	41.8%	42.8%	41.8%	42.8%	40.7%	38.4%
Slovak Republic	31.2%	31.2%	30.2%	31.2%	30.2%	0.0%	13.5%	27.4%
Slovenia	36.9%	36.9%	35.9%	36.9%	35.9%	36.9%	28.3%	19.6%
Spain	29.9%	29.9%	28.5%	29.9%	29.2%	29.9%	28.4%	26.8%
Sweden	37.5%	37.5%	36.7%	37.5%	36.7%	37.5%	36.0%	34.4%
Switzerland	28.2%	29.8%	25.5%	29.8%	25.5%	29.8%	21.1%	12.4%
Turkey	76.1%	76.1%	70.3%	76.1%	70.3%	70.4%	35.2%	0.0%
United Kingdom	0.0%	0.0%	0.0%	0.0%	0.0%	0.0%	0.0%	0.0%
United States	43.9%	43.9%	42.6%	43.9%	42.6%	26.3%	24.6%	22.8%
Argentina	0.0%	37.5%	37.5%	0.0%	0.0%	37.5%	37.5%	37.5%
Bulgaria	11.3%	0.0%	0.0%	0.0%	0.0%	7.0%	3.5%	0.0%
Colombia	7.0%	11.6%	10.9%	11.6%	10.9%	0.0%	0.0%	0.0%
Lithuania	0.0%	0.0%	0.0%	0.0%	0.0%	26.8%	13.4%	0.0%
South Africa	0.0%	0.0%	0.0%	0.0%	0.0%	60.8%	46.5%	31.9%

Table B.5. **Marginal effective tax rates by asset: 2% real return, 100% of average wage, 2016** *(cont.)*

Standard assumptions: country actual inflation, 5 years expected holding period (20 years for pensions and property)

Country	Investment funds	Pension funds		Tax-favoured savings accounts	Residential property			
					Equity-financed		Debt-financed	
		Deductible contributions	Non-deductible contributions		Owner-occupied	Rented	Owner-occupied	Rented
Australia	79.6%	-48.3%	30.6%	n.a.	20.9%	119.7%	83.0%	119.7%
Austria	47.0%	-11.1%	0.0%	47.9%	22.3%	73.1%	60.6%	45.3%
Belgium	0.0%	-78.6%	20.0%	26.5%	71.2%	73.0%	43.4%	107.8%
Canada	51.9%	0.0%	33.1%	0.0%	57.9%	102.2%	96.9%	102.2%
Chile	8.8%	0.0%	5.3%	n.a.	31.9%	31.9%	29.2%	29.2%
Czech Republic	8.3%	0.0%	15.5%	n.a.	15.6%	29.6%	15.6%	29.6%
Denmark	65.7%	23.9%	23.9%	n.a.	31.8%	59.1%	26.5%	65.0%
Estonia	31.6%	-31.3%	25.0%	n.a.	0.0%	27.4%	-34.5%	27.4%
Finland	45.2%	0.0%	32.9%	0.0%	17.6%	62.5%	38.5%	62.5%
France	58.7%	-13.4%	34.3%	0.0%	32.9%	62.4%	88.1%	114.7%
Germany	0.0%	0.0%	44.9%	n.a.	28.3%	88.0%	28.3%	28.6%
Greece	11.7%	0.0%	0.0%	n.a.	37.4%	32.5%	40.9%	36.1%
Hungary	16.2%	-62.5%	0.0%	0.0%	20.0%	39.3%	43.4%	62.0%
Iceland	43.1%	0.0%	55.0%	n.a.	23.2%	50.4%	59.2%	85.7%
Ireland	50.7%	22.9%	45.0%	n.a.	9.6%	70.3%	61.9%	71.6%
Israel	23.2%	-134.6%	0.0%	0.0%	15.0%	36.0%	34.6%	54.6%
Italy	32.1%	-12.1%	42.4%	n.a.	2.5%	65.0%	16.6%	100.8%
Japan	24.3%	-12.1%	11.0%	0.0%	28.3%	48.8%	5.1%	53.7%
Korea	25.1%	-19.9%	5.3%	16.2%	8.2%	12.2%	6.5%	34.2%
Latvia	15.0%	-59.7%	15.0%	n.a.	32.2%	44.7%	45.0%	57.5%
Luxembourg	0.0%	-79.9%	20.9%	0.0%	0.4%	58.0%	15.7%	11.4%
Mexico	22.1%	-54.3%	0.0%	n.a.	15.7%	61.5%	-20.4%	27.3%
Netherlands	60.0%	-10.8%	0.0%	n.a.	15.2%	74.2%	10.6%	74.2%
New Zealand	43.4%	43.4%	43.4%	n.a.	30.0%	61.5%	69.6%	61.5%
Norway	86.0%	-5.8%	90.6%	62.5%	24.4%	90.3%	62.2%	123.0%
Poland	25.9%	-24.4%	25.0%	n.a.	8.4%	19.9%	34.9%	33.9%
Portugal	42.0%	37.5%	0.0%	n.a.	22.1%	57.1%	59.6%	92.1%
Slovak Republic	27.4%	19.8%	19.8%	n.a.	0.5%	26.2%	28.7%	53.2%
Slovenia	19.6%	-46.2%	33.8%	n.a.	11.3%	44.6%	45.1%	76.2%
Spain	26.8%	0.0%	27.6%	0.0%	50.0%	63.4%	57.5%	75.3%
Sweden	38.9%	26.9%	26.9%	21.0%	5.5%	24.4%	5.5%	24.4%
Switzerland	28.2%	-57.2%	17.3%	n.a.	31.0%	30.3%	43.2%	42.4%
Turkey	34.4%	0.0%	0.0%	n.a.	10.5%	47.5%	47.1%	12.1%
United Kingdom	39.0%	-15.6%	17.1%	0.0%	42.0%	75.9%	42.0%	45.6%
United States	26.3%	0.0%	62.5%	0.0%	59.6%	76.3%	59.6%	76.3%
Argentina	37.5%	0.0%	0.0%	n.a.	42.5%	79.0%	-34.4%	79.0%
Bulgaria	0.0%	-27.8%	0.0%	n.a.	13.7%	31.7%	24.0%	41.9%
Colombia	0.0%	0.0%	0.0%	0.0%	25.5%	25.1%	30.1%	29.8%
Lithuania	0.0%	-44.1%	0.0%	n.a.	4.0%	24.3%	4.0%	24.3%
South Africa	57.5%	-29.3%	27.4%	0.0%	34.4%	81.2%	34.4%	23.1%

StatLink http://dx.doi.org/10.1787/888933662008

Table B.6. **Marginal effective tax rates by asset: 2% real return, 500% of average wage, 2016**

Standard assumptions: country actual inflation, 5 years expected holding period (20 years for pensions and property)

Country	Bank deposits	Corporate bonds		Government bonds		Shares		
		Issued at par	Issued at discount	Issued at par	Issued at discount	100% distribution	50% distribution	0% distribution
Australia	100.0%	100.0%	97.6%	100.0%	97.6%	38.8%	40.9%	43.1%
Austria	47.9%	52.7%	51.0%	52.7%	51.0%	52.7%	49.4%	46.0%
Belgium	47.7%	48.7%	47.3%	48.7%	47.3%	50.7%	26.7%	2.7%
Canada	94.7%	93.6%	80.9%	93.6%	80.9%	69.6%	55.9%	41.7%
Chile	64.1%	64.1%	61.8%	64.1%	48.0%	-40.4%	-9.9%	22.3%
Czech Republic	24.9%	24.9%	18.7%	24.9%	18.7%	24.9%	12.5%	0.0%
Denmark	65.7%	65.7%	64.3%	65.7%	64.3%	65.7%	62.9%	59.9%
Estonia	0.0%	36.4%	35.2%	36.4%	35.2%	0.0%	15.6%	31.6%
Finland	50.9%	50.9%	51.0%	50.9%	51.0%	43.2%	47.3%	51.5%
France	103.9%	103.9%	103.1%	103.9%	103.1%	80.1%	75.5%	70.8%
Germany	41.8%	41.8%	40.7%	41.8%	40.7%	41.8%	39.6%	37.3%
Greece	12.5%	12.5%	12.3%	0.0%	0.0%	28.4%	29.3%	30.3%
Hungary	28.6%	28.6%	21.4%	28.6%	21.4%	19.1%	17.6%	16.2%
Iceland	52.5%	52.5%	50.2%	52.5%	50.2%	52.5%	47.9%	43.1%
Ireland	54.9%	64.3%	58.5%	64.3%	48.2%	74.9%	62.8%	50.3%
Israel	21.4%	21.4%	20.8%	21.4%	20.8%	25.7%	24.5%	23.2%
Italy	43.8%	43.8%	42.7%	22.3%	21.6%	42.9%	40.6%	38.2%
Japan	27.0%	27.0%	26.3%	27.0%	26.3%	27.0%	25.7%	24.3%
Korea	68.2%	68.2%	66.5%	68.2%	66.5%	79.2%	44.6%	9.9%
Latvia	15.0%	15.0%	16.2%	15.0%	16.2%	15.0%	17.4%	19.9%
Luxembourg	17.2%	17.2%	12.9%	17.2%	12.9%	34.4%	17.2%	0.0%
Mexico	83.1%	83.1%	80.9%	83.1%	80.9%	27.7%	24.9%	22.1%
Netherlands	60.0%	60.0%	60.0%	60.0%	60.0%	60.0%	60.0%	60.0%
New Zealand	51.2%	51.2%	49.9%	51.2%	49.9%	7.8%	3.9%	0.0%
Norway	90.6%	90.6%	89.5%	90.6%	89.5%	42.5%	42.5%	42.5%
Poland	29.2%	29.2%	28.4%	29.2%	28.4%	29.2%	27.5%	25.9%
Portugal	42.8%	42.8%	41.8%	42.8%	41.8%	42.8%	40.7%	38.4%
Slovak Republic	31.2%	31.2%	30.2%	31.2%	30.2%	0.0%	13.5%	27.4%
Slovenia	36.9%	36.9%	35.9%	36.9%	35.9%	36.9%	28.3%	19.6%
Spain	32.8%	32.8%	31.3%	32.8%	31.3%	32.8%	29.8%	29.4%
Sweden	37.5%	37.5%	36.7%	37.5%	36.7%	37.5%	36.0%	34.4%
Switzerland	50.9%	52.4%	45.2%	52.4%	45.2%	52.4%	37.9%	23.4%
Turkey	76.1%	76.1%	70.3%	76.1%	70.3%	90.6%	45.3%	0.0%
United Kingdom	87.8%	87.8%	74.5%	87.8%	74.5%	93.3%	66.3%	38.5%
United States	64.6%	64.6%	63.0%	64.6%	63.0%	33.0%	30.9%	28.8%
Argentina	0.0%	62.5%	62.5%	0.0%	0.0%	62.5%	62.5%	62.5%
Bulgaria	11.3%	0.0%	0.0%	0.0%	0.0%	7.0%	3.5%	0.0%
Colombia	7.0%	11.6%	10.9%	11.6%	10.9%	0.0%	0.0%	0.0%
Lithuania	26.8%	26.8%	25.9%	26.8%	25.9%	26.8%	25.0%	23.2%
South Africa	157.2%	157.2%	130.5%	157.2%	130.5%	60.8%	55.3%	49.5%

Table B.6. **Marginal effective tax rates by asset: 2% real return, 500% of average wage, 2016** *(cont.)*

Standard assumptions: country actual inflation, 5 years expected holding period (20 years for pensions and property)

Country	Investment funds	Pension funds		Tax-favoured savings accounts	Residential property			
					Equity-financed		Debt-financed	
		Deductible contributions	Non-deductible contributions		Owner-occupied	Rented	Owner-occupied	Rented
Australia	100.0%	-28.0%	30.6%	n.a.	20.9%	135.6%	98.9%	135.6%
Austria	47.0%	-11.1%	0.0%	47.9%	22.3%	80.9%	60.6%	39.7%
Belgium	0.0%	-78.6%	20.0%	26.5%	71.2%	73.1%	105.2%	107.9%
Canada	93.6%	0.0%	65.0%	0.0%	59.5%	140.1%	129.4%	140.1%
Chile	52.2%	0.0%	32.3%	n.a.	37.1%	37.1%	64.6%	65.4%
Czech Republic	8.3%	0.0%	15.5%	n.a.	15.6%	29.6%	15.6%	29.6%
Denmark	65.7%	23.9%	23.9%	n.a.	31.8%	69.0%	34.3%	74.2%
Estonia	31.6%	-31.3%	25.0%	n.a.	5.7%	33.2%	5.7%	33.2%
Finland	51.5%	0.0%	32.9%	0.0%	24.5%	68.8%	41.8%	68.8%
France	100.5%	-23.9%	45.2%	103.9%	49.4%	92.8%	135.1%	169.9%
Germany	41.8%	0.0%	48.8%	n.a.	28.3%	92.5%	66.3%	66.6%
Greece	11.7%	0.0%	0.0%	n.a.	54.4%	49.1%	57.7%	52.5%
Hungary	16.2%	-62.5%	0.0%	0.0%	20.0%	39.3%	43.4%	62.0%
Iceland	43.1%	0.0%	68.3%	n.a.	23.2%	50.4%	59.2%	85.7%
Ireland	50.7%	33.3%	47.8%	n.a.	9.6%	73.6%	61.9%	74.9%
Israel	23.2%	-134.6%	0.0%	0.0%	32.1%	36.0%	50.8%	54.6%
Italy	32.1%	-93.8%	42.4%	n.a.	2.5%	65.0%	16.6%	100.8%
Japan	24.3%	-64.5%	36.9%	0.0%	28.3%	95.6%	5.1%	57.0%
Korea	68.2%	-19.9%	5.3%	16.2%	15.6%	71.1%	72.7%	103.4%
Latvia	15.0%	-59.7%	15.0%	n.a.	38.3%	50.1%	50.9%	62.7%
Luxembourg	0.0%	-83.3%	21.5%	0.0%	0.4%	59.5%	15.7%	11.3%
Mexico	22.1%	-30.9%	29.7%	n.a.	19.4%	84.8%	19.4%	84.8%
Netherlands	60.0%	0.0%	0.0%	n.a.	15.2%	74.2%	3.1%	74.2%
New Zealand	43.4%	43.4%	43.4%	n.a.	30.0%	64.7%	73.6%	64.7%
Norway	86.0%	0.0%	90.6%	62.5%	24.4%	90.3%	62.2%	123.0%
Poland	25.9%	-80.9%	25.0%	n.a.	8.4%	19.9%	34.9%	32.1%
Portugal	42.8%	-37.5%	0.0%	n.a.	38.6%	74.1%	74.3%	107.5%
Slovak Republic	27.4%	19.8%	19.8%	n.a.	0.5%	34.3%	28.7%	60.7%
Slovenia	19.6%	-125.0%	62.5%	n.a.	11.3%	44.6%	45.1%	76.2%
Spain	29.4%	0.0%	44.5%	0.0%	50.2%	71.0%	60.3%	77.9%
Sweden	38.9%	61.2%	61.2%	21.0%	5.5%	24.4%	5.5%	24.4%
Switzerland	50.9%	-135.0%	29.0%	n.a.	55.5%	52.8%	79.1%	75.6%
Turkey	34.4%	0.0%	0.0%	n.a.	10.5%	58.2%	47.1%	-1.6%
United Kingdom	87.8%	-51.1%	40.7%	87.8%	42.0%	114.3%	107.7%	114.3%
United States	33.0%	0.0%	82.5%	0.0%	50.5%	61.7%	50.5%	61.7%
Argentina	62.5%	0.0%	0.0%	n.a.	67.5%	114.8%	67.5%	114.8%
Bulgaria	0.0%	-27.8%	0.0%	n.a.	13.7%	31.7%	24.0%	41.9%
Colombia	0.0%	-97.2%	0.0%	-388.9%	28.7%	66.3%	-28.1%	14.0%
Lithuania	23.2%	-44.1%	0.0%	n.a.	24.0%	44.3%	45.9%	65.5%
South Africa	57.5%	-7.1%	66.5%	0.0%	59.6%	116.8%	137.9%	116.8%

StatLink http://dx.doi.org/10.1787/888933662027

Table B.7. **Marginal effective tax rates by asset: 4% real return, 67% of average wage, 2016**

Standard assumptions: country actual inflation, 5 years expected holding period (20 years for pensions and property)

Country	Bank deposits	Corporate bonds		Government bonds		Shares		
		Issued at par	Issued at discount	Issued at par	Issued at discount	100% distribution	50% distribution	0% distribution
Australia	52.4%	52.4%	50.2%	52.4%	50.2%	6.8%	13.7%	20.8%
Austria	36.4%	40.1%	38.3%	40.1%	38.3%	40.1%	36.5%	32.7%
Belgium	37.3%	37.9%	36.3%	37.9%	36.3%	38.9%	20.1%	1.3%
Canada	27.8%	27.6%	23.5%	27.6%	23.5%	0.0%	5.5%	11.1%
Chile	0.0%	0.0%	0.0%	0.0%	0.0%	-45.4%	-22.7%	0.0%
Czech Republic	20.0%	20.0%	15.0%	20.0%	15.0%	20.0%	10.0%	0.0%
Denmark	47.5%	47.5%	45.8%	47.5%	45.8%	53.9%	50.2%	46.3%
Estonia	0.0%	28.2%	26.9%	28.2%	26.9%	0.0%	11.2%	22.8%
Finland	40.4%	40.4%	38.8%	40.4%	38.8%	34.4%	34.0%	33.6%
France	35.3%	35.3%	33.9%	35.3%	33.9%	28.4%	25.4%	22.2%
Germany	0.0%	0.0%	0.0%	0.0%	0.0%	0.0%	0.0%	0.0%
Greece	13.8%	13.8%	13.3%	0.0%	0.0%	19.2%	19.8%	20.4%
Hungary	21.8%	21.8%	16.3%	21.8%	16.3%	14.5%	13.0%	11.5%
Iceland	0.0%	0.0%	6.7%	0.0%	6.7%	36.3%	32.1%	27.7%
Ireland	48.0%	29.8%	30.6%	29.8%	22.4%	35.6%	36.8%	38.0%
Israel	18.2%	18.2%	17.4%	18.2%	17.4%	25.7%	23.7%	21.6%
Italy	35.0%	35.0%	33.6%	17.5%	16.7%	34.5%	31.7%	28.7%
Japan	23.5%	23.5%	22.6%	23.5%	22.6%	12.5%	16.0%	19.7%
Korea	19.6%	19.6%	18.6%	19.6%	18.6%	25.7%	15.3%	5.0%
Latvia	12.5%	12.5%	13.2%	12.5%	13.2%	12.5%	13.9%	15.4%
Luxembourg	13.6%	13.6%	10.2%	13.6%	10.2%	23.1%	11.6%	0.0%
Mexico	0.9%	0.9%	0.9%	0.9%	0.9%	-17.3%	-1.8%	14.0%
Netherlands	30.0%	30.0%	30.0%	30.0%	30.0%	30.0%	30.0%	30.0%
New Zealand	22.3%	22.3%	21.3%	22.3%	21.3%	-13.4%	-6.7%	0.0%
Norway	57.8%	57.8%	56.4%	57.8%	56.4%	21.3%	21.3%	21.3%
Poland	24.1%	24.1%	23.0%	24.1%	23.0%	24.1%	22.0%	19.8%
Portugal	35.4%	35.4%	34.0%	35.4%	34.0%	35.4%	32.6%	29.7%
Slovak Republic	25.1%	25.1%	24.0%	25.1%	24.0%	0.0%	10.1%	20.5%
Slovenia	30.9%	30.9%	29.7%	30.9%	29.7%	30.9%	23.2%	15.3%
Spain	25.5%	25.5%	23.9%	25.5%	23.9%	25.5%	22.3%	19.1%
Sweden	33.8%	33.8%	32.6%	33.8%	32.6%	33.8%	31.4%	28.9%
Switzerland	14.6%	15.4%	11.8%	15.4%	11.8%	15.4%	8.1%	0.7%
Turkey	45.5%	45.5%	41.6%	45.5%	41.6%	31.5%	15.8%	0.0%
United Kingdom	0.0%	0.0%	0.0%	0.0%	0.0%	0.0%	0.0%	0.0%
United States	20.7%	20.7%	19.7%	20.7%	19.7%	0.0%	0.0%	0.0%
Argentina	0.0%	18.8%	18.8%	0.0%	0.0%	18.8%	18.8%	18.8%
Bulgaria	9.6%	0.0%	0.0%	0.0%	0.0%	6.0%	3.0%	0.0%
Colombia	7.0%	7.8%	7.3%	7.8%	7.3%	0.0%	0.0%	0.0%
Lithuania	0.0%	0.0%	0.0%	0.0%	0.0%	20.9%	10.4%	0.0%
South Africa	0.0%	0.0%	0.0%	0.0%	0.0%	38.0%	19.6%	13.2%

Table B.7. **Marginal effective tax rates by asset: 4% real return, 67% of average wage, 2016** *(cont.)*

Standard assumptions: country actual inflation, 5 years expected holding period (20 years for pensions and property)

Country	Investment funds	Pension funds		Tax-favoured savings accounts	Residential property			
					Equity-financed		Debt-financed	
		Deductible contributions	Non-deductible contributions		Owner-occupied	Rented	Owner-occupied	Rented
Australia	52.4%	-7.5%	22.8%	n.a.	11.5%	67.3%	49.6%	67.3%
Austria	35.0%	-5.5%	0.0%	36.4%	12.0%	46.3%	39.0%	34.7%
Belgium	0.0%	-39.3%	10.0%	0.0%	38.4%	39.4%	16.8%	64.6%
Canada	27.6%	0.0%	13.9%	0.0%	29.3%	50.3%	48.6%	50.3%
Chile	0.0%	0.0%	0.0%	n.a.	0.0%	0.0%	0.0%	0.0%
Czech Republic	6.7%	0.0%	10.1%	n.a.	8.8%	18.3%	8.8%	18.3%
Denmark	53.9%	19.6%	19.6%	n.a.	16.0%	42.0%	11.2%	46.9%
Estonia	22.8%	-15.6%	12.5%	n.a.	0.0%	19.7%	-25.2%	19.7%
Finland	33.6%	0.0%	21.2%	0.0%	9.3%	42.2%	24.9%	42.2%
France	29.7%	-1.7%	13.3%	0.0%	17.8%	32.9%	45.5%	59.5%
Germany	0.0%	0.0%	23.6%	n.a.	15.0%	47.5%	15.0%	10.8%
Greece	11.9%	0.0%	0.0%	n.a.	22.1%	22.7%	25.5%	26.2%
Hungary	11.5%	-31.3%	0.0%	0.0%	12.2%	25.6%	28.6%	41.3%
Iceland	27.7%	0.0%	31.6%	n.a.	11.7%	28.9%	35.4%	51.8%
Ireland	41.7%	8.6%	16.5%	n.a.	5.1%	33.3%	46.2%	54.4%
Israel	21.6%	-67.3%	0.0%	0.0%	7.5%	24.1%	22.6%	38.5%
Italy	24.3%	3.0%	32.5%	n.a.	1.4%	38.3%	11.4%	63.9%
Japan	19.7%	-3.7%	4.9%	0.0%	16.7%	26.1%	15.6%	35.5%
Korea	19.6%	-14.7%	3.3%	0.0%	4.3%	7.8%	3.1%	23.5%
Latvia	12.5%	-24.9%	12.5%	n.a.	13.6%	24.4%	23.5%	34.2%
Luxembourg	0.0%	-32.2%	11.6%	0.0%	0.2%	35.8%	11.3%	7.6%
Mexico	14.0%	-15.2%	0.0%	n.a.	8.7%	28.1%	-4.9%	15.1%
Netherlands	30.0%	-46.2%	0.0%	n.a.	8.1%	37.6%	-16.1%	37.6%
New Zealand	22.3%	22.3%	22.3%	n.a.	15.0%	28.6%	32.5%	28.6%
Norway	52.0%	-2.9%	57.8%	31.3%	12.8%	54.4%	30.9%	69.7%
Poland	19.8%	-12.2%	12.5%	n.a.	4.7%	12.5%	24.6%	22.2%
Portugal	35.4%	-18.8%	0.0%	n.a.	7.5%	34.2%	36.4%	60.3%
Slovak Republic	20.5%	12.8%	12.8%	n.a.	0.3%	17.8%	21.0%	37.3%
Slovenia	15.3%	-11.9%	10.0%	n.a.	6.2%	28.9%	31.8%	52.4%
Spain	19.1%	0.0%	15.2%	0.0%	29.8%	37.6%	35.7%	48.6%
Sweden	31.2%	15.8%	15.8%	10.5%	6.1%	23.5%	6.1%	23.5%
Switzerland	14.6%	-17.0%	14.6%	n.a.	10.2%	14.9%	10.2%	14.9%
Turkey	19.4%	0.0%	0.0%	n.a.	5.6%	24.6%	27.6%	15.4%
United Kingdom	29.5%	-7.8%	10.6%	0.0%	21.5%	45.1%	21.5%	23.6%
United States	0.0%	0.0%	18.8%	0.0%	33.8%	47.5%	33.8%	47.5%
Argentina	18.8%	0.0%	0.0%	n.a.	21.3%	42.5%	-17.3%	42.5%
Bulgaria	0.0%	-13.9%	0.0%	n.a.	7.5%	18.9%	15.4%	26.7%
Colombia	0.0%	0.0%	0.0%	0.0%	13.3%	13.2%	17.8%	17.7%
Lithuania	0.0%	-22.1%	0.0%	n.a.	2.0%	15.9%	2.0%	15.9%
South Africa	36.3%	-9.1%	10.2%	0.0%	17.2%	37.9%	17.2%	13.4%

StatLink http://dx.doi.org/10.1787/888933662046

Table B.8. **Marginal effective tax rates by asset: 4% real return, 100% of average wage, 2016**

Standard assumptions: country actual inflation, 5 years expected holding period (20 years for pensions and property)

Country	Bank deposits	Corporate bonds		Government bonds		Shares		
		Issued at par	Issued at discount	Issued at par	Issued at discount	100% distribution	50% distribution	0% distribution
Australia	59.3%	59.3%	56.9%	59.3%	56.9%	13.7%	18.5%	23.6%
Austria	36.4%	40.1%	38.3%	40.1%	38.3%	40.1%	36.5%	32.7%
Belgium	37.3%	37.9%	36.3%	37.9%	36.3%	38.9%	20.1%	1.3%
Canada	41.1%	40.8%	34.8%	40.8%	34.8%	8.9%	12.6%	16.5%
Chile	0.0%	0.0%	0.0%	0.0%	0.0%	-37.9%	-18.9%	0.0%
Czech Republic	20.0%	20.0%	15.0%	20.0%	15.0%	20.0%	10.0%	0.0%
Denmark	47.5%	47.5%	45.8%	47.5%	45.8%	53.9%	50.2%	46.3%
Estonia	0.0%	28.2%	26.9%	28.2%	26.9%	0.0%	11.2%	22.8%
Finland	40.4%	40.4%	38.8%	40.4%	38.8%	34.4%	34.0%	33.6%
France	53.9%	53.9%	52.2%	53.9%	52.2%	39.2%	34.7%	29.9%
Germany	0.0%	0.0%	0.0%	0.0%	0.0%	0.0%	0.0%	0.0%
Greece	13.8%	13.8%	13.3%	0.0%	0.0%	19.2%	19.8%	20.4%
Hungary	21.8%	21.8%	16.3%	21.8%	16.3%	14.5%	13.0%	11.5%
Iceland	36.3%	36.3%	34.2%	36.3%	34.2%	36.3%	32.1%	27.7%
Ireland	48.0%	53.2%	48.4%	53.2%	39.9%	58.8%	48.7%	38.0%
Israel	18.2%	18.2%	17.4%	18.2%	17.4%	25.7%	23.7%	21.6%
Italy	35.0%	35.0%	33.6%	17.5%	16.7%	34.5%	31.7%	28.7%
Japan	23.5%	23.5%	22.6%	23.5%	22.6%	19.0%	19.3%	19.7%
Korea	19.6%	19.6%	18.6%	19.6%	18.6%	25.7%	15.3%	5.0%
Latvia	12.5%	12.5%	13.2%	12.5%	13.2%	12.5%	13.9%	15.4%
Luxembourg	13.6%	13.6%	10.2%	13.6%	10.2%	26.5%	13.3%	0.0%
Mexico	0.9%	0.9%	0.9%	0.9%	0.9%	-4.1%	4.9%	14.0%
Netherlands	30.0%	30.0%	30.0%	30.0%	30.0%	30.0%	30.0%	30.0%
New Zealand	38.3%	38.3%	36.8%	38.3%	36.8%	2.6%	1.3%	0.0%
Norway	57.8%	57.8%	56.4%	57.8%	56.4%	21.3%	21.3%	21.3%
Poland	24.1%	24.1%	23.0%	24.1%	23.0%	24.1%	22.0%	19.8%
Portugal	35.4%	35.4%	34.0%	35.4%	34.0%	35.4%	32.6%	29.7%
Slovak Republic	25.1%	25.1%	24.0%	25.1%	24.0%	0.0%	10.1%	20.5%
Slovenia	30.9%	30.9%	29.7%	30.9%	29.7%	30.9%	23.2%	15.3%
Spain	25.5%	25.5%	23.9%	25.5%	24.4%	25.5%	23.4%	21.2%
Sweden	33.8%	33.8%	32.6%	33.8%	32.6%	33.8%	31.4%	28.9%
Switzerland	25.6%	26.4%	21.4%	26.4%	21.4%	26.4%	16.3%	6.2%
Turkey	45.5%	45.5%	41.6%	45.5%	41.6%	42.1%	21.1%	0.0%
United Kingdom	0.0%	0.0%	0.0%	0.0%	0.0%	0.0%	0.0%	0.0%
United States	34.4%	34.4%	32.9%	34.4%	32.9%	20.7%	18.7%	16.6%
Argentina	0.0%	18.8%	18.8%	0.0%	0.0%	18.8%	18.8%	18.8%
Bulgaria	9.6%	0.0%	0.0%	0.0%	0.0%	6.0%	3.0%	0.0%
Colombia	7.0%	7.8%	7.3%	7.8%	7.3%	0.0%	0.0%	0.0%
Lithuania	0.0%	0.0%	0.0%	0.0%	0.0%	20.9%	10.4%	0.0%
South Africa	0.0%	0.0%	0.0%	0.0%	0.0%	38.0%	28.4%	18.6%

Table B.8. **Marginal effective tax rates by asset: 4% real return, 100% of average wage, 2016** *(cont.)*

Standard assumptions: country actual inflation, 5 years expected holding period (20 years for pensions and property)

Country	Investment funds	Pension funds		Tax-favoured savings accounts	Residential property			
					Equity-financed		Debt-financed	
		Deductible contributions	Non-deductible contributions		Owner-occupied	Rented	Owner-occupied	Rented
Australia	59.3%	-16.7%	22.8%	n.a.	11.5%	72.2%	54.5%	72.2%
Austria	35.0%	-5.5%	0.0%	36.4%	12.0%	51.6%	39.0%	31.8%
Belgium	0.0%	-39.3%	10.0%	20.7%	38.4%	39.4%	16.8%	64.6%
Canada	40.8%	0.0%	21.1%	0.0%	29.3%	60.6%	57.9%	60.6%
Chile	5.5%	0.0%	3.0%	n.a.	15.9%	15.9%	13.4%	13.3%
Czech Republic	6.7%	0.0%	10.1%	n.a.	8.8%	18.3%	8.8%	18.3%
Denmark	53.9%	19.6%	19.6%	n.a.	16.0%	43.3%	11.2%	47.3%
Estonia	22.8%	-15.6%	12.5%	n.a.	0.0%	19.7%	-25.2%	19.7%
Finland	33.6%	0.0%	21.2%	0.0%	9.3%	43.2%	24.9%	43.2%
France	46.8%	-6.7%	23.3%	0.0%	17.8%	39.6%	60.2%	78.7%
Germany	0.0%	0.0%	29.6%	n.a.	15.0%	54.8%	15.0%	9.7%
Greece	11.9%	0.0%	0.0%	n.a.	22.1%	22.7%	25.5%	26.2%
Hungary	11.5%	-31.3%	0.0%	0.0%	12.2%	25.6%	28.6%	41.3%
Iceland	27.7%	0.0%	31.6%	n.a.	11.7%	28.9%	35.4%	51.8%
Ireland	41.7%	11.5%	31.6%	n.a.	5.1%	52.0%	46.2%	53.1%
Israel	21.6%	-67.3%	0.0%	0.0%	7.5%	24.1%	22.6%	38.5%
Italy	24.3%	3.0%	32.5%	n.a.	1.4%	38.3%	11.4%	63.9%
Japan	19.7%	-6.0%	7.6%	0.0%	16.7%	31.4%	15.6%	35.2%
Korea	19.6%	-9.9%	3.3%	12.6%	4.3%	7.8%	3.1%	23.5%
Latvia	12.5%	-24.9%	12.5%	n.a.	16.6%	27.2%	26.4%	36.8%
Luxembourg	0.0%	-40.0%	13.4%	0.0%	0.2%	41.1%	11.3%	6.9%
Mexico	14.0%	-27.2%	0.0%	n.a.	8.7%	37.5%	-15.1%	15.4%
Netherlands	30.0%	-5.4%	0.0%	n.a.	8.1%	37.6%	-16.1%	37.6%
New Zealand	35.7%	35.7%	35.7%	n.a.	15.0%	38.3%	44.9%	38.3%
Norway	52.0%	-2.9%	57.8%	31.3%	12.8%	54.4%	30.9%	69.7%
Poland	19.8%	-12.2%	12.5%	n.a.	4.7%	12.5%	24.6%	22.2%
Portugal	35.4%	-10.0%	0.0%	n.a.	11.5%	37.8%	39.8%	63.5%
Slovak Republic	20.5%	12.8%	12.8%	n.a.	0.3%	17.8%	21.0%	37.3%
Slovenia	15.3%	-23.1%	16.9%	n.a.	6.2%	28.9%	31.8%	52.4%
Spain	21.2%	0.0%	18.9%	0.0%	29.8%	39.3%	35.7%	48.5%
Sweden	31.2%	18.3%	18.3%	10.5%	6.1%	23.5%	6.1%	23.5%
Switzerland	25.6%	-28.6%	20.1%	n.a.	19.5%	25.9%	25.0%	31.4%
Turkey	19.4%	0.0%	0.0%	n.a.	5.6%	31.0%	27.6%	10.0%
United Kingdom	29.5%	-7.8%	10.6%	0.0%	21.5%	45.1%	21.5%	23.6%
United States	20.7%	0.0%	31.3%	0.0%	29.9%	48.4%	29.9%	48.4%
Argentina	18.8%	0.0%	0.0%	n.a.	21.3%	46.2%	-25.6%	46.2%
Bulgaria	0.0%	-13.9%	0.0%	n.a.	7.5%	18.9%	15.4%	26.7%
Colombia	0.0%	0.0%	0.0%	0.0%	13.3%	13.2%	17.8%	17.7%
Lithuania	0.0%	-22.1%	0.0%	n.a.	2.0%	15.9%	2.0%	15.9%
South Africa	36.3%	-14.6%	14.9%	0.0%	17.2%	47.3%	17.2%	11.4%

StatLink http://dx.doi.org/10.1787/888933662065

Table B.9. **Marginal effective tax rates by asset: 4% real return, 500% of average wage, 2016**

Standard assumptions: country actual inflation, 5 years expected holding period (20 years for pensions and property)

Country	Bank deposits	Corporate bonds		Government bonds		Shares		
		Issued at par	Issued at discount	Issued at par	Issued at discount	100% distribution	50% distribution	0% distribution
Australia	74.5%	74.5%	71.9%	74.5%	71.9%	28.9%	29.4%	29.9%
Austria	36.4%	40.1%	38.3%	40.1%	38.3%	40.1%	36.5%	32.7%
Belgium	37.3%	37.9%	36.3%	37.9%	36.3%	38.9%	20.1%	1.3%
Canada	74.1%	73.6%	63.2%	73.6%	63.2%	54.4%	42.8%	30.5%
Chile	43.5%	43.5%	41.4%	43.5%	32.6%	-19.2%	0.1%	20.7%
Czech Republic	20.0%	20.0%	15.0%	20.0%	15.0%	20.0%	10.0%	0.0%
Denmark	53.9%	53.9%	52.1%	53.9%	52.1%	53.9%	50.2%	46.3%
Estonia	0.0%	28.2%	26.9%	28.2%	26.9%	0.0%	11.2%	22.8%
Finland	40.4%	40.4%	39.9%	40.4%	39.9%	34.4%	36.3%	38.4%
France	79.2%	79.2%	77.8%	79.2%	77.8%	59.1%	54.0%	48.7%
Germany	34.1%	34.1%	32.7%	34.1%	32.7%	34.1%	31.3%	28.4%
Greece	13.8%	13.8%	13.3%	0.0%	0.0%	19.2%	19.8%	20.4%
Hungary	21.8%	21.8%	16.3%	21.8%	16.3%	14.5%	13.0%	11.5%
Iceland	36.3%	36.3%	34.2%	36.3%	34.2%	36.3%	32.1%	27.7%
Ireland	48.0%	56.2%	50.6%	56.2%	42.1%	61.7%	50.2%	38.0%
Israel	18.2%	18.2%	17.4%	18.2%	17.4%	25.7%	23.7%	21.6%
Italy	35.0%	35.0%	33.6%	17.5%	16.7%	34.5%	31.7%	28.7%
Japan	23.5%	23.5%	22.6%	23.5%	22.6%	23.5%	21.6%	19.7%
Korea	53.1%	53.1%	51.1%	53.1%	51.1%	58.9%	31.9%	5.0%
Latvia	12.5%	12.5%	13.2%	12.5%	13.2%	12.5%	13.9%	15.4%
Luxembourg	13.6%	13.6%	10.2%	13.6%	10.2%	27.2%	13.6%	0.0%
Mexico	56.6%	56.6%	54.3%	56.6%	54.3%	18.9%	16.4%	14.0%
Netherlands	30.0%	30.0%	30.0%	30.0%	30.0%	30.0%	30.0%	30.0%
New Zealand	42.1%	42.1%	40.5%	42.1%	40.5%	6.4%	3.2%	0.0%
Norway	57.8%	57.8%	56.4%	57.8%	56.4%	21.3%	21.3%	21.3%
Poland	24.1%	24.1%	23.0%	24.1%	23.0%	24.1%	22.0%	19.8%
Portugal	35.4%	35.4%	34.0%	35.4%	34.0%	35.4%	32.6%	29.7%
Slovak Republic	25.1%	25.1%	24.0%	25.1%	24.0%	0.0%	10.1%	20.5%
Slovenia	30.9%	30.9%	29.7%	30.9%	29.7%	30.9%	23.2%	15.3%
Spain	27.9%	27.9%	26.3%	27.9%	26.3%	27.9%	24.6%	23.3%
Sweden	33.8%	33.8%	32.6%	33.8%	32.6%	33.8%	31.4%	28.9%
Switzerland	44.6%	45.5%	37.0%	45.5%	37.0%	45.5%	28.6%	11.7%
Turkey	45.5%	45.5%	41.6%	45.5%	41.6%	54.3%	27.1%	0.0%
United Kingdom	66.4%	66.4%	56.0%	66.4%	56.0%	69.3%	48.1%	26.1%
United States	50.7%	50.7%	48.8%	50.7%	48.8%	25.9%	23.5%	21.0%
Argentina	0.0%	31.3%	31.3%	0.0%	0.0%	31.3%	31.3%	31.3%
Bulgaria	9.6%	0.0%	0.0%	0.0%	0.0%	6.0%	3.0%	0.0%
Colombia	7.0%	7.8%	7.3%	7.8%	7.3%	0.0%	0.0%	0.0%
Lithuania	20.9%	20.9%	19.9%	20.9%	19.9%	20.9%	18.9%	16.8%
South Africa	99.1%	99.1%	81.8%	99.1%	81.8%	38.0%	33.6%	29.0%

Table B.9. **Marginal effective tax rates by asset: 4% real return, 500% of average wage, 2016** *(cont.)*

Standard assumptions: country actual inflation, 5 years expected holding period (20 years for pensions and property)

Country	Investment funds	Pension funds		Tax-favoured savings accounts	Residential property			
					Equity-financed		Debt-financed	
		Deductible contributions	Non-deductible contributions		Owner-occupied	Rented	Owner-occupied	Rented
Australia	74.5%	-6.5%	22.8%	n.a.	11.5%	83.3%	65.6%	83.3%
Austria	35.0%	-5.5%	0.0%	36.4%	12.0%	57.8%	39.0%	28.2%
Belgium	0.0%	-39.3%	10.0%	20.7%	38.4%	39.4%	63.1%	64.7%
Canada	73.6%	0.0%	41.6%	0.0%	30.2%	87.4%	81.5%	87.4%
Chile	33.2%	0.0%	18.4%	n.a.	18.6%	18.6%	32.2%	32.6%
Czech Republic	6.7%	0.0%	10.1%	n.a.	8.8%	18.3%	8.8%	18.3%
Denmark	53.9%	19.6%	19.6%	n.a.	16.0%	52.0%	17.5%	55.4%
Estonia	22.8%	-15.6%	12.5%	n.a.	2.9%	22.6%	2.9%	22.6%
Finland	38.4%	0.0%	21.2%	0.0%	13.2%	46.7%	26.2%	46.7%
France	73.2%	-11.9%	30.8%	79.2%	26.1%	56.2%	85.7%	108.4%
Germany	34.1%	0.0%	32.2%	n.a.	15.0%	57.8%	43.1%	38.1%
Greece	11.9%	0.0%	0.0%	n.a.	30.6%	31.2%	33.8%	34.5%
Hungary	11.5%	-31.3%	0.0%	0.0%	12.2%	25.6%	28.6%	41.3%
Iceland	27.7%	0.0%	39.2%	n.a.	11.7%	28.9%	35.4%	51.8%
Ireland	41.7%	16.7%	33.7%	n.a.	5.1%	54.4%	46.2%	55.4%
Israel	21.6%	-67.3%	0.0%	0.0%	17.3%	24.1%	31.7%	38.5%
Italy	24.3%	-37.8%	32.5%	n.a.	1.4%	38.3%	11.4%	63.9%
Japan	19.7%	-32.3%	25.8%	0.0%	16.7%	63.9%	15.6%	32.7%
Korea	53.1%	-9.9%	3.3%	12.6%	8.0%	46.9%	49.1%	69.6%
Latvia	12.5%	-24.9%	12.5%	n.a.	19.6%	29.9%	29.3%	39.4%
Luxembourg	0.0%	-41.7%	13.8%	0.0%	0.2%	42.2%	11.3%	6.7%
Mexico	14.0%	-15.4%	17.0%	n.a.	10.7%	52.5%	10.7%	52.5%
Netherlands	30.0%	0.0%	0.0%	n.a.	8.1%	37.6%	-23.3%	37.6%
New Zealand	35.7%	35.7%	35.7%	n.a.	15.0%	40.6%	47.9%	40.6%
Norway	52.0%	0.0%	57.8%	31.3%	12.8%	54.4%	30.9%	69.7%
Poland	19.8%	-40.4%	12.5%	n.a.	4.7%	12.5%	24.6%	19.5%
Portugal	35.4%	18.8%	0.0%	n.a.	20.9%	48.9%	47.9%	73.3%
Slovak Republic	20.5%	12.8%	12.8%	n.a.	0.3%	23.4%	21.0%	42.3%
Slovenia	15.3%	-62.5%	31.3%	n.a.	6.2%	28.9%	31.8%	52.4%
Spain	23.3%	0.0%	30.6%	0.0%	30.1%	44.9%	38.0%	50.2%
Sweden	31.2%	43.6%	43.6%	10.5%	6.1%	23.5%	6.1%	23.5%
Switzerland	44.6%	-67.5%	33.7%	n.a.	34.5%	45.1%	45.4%	55.6%
Turkey	19.4%	0.0%	0.0%	n.a.	5.6%	38.3%	27.6%	3.0%
United Kingdom	66.4%	-25.6%	25.2%	66.4%	21.5%	71.8%	68.0%	71.8%
United States	25.9%	0.0%	41.3%	0.0%	25.3%	45.6%	25.3%	45.6%
Argentina	31.3%	0.0%	0.0%	n.a.	33.8%	66.1%	33.8%	66.1%
Bulgaria	0.0%	-13.9%	0.0%	n.a.	7.5%	18.9%	15.4%	26.7%
Colombia	0.0%	-48.6%	0.0%	-194.4%	15.0%	40.8%	-20.9%	8.7%
Lithuania	16.8%	-22.1%	0.0%	n.a.	12.0%	25.9%	27.8%	41.0%
South Africa	36.3%	-3.5%	35.9%	0.0%	31.7%	70.2%	80.5%	70.2%

StatLink http://dx.doi.org/10.1787/888933662084

Table B.10. **Marginal effective tax rates by asset: 6 months expected holding period (10 years for pensions and property), 67% of average wage, 2016**

Standard assumptions: 3% real return, country actual inflation

Country	Bank deposits	Corporate bonds		Government bonds		Shares		
		Issued at par	Issued at discount	Issued at par	Issued at discount	100% distribution	50% distribution	0% distribution
Australia	58.4%	58.4%	58.2%	58.4%	58.2%	7.6%	32.4%	57.5%
Austria	40.3%	44.3%	44.1%	44.3%	44.1%	44.3%	43.9%	43.5%
Belgium	40.8%	46.9%	46.7%	46.9%	46.7%	59.0%	38.5%	18.0%
Canada	30.3%	30.1%	26.2%	30.1%	26.2%	0.0%	7.4%	14.9%
Chile	0.0%	0.0%	0.0%	0.0%	0.0%	-52.6%	-26.3%	0.0%
Czech Republic	21.6%	21.6%	16.2%	21.6%	16.2%	21.6%	21.4%	21.2%
Denmark	50.9%	50.9%	50.8%	50.9%	50.8%	57.8%	57.5%	57.1%
Estonia	0.0%	30.9%	30.8%	30.9%	30.8%	0.0%	15.1%	30.4%
Finland	43.9%	43.9%	43.7%	43.9%	43.7%	37.3%	40.3%	43.2%
France	37.4%	37.4%	37.3%	37.4%	37.3%	30.1%	33.5%	36.9%
Germany	0.0%	0.0%	0.0%	0.0%	0.0%	0.0%	0.0%	0.0%
Greece	13.4%	13.4%	13.3%	0.0%	0.0%	142.2%	143.6%	145.0%
Hungary	24.1%	24.1%	23.9%	24.1%	23.9%	24.1%	23.8%	23.6%
Iceland	0.0%	0.0%	10.1%	0.0%	10.1%	41.7%	41.2%	40.6%
Ireland	50.3%	31.3%	33.4%	31.3%	23.5%	98.2%	102.1%	106.0%
Israel	19.3%	19.3%	19.2%	19.3%	19.2%	25.1%	24.9%	24.7%
Italy	49.9%	49.9%	49.7%	31.1%	30.9%	44.5%	44.2%	43.8%
Japan	24.7%	24.7%	24.6%	24.7%	24.6%	13.1%	18.7%	24.3%
Korea	21.4%	21.4%	21.3%	21.4%	21.3%	88.7%	77.4%	66.0%
Latvia	13.3%	13.3%	14.9%	13.3%	14.9%	13.3%	16.5%	19.6%
Luxembourg	14.8%	14.8%	23.4%	14.8%	23.4%	25.2%	37.3%	49.6%
Mexico	1.1%	1.1%	1.1%	1.1%	1.1%	-20.0%	0.6%	21.2%
Netherlands	40.0%	40.0%	40.0%	40.0%	40.0%	40.0%	40.0%	40.0%
New Zealand	23.9%	23.9%	23.8%	23.9%	23.8%	-14.4%	-7.2%	0.0%
Norway	68.8%	68.8%	68.6%	68.8%	68.6%	28.3%	28.3%	28.3%
Poland	25.8%	25.8%	25.7%	25.8%	25.7%	25.8%	25.6%	25.4%
Portugal	37.9%	37.9%	37.8%	37.9%	37.8%	37.9%	37.6%	37.3%
Slovak Republic	27.1%	27.1%	27.0%	27.1%	27.0%	0.0%	0.0%	0.0%
Slovenia	32.9%	32.9%	32.8%	32.9%	32.8%	32.9%	32.7%	32.4%
Spain	27.0%	27.0%	26.2%	27.0%	26.2%	27.0%	25.5%	24.0%
Sweden	35.0%	35.0%	34.9%	35.0%	34.9%	35.0%	34.8%	34.6%
Switzerland	13.9%	24.0%	20.5%	24.0%	20.5%	24.0%	17.0%	10.0%
Turkey	55.7%	55.7%	55.1%	55.7%	55.1%	38.5%	19.3%	0.0%
United Kingdom	0.0%	0.0%	0.0%	0.0%	0.0%	0.0%	0.0%	0.0%
United States	22.6%	22.6%	22.4%	22.6%	22.4%	0.0%	11.0%	22.1%
Argentina	0.0%	25.0%	25.0%	0.0%	0.0%	25.0%	25.0%	25.0%
Bulgaria	10.2%	0.0%	0.0%	0.0%	0.0%	6.4%	3.2%	0.0%
Colombia	7.0%	9.0%	9.0%	9.0%	9.0%	0.0%	0.0%	0.0%
Lithuania	0.0%	0.0%	0.0%	0.0%	0.0%	22.9%	11.4%	0.0%
South Africa	0.0%	0.0%	0.0%	0.0%	0.0%	60.6%	38.6%	16.6%

Table B.10. **Marginal effective tax rates by asset: 6 months expected holding period (10 years for pensions and property), 67% of average wage, 2016** *(cont.)*

Standard assumptions: 3% real return, country actual inflation

Country	Investment funds	Pension funds		Tax-favoured savings accounts	Residential property			
					Equity-financed		Debt-financed	
		Deductible contributions	Non-deductible contributions		Owner-occupied	Rented	Owner-occupied	Rented
Australia	58.4%	-55.3%	25.4%	n.a.	21.9%	91.3%	69.7%	91.3%
Austria	41.1%	-14.8%	0.0%	40.3%	21.1%	60.6%	54.7%	46.6%
Belgium	0.0%	-104.8%	26.7%	0.0%	67.8%	69.1%	44.0%	100.3%
Canada	30.1%	0.0%	21.7%	0.0%	41.3%	66.0%	65.9%	66.0%
Chile	0.0%	0.0%	0.0%	n.a.	0.0%	0.0%	0.0%	0.0%
Czech Republic	7.2%	0.0%	15.6%	n.a.	17.5%	28.5%	17.5%	28.5%
Denmark	57.8%	21.1%	21.1%	n.a.	22.3%	50.0%	18.5%	57.1%
Estonia	30.4%	-41.7%	33.3%	n.a.	0.0%	24.0%	-29.3%	24.0%
Finland	43.2%	0.0%	32.7%	0.0%	15.3%	53.9%	35.3%	53.9%
France	36.9%	-4.6%	19.9%	0.0%	32.0%	51.8%	64.4%	83.5%
Germany	0.0%	0.0%	35.8%	n.a.	29.3%	67.7%	29.3%	25.1%
Greece	13.2%	0.0%	0.0%	n.a.	32.0%	30.8%	35.5%	34.3%
Hungary	23.6%	-83.3%	0.0%	24.1%	22.8%	38.0%	43.1%	57.8%
Iceland	40.6%	0.0%	54.7%	n.a.	16.2%	40.3%	48.3%	71.9%
Ireland	49.7%	22.9%	24.1%	n.a.	8.2%	39.4%	55.1%	63.6%
Israel	24.7%	-179.5%	0.0%	0.0%	10.0%	40.5%	27.7%	57.1%
Italy	31.2%	-29.4%	38.6%	n.a.	2.8%	51.8%	26.1%	93.8%
Japan	24.3%	-9.9%	7.3%	0.0%	21.5%	31.9%	13.4%	42.8%
Korea	21.4%	-39.2%	5.3%	0.0%	7.3%	12.1%	5.9%	31.2%
Latvia	13.3%	-86.3%	13.3%	n.a.	21.0%	33.4%	32.8%	45.0%
Luxembourg	49.6%	-85.9%	18.1%	0.0%	0.3%	41.9%	13.6%	8.7%
Mexico	21.2%	-40.5%	0.0%	n.a.	16.7%	43.2%	-1.1%	25.7%
Netherlands	40.0%	-123.3%	0.0%	n.a.	13.7%	53.1%	-4.0%	53.1%
New Zealand	23.9%	23.9%	23.9%	n.a.	20.0%	35.2%	41.0%	35.2%
Norway	68.2%	-7.7%	68.8%	416.7%	20.7%	72.7%	46.4%	96.2%
Poland	25.4%	-32.5%	33.3%	n.a.	9.2%	18.2%	32.5%	29.4%
Portugal	37.9%	-50.0%	0.0%	n.a.	10.0%	40.4%	44.2%	72.9%
Slovak Republic	26.6%	19.8%	19.8%	n.a.	0.4%	20.6%	25.0%	44.5%
Slovenia	32.4%	-31.7%	26.7%	n.a.	13.4%	39.3%	43.3%	67.8%
Spain	24.0%	0.0%	22.6%	24.4%	52.8%	61.4%	59.5%	74.2%
Sweden	37.5%	22.5%	22.5%	14.0%	9.1%	26.9%	9.1%	26.9%
Switzerland	13.9%	-45.3%	13.9%	n.a.	11.6%	14.5%	11.6%	14.5%
Turkey	69.1%	0.0%	0.0%	n.a.	9.7%	31.6%	43.2%	17.7%
United Kingdom	32.7%	-20.8%	17.0%	0.0%	31.6%	60.3%	31.6%	33.1%
United States	0.0%	0.0%	50.0%	0.0%	45.6%	59.4%	45.6%	59.4%
Argentina	25.0%	0.0%	0.0%	n.a.	28.3%	52.9%	-30.8%	52.9%
Bulgaria	0.0%	-37.0%	0.0%	n.a.	13.6%	27.2%	22.8%	36.4%
Colombia	0.0%	0.0%	0.0%	0.0%	21.2%	20.9%	26.5%	26.2%
Lithuania	0.0%	-58.8%	0.0%	n.a.	2.7%	18.7%	2.7%	18.7%
South Africa	43.4%	-24.4%	19.2%	0.0%	22.9%	49.8%	22.9%	13.7%

StatLink http://dx.doi.org/10.1787/888933662103

Table B.11. **Marginal effective tax rates by asset: 6 months expected holding period (10 years for pensions and property), 100% of average wage, 2016**

Standard assumptions: 3% real return, country actual inflation

Country	Bank deposits	Corporate bonds		Government bonds		Shares		
		Issued at par	Issued at discount	Issued at par	Issued at discount	100% distribution	50% distribution	0% distribution
Australia	66.0%	66.0%	65.8%	66.0%	65.8%	15.2%	40.0%	65.0%
Austria	40.3%	44.3%	44.1%	44.3%	44.1%	44.3%	43.9%	43.5%
Belgium	40.8%	46.9%	46.7%	46.9%	46.7%	59.0%	38.5%	18.0%
Canada	44.9%	44.5%	38.8%	44.5%	38.8%	9.7%	15.8%	22.0%
Chile	0.0%	0.0%	0.0%	0.0%	0.0%	-43.8%	-21.9%	0.0%
Czech Republic	21.6%	21.6%	16.2%	21.6%	16.2%	21.6%	21.4%	21.2%
Denmark	50.9%	50.9%	50.8%	50.9%	50.8%	57.8%	57.5%	57.1%
Estonia	0.0%	30.9%	30.8%	30.9%	30.8%	0.0%	15.1%	30.4%
Finland	43.9%	43.9%	43.7%	43.9%	43.7%	37.3%	40.3%	43.2%
France	57.2%	57.2%	57.0%	57.2%	57.0%	41.6%	49.0%	56.5%
Germany	0.0%	0.0%	0.0%	0.0%	0.0%	0.0%	0.0%	0.0%
Greece	13.4%	13.4%	13.3%	0.0%	0.0%	142.2%	143.6%	145.0%
Hungary	24.1%	24.1%	23.9%	24.1%	23.9%	24.1%	23.8%	23.6%
Iceland	41.7%	41.7%	41.4%	41.7%	41.4%	41.7%	41.2%	40.6%
Ireland	50.3%	55.8%	51.9%	55.8%	41.9%	122.5%	114.3%	106.0%
Israel	19.3%	19.3%	19.2%	19.3%	19.2%	25.1%	24.9%	24.7%
Italy	49.9%	49.9%	49.7%	31.1%	30.9%	44.5%	44.2%	43.8%
Japan	24.7%	24.7%	24.6%	24.7%	24.6%	20.0%	22.1%	24.3%
Korea	21.4%	21.4%	21.3%	21.4%	21.3%	88.7%	77.4%	66.0%
Latvia	13.3%	13.3%	14.9%	13.3%	14.9%	13.3%	16.5%	19.6%
Luxembourg	14.8%	14.8%	25.3%	14.8%	25.3%	28.9%	42.8%	56.9%
Mexico	1.1%	1.1%	1.1%	1.1%	1.1%	-4.7%	8.2%	21.2%
Netherlands	40.0%	40.0%	40.0%	40.0%	40.0%	40.0%	40.0%	40.0%
New Zealand	41.0%	41.0%	40.9%	41.0%	40.9%	2.7%	1.4%	0.0%
Norway	68.8%	68.8%	68.6%	68.8%	68.6%	28.3%	28.3%	28.3%
Poland	25.8%	25.8%	25.7%	25.8%	25.7%	25.8%	25.6%	25.4%
Portugal	37.9%	37.9%	37.8%	37.9%	37.8%	37.9%	37.6%	37.3%
Slovak Republic	27.1%	27.1%	27.0%	27.1%	27.0%	0.0%	0.0%	0.0%
Slovenia	32.9%	32.9%	32.8%	32.9%	32.8%	32.9%	32.7%	32.4%
Spain	27.0%	27.0%	26.2%	27.0%	26.2%	27.0%	25.5%	24.0%
Sweden	35.0%	35.0%	34.9%	35.0%	34.9%	35.0%	34.8%	34.6%
Switzerland	26.5%	36.5%	31.7%	36.5%	31.7%	36.5%	26.9%	17.3%
Turkey	55.7%	55.7%	55.1%	55.7%	55.1%	51.5%	25.8%	0.0%
United Kingdom	0.0%	0.0%	0.0%	0.0%	0.0%	0.0%	0.0%	0.0%
United States	37.6%	37.6%	37.4%	37.6%	37.4%	22.6%	29.7%	37.0%
Argentina	0.0%	25.0%	25.0%	0.0%	0.0%	25.0%	25.0%	25.0%
Bulgaria	10.2%	0.0%	0.0%	0.0%	0.0%	6.4%	3.2%	0.0%
Colombia	7.0%	9.0%	9.0%	9.0%	9.0%	0.0%	0.0%	0.0%
Lithuania	0.0%	0.0%	0.0%	0.0%	0.0%	22.9%	11.4%	0.0%
South Africa	0.0%	0.0%	0.0%	0.0%	0.0%	60.6%	38.6%	16.6%

Table B.11. **Marginal effective tax rates by asset: 6 months expected holding period (10 years for pensions and property), 100% of average wage, 2016** *(cont.)*

Standard assumptions: 3% real return, country actual inflation

Country	Investment funds	Pension funds		Tax-favoured savings accounts	Residential property			
					Equity-financed		Debt-financed	
		Deductible contributions	Non-deductible contributions		Owner-occupied	Rented	Owner-occupied	Rented
Australia	66.0%	-79.9%	25.4%	n.a.	21.9%	97.1%	75.9%	97.1%
Austria	41.1%	-14.8%	0.0%	40.3%	21.1%	66.2%	54.7%	42.2%
Belgium	0.0%	-104.8%	26.7%	22.7%	67.8%	69.1%	44.0%	100.3%
Canada	44.5%	0.0%	32.9%	0.0%	41.3%	77.9%	77.6%	77.9%
Chile	8.5%	0.0%	5.3%	n.a.	21.2%	21.2%	18.2%	18.2%
Czech Republic	7.2%	0.0%	15.6%	n.a.	17.5%	28.5%	17.5%	28.5%
Denmark	57.8%	21.1%	21.1%	n.a.	22.3%	51.5%	18.5%	57.5%
Estonia	30.4%	-41.7%	33.3%	n.a.	0.0%	24.0%	-29.3%	24.0%
Finland	43.2%	0.0%	32.7%	0.0%	15.3%	53.9%	35.3%	53.9%
France	56.5%	-17.9%	34.5%	0.0%	32.0%	59.5%	81.5%	107.0%
Germany	0.0%	0.0%	44.6%	n.a.	29.3%	76.3%	29.3%	24.1%
Greece	13.2%	0.0%	0.0%	n.a.	32.0%	30.8%	35.5%	34.3%
Hungary	23.6%	-83.3%	0.0%	24.1%	22.8%	38.0%	43.1%	57.8%
Iceland	40.6%	0.0%	54.7%	n.a.	16.2%	40.3%	48.3%	71.9%
Ireland	49.7%	30.6%	45.3%	n.a.	8.2%	60.8%	55.1%	61.9%
Israel	24.7%	-179.5%	0.0%	0.0%	10.0%	40.5%	27.7%	57.1%
Italy	31.2%	-29.4%	38.6%	n.a.	2.8%	51.8%	26.1%	93.8%
Japan	24.3%	-16.1%	11.2%	0.0%	21.5%	37.9%	13.4%	42.3%
Korea	21.4%	-26.5%	5.3%	13.8%	7.3%	12.1%	5.9%	31.2%
Latvia	13.3%	-86.3%	13.3%	n.a.	25.1%	37.0%	36.7%	48.6%
Luxembourg	56.9%	-106.6%	20.9%	0.0%	0.3%	48.1%	13.6%	7.8%
Mexico	21.2%	-72.4%	0.0%	n.a.	16.7%	52.3%	-14.0%	22.7%
Netherlands	40.0%	-14.4%	0.0%	n.a.	13.7%	53.1%	-4.0%	53.1%
New Zealand	38.3%	38.3%	38.3%	n.a.	20.0%	46.0%	56.1%	46.0%
Norway	68.2%	-7.7%	68.8%	416.7%	20.7%	72.7%	46.4%	96.2%
Poland	25.4%	-32.5%	33.3%	n.a.	9.2%	18.2%	32.5%	29.4%
Portugal	37.9%	-50.0%	0.0%	n.a.	18.3%	48.3%	51.9%	80.2%
Slovak Republic	26.6%	19.8%	19.8%	n.a.	0.4%	20.6%	25.0%	44.5%
Slovenia	32.4%	-61.6%	45.0%	n.a.	13.4%	39.3%	43.3%	67.8%
Spain	24.0%	0.0%	27.9%	24.4%	52.8%	63.4%	59.5%	74.0%
Sweden	37.5%	25.9%	25.9%	14.0%	9.1%	26.9%	9.1%	26.9%
Switzerland	26.5%	-76.2%	19.2%	n.a.	23.3%	27.2%	30.9%	34.7%
Turkey	69.1%	0.0%	0.0%	n.a.	9.7%	39.0%	43.2%	7.4%
United Kingdom	32.7%	-20.8%	17.0%	0.0%	31.6%	60.3%	31.6%	33.1%
United States	22.6%	0.0%	83.3%	0.0%	40.4%	57.5%	40.4%	57.5%
Argentina	25.0%	0.0%	0.0%	n.a.	28.3%	57.1%	-42.9%	57.1%
Bulgaria	0.0%	-37.0%	0.0%	n.a.	13.6%	27.2%	22.8%	36.4%
Colombia	0.0%	0.0%	0.0%	0.0%	21.2%	20.9%	26.5%	26.2%
Lithuania	0.0%	-58.8%	0.0%	n.a.	2.7%	18.7%	2.7%	18.7%
South Africa	43.4%	-39.0%	28.1%	0.0%	22.9%	61.9%	22.9%	8.9%

StatLink http://dx.doi.org/10.1787/888933662122

Table B.12. **Marginal effective tax rates by asset: 6 months expected holding period (10 years for pensions and property), 500% of average wage, 2016**

Standard assumptions: 3% real return, country actual inflation

Country	Bank deposits	Corporate bonds		Government bonds		Shares		
		Issued at par	Issued at discount	Issued at par	Issued at discount	100% distribution	50% distribution	0% distribution
Australia	83.0%	83.0%	82.7%	83.0%	82.7%	32.2%	56.9%	81.9%
Austria	40.3%	44.3%	44.1%	44.3%	44.1%	44.3%	43.9%	43.5%
Belgium	40.8%	46.9%	46.7%	46.9%	46.7%	59.0%	38.5%	18.0%
Canada	81.0%	80.3%	70.1%	80.3%	70.1%	59.5%	49.7%	39.8%
Chile	50.4%	50.4%	37.8%	50.4%	37.8%	-2.2%	-1.1%	0.0%
Czech Republic	21.6%	21.6%	16.2%	21.6%	16.2%	21.6%	21.4%	21.2%
Denmark	57.8%	57.8%	57.6%	57.8%	57.6%	57.8%	57.5%	57.1%
Estonia	0.0%	30.9%	30.8%	30.9%	30.8%	0.0%	15.1%	30.4%
Finland	43.9%	43.9%	43.7%	43.9%	43.7%	37.3%	40.3%	43.2%
France	87.4%	87.4%	87.3%	87.4%	87.3%	66.1%	76.5%	86.9%
Germany	36.7%	36.7%	36.5%	36.7%	36.5%	36.7%	36.4%	36.1%
Greece	13.4%	13.4%	13.3%	0.0%	0.0%	142.2%	143.6%	145.0%
Hungary	24.1%	24.1%	23.9%	24.1%	23.9%	24.1%	23.8%	23.6%
Iceland	41.7%	41.7%	41.4%	41.7%	41.4%	41.7%	41.2%	40.6%
Ireland	50.3%	58.9%	54.2%	58.9%	44.2%	125.5%	115.8%	106.0%
Israel	19.3%	19.3%	19.2%	19.3%	19.2%	25.1%	24.9%	24.7%
Italy	49.9%	49.9%	49.7%	31.1%	30.9%	44.5%	44.2%	43.8%
Japan	24.7%	24.7%	24.6%	24.7%	24.6%	24.7%	24.5%	24.3%
Korea	58.1%	58.1%	57.9%	58.1%	57.9%	125.1%	95.5%	66.0%
Latvia	13.3%	13.3%	14.9%	13.3%	14.9%	13.3%	16.5%	19.6%
Luxembourg	14.8%	14.8%	25.6%	14.8%	25.6%	29.6%	43.9%	58.4%
Mexico	65.4%	65.4%	65.0%	65.4%	65.0%	21.8%	21.5%	21.2%
Netherlands	40.0%	40.0%	40.0%	40.0%	40.0%	40.0%	40.0%	40.0%
New Zealand	45.1%	45.1%	44.9%	45.1%	44.9%	6.8%	3.4%	0.0%
Norway	68.8%	68.8%	68.6%	68.8%	68.6%	28.3%	28.3%	28.3%
Poland	25.8%	25.8%	25.7%	25.8%	25.7%	25.8%	25.6%	25.4%
Portugal	37.9%	37.9%	37.8%	37.9%	37.8%	37.9%	37.6%	37.3%
Slovak Republic	27.1%	27.1%	27.0%	27.1%	27.0%	0.0%	13.3%	26.6%
Slovenia	32.9%	32.9%	32.8%	32.9%	32.8%	32.9%	32.7%	32.4%
Spain	29.5%	29.5%	28.1%	29.5%	28.1%	29.5%	26.8%	26.5%
Sweden	35.0%	35.0%	34.9%	35.0%	34.9%	35.0%	34.8%	34.6%
Switzerland	46.7%	56.8%	48.7%	56.8%	48.7%	56.8%	40.7%	24.6%
Turkey	55.7%	55.7%	55.1%	55.7%	55.1%	66.4%	33.2%	0.0%
United Kingdom	73.5%	73.5%	63.2%	73.5%	63.2%	107.1%	86.2%	65.2%
United States	55.3%	55.3%	55.1%	55.3%	55.1%	28.3%	35.4%	42.6%
Argentina	0.0%	41.7%	41.7%	0.0%	0.0%	41.7%	41.7%	41.7%
Bulgaria	10.2%	0.0%	0.0%	0.0%	0.0%	6.4%	3.2%	0.0%
Colombia	7.0%	9.0%	9.0%	9.0%	9.0%	0.0%	0.0%	0.0%
Lithuania	22.9%	22.9%	22.7%	22.9%	22.7%	22.9%	22.6%	22.4%
South Africa	118.5%	118.5%	88.9%	118.5%	88.9%	60.6%	38.6%	16.6%

Table B.12. **Marginal effective tax rates by asset: 6 months expected holding period (10 years for pensions and property), 500% of average wage, 2016** *(cont.)*

Standard assumptions: 3% real return, country actual inflation

Country	Investment funds	Pension funds		Tax-favoured savings accounts	Residential property			
					Equity-financed		Debt-financed	
		Deductible contributions	Non-deductible contributions		Owner-occupied	Rented	Owner-occupied	Rented
Australia	83.0%	-52.8%	25.4%	n.a.	21.9%	110.1%	89.8%	110.1%
Austria	41.1%	-14.8%	0.0%	40.3%	21.1%	72.7%	54.7%	37.0%
Belgium	0.0%	-104.8%	26.7%	22.7%	67.8%	69.2%	98.6%	100.4%
Canada	80.3%	0.0%	63.8%	0.0%	43.2%	109.7%	108.4%	109.7%
Chile	49.1%	0.0%	32.3%	n.a.	24.8%	24.8%	45.9%	46.2%
Czech Republic	7.2%	0.0%	15.6%	n.a.	17.5%	28.5%	17.5%	28.5%
Denmark	57.8%	21.1%	21.1%	n.a.	22.3%	61.3%	25.3%	66.6%
Estonia	30.4%	-41.7%	33.3%	n.a.	3.8%	27.8%	3.8%	27.8%
Finland	43.2%	0.0%	32.7%	0.0%	23.4%	62.8%	38.4%	62.8%
France	86.9%	-31.9%	45.2%	87.4%	43.0%	80.8%	116.6%	149.5%
Germany	36.7%	0.0%	48.4%	n.a.	29.3%	79.8%	62.3%	57.1%
Greece	13.2%	0.0%	0.0%	n.a.	43.4%	42.0%	46.7%	45.4%
Hungary	23.6%	-83.3%	0.0%	24.1%	22.8%	38.0%	43.1%	57.8%
Iceland	40.6%	0.0%	67.8%	n.a.	16.2%	40.3%	48.3%	71.9%
Ireland	49.7%	44.4%	48.1%	n.a.	8.2%	63.4%	55.1%	64.6%
Israel	24.7%	-179.5%	0.0%	0.0%	30.2%	40.5%	47.0%	57.1%
Italy	31.2%	-138.4%	38.6%	n.a.	2.8%	51.8%	26.1%	93.8%
Japan	24.3%	-86.0%	37.4%	0.0%	21.5%	75.1%	13.4%	39.2%
Korea	58.1%	-26.5%	5.3%	13.8%	12.2%	57.7%	62.6%	86.9%
Latvia	13.3%	-86.3%	13.3%	n.a.	29.1%	40.7%	40.6%	52.1%
Luxembourg	58.4%	-111.1%	21.5%	0.0%	0.3%	49.3%	13.6%	7.6%
Mexico	21.2%	-41.1%	29.8%	n.a.	20.5%	75.4%	20.5%	75.4%
Netherlands	40.0%	0.0%	0.0%	n.a.	13.7%	53.1%	-10.9%	53.1%
New Zealand	38.3%	38.3%	38.3%	n.a.	20.0%	48.6%	59.7%	48.6%
Norway	68.2%	-20.1%	68.8%	416.7%	20.7%	72.7%	46.4%	96.2%
Poland	25.4%	-107.8%	33.3%	n.a.	9.2%	18.2%	32.5%	26.3%
Portugal	37.9%	-50.0%	0.0%	n.a.	37.7%	69.6%	69.7%	100.0%
Slovak Republic	26.6%	19.8%	19.8%	n.a.	0.4%	27.0%	25.0%	50.5%
Slovenia	32.4%	-166.7%	83.3%	n.a.	13.4%	39.3%	43.3%	67.8%
Spain	26.5%	0.0%	44.6%	27.0%	53.2%	69.7%	62.1%	75.8%
Sweden	37.5%	59.8%	59.8%	14.0%	9.1%	26.9%	9.1%	26.9%
Switzerland	46.7%	-179.9%	32.1%	n.a.	41.5%	47.6%	56.3%	62.2%
Turkey	69.1%	0.0%	0.0%	n.a.	9.7%	47.4%	43.2%	-5.6%
United Kingdom	73.5%	-68.2%	40.3%	73.5%	31.6%	91.6%	91.1%	91.6%
United States	28.3%	0.0%	110.0%	0.0%	34.3%	50.2%	34.3%	50.2%
Argentina	41.7%	0.0%	0.0%	n.a.	45.0%	82.3%	45.0%	82.3%
Bulgaria	0.0%	-37.0%	0.0%	n.a.	13.6%	27.2%	22.8%	36.4%
Colombia	0.0%	-129.6%	0.0%	-2592.6%	23.4%	53.1%	-23.8%	8.5%
Lithuania	22.4%	-58.8%	0.0%	n.a.	16.0%	32.0%	35.6%	51.2%
South Africa	43.4%	-9.4%	68.4%	0.0%	53.3%	103.4%	125.7%	103.4%

StatLink http://dx.doi.org/10.1787/888933662141

Table B.13. **Marginal effective tax rates by asset: 10 years expected holding period (30 years for pensions and property), 67% of average wage, 2016**

Standard assumptions: 3% real return, country actual inflation

Country	Bank deposits	Corporate bonds		Government bonds		Shares		
		Issued at par	Issued at discount	Issued at par	Issued at discount	100% distribution	50% distribution	0% distribution
Australia	58.4%	58.4%	54.7%	58.4%	54.7%	7.6%	13.8%	20.2%
Austria	40.3%	44.3%	41.4%	44.3%	41.4%	44.3%	38.3%	31.9%
Belgium	40.8%	41.2%	38.6%	41.2%	38.6%	42.0%	21.4%	0.9%
Canada	30.3%	30.1%	25.3%	30.1%	25.3%	0.0%	5.3%	10.7%
Chile	0.0%	0.0%	0.0%	0.0%	0.0%	-52.6%	-26.3%	0.0%
Czech Republic	21.6%	21.6%	16.2%	21.6%	16.2%	21.6%	10.8%	0.0%
Denmark	50.9%	50.9%	48.2%	50.9%	48.2%	57.8%	51.9%	45.3%
Estonia	0.0%	30.9%	28.8%	30.9%	28.8%	0.0%	10.8%	22.1%
Finland	43.9%	43.9%	41.3%	43.9%	41.3%	37.3%	35.1%	32.7%
France	37.4%	37.4%	35.4%	37.4%	35.4%	30.1%	24.8%	19.2%
Germany	0.0%	0.0%	0.0%	0.0%	0.0%	0.0%	0.0%	0.0%
Greece	13.4%	13.4%	12.7%	0.0%	0.0%	15.6%	15.9%	16.2%
Hungary	24.1%	24.1%	18.0%	24.1%	18.0%	16.0%	13.6%	11.1%
Iceland	0.0%	0.0%	6.5%	0.0%	6.5%	41.7%	34.5%	27.0%
Ireland	50.3%	31.3%	31.4%	31.3%	23.5%	35.5%	35.3%	35.0%
Israel	19.3%	19.3%	18.1%	19.3%	18.1%	26.3%	23.3%	20.2%
Italy	37.3%	37.3%	35.0%	18.4%	17.2%	36.9%	32.4%	27.6%
Japan	24.7%	24.7%	23.2%	24.7%	23.2%	13.1%	15.9%	18.8%
Korea	21.4%	21.4%	19.9%	21.4%	19.9%	26.0%	14.7%	3.3%
Latvia	13.3%	13.3%	13.6%	13.3%	13.6%	13.3%	14.0%	14.7%
Luxembourg	14.8%	14.8%	11.1%	14.8%	11.1%	25.2%	12.6%	0.0%
Mexico	1.1%	1.1%	1.0%	1.1%	1.0%	-20.0%	-3.4%	13.5%
Netherlands	40.0%	40.0%	40.0%	40.0%	40.0%	40.0%	40.0%	40.0%
New Zealand	23.9%	23.9%	22.4%	23.9%	22.4%	-14.4%	-7.2%	0.0%
Norway	68.8%	68.8%	66.5%	68.8%	66.5%	28.3%	28.3%	28.3%
Poland	25.8%	25.8%	24.2%	25.8%	24.2%	25.8%	22.5%	19.1%
Portugal	37.9%	37.9%	35.7%	37.9%	35.7%	37.9%	33.5%	28.7%
Slovak Republic	27.1%	27.1%	25.3%	27.1%	25.3%	0.0%	9.7%	19.8%
Slovenia	32.9%	32.9%	31.0%	32.9%	31.0%	32.9%	21.4%	9.6%
Spain	27.0%	27.0%	24.9%	27.0%	24.9%	27.0%	22.7%	20.4%
Sweden	35.0%	35.0%	33.2%	35.0%	33.2%	35.0%	31.4%	27.6%
Switzerland	13.9%	14.5%	11.0%	14.5%	11.0%	14.5%	7.5%	0.5%
Turkey	55.7%	55.7%	48.9%	55.7%	48.9%	38.5%	19.3%	0.0%
United Kingdom	0.0%	0.0%	0.0%	0.0%	0.0%	0.0%	0.0%	0.0%
United States	22.6%	22.6%	21.0%	22.6%	21.0%	0.0%	0.0%	0.0%
Argentina	0.0%	25.0%	25.0%	0.0%	0.0%	25.0%	25.0%	25.0%
Bulgaria	10.2%	0.0%	0.0%	0.0%	0.0%	6.4%	3.2%	0.0%
Colombia	7.0%	9.0%	8.1%	9.0%	8.1%	0.0%	0.0%	0.0%
Lithuania	0.0%	0.0%	0.0%	0.0%	0.0%	22.9%	11.4%	0.0%
South Africa	0.0%	0.0%	0.0%	0.0%	0.0%	44.8%	28.6%	12.2%

Table B.13. **Marginal effective tax rates by asset: 10 years expected holding period (30 years for pensions and property), 67% of average wage, 2016** *(cont.)*

Standard assumptions: 3% real return, country actual inflation

Country	Investment funds	Pension funds		Tax-favoured savings accounts	Residential property			
					Equity-financed		Debt-financed	
		Deductible contributions	Non-deductible contributions		Owner-occupied	Rented	Owner-occupied	Rented
Australia	58.4%	-1.5%	25.4%	n.a.	12.3%	79.0%	53.7%	79.0%
Austria	37.4%	-4.9%	0.0%	21.3%	13.6%	50.1%	42.8%	37.6%
Belgium	0.0%	-34.9%	8.9%	0.0%	43.2%	44.4%	19.6%	71.4%
Canada	30.1%	0.0%	13.5%	0.0%	38.0%	61.7%	58.0%	61.7%
Chile	0.0%	0.0%	0.0%	n.a.	0.0%	0.0%	0.0%	0.0%
Czech Republic	7.2%	0.0%	9.8%	n.a.	8.9%	19.9%	8.9%	19.9%
Denmark	57.8%	21.1%	21.1%	n.a.	20.9%	46.1%	15.5%	51.2%
Estonia	22.1%	-13.9%	11.1%	n.a.	0.0%	21.4%	-27.8%	21.4%
Finland	32.7%	0.0%	20.6%	0.0%	11.0%	46.6%	27.9%	46.6%
France	28.7%	-1.5%	12.9%	0.0%	19.8%	34.7%	49.5%	63.1%
Germany	0.0%	0.0%	22.9%	n.a.	17.5%	55.5%	17.5%	15.8%
Greece	10.8%	0.0%	0.0%	n.a.	25.6%	24.8%	29.0%	28.4%
Hungary	11.1%	-27.8%	0.0%	0.0%	11.8%	27.3%	29.8%	44.4%
Iceland	27.0%	0.0%	30.7%	n.a.	15.3%	33.8%	40.8%	58.5%
Ireland	40.3%	7.6%	16.0%	n.a.	6.0%	36.0%	50.1%	58.7%
Israel	20.2%	-59.8%	0.0%	0.0%	10.0%	24.5%	26.2%	39.9%
Italy	23.5%	7.1%	34.2%	n.a.	1.4%	45.7%	12.2%	72.7%
Japan	18.8%	-3.3%	4.7%	0.0%	20.3%	31.0%	12.4%	41.0%
Korea	21.4%	-13.1%	3.3%	0.0%	5.1%	8.1%	3.8%	25.3%
Latvia	13.3%	-19.9%	13.3%	n.a.	16.7%	28.0%	27.3%	38.4%
Luxembourg	0.0%	-28.6%	11.3%	0.0%	0.3%	40.1%	12.3%	9.4%
Mexico	13.5%	-13.5%	0.0%	n.a.	9.1%	32.6%	-5.8%	18.4%
Netherlands	40.0%	-41.1%	0.0%	n.a.	9.4%	48.7%	-8.3%	48.7%
New Zealand	23.9%	23.9%	23.9%	n.a.	20.0%	35.2%	38.4%	35.2%
Norway	59.3%	-2.6%	68.8%	20.8%	15.3%	63.8%	39.2%	83.2%
Poland	19.1%	-10.8%	11.1%	n.a.	4.8%	13.9%	26.4%	25.0%
Portugal	37.9%	-16.7%	0.0%	n.a.	10.0%	39.3%	40.9%	67.1%
Slovak Republic	19.8%	12.5%	12.5%	n.a.	0.4%	20.6%	22.9%	41.7%
Slovenia	9.6%	-10.6%	8.9%	n.a.	6.8%	33.1%	34.5%	58.1%
Spain	20.4%	0.0%	14.7%	0.0%	31.1%	40.1%	37.4%	52.0%
Sweden	30.8%	16.1%	16.1%	14.0%	4.9%	23.1%	4.9%	23.1%
Switzerland	13.9%	-15.1%	13.9%	n.a.	11.6%	15.3%	11.6%	15.3%
Turkey	18.0%	0.0%	0.0%	n.a.	6.4%	28.3%	30.0%	18.3%
United Kingdom	32.7%	-6.9%	10.3%	0.0%	27.3%	53.3%	27.3%	30.6%
United States	0.0%	0.0%	16.7%	0.0%	44.8%	60.7%	44.8%	60.7%
Argentina	25.0%	0.0%	0.0%	n.a.	28.3%	52.9%	-12.2%	52.9%
Bulgaria	0.0%	-12.3%	0.0%	n.a.	8.2%	21.8%	16.8%	30.2%
Colombia	0.0%	0.0%	0.0%	0.0%	15.6%	15.5%	19.7%	19.7%
Lithuania	0.0%	-19.6%	0.0%	n.a.	2.7%	18.7%	2.7%	18.7%
South Africa	43.4%	-8.1%	9.9%	0.0%	22.9%	46.3%	22.9%	20.3%

StatLink http://dx.doi.org/10.1787/888933662160

Table B.14. **Marginal effective tax rates by asset: 10 years expected holding period (30 years for pensions and property), 100% of average wage, 2016**

Standard assumptions: 3% real return, country actual inflation

Country	Bank deposits	Corporate bonds		Government bonds		Shares		
		Issued at par	Issued at discount	Issued at par	Issued at discount	100% distribution	50% distribution	0% distribution
Australia	66.0%	66.0%	62.0%	66.0%	62.0%	15.2%	19.0%	22.9%
Austria	40.3%	44.3%	41.4%	44.3%	41.4%	44.3%	38.3%	31.9%
Belgium	40.8%	41.2%	38.6%	41.2%	38.6%	42.0%	21.4%	0.9%
Canada	44.9%	44.5%	37.5%	44.5%	37.5%	9.7%	12.8%	16.0%
Chile	0.0%	0.0%	0.0%	0.0%	0.0%	-63.0%	-21.9%	0.0%
Czech Republic	21.6%	21.6%	16.2%	21.6%	16.2%	21.6%	10.8%	0.0%
Denmark	50.9%	50.9%	48.2%	50.9%	48.2%	57.8%	51.9%	45.3%
Estonia	0.0%	30.9%	28.8%	30.9%	28.8%	0.0%	10.8%	22.1%
Finland	43.9%	43.9%	41.3%	43.9%	41.3%	37.3%	35.1%	37.5%
France	57.2%	57.2%	54.5%	57.2%	54.5%	41.6%	33.1%	24.1%
Germany	0.0%	0.0%	0.0%	0.0%	0.0%	0.0%	0.0%	0.0%
Greece	13.4%	13.4%	12.7%	0.0%	0.0%	15.6%	15.9%	16.2%
Hungary	24.1%	24.1%	18.0%	24.1%	18.0%	16.0%	13.6%	11.1%
Iceland	41.7%	41.7%	38.1%	41.7%	38.1%	41.7%	34.5%	27.0%
Ireland	50.3%	55.8%	50.2%	55.8%	41.9%	59.8%	47.9%	35.0%
Israel	19.3%	19.3%	18.1%	19.3%	18.1%	26.3%	23.3%	20.2%
Italy	37.3%	37.3%	35.0%	18.4%	17.2%	36.9%	32.4%	27.6%
Japan	24.7%	24.7%	23.2%	24.7%	23.2%	20.0%	19.4%	18.8%
Korea	21.4%	21.4%	19.9%	21.4%	19.9%	26.0%	14.7%	3.3%
Latvia	13.3%	13.3%	13.6%	13.3%	13.6%	13.3%	14.0%	14.7%
Luxembourg	14.8%	14.8%	11.1%	14.8%	11.1%	28.9%	14.4%	0.0%
Mexico	1.1%	1.1%	1.0%	1.1%	1.0%	-4.7%	4.3%	13.5%
Netherlands	40.0%	40.0%	40.0%	40.0%	40.0%	40.0%	40.0%	40.0%
New Zealand	41.0%	41.0%	38.7%	41.0%	38.7%	2.7%	1.4%	0.0%
Norway	68.8%	68.8%	66.5%	68.8%	66.5%	28.3%	28.3%	28.3%
Poland	25.8%	25.8%	24.2%	25.8%	24.2%	25.8%	22.5%	19.1%
Portugal	37.9%	37.9%	35.7%	37.9%	35.7%	37.9%	33.5%	28.7%
Slovak Republic	27.1%	27.1%	25.3%	27.1%	25.3%	0.0%	9.7%	19.8%
Slovenia	32.9%	32.9%	31.0%	32.9%	31.0%	32.9%	21.4%	9.6%
Spain	27.0%	27.0%	25.4%	27.0%	25.4%	27.0%	23.7%	20.4%
Sweden	35.0%	35.0%	33.2%	35.0%	33.2%	35.0%	31.4%	27.6%
Switzerland	26.5%	27.0%	22.2%	27.0%	22.2%	27.0%	17.4%	7.8%
Turkey	55.7%	55.7%	48.9%	55.7%	48.9%	51.5%	25.8%	0.0%
United Kingdom	0.0%	0.0%	0.0%	0.0%	0.0%	0.0%	0.0%	0.0%
United States	37.6%	37.6%	35.2%	37.6%	35.2%	22.6%	19.4%	16.1%
Argentina	0.0%	25.0%	25.0%	0.0%	0.0%	25.0%	25.0%	25.0%
Bulgaria	10.2%	0.0%	0.0%	0.0%	0.0%	6.4%	3.2%	0.0%
Colombia	7.0%	9.0%	8.1%	9.0%	8.1%	0.0%	0.0%	0.0%
Lithuania	0.0%	0.0%	0.0%	0.0%	0.0%	22.9%	11.4%	0.0%
South Africa	0.0%	0.0%	4.1%	0.0%	4.1%	44.8%	31.3%	17.4%

Table B.14. **Marginal effective tax rates by asset: 10 years expected holding period (30 years for pensions and property), 100% of average wage, 2016** *(cont.)*

Standard assumptions: 3% real return, country actual inflation

Country	Investment funds	Pension funds		Tax-favoured savings accounts	Residential property			
					Equity-financed		Debt-financed	
		Deductible contributions	Non-deductible contributions		Owner-occupied	Rented	Owner-occupied	Rented
Australia	66.0%	-9.7%	25.4%	n.a.	12.3%	84.5%	59.1%	84.5%
Austria	37.4%	-4.9%	0.0%	21.3%	13.6%	56.1%	42.8%	34.5%
Belgium	0.0%	-34.9%	8.9%	22.7%	43.2%	44.4%	19.6%	71.4%
Canada	44.5%	0.0%	20.5%	0.0%	38.0%	73.1%	67.6%	73.1%
Chile	5.3%	0.0%	3.0%	n.a.	21.2%	21.2%	18.9%	18.8%
Czech Republic	7.2%	0.0%	9.8%	n.a.	8.9%	19.9%	8.9%	19.9%
Denmark	57.8%	21.1%	21.1%	n.a.	20.9%	47.4%	15.5%	51.6%
Estonia	22.1%	-13.9%	11.1%	n.a.	0.0%	21.4%	-27.8%	21.4%
Finland	37.5%	0.0%	20.6%	0.0%	11.0%	47.4%	27.9%	47.4%
France	45.6%	-6.0%	22.6%	0.0%	19.8%	42.3%	65.1%	83.9%
Germany	0.0%	0.0%	28.7%	n.a.	17.5%	64.0%	17.5%	15.3%
Greece	10.8%	0.0%	0.0%	n.a.	25.6%	24.8%	29.0%	28.4%
Hungary	11.1%	-27.8%	0.0%	0.0%	11.8%	27.3%	29.8%	44.4%
Iceland	27.0%	0.0%	30.7%	n.a.	15.3%	33.8%	40.8%	58.5%
Ireland	40.3%	10.2%	30.5%	n.a.	6.0%	57.4%	50.1%	58.5%
Israel	20.2%	-59.8%	0.0%	0.0%	10.0%	24.5%	26.2%	39.9%
Italy	23.5%	7.1%	34.2%	n.a.	1.4%	45.7%	12.2%	72.7%
Japan	18.8%	-5.4%	7.3%	0.0%	20.3%	37.1%	12.4%	41.1%
Korea	21.4%	-8.8%	3.3%	13.8%	5.1%	8.1%	3.8%	25.3%
Latvia	13.3%	-19.9%	13.3%	n.a.	20.7%	31.7%	31.1%	41.9%
Luxembourg	0.0%	-35.5%	13.0%	0.0%	0.3%	46.1%	12.3%	8.7%
Mexico	13.5%	-24.1%	0.0%	n.a.	9.2%	41.1%	-17.2%	17.0%
Netherlands	40.0%	-4.8%	0.0%	n.a.	9.4%	48.7%	-8.3%	48.7%
New Zealand	38.3%	38.3%	38.3%	n.a.	20.0%	46.0%	51.6%	46.0%
Norway	59.3%	-1.9%	68.8%	20.8%	15.3%	63.8%	39.2%	83.2%
Poland	10.1%	-10.8%	11.1%	n.a.	4.8%	13.9%	26.4%	25.0%
Portugal	37.9%	-16.7%	0.0%	n.a.	13.9%	42.9%	44.3%	70.1%
Slovak Republic	19.8%	12.5%	12.5%	n.a.	0.4%	20.6%	22.9%	41.7%
Slovenia	9.6%	-20.5%	15.0%	n.a.	6.8%	33.1%	34.5%	58.1%
Spain	20.4%	0.0%	18.2%	0.0%	31.1%	42.1%	37.4%	51.9%
Sweden	30.8%	18.4%	18.4%	14.0%	4.9%	23.1%	4.9%	23.1%
Switzerland	26.5%	-25.4%	19.2%	n.a.	23.3%	28.2%	31.1%	35.9%
Turkey	18.0%	0.0%	0.0%	n.a.	6.4%	35.7%	30.0%	12.9%
United Kingdom	32.7%	-6.9%	10.3%	0.0%	27.3%	53.3%	27.3%	30.6%
United States	22.6%	0.0%	27.8%	0.0%	39.6%	58.5%	39.6%	58.5%
Argentina	25.0%	0.0%	0.0%	n.a.	28.3%	57.1%	-21.1%	57.1%
Bulgaria	0.0%	-12.3%	0.0%	n.a.	8.2%	21.8%	16.8%	30.2%
Colombia	0.0%	0.0%	0.0%	0.0%	15.6%	15.5%	19.7%	19.7%
Lithuania	0.0%	-19.6%	0.0%	n.a.	2.7%	18.7%	2.7%	18.7%
South Africa	43.4%	-4.0%	19.7%	0.0%	22.9%	56.8%	22.9%	18.8%

StatLink http://dx.doi.org/10.1787/888933662179

Table B.15. **Marginal effective tax rates by asset: 10 years expected holding period (30 years for pensions and property), 500% of average wage, 2016**

Standard assumptions: 3% real return, country actual inflation

Country	Bank deposits	Corporate bonds		Government bonds		Shares		
		Issued at par	Issued at discount	Issued at par	Issued at discount	100% distribution	50% distribution	0% distribution
Australia	83.0%	83.0%	78.5%	83.0%	78.5%	32.2%	30.7%	29.2%
Austria	40.3%	44.3%	41.4%	44.3%	41.4%	44.3%	38.3%	31.9%
Belgium	40.8%	41.2%	38.6%	41.2%	38.6%	42.0%	21.4%	0.9%
Canada	81.0%	80.3%	68.2%	80.3%	68.2%	59.5%	45.1%	29.7%
Chile	50.4%	50.4%	46.4%	50.4%	37.8%	-23.0%	-2.8%	19.3%
Czech Republic	21.6%	21.6%	16.2%	21.6%	16.2%	21.6%	10.8%	0.0%
Denmark	57.8%	57.8%	54.9%	57.8%	54.9%	57.8%	51.9%	45.3%
Estonia	0.0%	30.9%	28.8%	30.9%	28.8%	0.0%	10.8%	22.1%
Finland	43.9%	43.9%	42.4%	43.9%	42.4%	37.3%	37.4%	37.5%
France	87.4%	87.4%	85.3%	87.4%	85.3%	66.1%	56.1%	45.5%
Germany	36.7%	36.7%	34.5%	36.7%	34.5%	36.7%	32.2%	27.5%
Greece	13.4%	13.4%	12.7%	0.0%	0.0%	15.6%	15.9%	16.2%
Hungary	24.1%	24.1%	18.0%	24.1%	18.0%	16.0%	13.6%	11.1%
Iceland	41.7%	41.7%	38.1%	41.7%	38.1%	41.7%	34.5%	27.0%
Ireland	50.3%	58.9%	52.5%	58.9%	44.2%	62.8%	49.5%	35.0%
Israel	19.3%	19.3%	18.1%	19.3%	18.1%	26.3%	23.3%	20.2%
Italy	37.3%	37.3%	35.0%	18.4%	17.2%	36.9%	32.4%	27.6%
Japan	24.7%	24.7%	23.2%	24.7%	23.2%	24.7%	21.8%	18.8%
Korea	58.1%	58.1%	54.8%	58.1%	54.8%	62.4%	32.8%	3.3%
Latvia	13.3%	13.3%	13.6%	13.3%	13.6%	13.3%	14.0%	14.7%
Luxembourg	14.8%	14.8%	11.1%	14.8%	11.1%	29.6%	14.8%	0.0%
Mexico	65.4%	65.4%	60.9%	65.4%	60.9%	21.8%	17.7%	13.5%
Netherlands	40.0%	40.0%	40.0%	40.0%	40.0%	40.0%	40.0%	40.0%
New Zealand	45.1%	45.1%	42.6%	45.1%	42.6%	6.8%	3.4%	0.0%
Norway	68.8%	68.8%	66.5%	68.8%	66.5%	28.3%	28.3%	28.3%
Poland	25.8%	25.8%	24.2%	25.8%	24.2%	25.8%	22.5%	19.1%
Portugal	37.9%	37.9%	35.7%	37.9%	35.7%	37.9%	33.5%	28.7%
Slovak Republic	27.1%	27.1%	25.3%	27.1%	25.3%	0.0%	9.7%	19.8%
Slovenia	32.9%	32.9%	31.0%	32.9%	31.0%	32.9%	21.4%	9.6%
Spain	29.5%	29.5%	27.3%	29.5%	27.3%	29.5%	26.1%	22.4%
Sweden	35.0%	35.0%	33.2%	35.0%	33.2%	35.0%	31.4%	27.6%
Switzerland	46.7%	47.3%	39.2%	47.3%	39.2%	47.3%	31.2%	15.1%
Turkey	55.7%	55.7%	48.9%	55.7%	48.9%	66.4%	33.2%	0.0%
United Kingdom	73.5%	73.5%	61.4%	73.5%	61.4%	75.6%	50.8%	24.6%
United States	55.3%	55.3%	52.2%	55.3%	52.2%	28.3%	24.4%	20.3%
Argentina	0.0%	41.7%	41.7%	0.0%	0.0%	41.7%	41.7%	41.7%
Bulgaria	10.2%	0.0%	0.0%	0.0%	0.0%	6.4%	3.2%	0.0%
Colombia	7.0%	9.0%	8.1%	9.0%	8.1%	0.0%	0.0%	0.0%
Lithuania	22.9%	22.9%	21.2%	22.9%	21.2%	22.9%	19.6%	16.2%
South Africa	118.5%	118.5%	96.4%	118.5%	96.4%	44.8%	36.3%	27.3%

Table B.15. **Marginal effective tax rates by asset: 10 years expected holding period (30 years for pensions and property), 500% of average wage, 2016** *(cont.)*

Standard assumptions: 3% real return, country actual inflation

Country	Investment funds	Pension funds		Tax-favoured savings accounts	Residential property			
					Equity-financed		Debt-financed	
		Deductible contributions	Non-deductible contributions		Owner-occupied	Rented	Owner-occupied	Rented
Australia	83.0%	-0.7%	25.4%	n.a.	12.3%	97.0%	71.1%	97.0%
Austria	37.4%	-4.9%	0.0%	21.3%	13.6%	63.0%	42.8%	30.9%
Belgium	0.0%	-34.9%	8.9%	22.7%	43.2%	44.5%	69.3%	71.4%
Canada	80.3%	0.0%	40.4%	0.0%	38.9%	103.1%	92.0%	103.1%
Chile	32.3%	0.0%	17.9%	n.a.	24.8%	24.8%	41.4%	42.0%
Czech Republic	7.2%	0.0%	9.8%	n.a.	8.9%	19.9%	8.9%	19.9%
Denmark	57.8%	21.1%	21.1%	n.a.	20.9%	56.2%	22.3%	59.7%
Estonia	22.1%	-13.9%	11.1%	n.a.	3.8%	25.3%	3.8%	25.3%
Finland	37.5%	0.0%	20.6%	0.0%	14.8%	50.8%	28.9%	50.8%
France	77.8%	-10.6%	29.8%	87.4%	30.8%	63.3%	96.2%	119.3%
Germany	36.7%	0.0%	31.3%	n.a.	17.5%	67.5%	48.4%	46.3%
Greece	10.8%	0.0%	0.0%	n.a.	36.9%	36.1%	40.2%	39.4%
Hungary	11.1%	-27.8%	0.0%	0.0%	11.8%	27.3%	29.8%	44.4%
Iceland	27.0%	0.0%	38.0%	n.a.	15.3%	33.8%	40.8%	58.5%
Ireland	40.3%	14.8%	32.5%	n.a.	6.0%	60.1%	50.1%	61.2%
Israel	20.2%	-59.8%	0.0%	0.0%	19.6%	24.5%	35.0%	39.9%
Italy	23.5%	-29.2%	34.2%	n.a.	1.4%	45.7%	12.2%	72.7%
Japan	18.8%	-28.7%	24.9%	0.0%	20.3%	74.4%	12.4%	42.0%
Korea	58.1%	-8.8%	3.3%	13.8%	10.0%	53.8%	54.3%	78.0%
Latvia	13.3%	-19.9%	13.3%	n.a.	24.7%	35.3%	34.9%	45.4%
Luxembourg	0.0%	-37.0%	13.4%	0.0%	0.3%	47.3%	12.3%	8.6%
Mexico	13.5%	-13.7%	16.6%	n.a.	11.3%	57.1%	11.3%	57.1%
Netherlands	40.0%	0.0%	0.0%	n.a.	9.4%	48.7%	-15.8%	48.7%
New Zealand	38.3%	38.3%	38.3%	n.a.	20.0%	48.6%	54.8%	48.6%
Norway	59.3%	0.0%	68.8%	20.8%	15.3%	63.8%	39.2%	83.2%
Poland	19.1%	36.0%	11.1%	n.a.	4.8%	13.9%	26.4%	22.9%
Portugal	37.9%	-16.7%	0.0%	n.a.	23.2%	53.1%	52.1%	79.0%
Slovak Republic	19.8%	12.5%	12.5%	n.a.	0.4%	27.0%	22.9%	47.4%
Slovenia	9.6%	-55.6%	27.8%	n.a.	6.8%	33.1%	34.5%	58.1%
Spain	22.4%	0.0%	29.6%	0.0%	31.3%	48.3%	39.8%	54.0%
Sweden	30.8%	43.0%	43.0%	14.0%	4.9%	23.1%	4.9%	23.1%
Switzerland	46.7%	-60.0%	32.1%	n.a.	41.5%	48.8%	56.7%	63.3%
Turkey	18.0%	0.0%	0.0%	n.a.	6.4%	44.1%	30.0%	5.8%
United Kingdom	73.5%	-22.7%	24.5%	73.5%	27.3%	83.5%	76.5%	83.5%
United States	28.3%	0.0%	36.7%	0.0%	38.2%	52.3%	38.2%	52.3%
Argentina	41.7%	0.0%	0.0%	n.a.	45.0%	82.3%	45.0%	82.3%
Bulgaria	0.0%	-12.3%	0.0%	n.a.	8.2%	21.8%	16.8%	30.2%
Colombia	0.0%	-43.2%	0.0%	-129.6%	17.8%	47.6%	-22.5%	12.0%
Lithuania	16.2%	-19.6%	0.0%	n.a.	16.0%	32.0%	32.9%	48.1%
South Africa	43.4%	-3.1%	34.6%	0.0%	45.9%	78.7%	95.8%	78.7%

StatLink http://dx.doi.org/10.1787/888933662198

ANNEX C

Financial institutions, financial accounts, and the common reporting standard

Financial institutions and the common reporting standard

Financial Institutions that are specifically included in the Common Reporting Standard

Depository institution[1]

A depository institution is any entity that accepts deposits in the ordinary course of a banking or similar business. This category includes savings banks, commercial banks, savings and loan associations and credit unions.

Custodial institution

A custodial institution is any entity that holds as a substantial portion of its business financial assets for the account of others. This category includes entities that keep financial assets for the account of others, such as custodian banks, brokers and central securities depositories.

Investment entities

An investment entity is any entity that primarily conducts as a business investment activities or operations on behalf of other persons, and entities that are managed by those entities or other FIs. An entity would generally be considered within this category if it functions or holds itself out as a collective investment vehicle, mutual fund, exchange traded fund, private equity fund, hedge fund, venture capital, fund leveraged buy-out fund or any similar investment vehicle established with an investment strategy or investing, reinvesting or trading in financial assets.

Specified insurance companies

A specified insurance company is any entity that is regulated as an insurance business under the laws, regulations or practices of any jurisdiction in which the entity does business (or the holding company of an insurance company) that issues, or is obligated to make payments with respect to a cash value insurance contract or an annuity contract. Most life insurance companies would generally be considered within this category.

Financial Institutions that are specifically excluded from in the Common Reporting Standard

Broad participation retirement funds

Non-reportable broad participation retirement funds: these include funds established to provide retirement, disability, or death benefits to beneficiaries that are current or former employee, in consideration for services rendered provided that the fund: i) does not have a single beneficiary with a right to more than 5% of the fund's assets; ii) is subject to government regulation and provides information to tax authorities; and iii) fulfils one of the following requirements: a) is exempt from tax on investment income; or b) receives at least 50% of total contributions from sponsoring employers; or c) withdrawals are allowed upon occurrence of specified events or penalties apply; or d) contributions by the employees are limited by reference to earned income of the employee or may not exceed USD 50 000.

Narrow participation retirement funds

Non-reportable narrow participation retirement fund: these include funds established to provide retirement, disability, or death benefits to beneficiaries that are current or former employees, in consideration for services rendered, provided that the fund: i) has fewer than 50 participants; ii) is sponsored by employers that are not investment entities or passive non-financial entities; iii) contributions to the fund are limited by reference to earned income and compensation of employee; iv) participants that are not residents are not entitled to more than 20% of the fund's assets; and v) is subject to government regulation and provides information reporting to the tax authorities.

Qualified credit card issuers

Non-reportable qualified credit card issuers these include a financial institution that is solely a financial institution because it is an issuer of credit cards that accepts deposits only when a customer makes a payment in excess of the balance due, and the overpayment is not immediately returned, and financial institution implements policies and procedures either to prevent a customer from making an overpayment in excess of USD 50 000 or to ensure that any payment in excess of this amount is refunded to the customer within 60 days.

Exempt collective investment vehicles

Non-reportable exempt collective investment vehicles are investment entities that are regulated as collective investment vehicles, provided that all of the interests in the vehicle are held by or through individuals or entities that are not RPs (e.g. because they are FIs).

Trustee documented trust

A trust that is a financial institution (e.g. because it is an investment entity) is a non-reporting financial institution to the extent that the trustee of the trust is a RFI and reports all information required to be reported with respect to all the RFAs held by the trust.

Low-risk non-reporting financial institutions

Any other entity that substantially has similar characteristics to any of the entities described as non-reportable FIs that present a low risk of being used to evade taxes, and is defined in domestic law as a non-reporting FIs, provided that the status of such entity as a non-reporting financial institution does not frustrate the purposes of the CRS. The commentaries to the CRS describe the following as low-risk factors as: i) the financial institution is subject to regulation; and ii) information reporting by the financial institution to the tax authorities is required.

Financial accounts and the common reporting standard

Financial accounts that are specifically included in the Common Reporting Standard

Depository account[2]

A depository account refers to any commercial, checking, savings, time, or thrift account, or an account that is evidenced by a certificate of deposit, thrift certificate, investment certificate, certificate of indebtedness, or other similar instruments maintained by a financial institution in the ordinary course of a banking or similar business. A depository account also includes an amount held by an insurance company pursuant to a guaranteed investment contract or similar agreement to pay or credit interest thereon.

Custodial account

A custodial account is any account that holds one or more financial assets for the benefit of another person.

Equity interest

Equity interests refer to interests in investment entities, including partnerships and trusts.

Cash value insurance

Cash value insurance is an insurance contract that has a cash value. The term "cash value" is defined as the greater of the amount that the policy holder is entitled to receive upon surrender or termination of the contract, and the amount the policyholder can borrow under or with regards to the contract.

Financial accounts that are specifically excluded from the Common Reporting Standard

Retirement and pension accounts[3]

A retirement or pension account can be excluded from CRS reporting, provided that it satisfies all the following requirements: i) the account is subject to regulation as a personal retirement account or is part of a registered or regulated retirement or pension plan for the provision of retirement or pension benefits; ii) the account is tax-favoured; iii) information reporting is required to the tax authorities with respect to the account; iv) withdrawals are conditions on reaching a specified retirement age, disability, or death, or penalties apply to withdrawals made before such specified events; and v) either contributions are limited to USD 50 000 or less, or there is a maximum lifetime contribution limit to the account of USD 1 000 000 or less, excluding rollovers.

Non-retirement tax-favoured accounts

Non-retirement accounts may be excluded provided the account i) is subject to regulation as an investment vehicle or as a savings account for purposes other than for retirement; ii) the account is tax-favoured; iii) withdrawals are conditioned or penalties apply; and iv) annual contributions are limited to USD 50 000 or less.

Term life insurance contracts

A life insurance contract with a coverage period that will end before the insured individual attains age 90, can be excluded provided that it fulfils all the following requirements: i) the contract has no contract value that any person can access without terminating the contract; ii) the amount payable upon cancellation or termination of the contract cannot exceed the aggregate premiums paid for the contract, less the sum of mortality, morbidity, and expenses changes; and iii) the contract is not held by a transferee for value.

Estate accounts

An account that is held solely by an estate can be an excluded account if the documentation of such account includes a copy of the deceased's will or death certificate.

Escrow accounts

An account where money is held by a third party on behalf of transacting parties provided they are established in connection with any of the following i) a court order or judgment; ii) a sale, exchange, or lease of real or personal property; iii) or there is an obligation of a FI solely to facilitate the payment of taxes at a later time.

Depository accounts due to not-returned overpayments

The account exists solely because a customer makes a payment in excess of a balance due with respect to a credit card or other revolving credit facility and the overpayment is not immediately returned to the customer, and the FI implements policies and procedure to prevent a customer from making an overpayment in excess of USD 50 000 or ensures the overpayment is refunded to the customer within 60 days.

Low-risk accounts

An account can be excluded provided that i) the account presents a low risk of being used to evade taxes; ii) the account is similar to the other excluded accounts; iii) the account is defined in domestic law as an excluded account; iv) the status of the account as an excluded account does not frustrate the purposes of the CRS.

Notes

1. This discussion is based on Section VIII(A) of the Common Reporting Standard.
2. This discussion is based on Section VIII(C) of the Common Reporting Standard.
3. This discussion is based on Section VIII(C)(17) of the Common Reporting Standard.

ORGANISATION FOR ECONOMIC CO-OPERATION AND DEVELOPMENT

The OECD is a unique forum where governments work together to address the economic, social and environmental challenges of globalisation. The OECD is also at the forefront of efforts to understand and to help governments respond to new developments and concerns, such as corporate governance, the information economy and the challenges of an ageing population. The Organisation provides a setting where governments can compare policy experiences, seek answers to common problems, identify good practice and work to co-ordinate domestic and international policies.

The OECD member countries are: Australia, Austria, Belgium, Canada, Chile, the Czech Republic, Denmark, Estonia, Finland, France, Germany, Greece, Hungary, Iceland, Ireland, Israel, Italy, Japan, Korea, Latvia, Luxembourg, Mexico, the Netherlands, New Zealand, Norway, Poland, Portugal, the Slovak Republic, Slovenia, Spain, Sweden, Switzerland, Turkey, the United Kingdom and the United States. The European Union takes part in the work of the OECD.

OECD Publishing disseminates widely the results of the Organisation's statistics gathering and research on economic, social and environmental issues, as well as the conventions, guidelines and standards agreed by its members.

OECD PUBLISHING, 2, rue André-Pascal, 75775 PARIS CEDEX 16
(23 2018 05 1 P) ISBN 978-92-64-28952-9 – 2018

www.ingramcontent.com/pod-product-compliance
Ingram Content Group UK Ltd.
Pitfield, Milton Keynes, MK11 3LW, UK
UKHW051500290926
15471UKWH00008B/1317

9 789264 289529